The New Detente

V

The United Nations University's Programme on Peace and Global Transformation was a major world-wide project whose purpose was to develop new insights about the interlinkages between questions of peace, conflict resolution, and the process of transformation. The research in this project, under six major themes, was co-ordinated by a 12-member core group in different regions of the world: East Asia, South-East Asia (including the Pacific), South Asia, the Arab region, Africa, Western Europe, Eastern Europe, North America, and Latin America. The themes covered were: Conflicts over Natural Resources; Security, Vulnerability, and Violence; Human Rights and Cultural Survival in a Changing Pluralistic World; The Role of Science and Technology in Peace and Transformation; The Role of the State in Peace and Global Transformation; and Global Economic Crisis. The project also included a special project on Peace and Regional Security.

The New Detente

Rethinking East–West Relations

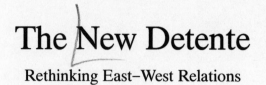

Edited by
MARY KALDOR, GERARD HOLDEN
and RICHARD FALK

WITHDRAWN

VERSO

London · New York

THE UNITED NATIONS UNIVERSITY

Tokyo

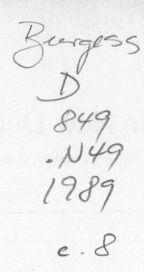

Published in 1989 by Verso and The United Nations University
© United Nations University, Tokyo, 1989
All rights reserved

Verso
UK: 6 Meard Street, London W1V 3HR
USA: 29 West 35th Street, New York, NY 10001-2291

Verso is the imprint of New Left Books

The United Nations University
Toho Seimei Building, 15-1, Shibuya 2-chome,
Shibuya-ku, Tokyo 150, Japan

British Library Cataloguing in Publication Data
The New detente: rethinking East–West relations.
   1. Western bloc countries. Foreign relations with
Soviet Union
   2. Soviet Union. Foreign relations with Western bloc
countries
   I. Kaldor, Mary II. Holden, Gerard III. Falk, Richard
A. (Richard Anderson), *1930–*
327′.09171′3

ISBN 0-86091-247-7
ISBN 0-86091-962-5 pbk

US Library of Congress Cataloging in Publication Data
The New detente: rethinking East–West relations/edited by Mary
   Kaldor, Gerard Holden, and Richard Falk.
   p.   cm.
      ISBN 0-86091-247-7: — ISBN 0-86091-962-5 (pbk.):
       1. World politics—1985–1995.   2. Detente.   I. Kaldor, Mary.
  II. Holden, Gerard.   III. Falk, Richard A.
  D849.N49 1989
  327′.09′048—dc20

Typeset by Leaper & Gard Limited, Bristol, England
Printed in Great Britain by Bookcraft (Bath) Ltd

Contents

Acknowledgements

This book is the final project of the West European network of the United Nations University's Peace and Global Transformation Sub-programme; we are grateful to the UNU for its intellectual and financial support. We are also grateful to the Transnational Institute, Amsterdam for hosting a valuable meeting for our contributors in January 1988; to the translators of several of the chapters: Caesar Voute, A.G. Brain, Rick Simon, Witold Zbironowski-Kościa, Pavel Stránský; and to all those who have helped in Princeton, Sussex and Amsterdam: Claire Trevelyan, Suki Pollard, June Garson, Sara Henley, Sue Romer, and Laurian Zwart.

Introduction

Mary Kaldor

'The Cold War is over . . . The post-war era has come to an end.' So commented Franz Josef Strauss on his visit to Moscow a few months before his death. Strauss was the man who proposed nuclear weapons for West Germany in the 1950s, who argued for a Franco–German nuclear force in the 1960s, and who described the students of 1968 as 'animals, who cannot be handled by laws made for humans'.

His view that the Cold War is over has been echoed throughout the political spectrum of Western Europe and the United States. Politicians compete with each other for the privilege of making triumphant visits to the Soviet Union and Eastern Europe. The implacable enemy of the evil empire has applauded the songs of Soviet schoolchildren and the Iron Lady has allowed herself to be kissed by a soldier in the Caucasus. Even more astonishing has been the sight of cruise missiles wheeled out of Molesworth and of SS-12 and SS-23 missiles, formerly deployed in Czechoslovakia and East Germany, being blown up in central Asia – all of this observed by military inspectors from both sides and by disbelieving peace activists and journalists.

So is it true? Is the Cold War coming to an end? Are we witnessing a watershed in international relations – one of those moments in history when long-standing institutions and arrangements seem to crumble and when new relationships are established more in keeping with changed economic and social realities? Or is this just another phase in the alternating cycle of detente and Cold War that has characterized the East–West conflict in Europe up to now? How does the present period differ from the post-Stalin thaw when Khrushchev enunciated the doctrine of peaceful coexistence, or from the detente of the early 1970s when Nixon and Kissinger went to Moscow and the Helsinki Final Act was signed in

1

Europe? Will this phase of detente last? Or will it revert to confrontation, as happened in the late 1950s and the late 1970s?

The essays in this book are focused around these questions. They represent a variety of opinions from within what might be described as a liberal or democratic perspective. One of the signs of flux in politics is the fact that labels are difficult to apply. The Westerners contributing to this book would probably prefer to be called left or radical or socialist. But for their counterparts in Eastern Europe, these terms have been tainted by what actually exists and by the use of such terms on the part of the ruling establishments. What I mean by 'liberal' or 'democratic' broadly covers those who are in some way committed to the establishment of democracy in the East and the reinvigoration of democracy in the West. The authors include those who are active in Socialist or Social Democrat parties in the West, those who could be described as official reformers in the East, as well as those who are active in new social movements (peace, green, human rights and so on).

The essays share two main preoccupations. One is with the future of Europe. The changes in international relations that are described in this book centre around changes in Europe. What happens in Europe, the political direction of individual European countries and the political relations between groups of European countries as well as between individual countries, the nature of European institutions that are created, will have a profound influence on East–West relations and on global political arrangements. Will Europe remain divided between a capitalist West and a socialist East? Will the military confrontation continue? Will Western Europe acquire an independent status backed by independent military forces? Or can we envisage a diverse, pluralistic Europe in which the division between East and West withers away, to coin a phrase?

A second and related preoccupation is with the relationship between state and society. What distinguishes this book from many other studies of East–West relations is the emphasis on the role played by domestic political processes, the notion that international postures and perceptions have to be understood in a social context and not merely in terms of some abstract definition of what constitutes national or bloc interests. Most of these essays argue that whether or not Europe is able to move beyond the Cold War will depend on the extent to which we are able to reconstruct the relationship between governments, political parties and social movements, on what is often described as the re-emergence of civil society.[1]

The International Context

The new detente –,or as the Germans call it, the second phase of detente – seems to have emerged from a specific international conjuncture which can be characterized in terms of three broad developments.

The first is the relative decline of the United States and the growing rivalry between the United States, Western Europe and Japan over economic issues as well as over relations with the countries of the East and the South. At the end of the Second World War, the United States accounted for over one-third of global output and enjoyed a massive trade surplus with the rest of the world. Through the system of military alliances, the stationing of troops overseas, the provision of economic and military aid, the USA was able to stimulate the recovery of Western Europe and Japan and to underpin global financial and trading arrangements. Dollars spent overseas in support of the US global role returned to the United States in the form of purchases of American goods and services.

Today, the USA remains the single largest economic entity but its output has declined to less than a quarter of global output, and in recent years it has experienced a series of substantial balance-of-payments deficits. Western Europe and Japan are now nearly as rich as the United States (in terms of *per capita* incomes) and represent much larger trading blocs. The American external deficit is matched by the surpluses of West Germany and Japan.

During the Reagan years, the American administration was able to use its political and military clout to 'compensate' for economic weakness. Because of the role of the dollar and the ability to insist on trading terms (Voluntary Export Restraints, for example) the USA was able to sustain high rates of economic growth and relatively low levels of unemployment. Demand was stimulated by budgetary deficits caused by high military spending and tax cuts. Because of the declining competitiveness of US products, even despite protectionism, this resulted in substantial balance-of-payments deficits which were financed by foreign borrowing. The USA could get away with a scale of borrowing undreamed of by Third World countries because of its predominant global position.

The 1987 Wall Street Crash gave rise to a new questioning of America's global role and popularized an ongoing scholarly debate about the rise and fall of empires.[2] (This debate is further described in Richard Falk's chapter.) International relations theorists like Robert Keohane or Robert Gilpin have, for some time, put forward theories of hegemonic stability.[3] The argument is that the global economic system requires a 'hegemon', a successful industrial nation to guarantee its

smooth functioning. Britain played such a role in the nineteenth century
and Holland in the seventeenth. However, the burdens of empire, the
cost of being a hegemon, lead to economic decline and global economic
anarchy until a new hegemon emerges.

Today, it is argued, American overseas military commitments are the
main reason for the balance-of-payments deficits. Moreover, overseas
military spending no longer returns to the United States in the form of
increased American exports. Instead, it is spent on German and
Japanese products. The problem, today, is how to reduce America's
military commitments without any obvious hegemonic successor and
how a transition to a new global system can be achieved without the
kind of destructive convulsions that characterized earlier transitions.

There is a seductive logic to these theories of hegemonic cycles. They
are, however, curiously ahistorical in the way they fail to convey a sense
of long-term social and political change. The reason the United States
cannot afford to maintain its overseas commitments is the declining
competitiveness of American products. And that has to be explained in
terms of deeper, more structural reasons – the exhaustion of the
American model of development, for example, or even the domestic
rigidities and distortions introduced by military spending, and particularly by the absorption of scientific and technological resources. It
could equally well be argued that the overseas military commitments
offset the structural decline of the American economy by upholding
America's political position, stimulating demand, and allowing the
United States to maintain high levels of borrowing. Likewise, the
problems of renewing hegemony, transition to a new hegemony, or even
the possibility of developing a global economic system that does not
require hegemony cannot be fully explored except in a broader, more
historical social and political context.

Be that as it may, some American authors are using the debate about
hegemonic cycles to point out that hegemonic stability is a myth because
it cannot last. What is needed is shared hegemony in order to balance
the role of debtors and creditors and to provide a more stable long-term
system. Hence there is talk of a 'bigemony' of the United States and
Japan[4] or of a 'devolution' of military and political power to both
Western Europe and Japan.[5]

The notion of 'devolution' also has its adherents in Western Europe.
For many years there have been proposals for a 'West European pillar'
and a more equal relationship between Western Europe and the United
States. In recent years these proposals have gained substance. On the
initiative of the French, the Western European Union (created in 1954
as a device to contain the rearmament of West Germany) has been
revived. In October 1987 the Western European Union adopted the

Hague Platform on European security interests. It emphasized co-operation in conventional military capabilities and commended the role of British and French nuclear forces. Parallel to the revival of the WEU has been intensified Franco–German military co-operation – frequent consultations, joint exercises, the formation of a joint brigade, a joint council, and so forth.

The West European pillar concept is linked with concerns about the integration of the European arms industry. National markets are too small to provide sufficient economies of scale for domestic arms production. Most European countries, especially Britain and France, are heavily dependent on arms exports to the Third World. However, given the continuing economic crisis in the Third World, this market does not offer long-term potential for expansion. If European arms firms are to compete with American companies they need a common European, as opposed to NATO, procurement policy. France recently found it necessary to make substantial increases in domestic defence spending, following a slump in overseas orders. Britain, on the other hand, is enjoying an unprecedented export boom and this has facilitated a stabilization of defence spending.

In addition to arms-industry interests, there seems also to be an interest in asserting an independent West European role in the Third World. Advocates of the West European pillar often emphasize the 'out-of-area' component of the concept.[6] It is worth noting that one of the first initiatives of the revived Western European Union was to send minesweepers to the Persian Gulf.

Finally, of course, the West European pillar concept also relates to the economic integration of Western Europe. By 1992, the twelve members of the European Community will abolish internal customs and create a single European market. This economic integration is not paralleled by political integration. Some advocates of the West European pillar see military co-operation as a vehicle for achieving political co-operation. It is a move towards creating a West European state. Is it possible to create a state without a military arm?

This whole discussion about 'burden-sharing' and about the Atlantic relationship takes place almost without reference to the Soviet Union. The Soviet threat is a given or even an afterthought. It seems to be taken for granted that a hegemon, in an economic sense, needs to base its power on military capabilities and that these military capabilities are directed against an external threat to the system, or alternatively against a competing hegemon or a 'latecomer'.[7] But the Soviet Union can hardly be described as a competitor for economic hegemony. (This is the role of Western Europe and Japan.) Moreover, the current efforts of the Soviet Union and Eastern Europe to join the global economic system call into question whether the Soviet Union can continue to be assumed as an external threat to the system. At the very least, the changing Soviet role needs to be taken into account in these discussions.

Thus the second broad development concerns the advent of Gorbachev and the domestic and international openings in the formerly closed systems of the Soviet Union and Eastern Europe.

Several writers have drawn a parallel between the United States and the Soviet Union. Both superpowers are declining and both are suffering from the burdens of imperialism; both are seeking ways to withdraw from their military commitments in Europe and the Third World. (Gian Giacomo Migone makes the same point in his chapter.) This is, of course, true but, put in this way, it conceals the enormous asymmetry between the Eastern and Western blocs. The Soviet Union may be considered roughly equivalent to the United States as a military superpower, but in economic terms it is more like a Third World country. If the American empire was based on economic strength, the Soviet empire was born from economic weakness – from fear (and paranoia) about external attack and from the need to exploit the more advanced industries of its East European satellites. In the years immediately following the Second World War, the Soviet Union extracted from its East European satellites – in the form of reparations, joint-stock companies, unfair terms of trade – an amount estimated to be equivalent to the amount the United States gave to Western Europe as Marshall Aid.[8]

There is not the space here to enter into a discussion of the nature of actually existing socialist societies, but in a sense it can be said that ever since 1945 the socialist countries have faced a permanent economic and political crisis concealed by mammoth 'administrative' controls. The system that was imposed on Eastern Europe in the late 1940s emerged in the Soviet Union in the 1930s in preparation for war. The emphasis was on industrial growth and the production of armaments. Consumption was kept low and the collectivization of agriculture was designed to extract maximum resources from the countryside.

All these countries did succeed in achieving very rapid rates of growth in the 1950s and 1960s, in transforming peasants into workers, and in raising educational standards. So much so that socialist leaders at the end of the 1950s and early 1960s expressed unbounded optimism about the possibility for socialism to overtake capitalism – an optimism reflected in Isaac Deutscher's book *The Great Contest.*[9]

But these gains were achieved at enormous human cost. Moreover, it turned out in the 1970s and 1980s to be extremely hard to sustain such rapid rates of growth or translate economic growth into tangible material benefits for the population. What the Soviet Union and Eastern Europe experienced, alongside the cycles of detente and Cold War, was a cycle of domestic reform and relaxation followed by 'normalization'. These cycles were not contiguous, although they were evidently connected in some way – a point addressed by several authors in this book. Reform and relaxation were necessary to restructure the economy, to stimulate innovation, and indeed to lessen the rigidifying atmosphere of fear in which officials as well as ordinary people existed. Reform and relaxation tended to be accompanied by greater openness towards the West, although this was not necessarily reciprocated. It is interesting to speculate, for example, on how post-war history might have been different had the West been more responsive to the de-Stalinization process in the 1950s. Reform also involved greater tolerance towards socialist experiment: Khrushchev's 'New Course' was symbolized by the *rapprochement* with Yugoslavia.

Every period of reform and relaxation produced shortages, inflation, spiralling demands for imports and political protest. Hence the reforms of the mid 1950s produced the Hungarian and Polish crises of 1956. The reforms of the mid 1960s culminated in the Prague Spring. The detente of the 1970s, initiated by the West, seems to have been viewed as a substitute for reform; in particular, improved East–West economic relations were a way of postponing reform. But the effect of detente seems to have been similar; it resulted in the Polish crisis of 1980–81 – an argument explored by Michnik – and a reversion to Cold War and 'normalization'.

It would be wrong to suggest that these cycles have not evolved. Reforms have had varying degrees of success in different countries – probably going furthest in Hungary. Political and financial controls have increasingly replaced administrative controls. These post-Stalinist societies are better described today as authoritarian rather than totalitarian. But perhaps for this very reason, the political and economic crisis of socialist societies is more acute today than at any time since the Second World War.

Likewise, international cycles have also evolved. Over time, the unity of the socialist bloc has loosened, so that the development of individual countries has depended increasingly on the domestic political conjuncture. What is remarkable is the growing diversity of actually existing socialism – the contrast between Czechoslovakia and the GDR, say, where Stalinist political elites have tried to retain power, and, on the other hand, Hungary and Poland.

The advent of Gorbachev marks the beginning of a new reform period. The significance of his reforms is open to widely differing interpretations. What is important is that the reform has been initiated in the metropolis – something that has not happened since Khrushchev – and this has increased the freedom of manoeuvre for reform tendencies in all the European socialist countries. In opposition circles in Eastern Europe and among some commentators in the West, there is scepticism about how much can be achieved by what is known as reform from above. Gorbachev's reforms – far-reaching as they are in their cultural, economic and foreign-policy dimensions – have been analysed as a permission.[10] Whether or not they can initiate an irreversible process of democratization and economic restructuring depends to a large extent on the emergence of new social institutions generating and safeguarding such a process – otherwise, permission can always be withdrawn. This is the thrust of Boris Kagarlitsky's argument in chapter 15. It is interesting to note that Milan Šimečka is more optimistic. He argues that reforms in Eastern Europe have never been reversed as a result of domestic contest but always as a consequence of external intervention. The Soviet Union is the one socialist country that does not need to fear external intervention.

All the same, it is in Eastern Europe, it can be argued, especially Poland and Hungary, that the potential for democratization is greatest. This is because, for a combination of reasons – historical experience, more advanced reforms, access to the West, and so on – pressures from below are much more developed. Solidarity remains the best, but by no means the only, example of the kind of independent social institution that is required. The advent of Gorbachev offers time, or permission, for these pressures from below to organize. How long or how much is again a subject for debate.

This brings us to the third broad development that characterizes the current international conjuncture – a parallel, although not symmetrical, process in the domestic politics of Europe, both East and West. This process can be most easily observed in the emergence of new social movements in both East and West, but the process is more than just the growth of new movements. It is also a growing disjuncture between formal and informal political processes – an erosion of the political institutions created in the post-war period.

The Hungarian sociologist Elemer Hankiss uses the term 'Second Society' to describe the combination of small-scale private enterprises, black-market enterprises, samizdat publishing, informal welfare networks, political and intellectual clubs that have grown up outside the realm of state and party.[11] The activities of the Second Society are virtually invisible, except in an immediate everyday sense. They are not reported by the media and are rarely acknowledged by officialdom. Indeed, in so far as they are acknowledged, they are harassed by the authorities: participants in the Second Society face penalties such as imprisonment, loss of job or promotion, loss of passport, and so forth.

The very existence of the Second Society is fragile.

Although there are significant differences, the concept of a second society could also be applied in the West. The growth of the service economy, the unemployed, the new information workers, the new movements (especially peace, green and women's) are hardly visible either in the mass media or in ongoing public political debates. This second society is not harassed in the same way, and does not face threats to its existence, but it is ignored and neglected. It constitutes an experience of marginalization and powerlessness. The electoral system and established political parties seem less and less capable of expressing and channelling popular aspirations – they seem increasingly remote from an everyday social context.

In the West, this growing disjuncture between formal and informal political processes can be viewed, in part, as a consequence of the decline of the traditional parties of the left. In the post-war period, domestic politics in the West was dominated by the philosophy and activities of Socialist and Social Democrat parties. The bipartisan consensus about managed capitalism could be said to have been a victory for social democracy. In the early 1980s Socialist and Social Democrat parties, at least in North-West Europe, suffered a series of electoral defeats. More importantly, the philosophy of managed capitalism was challenged on the right, by the new privatizers and the de-regulators in the established right-wing parties, and from underneath (since left is not quite the right term) by new preoccupations about peace, the environment, gender, democracy, and so on. The new social movements, especially the peace and green movements, had no access to the formal political process – Parliament and the mass media – *except* through the established political parties. (Although it is true that in several countries, especially West Germany, Green parties have made some inroads.) The anti-missile demonstrations in 1981 and 1983 did provide some visibility, although less than might have been expected considering the unprecedented transnational scale of the protests. But by and large, the activities of these mass movements are rarely observed in the public or official arena. Moreover, the decline of Socialist and Social Democrat parties has further obscured their political impact.

The peace issue was particularly troubling for these parties. The bipartisan consensus about managed capitalism also included a commitment to Atlanticism. The 1945 Labour government had, after all, helped to engineer the Cold War. The German Social Democrats were able to enter power only after they had abandoned, at least in practice, their commitment to a united socialist Germany. In the early 1980s the consensus about managed capitalism was broken by the right, while the commitment to Atlanticism was challenged by the peace movement.

Although most of these parties did, in the end, oppose the deployment of cruise and Pershing missiles, their new-found peace policies somehow seemed confusing and unconvincing and this also contributed to their defeats. Indeed, in some cases, especially in Britain, the peace issue became the expression of deep internal divisions. (The experience of Southern Europe is rather different. There, it is the Communist parties that face decline, while Socialist parties entered government in every Southern European country during the 1980s. Initially these parties were committed to socialist economic policies, and in some cases, notably Greece and Spain, to radical peace policies. Pasok in Greece was committed to the Balkan nuclear-free zone and the removal of nuclear weapons from Greece, while the Spanish Socialist Party promised to oppose Spanish membership of NATO. In practice these parties in power have become enthusiastic free-marketeers and their peace policies have been whittled down. Although both the French and Italian Socialist parties have strongly supported the notion of an independent Western Europe, they played a shameful role in the Euromissile debate. Mitterrand even spoke in favour of deployment in the Bundestag in 1983, an election year, to the shock and bewilderment of his Social Democrat colleagues. In all the Southern European countries, except France and Portugal, peace and green movements grew rapidly in the early 1980s. Their ability to influence politics was, however, nullified by the role of Socialist parties and the decline of Communist parties.)

The decline of social democracy in the West is paralleled by a decline of ideology in the East. On the one hand, it is possible to observe a growth in reformist tendencies within Communist parties – tendencies which sometimes seem to echo the belief in markets and private ownership that is heard on the Western right. On the other hand, except in the GDR and Czechoslovakia, the use of Marxist–Leninist ideology has increasingly been replaced by a more pragmatic and, in Gorbachev's case, humanitarian language. This change in the formal political process has been accompanied by an opening up of informal political space in East European societies, especially in the last two or three years – the emergence of mass peace and green movements (like Freedom and Peace in Poland, or the Danube circle and Blues in Hungary) and of independent trade unions and youth groups, the growth of underground publishing, and the mushrooming of informal intellectual circles and clubs.

(Again, there also seems to be a difference between North and South within the socialist system, and sometimes this difference is exhibited within the same country – as in the contrast between Serbia and Slovenia in Yugoslavia, or between Azerbaijan and Armenia, on the one hand,

and the Baltic States, on the other. The difference can be described in terms of a differing balance between the new type of democratic social movements, on the one hand, and nationalist, chauvinistic and even totalitarian tendencies on the other. In the poorer, more under-developed socialist regions – in some cases, under considerable pressure from Western creditors – the balance seems to be tipped towards the nationalistic tendencies. The most extreme example is Romania.)

Compared with Western social movements, the new groups in the East are embattled. Their efforts to exist are based on great individual courage. For Eastern social movements, the central issue is to be allowed to exist. For Western social movements, the problem is how to be heard. Both, however, share a common original insight which seems to have emerged quite independently from the experience of the Western peace movement and the experience of Polish Solidarity. This is the notion that the task of social movements is not to capture state power, but rather to change the relationships of state to society so that the state is more responsive to social demands, to allow for wider par-ticipation in the political process – a sharing of state power. Linked to this notion is the commitment to non-violence, to finding ways of acting politically that can contribute to the evolution of democracy.

The INF Treaty of December 1987 represented an expression of all these developments. Gorbachev was the immediate begetter of the treaty and it was the most positive outcome of his 'New Thinking' on security issues (described by Gerard Holden in chapter 10). Funda-mentally, Gorbachev has accepted the peace-movement argument that numbers of nuclear weapons have no military (or political) value in an era of overkill; hence he was willing to give up many more nuclear weapons than the West. And this made an agreement possible.

But the significance of the agreement lay in the fact that it removed the very missiles which had been the target of the demonstrations of the early 1980s and the subject of a bitter political debate in West European societies. The debate was not just about the role of nuclear weapons; it was about the political relationship between Western Europe and the United States. Originally, the missiles were deployed to 'couple' the United States and Western Europe, as a way of reassuring Western Europeans of the American commitment to defend them in the face of growing fissures over trade, the dollar, the Middle East, and so on. The missiles were said to be the 'symbol' of Atlantic unity. Moreover, an elaborate military rationale was developed to show that *only* intermediate-range land-based nuclear missiles could ensure the credi-bility of NATO's flexible-response strategy.

Hence their removal has been 'decoupling'. It has left the NATO establishment in disarray. It has reopened the issue of US–West European relations and stimulated interest in the West European pillar. It has legitimized the alternative security debate and opened up the possibility of a realistic agenda for disarmament and detente and a dialogue with the new social movements, especially the peace movement.

The prospects for detente – and this theme is developed in several of the chapters in this book – depend on the interrelationship of all these three developments. The success of the reform process in Eastern Europe and the Soviet Union depends primarily on internal factors in socialist societies – on the development of pressures from below and on the durability of autonomous social institutions. Nevertheless, if the West continues to arm and to justify its armament in terms of a Soviet threat, this reduces the possibilities for economic restructuring and strengthens the hardliners – the advocates of 'normalization'. On the other hand, the argument for militarization, especially in the West European context, rests both on the continued Soviet presence in Eastern Europe and on the oppressive nature of their political systems. The more successful the reforms, the weaker the case for a West European pillar. And finally, of course, both these interdependent issues, demilitarization and democratization, depend on the visibility of social movements – their ability to mobilize, to penetrate political consciousness and, *pari passu*, to reinforce each other through East–West links.

Differing Conceptions of Detente

In spelling out these interrelationships, it is useful to distinguish different ways of thinking about the detente process. It is possible broadly to identify two different conceptions of detente. Most of the essays in this book are based on a combination of both conceptions, although some would veer more to one or the other. The first conception tends to be prevalent within Socialist and Social Democrat parties and among official reformers in the East. This is a conception of detente between governments – sometimes described as detente from above or official detente. Considerable emphasis is placed on arms control and disarmament. Those who conceive of detente in this way tend to argue that earlier periods of detente, especially the detente of the 1970s, failed because the arms race was not controlled. There was no 'military detente', to use the Soviet phrase.

The second conception, which tends to be prevalent among the new social movements, is a conception of detente between societies – sometimes known as detente from below, or citizens' detente. This represents a broader approach to detente in which disarmament and demilitarization constitute one element of a package involving greater economic and ecological co-operation, settlement of outstanding political disputes, increased tolerance and pluralism, and so forth.

These two different conceptions stem from differing interpretations of the nature of the East–West conflict. Advocates of detente from above tend to see the East–West conflict as a deep underlying clash, either between capitalism and socialism or, more traditionally, between competing great powers. Their views tend to be shaped by the institutions to which they belong – institutions which more or less established their present forms at the height of the Cold War period in the late 1940s and 1950s. In so far as the East–West conflict is a clash between capitalism and socialism, advocates of official detente can see the possibility of demilitarizing this conflict. It is, after all, a debate about how to organize society, about the role of the state versus the role of the market as an economic regulator. It is a debate which is carried on *within* societies as much as *between* societies. The debate will not and should not cease because the military confrontation has lessened but, especially in the nuclear era, it need no longer be a *casus belli*.

For those who see the clash as a traditional balance-of-power conflict, detente is viewed as a way of managing this conflict. It is a kind of re-creation of the Concert of Europe, along the lines envisaged by Henry Kissinger in the early 1970s. Further measures of arms control, beyond what was achieved in the 1970s, are required to establish a basis of trust between the great powers.

For advocates of official detente, the primary aim is the prevention of war and the reduction of the economic burden of military spending.

An alternative interpretation would represent the East–West conflict as not so much a clash but an implicit collusion between two complementary systems. On this interpretation, Atlanticism – the specific variant of managed capitalism that came into being after the Second World War in the Atlantic region – and Stalinism, which was brutally imposed on the countries of East–Central Europe, were the outcomes of a shared historical experience and were mutually dependent in so far as they provided each other with a legitimizing external threat. Indeed, the new political tendencies that have evolved in the 1980s can be viewed as a reaction to characteristics of society that are common to *both* Atlanticism and Stalinism or post-Stalinism. These include big government, mass production, high levels of military spending, the wastage of resources, the pollution of the atmosphere, the belief in universalistic solutions, and so on. They are also a reaction to the exhaustion or stagnation of both systems – the difficulty of responding to new concerns within the existing political and social framework. The free-market option is viewed as one way of shaking up the existing framework – and this, perhaps, explains why political leaders like Mrs Thatcher, who combine a commitment to capitalism with an authoritarian style of government, are so enamoured of official reformers. The alternative option of democratization, which allows citizens and citizens' groups to reshape society, is put forward by the new social movements.

On this interpretation of the East–West conflict, detente has to be more than just agreements between governments. It has to resolve the East–West conflict if it is not to revert to Cold War as a way of sustaining the status quo. That means that detente has to permit an evolution of society beyond Atlanticism and post-Stalinism. This does not imply some sort of convergence of systems or the victory of one or other system – which would be a solution for those who view the East–West conflict as a systematic clash. Rather, it implies tolerance of diversity and experiment.

It is interesting to note that some American authors are implying that the USA has won the Cold War. The Western system, according to this line of thought, has proved superior in both economic and ideological terms.[12] Such a view ignores the critical domestic debates on both sides of the East–West divide. It presupposes that the East–West conflict is really about the role of the market. But it is difficult to believe that Cold War will be replaced by global unification on the American model; it is much more likely to involve changes in *both* Western and Eastern systems.

According to this alternative interpretation of the East–West conflict, the detente of the 1970s failed because governments were unwilling to permit an evolution of society in both East and West. A social detente *was* achieved between European countries, but not between the United States and the Soviet Union. Western Europe was drifting Eastwards away from the United States in a geopolitical, and economic and social sense. And in Eastern Europe, the emergence of Solidarity seemed to open up the prospect of an entirely new social contract.

For advocates of detente from below, then, the aim of detente is not just prevention of war, although that is very important, but the elimination of the Cold War system which upholds the social and political status quo in both East and West, but especially in the East. Demilitarization is essential to create the conditions for peaceful social change, but only tolerance of peaceful change through respect for democratic rights and as a result of increased co-operation can create the conditions in which demilitarization is possible. It is not one or the other, but a choice of vicious or virtuous circles.

Evidently, the political strategies for achieving detente depend on the conception of detente. For advocates of detente from above, the task is to install detente-minded governments. Gorbachev is, for the present, detente-minded. So are Erich Honecker, Karoly Grosz and even Helmut

Kohl. Margaret Thatcher, François Mitterrand, and Ronald Reagan and George Bush have been pushed into a detente mode, but their inclinations have lain elsewhere. Social movements, especially the peace movement, have an important role in pressurizing governments to adopt detente policies and in generating new proposals for arms control and disarmament. From this point of view, an effective political strategy for detente involves the development of concrete proposals which are capable of generating public support *and* of providing a basis for East–West agreement.

Detente from below, on the other hand, is a policy for social movements. It is not addressed to governments except in so far as they are asked to guarantee freedom of travel and freedom of assembly so that citizens' groups can meet and communicate. It is a strategy of dialogue, an attempt to change society through the actions of citizens rather than governments, to change ideas and to develop new institutions; in short, to create a new political culture. Increasingly, advocates of detente from below are talking about an all-European civil society.

The term 'civil society' is sometimes used to mean society as opposed to the state, and sometimes – this is the Hegelian sense – to mean a society that comes into being as a result of the existence of a state. The sense in which it is used in connection with the debate about detente seems to mean the autonomy of citizens or social groups – an autonomy, however, which exists only by virtue of its recognition by the state. Hence we seem to be talking about a 'second society' which has a formal, legal existence. The idea of an all-European second society is the idea of integration at the level of society – a second society in which East–West divisions no longer exist except at the level of governments. An all-European civil society would be, as it were, official recognition of this all-European second society. In such a situation, the behaviour of governments either changes or becomes less and less relevant.

These two different approaches are *not* mutually exclusive. On the contrary, as I pointed out above, most of the contributors to this book would advocate a combination of approaches, although the emphasis varies greatly in the different chapters.

What is the New Detente?

The new detente can perhaps be described as a conversation – the opening up of real dialogue between East and West. In a sense, this book is a series of unfinished discussions which have to be continued in the coming years.

In trying to define the content of this conversation, certain preliminary

hesitations and qualifications become apparent. First, a major theme
of this book is uncertainty. The certainties of the post-war period
are dissolving; we are not searching for new ones. Trying to increase
mutual understanding between, say, the Western left and Eastern opposition groups, or between Eastern reformers and Western liberals, calls
into question many of the political assumptions of the past, the political
styles and goals we have taken for granted. Yet at the same time there
have to be some certainties, some continuities, if we are to shape and
participate in a new detente.

Secondly, the chapters of this book are both descriptive and pre-
scriptive. Is the new detente what *is* happening in the post-INF era? Or
is it about what *ought* to happen? The world is changing so rapidly that
the distinction may no longer be relevant. How we describe the new
detente is also a way of influencing the process. The goals of a new
detente have to be ambitious and yet rooted in what is actually happening – 'responsibly utopian' is the term used by Radmila Nakarada in the
concluding chapter. Thirdly, what are the limits to tolerance? Is it possible to reconcile a belief in diversity and experiment and a rejection of
universalistic answers with a commitment to basic shared human values,
as expressed in international laws or declarations like the Helsinki Final
Act? Do we tolerate the Ceausescu regime in Romania, apartheid, or
the genocide of Kurds? Does tolerance merely mean non-violence, an
unwillingness to intervene with physical force? Would the new detente
be better described as an argument or a struggle? The term conversation
implies, perhaps, too much underlying empathy.

Finally, in what sense can a conversation constitute a form of political
action? In a certain respect this is a Western question. For East Europeans, talking, creating the autonomy in which to talk, is itself a political
act. Being non-political, in the sense described by George Konrád and
Vaclav Havel, is political, because everything is political.[13] Western
society, on the other hand, can perhaps be described as non-political –
atomized and individualized. Talking is permitted; so is the creation of
subcultures. But how does this influence politics? Is it enough to join a
demonstration, to give a donation to CND, Greenpeace or Band Aid?
How are these concerns politicized? How are they translated into social
and political change?

Taking into account these qualifications and hesitations, it is possible
to draw up an agenda for discussion, a series of topics that ought to be
covered in the forthcoming conversation. This book is roughly divided
into such a set of topics.

The chapters in Part I explore differing conceptions of detente both
now and in the 1970s, as well as differing futures for Europe. Can we
conceive of changes in international relations, in the relations between

states in East and West, without taking into account the influence of and consequences for internal domestic changes? What are the connections between cycles of detente and Cold War, and cycles of reform and 'normalization'? Or, more specifically – and ambitiously – what is the connection between demilitarization and democratization, in the European context? Pavel Podlesnyi and Adam Michnik offer almost opposite ways of answering these questions from an Eastern perspective. Podlesnyi is preoccupied with interstate relations and the obstacles to detente posed by Western governments – an orthodox, seemingly pre-Gorbachevian Soviet view. Michnik is concerned with the relationship between detente and internal change in Soviet-type societies. While he interprets the ostpolitik of the SPD in the early 1970s as beneficial for the domestic evolution of Polish society, he points out the limits to detente in the 1970s – the way in which detente appeared to accept oppression in the East – and he is wary of disarmament moves in the West which might, he thinks, strengthen hardliners in the East. The chapters by Mient Jan Faber, Egbert Jahn and Jaraslav Šabata all in different ways make what they regard as a necessary connection between international and domestic changes, between disarmament and democracy, in Europe as a whole and the two Germanies in particular. Šabata proposes practical ways in which state detente and citizens' detente could interact.

Part II covers the more conventional subjects of international relations literature and of those concerned about detente between governments – that is to say, geopolitics and militarization. By geopolitics, we mean the global context of a new detente in Europe, changing relations with the superpowers and the Third World. The first three essays address the issue of superpower withdrawal from Europe and the Third World. Is there a tendency on the part of the superpowers to withdraw from Europe, and how can superpower withdrawal be encouraged and yet managed so as to ensure that *both* withdraw? Does withdrawal from Europe imply withdrawal from the Third World, or a shift of strategic interest *towards* the Third World? It seems that the Soviet Union is engaged in a general retreat, a loss of interest in the Third World. But, as Richard Falk suggests, the opposite may be true for the United States. It is important in setting out the global context to emphasize the asymmetry between East and West. Developments in East and West are parallel and interconnected, but not at all the same. In Europe, the Western part is economically strong and has an independent voice in world affairs. Western Europe, for example, accounts for over 40 per cent of world manufactured trade. Western Europe is both object and subject, actor and victim. Eastern Europe is object and victim.

A similar asymmetry may be observed in relation to the Third World. In particular, the Soviet role is seen there as relatively more progressive than the Western role. The war in Afghanistan is hideous and tragic and has to be resolved. Nevertheless, as Muchie and van Zon point out, some parts of the Third World fear the retreat of a counter to Western involvement.

The main form of geopolitical withdrawal is demilitarization. The chapters by Gerard Holden and Karsten Voigt describe the 'New Thinking' in Soviet reform circles and West German Social Democratic circles, respectively. There is a remarkable parallelism in these two types of 'New Thinking'. Both emphasize the importance of non-provocative defence, alternatively known as sufficient defence or structural inability to attack. Both envisage that this change in defence posture will be achieved within the framework of existing alliances and through a combination of multilateral agreements, as in the Conventional Armed Forces talks in Vienna, and unilateral steps – what Voigt calls 'defensive re-armament'. This approach to demilitarization is very much in keeping with official detente concepts. The aim is to lessen the risk of war and the danger of misperception of each other's intentions while maintaining current military-political arrangements more or less intact. Of course, a restructuring of military postures and a reduction in mutual provocation would open up new political opportunities, not least because the legitimation of the external threat, the 'other', is reduced. Also, the most provocative elements in the postures of NATO and the Warsaw Pact tend to be associated with the superpowers – in the case of NATO, American nuclear weapons and 'deep-strike' conventional weapons; in the case of the Warsaw Pact, Soviet tanks. All the same, it is possible to envisage a process of demilitarization that would be more in keeping with an erosion of the blocs and of the sharp distinction between East and West. Such a process would put more emphasis on lowering military capabilities rather than transforming military postures, and on measures which would lessen the integration of alliances such as troop withdrawals. This sort of approach is, for example, suggested in Mient Jan Faber's essay.

Part III, entitled European Co-operation and Domestic Change, deals with subjects that broadly come under the auspices of detente between societies or detente from below. Co-operation on common problems – especially economic, ecological and cultural co-operation – is often seen as an important way of drawing together the two halves of Europe, especially at the level of citizen and society. But co-operation is not as straightforward as it sometimes appears.

First of all, it is not obvious that both sides do in fact share common problems. It may be that Eastern Europe needs Western Europe more than the other way round – at least, this is how it is perceived. In economic terms, Eastern Europe needs access to the global economy, to Western science and technology and to Western sources of credit. East Europeans also feel as though they have been denied their cultural heritage –'kidnapped West' is the term used by Milan Kundera.[14] There are common ecological problems, of course – pollution of rivers and seas, acid rain, the fallout from Chernobyl – but is this the extent of shared concern? After all, the East European market accounts for a rather small share of West European exports, except for West Germany. What is more, Eastern Europe does not have much to offer in return, at least in an economic sense. Increased economic co-operation in the 1970s merely led to increased indebtedness on the part of Eastern Europe. Some in the West perhaps hanker for the cultural and intellectual traditions of Central Europe, but how much? Is there, in fact, likely to be a further divergence between Eastern and Western Europe – a growing income gap? Can we anticipate the marginalization or the 'Third Worldization' of Eastern Europe? There is, of course, the common problem of the arms race. In so far as West European establishments favour high levels of armament and, indeed, depend on the divison of Europe for their legitimacy, there is a vested interest in *not* co-operating. However, the prospects for demilitarization and change in Eastern Europe do offer the possibility of a changed balance of domestic political forces in Western Europe. Those groups favouring internal change in Western Europe do have an interest in co-operation.

This relates to a second problem: the difficulty of co-operation between different economic and political systems. A concrete example is provided in Andras Köves's chapter, where he points out that economic co-operation began to stagnate and decline even before the political detente of the 1970s came to an end. This was because of growing indebtedness. The reason why Eastern Europeans were unable to export enough to pay for the upsurge in imports had to do both with the nature of socialist economic systems *and* with socialist policies. He argues that internal economic reform, liberalization of markets to deal with shortage, as well as reorientation towards Western markets, are a necessary precondition for successful economic change. Hence co-operation cannot be separated from domestic change – what we refer to as pluralism.

Pluralism may not be the right term. What we mean is a process of internal change within the different localities, regions and nations of Europe, at different paces and in different directions. The end result is a variety, or pluralism, of economic and political systems in place of the two rather homogeneous models of Atlanticism and post-Stalinism that can be observed in Europe today.

Pluralism does not necessarily mean that change will be progressive – herein lies the contradiction of uncertainty and diversity. On the contrary, this will depend on local and particular circumstances. Moreover, pluralism, especially in Eastern Europe, could bring out into the open long-suppressed nationalistic and anti-Semitic tendencies – observable, for example, in some sections of Pamiat (Soviet Union), Grunewald (Poland) or among the Populists (Hungary). If these tendencies are somehow to be managed they need, perhaps, to come out into the open. They underline the need for dialogue, for a sense of internationalism and for individual responsibility.

On the other hand, pluralism is a necessary condition for a renewed creativity, to reverse the stagnation and, indeed, involution of European and global civilization. Pluralism allows for experimentation and for observation. In this respect, our deliberations about the state versus the market, and about the state versus civil society, are particularly important. There is so much to learn. Can we envisage a social sector that is neither public (belonging to the state) nor private (belonging to the individual and the realm of profit)? Can we envisage a public sector that is truly accountable and participatory? The chapters concerned with economic and ecological issues focus on these questions. They illuminate the divergence between Western socialists, who are interested in the construction of an empowering or flexible state, and Eastern radicals, who see markets as necessary both to solve economic problems and to provide non-political space. In fact, the divergence is smaller than it appears once issues are talked through – it arises precisely out of the differing and asymmetric political and social contexts. Indeed, the differences between official reformers in the East and representatives of Eastern social movements are greater than the differences between social movements in East and West.

There is an enormous problem of language which obscures or, alternatively, widens differences. Words like 'markets' are used differently according to different political situations and priorities. A particular problem arises from the term 'socialist'. Many of the activists in social movements would describe themselves as socialist in a Western context, but the term is less and less used in an Eastern context because of its associations. (It is used much more among the Soviet clubs than in Eastern Europe.) But this does not mean that the Eastern activists are liberals in a Western sense, as Timothy Garton Ash has suggested in a recent article.[15] This is easily revealed by a study of the content of their concerns. These chapters, especially those by Istvan Rev, Kate Soper and Martin Ryle, Hilary Wainwright and Boris Kagarlitsky, illuminate these problems of language. Developing a common language could be the most important outcome of a new detente.

At the heart of the pluralist conception is the problem of how to create the rules, norms and organizations necessary for democratic politics. East European societies have to learn how to adapt to and evolve democratic institutions. Western societies enjoy the trappings of democracy, yet they have to learn how to be political, how to engage in a process of political change, how to overcome apathy, alienation and depoliticization. (Mrs Thatcher won her three elections on a much smaller proportion of the eligible voters than Jaruselzki obtained when he lost the referendum about political and economic reform in Poland.) At root, this is a problem of political culture – something specifically addressed by Milan Šimečka, Boris Kagarlitsky and Istvan Rev. Elisabeth Gerle describes one particular subculture, that of the women's peace movement, and how this might challenge the cultural norms of European society.

In the concluding chapter Radmila Nakarada recapitulates the conversation, describing and prescribing past and future approaches to East–West dialogue.

It may be that what we require is some form of concrete proposal – some way of institutionalizing the conversation. Charter 77 in Czechoslovakia have put forward an interesting suggestion. They say that what we need is a formal gathering of social movements, a Citizens' Assembly or a Helsinki Parliament. Such a gathering would comprise all autonomous movements in Europe, including the Soviet Union, committed to certain principles such as democracy, disarmament, the withdrawal of foreign troops – that is, principles which, if applied, could end the East–West division of Europe. Such an Assembly would deal with many European problems (national minorities, ecological questions, and so on) through its own deliberations, address proposals to governments, and constitute a formal recognition of the existence of such movements. Governments would be asked formally to guarantee the safety of such an Assembly through, for example, the continuing Helsinki process.

The point of a proposal of this kind is to make visible the second political society of social movements – to provide an institutional expression of an all-European civil society. Or, to put it another way, along with this book and a plethora of invisible or hardly visible efforts to increase the communication between citizens and citizens' groups in East and West that *already* exist, it is an attempt to secure a deep-rooted social and cultural interest in a Europe beyond the Cold War and beyond detente.

Notes

1. See John Keane, *Democracy and Civil Society*, London 1988.

2. Paul Kennedy, *The Rise and Fall of the Great Powers: Economic Change and Military Conflict from 1500 to 2000*, New York 1987.

3. See, especially, Robert Gilpin, *War and Change in World Politics*, Cambridge 1982, and Robert Keohane, *After Hegemony: Cooperation and Discord in the World Political Economy*, Princeton, NJ 1984.

4. C. Fred Bergsten, 'Economic Imbalances', *Foreign Affairs*, Spring 1987.

5. David P. Calleo, *Beyond American Hegemony: The Future of the Western Alliance*, Brighton 1987.

6. See 'Part III, Europe and the World Outside', in Jonathan Alford and Kenneth Hunt, eds, *Europe in the Western Alliance, Towards European Defence Entity?* London 1987.

7. W.W. Rostow, 'On Ending the Cold War', *Foreign Affairs*, Spring 1987.

8. Paul Marer, 'Intrabloc Economic Relations and Prospects', in David Holloway and Jane M.O. Sharp, eds, *The Warsaw Pact: Alliance in Transition?* London 1984.

9. London 1960.

10. Kate Soper, 'Contradictions of Perestroika', *END Journal*, no. 28/29, Summer 1987.

11. Ferenc Miszlivetz, *Reform, Crisis and the Second Society in Hungary*, paper presented to the conference on 'Withdrawal of the Developmental State', Institute of Development Studies, Brighton, July 1987.

12. 'We have won the ideological war; we are close to winning the geopolitical contest in the Third World, except for the Middle East. We long ago won the economic competition.' William G. Hyland, 'Reagan–Gorbachev III', *Foreign Affairs*, Autumn 1987.

13. George Konrád, *Anti-Politics*, London 1984; Vaclav Havel, in J. Keane, ed., *The Power of the Powerless: citizens against the state in Central-Eastern Europe*, London 1985.

14. Milan Kundera, '"A Kidnapped West or Culture Bows Out"', *Granta*, no. 11.

15. Timothy Garton Ash, 'Empire in Decay', *New York Review of Books*, 29 September 1988.

PART I
Concepts of Detente

1

Detente in Europe

Mient Jan Faber

The period after the Cold War is usually called 'detente', but when exactly did the Cold War end? Did the Cold War ever end, if by Cold War we mean its structural consequences: a Europe divided into two military alliances under the leadership of the superpowers? In any case, historians still argue about when the 'thaw' began.

One problem is, of course, that the term 'thaw' or detente means different things to different sections of society and in different parts of the world. There is detente between the superpowers, which involves a less confrontational stance between the United States and the Soviet Union as well as a series of arms-control agreements. And there is the detente in Europe initiated by Willy Brandt's Ostpolitik and culminating in the 1975 Helsinki Final Act, which not only settled outstanding geopolitical disputes in Europe but also led to a deeper, more far-reaching social detente because it involved increased co-operation and communication between European societies.

A major concern of this chapter is whether this deeper social detente can be sustained in the future without a real attempt to dismantle the structural consequences of the Cold War – that is to say, without lowering the level of militarization in Europe and especially in Central Europe, and without loosening the integrated military structures of the two alliances.

The Superpowers

It is generally recognized that Stalin's death in 1953 and the liquidation of Beria, the head of the secret police (KGB), in June of that year were the essential preconditions for detente. In 1956, at the 20th Congress of the CPSU, Stalinism was rejected and a policy of peaceful coexistence (detente) was proclaimed. A year earlier the USSR had agreed to the Austrian State Treaty. Territorial disputes with Finland and China were resolved and Yugoslavia's 'own way' was respected. The unilateral demobilization of 1.2 million Russian soldiers was also a gesture of goodwill towards the USA. But detente was more than that; it had psychological significance too. Khrushchev's foreign policy was characterized by what soon became known as 'the diplomacy of the smile'. In 1959 America's Vice-President Nixon travelled to the USSR, and in December of that year Khrushchev visited the USA. The main purpose of his journey was to discuss – and resolve if possible – the German problems, especially the 'tinderbox' Berlin.

But in spite of the good atmosphere the Berlin question remained a source of conflict. Many thousands of GDR citizens left their country via Berlin to settle in West Germany. After some five years of careful thaw, the weather changed. On 2 and 3 June 1961 an 'informal' meeting took place in Vienna between Kennedy and Khrushchev. It failed. On 15 June Khrushchev delivered a speech in Moscow and gave the West an ultimatum regarding Berlin. He also denied the Western allies the right to control access to the city. The following month the USSR announced a substantial increase in the defence budget. On 23 July Kennedy asked for reinforcement of NATO forces. Early in August, Khrushchev even threatened to start general mobilization in the USSR. Was the Cold War about to become hot? But then, on 13 August, the GDR sealed off the Eastern sector of Berlin and began to build 'the Wall'. However shocking and inhuman, this reduced the risk of armed confrontation. But once again the people had to pay the bill: *Abgrenzung*, or the cutting-off of East from West Germany. In mid-October international tension decreased when the USSR withdrew the Berlin ultimatum.

In summer 1962 reconnaissance photographs showed that the USSR was sending large shipments of bombers and nuclear missiles to Cuba, to be based there. The American administration felt this was a direct threat to its security. On 22 October Kennedy announced a total blockade of Cuba and demanded that the Soviet Union withdraw the offensive weapons from the island. Four days later Khrushchev made a counter-proposal, in which he made the withdrawal of Russian weapons dependent on the removal from Turkey of fifteen American Jupiter missiles which had been stationed there in 1958. The American government refused this condition. For the next two days the world was balanced on the brink of war between the USA and the USSR. But then, on 28 October, the Russian ships changed course. Khrushchev declared that he was willing to dismantle the missiles in Cuba on condition that the USA lifted the blockade and undertook not to invade the island. About a month later the Americans ended the blockade and the Russian missiles, which had already been dismantled, left Cuba. A little later the USA withdrew the medium-range Thor and Jupiter missiles from Europe.

In their bilateral relations after the Cuba crisis, the USA and the USSR refrained from a 'brinkmanship strategy' for almost eleven years. This did happen once again, through bad crisis management, in 1973 in the Middle East. But that was the last time, in spite of the many conflicts between the two countries.

It seems to me that detente between the superpowers is therefore principally based on the virtual absence of brinkmanship strategies. In that sense we can say that there is *structural detente*. No doubt the realization that such a war could be a nuclear one in which both sides would be losers has contributed to this state of affairs. The nuclear MAD (Mutual Assured Destruction) philosophy has (implicitly) been accepted by both sides.

In summer 1973 the political climate in the Middle East deteriorated. The USSR was shipping cargoes of modern Russian weapons to the Arab states, notwithstanding doubts about the Arabs' military competence and Arab doubts about Moscow in 1972, when Sadat had dismissed 20,000 Soviet military advisers. However, even a limited victory by Egypt and Syria in the territories occupied by Israel would have severely undermined the USA's prestige in the region. This is presumably why the USSR did nothing to prevent war from breaking out, even though it was probably informed a few days in advance, since many Soviet citizens departed from Syria in the first days of October. Hostilities started on 6 October 1973. Although President Nixon was furious, he did appeal to Brezhnev to work together for a cease-fire. After all, the superpowers had an agreement to co-operate in trying to avoid conflicts of this type! Brezhnev responded positively, but at the same time he encouraged the Arabs, in a letter to the Algerian President Boumédienne, to give Egypt and Syria all possible support. From 10 October onwards Russian aircraft were flying to and from the Middle East – more than 1,000 flights that month! – to supply the Arab countries with military equipment. When Israel gained the initiative in the war, Moscow began to advocate a political solution for the conflict. In the meantime the USA too had set up an extensive airlift to Israel.

At Brezhnev's request Kissinger went to Moscow, where both countries tried to reach agreement about a resolution for the Security Council. In addition to a cease-fire, Brezhnev also wanted direct negotiations between Israel and the Arab countries. On 22 October the Security

Council adopted a cease-fire resolution, but Israel ignored it. From the bridgehead on the west bank of the Suez Canal its forces started to encircle Egypt's Third Army. Egypt's military collapse was finally prevented because of the risk of direct military confrontation between the superpowers. The American intelligence services had reported that even though the USSR had recalled a large part of its air fleet, seven Russian airborne divisions had been put on alert. Brezhnev wrote in a harsh letter to Nixon that the USSR could be compelled to initiate unilateral (military) action if Israel did not climb down. In response, all US forces worldwide – nuclear ones included – were put on a state of alert. NATO allies were not informed in advance. In the tense hours which followed, American and Soviet diplomats worked with frenzied haste on a new resolution: a UN peacekeeping force (without Americans and Russians) was to separate the opposing sides. This resolution was accepted by the Security Council and, under US pressure, also by Israel.

Arms Control

Despite the acceptance of the MAD philosophy, the arms race did not come to an end, but MAD did provide a basis for arms control. Today, that function is supposed to be provided by the concept of 'common security' – a more benign concept than MAD. But both concepts share the same assumption: that in the nuclear era, one-sided security does not exist. Arms control became the unique instrument for taming an unrestrained arms race, but it is an instrument with major flaws. After all, the obvious arms-control technique is one which is mainly determined by mathematics. Numbers (of weapons) and (tactical combat) options are compared and efforts are made to establish some kind of measurable equality. Sometimes this could even mean elimination, as happened with the INF missiles. But the MAD situation does not depend on equilibria in weaponry and capabilities. There is also, for example, a MAD situation between France and the USSR. In view of the relatively small number of weapons and options they have available, it is therefore not surprising that the French are not at all inclined to get involved in arms-control negotiations.

A not unimportant side-effect of arms control is that MAD gets 'overinsured'. The possession of at least as many options (and numbers) as the opponent becomes an objective which hypnotizes the military and the politicians. The process of continuous regulation of all these options pushes the arms race forward.

Arms control came increasingly to replace MAD, which turned out to be the closing item on the balance sheet. MAD could not stand up against the political and psychological pressures of the arms race and arms control. The structural detente between the superpowers became overshadowed by the alternation of sunshine and cloud in the arms-race and arms-control processes. The 'weather' (arms control) determined the relationship – or rather the mood – between East and West. And the weather is changeable, especially because brinkmanship strategies *within* the arms-race and -control process are very popular. The opponent must be forced to submit by a strategy of developing new weapons or by increasing the number of weapons. Each side tries to gain a numerical advantage within the arms-control game. If the opponent does not give in, however, the risk is *not* war. If the opponent does not climb down, *nothing* happens, only arms control fails and the arms race proceeds 'normally': that is, without restraint in a certain area. It is usually forgotten in the heat of the political conflict that because of MAD, these controversies about weapons are just a sham. It is still assumed, somehow, that political power can be measured in numbers of weapons.

In the USSR a profound political change was necessary before the 'New Thinking' could break through this arms-control myopia, and it was realized that the confrontation about land-based medium-range missiles was rather absurd. The governments of most of the NATO countries still have not understood this insight. They still swear by the INF brinkmanship strategy, which they believe worked like this: increasing understanding between the USA and the USSR that nuclear war between them was out of the question led in the late 1970s to the SALT II Treaty. Through this arms-control agreement the arms race in the area of strategic systems was restrained. This gave the USSR the opportunity to strengthen its position in Europe in the field of medium-range weapons. By means of a new tactical option – the SS-20 missiles – pressure could be put on Western Europe in times of tension. The most important Western European government leaders (Schmidt, Giscard d'Estaing, Callaghan) convinced the Carter administration in early 1979, in Guadeloupe, of the necessity of an INF brinkmanship strategy to make the USSR back down. On 12 December 1979 the NATO countries decided to deploy in Western Europe large numbers (572) of Pershing II missiles with their surgical precision and ultra-short warning time, and the GLCMs (Ground-Launched Cruise Missiles) with first-use missions. On 18 November 1981 the USSR was offered only one way to escape from this threat: to dismantle all its SS-20 missiles, the so-called Zero Option. After six years of political pressure, from 1981 to 1987, the USSR finally gave in. An agreement was signed by Reagan and Gorbachev in Washington on 8 December 1987. All the missiles will be destroyed.

This line of reasoning is highly dubious, even though it is very useful for public consumption. After all, unlike the Cold War brinkmanship of the 1950s, an arms-control brinkmanship strategy can fail, because the ultimate sanction, war, is out of the question. I remember a discussion with the Dutch Defence Minister in September 1983, in which he said: 'I give you my guarantee that after the stationing of Pershing II and GLCM war will not break out in Europe.' He most definitely believed that MAD continued to function. And the brinkmanship strategy did indeed fail, in late 1983. In November that year the Geneva negotiations collapsed, the first cruise missiles and Pershing IIs were stationed in Western Europe, and in turn the USSR took countermeasures by stationing SS-12/22 missiles in Czechoslovakia and the GDR – the 'normal' process of the arms race, nothing 'serious'! The brinkmanship strategy had collapsed like a house of cards, and nobody was surprised. Moreover, the West had already for some time been indicating, in a variety of ways, that a different outcome from the Geneva negotiations – different from the Zero Option – would be quite acceptable. A degree of parity between the SS-20s on one side and Pershing II and the GLCMs on the other side in Europe fitted in very well with NATO's flexible-response strategy. The private 'Walk in the Woods' agreement between the negotiators Nitze and Kvitsinski in Geneva, in summer 1982, allowed for hundreds of warheads on both sides, and after it was disclosed to the public it met with much approval from the political leaders in Western Europe at that time. It seems that they did not at all feel that the SS-20s took them to the edge of the precipice, and brink-manship was a kind of theatre, performed for the sake of arms control. If Brezhnev had lived longer, it is more than probable that we would still be surrounded by medium-range missiles. It is ultimately Gorbachev's achievement that this theatre came to an end.

The signing of the INF Accord in Washington on 8 December 1987 has given 'arms control' some new credit. The main criticism from within the Western security establishment concerns the unusual nature of the INF Accord. A strategic option is being eliminated. This is incon-sistent with the logic of the arms race and associated arms-control measures. Although options should be kept under control, they should not be eliminated. It is feared that this new form of arms control might be the start of a process leading to a nuclear-free world. In other words, agreements of this type undermine MAD, and MAD is supposed to be responsible for the elimination of war – at least between the nuclear powers!

The Strategic Defense Initiative (SDI) was attacked for the same reason a few years ago. President Reagan's sharp criticism of 'arms control' – he particularly attacked SALT II – was one of the factors which helped him to gain power in 1980. Initially he did not oppose

MAD, it was only in 1983 that he added a fundamental criticism of MAD to his dislike of arms-control agreements with the Russians. SDI was to make nuclear weapons 'impotent and obsolete'. All this, combined with strong anti-Soviet rhetoric, inevitably gave the impression that the president was hankering back to the time of *real* brinkmanship strategies. Only the risk of nuclear destruction had to be avoided (at least for the USA!).

SDI – and 'Reagan's dream' even more so – sent shock waves of dismay through Western Europe's security elites, and also amongst many in the USA. It was, as the Germans would put it, an *Umwertung aller nuklearen Werten* – a revision of all nuclear principles.

At the time of writing, the 1972 ABM Treaty seems to have won the battle against SDI. For the time being, SDI will consist of research only. The ABM Treaty can properly be called the cornerstone of MAD. The US Congress wants to stick to a strict interpretation of the treaty and the Reagan administration appears to accept this, despite some verbal violence. The USSR too displays loyalty to the ABM Treaty, but it is not clear to what extent this standpoint is consistent with the USSR's aim of a nuclear-free world. After all, the ABM Treaty has meaning only when coupled to MAD. The treaty guarantees 'common (in)security' because it makes defence against strategic nuclear weapons impossible.

It looks as if, after all the commotion, both superpowers have returned to the discipline of MAD, including the rules of the game of arms control. The reduction in strategic weapons aimed for is 'only' 50 per cent (overall), not total elimination. This, and also the forthcoming 'stability/reduction talks' in the field of conventional forces' ratios (in Europe), indicate that the traditional approach to arms control has been resumed. It is possible, however, that both sides will take some unilateral steps for economic reasons.

Europe

Because of their worldwide interests, the superpowers are often 'trouble-makers'. Their interference in regional problems can easily lead to a worsening of the situation, instead of improvement. There are numerous examples: Vietnam, Afghanistan, Nicaragua, and so on. But because of their relationship of structural detente it is in the interest of both super-powers that the conflicts do not escalate. They also fulfil a role as 'troubleshooters'.

Europe's post-war history is a good illustration of 'troubles' being created and then eased by one superpower or both. Stable relations between East and West in Europe came about both in spite of this involvement by the USSR and the USA and because of it; they now are guarded with great care by the European countries themselves. Whereas the USA and the USSR often continue to perceive the arms race as a key instrument in their power struggle for influence in Europe, their European allies regard arms control as an excellent opportunity to bring about detente. European governments, particularly in the West, are so much under the spell of parity in military capabilities that all other problems are considered secondary or completely separate. Detente turns out to be highly divisible. The Russian occupation of Afghanistan in 1979 was obviously not glossed over in Western Europe, but many countries refused to make too big an issue of it and to join the USA in boycotting the 1980 Olympic Games in Moscow. And when, in 1981, a state of martial law was proclaimed in Poland and the independent trade union Solidarność was suppressed, the Chancellor of West Germany at that time, Helmut Schmidt, spoke from the heart on that very same day (13 December) when he said that this was primarily an internal matter. In other words, East–West relations in Europe were not put to the test by the events in Poland. Neither was the NATO dual-track decision of 1979, in which arms-race deployment and arms control (negotiations) were combined, allowed to suffer a setback, for it depended more than anything else on whether or not there would be detente in Europe.

The Western responses to Afghanistan and Poland were not so unlike the earlier European reactions to the Warsaw Pact invasion of Czecho-slovakia in 1968. The French Prime Minister at that time, Michel Debré, described the invasion as 'an accident on the road to detente'.

It seems as if Europe has accepted its division for the time being. During his visit to the Federal Republic in 1987, Honecker character-ized the differences between East and West as 'water and fire'. If the fire heats the water long enough, the water will evaporate; and water is in turn able to extinguish fire. So the two must be kept apart by creating political and military barriers: closed borders (visa requirements) and parity in armaments.

In December 1967 the NATO Council accepted the Harmel Report. Article 5 reads:

> The Atlantic Alliance has two main functions. Its first function is to maintain adequate military strength and political solidarity to deter aggression and other forms of pressure and to defend the territory of member countries if aggression should occur. Since its inception, the Alliance has successfully fulfilled this task. But the possibility of a crisis cannot be excluded as long as the central political issues in Europe, first and foremost the *German Question*, remain unsolved. Moreover, the situation of instability and uncertainty still precludes a balanced reduction of military forces. Under these conditions, the Allies will maintain as necessary a suitable military capability to assure the

balance of forces, thereby creating a climate of stability, security and confidence. In this climate the Alliance can carry out its second function, to
pursue the search for progress towards a more stable relationship in which the
underlying political issues can be contradictory but complementary. Collective
defence is a stabilizing factor in world politics. It is the necessary condition of
effective policies directed towards a greater relaxation of tensions. The way to
peace and stability in Europe rests in particular on the use of the Alliance
constructively in the interest of detente. The participation of the USSR and
the USA will be necessary to achieve a settlement of the political problems of
Europe.

Now, twenty years later, many of the underlying political issues
described in Article 5 of the Harmel Report have been resolved. The
24th Party Congress of the Communist Party of the USSR, which took
place from 30 March to 9 April 1971, approved Brezhnev's 'peace
programme', which had as its main aim 'the final recognition of the territorial changes that took place in Europe as a result of the Second World
War. To bring about a radical turn towards detente and peace on this
continent.' The overriding aim of the USSR was to make the West
accept that the division of Germany – 'the German Question' – was an
established fact, and also to accept the other territorial and political
changes in Central and Eastern Europe that took place as a result of the
Second World War. This programme yielded results in the 1970s.

In 1969 the SPD gained a majority in the Bundestag and Willy
Brandt became Federal Chancellor. The long-cherished desire for
German reunification – still implicit in the Harmel Report – was no
longer realistic. Instead a policy of reconciliation was developed. In the
words of Egon Bahr of the SPD: *Wandel durch Annäherung* (change
through *rapprochement*). The idea of one German nation was of course
maintained, but it was quite acceptable that this one nation would for
the time being consist of two independent states. According to the SPD
this need not lead to a *de jure* recognition of the GDR – which would,
after all, require a revision of the West German Constitution – but the
GDR was *de facto* recognized by the FRG. Erich Honecker's first
official visit to the FRG in 1987 was the highest achievement of this
policy. For Willy Brandt and for all his successors reunification is now
only a distant goal, the precise form of which is left open for the future.
Since the two regimes in East and West Germany are now unlikely to
merge, the problem is how to reduce the barriers between the peoples of
both states so that they will at least be able to become reconciled. On 12
August 1970 Brandt and Brezhnev signed a non-aggression treaty.
Article 1 stated explicitly that 'detente' was the primary objective of
Russo–German political relations. Both parties undertook to refrain
from the use of force; the frontiers of all states in Europe were said to be

inviolable, including the Oder–Neisse border between Poland and the GDR. In this way West Germany confirmed the division of the German nation into two states and the loss of territories to Poland. Three months later Chancellor Brandt visited Warsaw and knelt down before the monument for victims of the war, bearing witness to German guilt. '*Ost Verträge*' ('Treaties with the East') were concluded not only with Poland but also with other East European countries.

The Treaty of Moscow was a great success for Brezhnev's policies, but the West Germans demanded a *quid pro quo* and were prepared to ratify the treaty only if a satisfactory agreement regarding Berlin was reached. On 26 March 1970 the four occupying powers (the UK, France, the USA and the USSR) began discussions, but these were greatly complicated by Walter Ulbricht's inflexible stance. The East German leader demanded – as a precondition – Bonn's full recognition of the GDR as a sovereign state. The Western powers were prepared to accept East Berlin's status as the capital of the GDR, but only if the Soviet Union would recognize West Berlin as a part of West Germany. Moscow refused. The negotiations became deadlocked, and could proceed again only when, under pressure from Moscow, Walter Ulbricht was replaced by Erich Honecker. On 3 September 1971 an agreement was reached which called upon East and West to make the necessary arrangements to facilitate the movement of traffic to Berlin. The 'Final Quadripartite Protocol' was signed on 3 June 1972. Moscow had its way: West Berlin did not become a 'constituent part of the Federal Republic of Germany' and there would be only a limited official presence of the FRG in West Berlin. Conversely, the USSR had made concessions too, including a promise of no hindrance to traffic between West Germany and West Berlin. The USSR further recognized the special financial, economic and cultural links between West Berlin and the FRG, which could be maintained and extended. Citizens of West Berlin were given the same rights of access to East Berlin and the GDR as those of West Germany already possessed. It was generally agreed that the Berlin question, despite the limitations of the agreements, was now no longer a source of tension between East and West which could lead to war. Even in 1988, however, West Berlin's definitive status was still a source of dispute between East and West: it delayed the reaching of an agreement between the EEC and Comecon which was finally signed in Luxembourg on 25 June. The USSR has always seen West Berlin as a distinct entity, and continues to do so.

Still outstanding in the early 1970s was a formal treaty between the two Germanies. Talks commenced in August 1972 and a preparatory treaty was signed as early as 21 September of that same year. It was a political compromise; a definitive legal basis for the status of both

Germanies was not and still is not possible. The most important provisions were:

- the exchange of permanent legations (not embassies);
- the GDR kept the EEC advantages it had by virtue of 'inter-German trade';
- both countries became members of the United Nations.

The most important preparatory work for an agreement between *all* countries of East and West had now in fact been completed. On 1 August 1975 the Final Act of the Conference for Security and Co-operation in Europe (CSCE) was signed in Helsinki by thirty-five countries – by the US and Canada and all European countries, except Albania.

The Final Act of Helsinki was the outcome of a process which had been going on for the previous thirty years. The territorial status quo in Europe was confirmed and the post-war borders were ratified. In addition, the political systems which had emerged under Soviet pressure in the Warsaw Pact countries were finally accepted by the West. But the Final Act also contained ten principles – such as respect for human rights and fundamental freedoms, equal rights and the right of self-determination for nations – which, of course, also challenged aspects of the system. In addition, the 'third basket' of the Accord contained a commitment to humanitarian, social and cultural co-operation. It was agreed to stimulate contacts between people and educational and cultural exchanges, and finally to give everybody access to information. The irreconcilable was in fact reconciled in Helsinki. Under pressure from the East the geopolitical status quo, the *partition* of Europe, had been accepted, but under pressure from the West the cultural and historical *unity* (Gorbachev's expression) was implicitly established. 'If we have no option other than to go our separate ways politically and as *states*, let us then at least try to preserve the unity of European *society*', seems to have been the thinking in the West.

> Europe is partitioned politically, but it is not divided and is indivisible in spirit. . . . What unites us is a common history, the unity in a diversity of national cultures and the indivisible fate of the future on this small piece of land. . . . What matters is that the borders are stripped of their divisive and inhuman characteristics.

Thus Federal President Von Weizsäcker summarized concisely the Helsinki Accords in a speech in Moscow in 1987.

It is an intriguing compromise. The East European states either did not fathom its scope, or thought they could live with it in a Machiavellian manner. They had, after all, been sold an intellectual notion from the French Revolution (and Enlightenment): the separation of state and society; and also the separation of state and individual. Translated into legal terms it means: the individual and the 'free' spheres of society have the *right* (qualified by circumstances) of protection against the state. In the Marxist–Leninist model, however, society and the individual are largely subordinate to the state; they are, as it were, part of the state, or integrated with the state. Individual rights have been replaced by collective rights; the individual (in better times) is bestowed favours. Against this background it is remarkable and intriguing that Gorbachev appears to subscribe to this Western interpretation of the Helsinki Accords in his book *Perestroika*. 'Europe is our common home', he writes, and he came to think this 'after meeting many European leaders':

> Contemplating the vistas of this long-suffering continent and also thinking about the common roots of the multifaceted but essentially collective European civilization, I came to realize more and more how artificial the confrontation between the blocs is after all, the extent to which it is an interim situation, and how much the Iron Curtain is out of date. . . . The idea of a *common European home* most of all suggests a degree of unity, even if the countries belong to different social systems and opposing political–military alliances.

It seems that this unity should be sought not between states, but elsewhere in society.

The current debate in East Europe, in which the USSR (under Gorbachev) is now participating so actively, returns again and again to the relationship between state and society. The need for governments to withdraw, even partially, from a variety of areas, and thus the distinction between state and society, is repeatedly emphasized.

Europe, our common home; if you say that you should not be surprised if all sorts of people, groups and organizations from East and West want to begin to put this unity into practice. Parts of the Western peace movement have allied themselves with self-supporting and independent groups in East Europe, to register Europe's unity and to fight against the obstacles imposed by the military and political separation.

During the follow-up conferences to the Helsinki Accord (Belgrade: June 1977–March 1978; Madrid: 1980–March 1983; Vienna: since November 1986) there has been an avalanche of complaints about the East European countries' poor record in respecting the 'third basket' of the Helsinki Final Act. These complaints have primarily concerned the problems of individual citizens who have had to wait months and years to reunite families, for exit visas, emigration permits, and suchlike. The treatment of individual citizens in various countries has now, however, in the era of glasnost and perestroika, become more flexible. The obvious next step would be to make all sorts of initiatives for self-organization a topic for discussion at the follow-up conferences, especially since these are still being kept in check in Eastern Europe.

I remember, early in 1955, having a discussion about the Cold War in our religious studies lesson at the Protestant grammar school I attended in the Dutch provincial town of Emmen. In those days there was no subject called 'social studies' and history had to cover everything, so that we never got further than the French Revolution. Modern times remained shrouded in mystery, but an attempt was made to use religious studies lessons to cover this gap. Although Stalin had died, the German Question was very much alive. The Western powers – the USA, the UK and France – had decided to conclude unilaterally a peace treaty with West Germany (the Paris Accords of 23 October 1954). The occupation would come to an end. West Germany would join the West European Union, and was also invited to join NATO. The UK and the USA promised to leave their military forces in Europe for as long as necessary. With keen interest, we discussed in the classroom the USSR's possible and most probable responses to these events. War was a real possibility. The thought made us shiver. But the religious studies teacher had reassurance up his sleeve. He explained that Lenin had set up state communism using the model of the Roman Catholic Church – another, and a competing, (spiritual) *world* power. And hatred between the Vatican and Moscow went much deeper than that between Moscow and the Protestants. If the Russians were to occupy our country, they would no doubt leave us – the Protestants – alone for some time to come; the Catholics were in much greater danger. It was the height of the Cold War, the time of brinkmanship strategies. War was a distinct possibility, and that was how we experienced it too.

We have now been living for a long time in the era of MAD. If nuclear wars were to break out between the superpowers, that would be the end of both of them. For that reason the superpowers have (almost) eliminated the option of war in their mutual relations. This is a re-assurance for Europe too, albeit a relative one. It remains, after all, in principle possible and thinkable that a war could break out between the superpowers, perhaps even one limited to Europe. It is the perception of almost all Europeans that the chance of this happening must be reduced further and further. The Federal German Republic has, in particular, understood that it, and no one else, has to bandage Europe's post-war wounds, even though a complete healing may not be possible. The Bonn government's Deutschland-Politik and Ostpolitik have achieved a good deal. The great tinderboxes between East and West have been extinguished. 'Berlin' has been sorted out (1972). Of course, there is always room for improvement, but the essential point is that working towards a solution has entered the realm of rational and peaceable discussion. The same applies to the German Question. Full recognition of the GDR by the FRG has not yet taken place, and we may have to wait a long time. The development of bilateral relations and making 'the Wall' more penetrable, however, seem more important. The struggle for a free and decent existence in the GDR and an *open* border between the two German states continues to exercise many minds permanently on both sides of the dividing line.

The fact that the East German system is such a closed one – both internally and externally – is one reason why an estimated 80,000 people have applied for exit permits, and the FRG's constitution provides the opportunity to settle in the West without obstruction. The political and socio-economic malaise in other East European countries threatens to lead to mass exodus too. It is expected that in 1988 as many as 150,000 Poles will have settled in the FRG, most of them young and arriving without valid exit permits. The second basket of the Helsinki Accords, which calls for the intensification of scientific, economic and technological links, might be able to help in this situation, if West Europe were to show genuine interest in a socio-economic programme of reconstruction for East Europe. But so far there have been no concrete signs of this.

Militarization

The Helsinki Accords (1975) registered that everything was politically in the right place in Europe. A logical consequence of this ought to be an adjustment in the integrated military apparatus, which was constructed because of Europe's lack of political stability. As the Harmel Report put it: 'Moreover, the situation of instability and uncertainty still precludes a balanced reduction of military forces', and reference was made to the German Question. But more is involved than just 'balanced reductions'. The military edifices themselves – of NATO and the Warsaw Pact – must be adapted, for these structures are the obvious remains of the unstable period of the Cold War. NATO's forward defence positions, in which many member states participate, the massed presence of American troops and equipment in the FRG, the nineteen divisions of the USSR in the GDR and the offensive strategy of the

Warsaw Pact – all are features of a war-on-paper which still rages on under the leadership of the superpowers, in spite of the changed political situation. What would have been more logical than the evacuation of a large part of the foreign troops from Central Europe after 'Helsinki'? But the reality of the situation has shown that the adjustment of NATO's and the WTO's military structures does not necessarily proceed in parallel with the creation of political stability in Europe. During Nixon's and Brezhnev's 1972 Summit in Moscow, Nixon agreed to convene the CSCE Conference under the implicit condition that there would be parallel negotiations about a balanced reduction in troops and weapons in Europe – not so much because the West was keeping an eye on the relationship between 'political stability' and 'military adjustment', but rather because of the West's suspicion that the USSR would make political use of its superior conventional military power, especially as increasingly strong voices in the USA were advocating the withdrawal of American troops.

Since 30 October 1973, NATO and the Warsaw Pact have met regularly in Vienna for the 'Negotiations on the mutual reductions of forces and armaments and associated measures in Central Europe'. Central Europe, in this context, consists of seven countries: the Benelux countries, the FRG, the GDR, Poland and Czechoslovakia. From the beginning NATO used the term M(B)FR negotiations, thus indicating that its main aim was to achieve a 'balanced' outcome. In terms of numbers the Warsaw Pact has superiority, sometimes considerable, in a variety of types of arms – especially tanks and artillery, which are considered offensive weapons. After more than fifteen years of negotiation no progress has in fact been made, and even disagreement about the precise numbers of men on each side still persists. Only in the area of CSBMs (Confidence and Security Building Measures) – comparable with what were earlier called 'associated measures' – has some progress been made, but this was mainly in Stockholm at the so-called European Disarmament Conference (EDC) which took place as an offshoot of the second CSCE review conference in Madrid from 17 January 1986. The official title was 'Conference on Confidence and Security Building and Disarmament in Europe', and all thirty-five 'Helsinki' countries took part. On 22 September 1986 the EDC came to a successful conclusion. Considerable progress has been made on information, notification and verification of military activities. Even 'on-site inspections at short notice' have been accepted by all parties. The Warsaw Pact countries were previously not prepared to accept this. In 1987 the USA and UK used this opportunity to carry out inspections of military exercises in the USSR and GDR. The USSR in turn carried out inspections in West Germany and Turkey, and the GDR too visited an exercise in the

Federal Republic at short notice. In other words, a climate of openness
is emerging in military relations, but this still does not mean that we can
also expect early results in the reduction of forces. It seemed likely that
M(B)FR would fade out quietly in 1988.

It seems that the CSCE review conference in Vienna is likely to
create a new forum in which there will be negotiations about 'military
stability and reductions', but over a much larger territory than 'Central
Europe': from the Atlantic to the Urals. The USSR has now admitted
that there are military imbalances and that these should be eliminated
through reductions, but it is generally recognized that comparing the
various weapons systems of East and West is a highly complex matter.
NATO emphasizes inequalities in tanks and artillery, while the Warsaw
Pact draws attention to combat aircraft, about which NATO in turn
prefers not to negotiate for the time being. Whatever the case may be,
the main issue is an extension of the M(B)FR negotiations: 'parity, at a
lower level if possible'. To this has now been added the desirability of
giving priority in the discussions to reductions on the most offensive
weapons systems which could be decisive in a surprise attack: tanks,
artillery, aircraft (and missiles). It is generally thought that results, if
possible at all, will be achieved only over many years.

Discussions about the level of armaments seem, however, to have
little to do with the basic question about the continued existence of the
military structures of the alliances in their present form. As previously
argued, after 'Helsinki' this would have been the obvious question to
tackle next. It sometimes seems as if both parties have resigned themselves to the fact that the military alliances have acquired lives of their
own. Gorbachev wrote in *Perestroika*: 'We have ... repeatedly
proposed to dissolve the military blocs, or at least the military wings of
the two alliances. But because our proposal has not been accepted, we
must take this reality into account as well.' And this reality shows us a
Europe which was able to find solutions to a number of serious political
problems in a peaceful and creative way, but which nevertheless did not
have the will or the courage to face up to the fundamental military
consequences. After 1975 (Helsinki) the *military* partition of Europe
virtually became an independent axiom, because it could no longer be
related to the political instabilities of the past: the German Question,
Berlin and the post-war borders. And the military competition began to
determine the East–West climate more and more, for the development
of weaponry, be it medium-range missiles or tanks, creates new instabilities again and again.

The emerging new peace movement in Western Europe, and
certainly in the Netherlands, was also a response to this phenomenon: a
response to a policy (of both NATO and Warsaw Pact countries) which

made peace and security in Europe dependent on the arms race and on military power relations between East and West. After 1975 it became clear that NATO and Warsaw Pact countries had become militarized. They armed themselves for the sake of arming. The arms race and arms control had become autonomous, a process from which the USA and the USSR were thought to derive power and influence in Europe. Virtually the entire security establishment, from the political left to the right, is convinced that the situation in Europe is very stable. The risk of war breaking out is extremely small. But the reason for this is increasingly said to be the existence of a military equilibrium between East and West, one in which nuclear weapons play a special role. There is no need to supply evidence for this assertion, for it is proved by the European situation itself. In a tit-for-tat fashion both parties are now of the opinion that neither they themselves nor their opponent harbours aggressive intentions towards the other side. But – their reasoning goes – that is, of course, also because of the existing military balance. And that completes the circle. Even the thought processes have been militarized.

East and West have by now become so used to 'arms-thinking' that they are beginning to feel that they are not arming themselves against the other any more, but that they are arming Europe together – hand in hand, as it were – to make Europe secure. But secure against what? That has become unclear. The main thing seems to be the maintenance of the status quo. The notion 'common security' is gaining currency: our security in Europe is a shared one; one side is secure only if the other side is. On the basis of such thinking the armies of NATO and the WTO ought to be more each other's mirror-image, but without forming a threat to the other side. That is called 'defensive defence'. This philosophy will no doubt soon play a role in the 'stability/reduction talks'. The allied armies are meant to stay in Central Europe. The stalemate which has evolved has, after all, been equated with 'security', and such an important 'benefit' must be conserved. A remark in a letter of 30 March 1988 from the WTO foreign ministers addressed to the NATO countries, saying that the old proposals for 'the removal of military bases and withdrawal of foreign troops from the territory of other countries' still stand, seems to be no more than a ritual.

The Most Recent Phase of Detente

The military partition of Europe and the militarization of political thought about East–West relations is likely to frustrate the most recent stage on the post-war road to detente. This latest stage can be described as: the reconstruction of the unity of European (civil) society, the rebuilding of the common European home (Gorbachev), the unity in diversity of national cultures (Von Weizsäcker). A necessary condition for this reconstruction is the '*democratization of society*' in the states of East and Central Europe. There society, just as elsewhere in Europe, must be given the right and space by the state to develop its own forms of organization, so that the richness of cultural values and achievements can be genuinely expressed and can also be linked to developments in other countries. The state should no longer function as a funnel and a filter for all the things which happen in society. The question of how the relations between state and society should be organized, in terms of both law and administration, is in essence a matter only for those directly involved; there are no perfect blueprints, only preferences. A fascinating question for international discussion!

The most recent history of East and Central Europe has shown that the democratization of society proceeds in an awkward and arduous way. Dubček demonstrated in 1968 that it is possible for a socialist regime to take that road. It is unfortunate that the other Warsaw Pact countries soon deprived him of the opportunity to display to the world 'the human face' of a socialist society. Hungary under the leadership of Kádár (1956–88) and Grosz (1988–), Poland under Jaruzelski and the USSR under Gorbachev, each in their own way, have been confronted with similar processes and they too (even Jaruzelski!) have been giving the impression of wanting to create space for them, although there are uncertainties about their real intentions.

Ever since the first strikes, in June 1980, the position of the Polish army command, under the leadership of Jaruzelski, was a decisive factor in whether or not Solidarność was to be liquidated and for the chances of survival of the moderate Kania government. Jaruzelski and Kania thought that the Gdansk Agreements, which were signed on 30 August 1980 by representatives of the strikers and the government, were a starting point for a controlled reform of socialism. On 4 and 5 September 1980 Jaruzelski pushed through the appointment of Kania as the new leader of the party and the government, without gaining Moscow's consent or even consulting Moscow. This cleared the way for the experiment which was going to be called Solidarność. The unstoppable growth of the free trade-union movement, the strikes and chaos, however, led to increased pressure on Kania to intervene quickly. But General Jaruzelski and Admiral Janczysn declared in the Central Committee on 6 October: 'The armed forces advocate a political solution. We are now faced with 500 factories on strike. But if we start military actions, we will have to confront 500 strongholds.' It has been established that not long after the legalization of Solidarność, on 10 November 1980, the armed forces command made it clear to Moscow that if need be they would

offer military resistance if the forces of the Warsaw Pact were to intervene. In December 1980, and again in March 1981, the Polish army
command refused to participate in Russian plans for combined Soviet–
Polish military action against Solidarność.

As early as August 1980 a military infrastructure began to be built in
the Western military districts of the Soviet Union, and it remained in use
until the end of 1981. Although Moscow was acutely aware that direct
intervention in Poland was not only unattractive from a military point of
view but would also cause great damage to Brezhnev's policy of detente,
if it came to the crunch the USSR would not recoil from it. Poland's
strategic position in the WTO required a high degree of reliability,
especially in the matter of railway lines between the Soviet Union and its
forces (nineteen divisions) in the GDR. It gradually became clear that it
was possible to intervene against Solidarność only if the Soviet Union
could count on the Polish army's – and therefore Jaruzelski's – active
co-operation. It was therefore important for Moscow to create, in and
around Poland, the kind of situation in which Kania and Jaruzelski
would be forced to proclaim the state of siege themselves for fear of a
Russian intervention. Large-scale military manoeuvres and numerous
attempts to force the issue inside Poland followed.

In May 1981 the Polish Communist Party's Politburo took, in
Jaruzelski's absence, a decision to proclaim martial law, but Jaruzelski's
speedy return prevented this decision from being implemented. There
was, however, a growing readiness to intervene, and this was true of the
general as well. Kania was replaced on 17 October 1981 because he
remained opposed to the state of siege as a matter of principle.
Jaruzelski took over. It was clear then that the political experiment
around Solidarność was coming to an end.

Two events finally made the proclamation of martial law inevitable.
The first was itself an action by Solidarność which could (or would) have
led to direct intervention by the USSR. The union's national executive
had announced a general strike, to commence on 17 December 1981.
Unlike all previous strikes, this one was also going to paralyse the railway routes between the USSR and the GDR. One year earlier, on 20
November 1980, the Soviet Union had made an extremely sharp
response, via Tass and *Izvestiya*, when Solidarność called a railway
strike. The result had been a tacit agreement between Solidarność, the
Polish government and the Soviet Union to respect military interests in
future, but this time the agreement was put to the test.

The second event involved General Jaruzelski directly. A *coup d'état*
had been planned, also for 17 December and probably not accidentally
so, by dogmatic opponents of the general. The opportunity of
Jaruzelski's presence in Moscow, for Brezhnev's birthday, was to be

used to occupy the government buildings and the radio and television stations. The Soviet Union would then be invited to give fraternal military assistance. On 13 December 1981 Jaruzelski proclaimed the state of siege. Solidarność was banned.

Of course, no one can say with certainty that an intervention by the Soviet Union in Poland would have been less likely if no demonstrable military interests had been at stake. But if this had been true, an important rationale for intervention would have disappeared. Whatever the case may be, it remains an intriguing question whether the prospects for a process of democratization in Poland and other WTO countries would be more favourable in a more demilitarized Europe where the military wings of NATO and the WTO are curtailed and the superpowers' troops have to a large extent been withdrawn from Central Europe. It is certain that up to now the military factor has played an important role when profound changes of the kind experienced in Poland and Czechoslovakia failed.

Brezhnev has been credited with the doctrine that the other Warsaw Pact countries have only limited sovereignty. Under this doctrine it is forbidden to make drastic changes to the Marxist–Leninist system; the leading role of the Communist Party is not up for discussion. In early 1988 the East European media – especially *Pravda* – declared, with a multitude of arguments that the 'Prague Spring' twenty years before had led to the inevitable fiasco because Dubček and his supporters were undermining socialism. But is the Brezhnev Doctrine still in force? 'The entire structure of political relations between the socialist countries must be strictly based on absolute independence', wrote Gorbachev in *Perestroika*, and during a visit to Yugoslavia in March 1988 the party secretary emphasized that socialism can have many forms. But what would happen if one of these countries started to behave in a less *socialist* manner in the eyes of the Soviet Union? Would 'absolute independence' still apply? To quote *Perestroika* once more:

> The socialist community will only succeed in its aims . . . if every party and every state respects its friends and allies, takes their interests into account and pays attention to the experience of others. . . . In the complicated international situation the unanimously decided extension of the duration of the Warsaw Pact was of crucial significance.

Are these mere words? Or does this contain a demand for uniformity and discipline? Only time will tell.

Nevertheless, the price to be paid for military intervention seems to go up all the time – even if it is called 'fraternal assistance'. The old justifications have, after all, lost their force. Even the late Franz Joseph

Strauss could hardly any longer be accused of revanchist intentions after he embraced Gorbachev in Moscow, in January 1988. The borders have been recognized and are respected by all Western countries; 'Helsinki' works. In addition, the cultural–historical unity of Europe has been displayed as a precious asset by Gorbachev too, which legitimizes mutual involvement instead of treating it as cause for suspicion. In short, classical Cold War rhetoric does not work any more, and – most important of all – it does not work any more for those who would have to use it under certain circumstances.

The cost of military intervention would become higher still if NATO and the WTO were to change and loosen the present military structures. Lessening the degree of military integration would still not dissolve the blocs; national military forces would in principle remain the same size. (Agreed national upper limits are highly desirable!) But this could create political space, beneficial for the reduction of tension in Europe. It might also stimulate the democratization of *society* in the Warsaw Pact countries and in any case lessen the obstacles 'from the outside'. It follows that the process of *rapprochement* between East and West should be accelerated. But it may, perhaps temporarily, stiffen the domestic policies of some Central East European regimes, as we see in the GDR and Czechoslovakia at the time of writing; partly because the oppressive protection of the USSR no longer fulfils that role. Moreover, 'it takes two to tango'. It is true that the West is set on repairing 'the unity in a diversity of national cultures' (Von Weizsäcker) and wants to strip the borders of their divisive and inhuman characteristics, but is the West also willing to remove the political and military obstacles which stand in the way of the pursuit of unity? We certainly have good reasons to doubt this.

Much work was initially done after the Second World War towards combining West European forces in the area of security. The Treaty of Brussels (1948) resulted in an alliance between the UK, France and the Benelux countries, joined in 1954 by Italy and West Germany: the Western European Union (WEU). The 1952 European Coal and Steel Community (ECSC) was also based on considerations of security politics. The new Federal Republic had to be integrated in the post-war reconstruction of West Europe – also in order to make sure that 'coal and steel' could not serve any conceivable future German expansionist policy.

The Schuman plan provided for a supranational management over coal and steel production of the six participating countries (France, Italy, the FRG and Benelux) and also met the desire to base future Franco–German relations on lasting co-operation instead of mutual threats. The Federal Republic was also regarded as indispensable for the security of

Western Europe against the Russian threat. With the USA's consent, the six member states of the ECSC decided to create the European Defence Community (EDC). The EDC was intended to manage a West European army, to which West German units would be added. But this never materialized, for in August 1954 the French National Assembly rejected the idea of an EDC. From that time onwards the defence of Western Europe became exclusively a NATO matter, in which the USA played a dominant role. But once again it was France which did not feel happy with this new security arrangement. In 1966, under the leadership of de Gaulle, it left the military wing of NATO and developed a security doctrine which on the one hand was based on its own nuclear weapons (*Force de Frappe*) but on the other relied on the NATO context, and especially American–German co-operation.

Intergovernmental co-operation in foreign policy started again in (Western) Europe only in the early 1970s, in the context of the European Political Co-operation group (EPC). The EPC, to which all EEC countries belong, resulted from the Luxembourg Report (1969). Initially it kept a careful distance from security politics in the narrow sense. It co-ordinates, for example, the negotiating positions for the CSCE reviews, but the military aspects (First Basket) are not discussed; these are dealt with by NATO. The Tindemans Report (1975) about the creation of a European Union advocated, for the first time in twenty years, a common European security policy. But not until the end of 1981 did the EPC countries agree, in the London Report, to raise 'security' as a theme for discussion, at least its political aspects. The economic aspects were added in the Stuttgart 'Solemn Declaration' (1983). A further step was made in February 1986 when, through the implementation of the so-called 'European Single Act', European political co-operation between member states of the EEC was formally incorporated in European treaties. 'Inspired by the desire' to transform all their relations in European union, they are prepared 'to increase co-ordination of their standpoints in the political and economic aspects of security', and it is stated by the twelve EEC countries in the Single Act that they regard this as an essential contribution to the 'development of a European identity in foreign policy'.

> We reiterate our obligation to create a European Union according to the European Single Act. . . . We are convinced that the edifice of an integrated Europe will remain unfinished whilst security and defence do not form part of it. An important means to achieve this aim is the Amended Treaty of Brussels, the WEU Treaty.

This was the first article of the 'Platform for European security interests', which was accepted by the WEU countries on 27 October

1987 in The Hague. In 1984 the WEU was roused from a long sleep, primarily through a French initiative. France perceives a tendency towards a reduction in the American involvement in Europe, and appears to have the intention of filling the gap to some extent. This is also to prevent 'neutralist' tendencies in the Federal Republic and an emerging Bonn–Moscow axis.

Although formally the WEU has nothing to do with the EPC, Article 1 of the Platform gives the impression that the WEU regards itself as an organization in which like-minded countries can work together in the field of security to create a European union. (After all, countries such as Greece and Denmark, which often do not hesitate to make dissident noises, also belong to EPC; and Ireland is not even a member of NATO.) Besides, the chairman of the European Commission, the Frenchman Delors, sees the consultations within the WEU as an unavoidable and useful intermediate state towards a fully developed European Community, which includes a collective defence and security policy. Entirely in line with French policy, Article 5 of the Platform states that a 'considerable presence of the USA's conventional and nuclear forces plays an irreplaceable role in the defence of Europe.' This presence is intended to be mainly in the Federal Republic. Article 8 emphasizes that for the foreseeable future nuclear restraint by France and Britain is out of the question, with the words: 'they definitely want to maintain the credibility [of their nuclear forces]'.

Just as in the first years after the Second World War, France is once again the main instigator of a rethinking of European security. It wants to play the leading role in a Europe which must begin to act in a more assertive manner, all over the world. For this, close co-operation with the Federal Republic is of great importance. The 1963 Élysée Treaty between Adenauer and de Gaulle has been rediscovered and since 1982 the defence ministers and chiefs of staff have been meeting regularly, as have three working groups set up for co-operation in the fields of equipment and operations and for consultations about security policies and strategy. The Franco–German Defence Council, set up in January 1988, functions as a kind of co-ordinating body for these working groups. Following a German proposal, a start has been made to form a mixed Franco–German brigade, although this has now been 'demoted' to an integrated military unit. It remains unclear how this unit is supposed to become operational, side by side with the existing NATO units. In addition, the military are doubtful whether it is at all possible to form one army out of two different cultures and languages. Up until now the Franco–German military exercises have mainly demonstrated its impossibility!

Even so, Chancellor Kohl emphasized the 'common destiny' of

France and Germany on 4 February 1988. The future Franco–German brigade is to be 'a stimulus for the forming of other European multi-national units. . . . At the end of this road a common European defence must be in existence, if possible with a European army.'

But France does not have only the FRG in mind for military co-operation. In January 1988, for the first time for more than twenty years, it once again made its territory available for the transit of NATO reinforcements. Initially, British units can now use French ports to travel to the Continent. In February 1988 some 1,000 US marines encamped in French barracks near Limoges for two weeks of exercises, after which they boarded the 6th Fleet again. The exercises were part of a new agreement which, for the first time since 1966, enables American troops to train in France.

Last year Mitterrand and Thatcher began consultations about modest nuclear co-operation: for instance, on targeting doctrines. France and Britain together discussed the possibilities of developing a nuclear stand-off weapon for Tornado and Mirage. Likewise, an *ad hoc* working group has been set up with another neighbouring country, Spain, for the study of Mediterranean security. French and Spanish radar warning systems will be linked. Yet another important multinational example is the French project for an observation satellite. Most of the member states of the WEU and Spain will actively support the project. This is of great significance, for it will give France the capability to aim its new MIRV-ed missiles accurately on targets in the USSR, using a (European) satellite of its own. In short: in military matters France is participating again in Europe, even though it is doing so mainly according to its own views and together with those allies with whom French interests can best be realized.

Thus, parallel to military co-operation in the framework of NATO, a second track of military co-operation is emerging in Europe, which has to do with the creation of West European unity and not just with French interests. The military element, following the classical pattern, is seen to act as a kind of catalyst in the process of 'union-building' which is now taking place in Europe, with France as the spider in the web. The effect of this on relations with Eastern Europe has hardly been discussed, and the question of whether this military approach to union-building is at this time the right contribution towards a solution of the East–West conflict is not posed at all. It seems as if Western Europe wants to bet on three horses simultaneously. A European defence and security policy, with a good deal of military co-operation, is to be created; the level of US presence in Europe, both conventional and nuclear, is to be maintained; and relations with Eastern Europe must be normalized further (detente).

Recently there has been much demand for a new Harmel Report. In 1967 Harmel was able to express the Western countries' objectives very well: defence and detente, against the background of political instabilities in East–West relations. The 'new Harmel' will have to try to set out the logic and consistency of the present priorities. This will not be easy, for a continued process of East–West relaxation is not well served by the militarization of Western Europe; neither is it helped by the continued presence of an excess of American weapons and soldiers. In any case, we may well ask whether Kohl's vision of a European army will ever materialize as long as NATO, under American command, continues to claim most of the European troops.

On closer inspection Western Europe, if it has to choose between the three horses, seems most likely to choose itself. In 1992 its internal borders will be opened and the Common Market will genuinely be established. All Europe's energy is invested in this ambitious project. The integration of the existing defence and security interests is likely to follow, and may even have to function as a trigger for unification. The clearing away of obstacles and barricades – political and military – between East and West can easily be overlooked.

'The West is the petitioning party', said the Dutch ambassador at the CSCE Review Conference in Vienna, when asked about this. The West does indeed seem to have little to offer. It does not want to talk about nuclear weapons in the framework of the forthcoming stability/ reduction talks. Trade treaties between the EEC and the Comecon countries are acceptable because the 'fair-swap' principle is applicable. But there is much reticence with regard to more wide-ranging treaties concerning economic co-operation: treaties in which matters such as investment, loans, management, research, transport and technology provisions can be arranged. So far only Hungary has been able to conclude a somewhat more extensive agreement with the EEC, in July 1988. On 10 March 1988 the deputy chairman of the Soviet Foreign Economic Commission, Ivan D. Ivanov, said, after discussions with the EEC in Brussels were concluded:

> With perestroika under way, access to the future Soviet market will be feasible not through old-fashioned merchant exchange, diminishing nowadays in its volume and attraction, but predominantly through new types of business arrangements, conducive to industrial, investment and technological co-operation.

I would not be surprised if, in the next decade, the development of this and other new types of business arrangement will turn out to be of great significance in opening up possibilities for liberalization and democratization of society in the East. The *rapprochement* of the societies of East and West will be accelerated.

In the USSR and a few other East European countries the 'human-rights issue' is being depoliticized and stripped of its ideological content at an unexpected speed, so that problems in this area can be discussed in a 'normal' manner – for example in the context of the CSCE. The USSR has accommodated the West to a large extent at the Review Conference in Vienna and has agreed to the creation of a permanent mechanism to deal with human-rights problems. During my visit to Moscow in April 1988, the second most senior member of the Soviet delegation in Vienna assured me that the USSR also agrees to a specific aspect of this mechanism: the holding of bilateral conferences on the initiative of any country which wishes to do so in order to investigate, discuss and solve human-rights problems in the other country.

The USSR, Poland, Hungary, Bulgaria and also Czechoslovakia emphasize to a greater or lesser degree that economic reforms in their countries will have to be accompanied by political reforms, and a certain amount of liberalization in various areas – freedom of expression, opportunities for travel, small private enterprises, informal self-organization – can be observed. But liberalization also has its risky side for these regimes, for many people now feel (at long last) sufficiently free to express their dissatisfaction with the present situation, especially the deplorable socio-economic conditions. If the governments of Eastern Europe are unable to steer their economies out of their blind alley in a relatively short time, liberalization will probably turn against them and the socialist system itself will become the real scapegoat. However justified many of the criticisms may be, it remains to be seen whether this monolithic system is both capable and willing to adjust to the heavy pressure to accommodate the needs of society.

In an article in *Le Monde*, M. Tatu has advocated something along the lines of a 'Marshall Plan' devised by West Europe for East Europe. I support this idea, but such a plan should be subject to two conditions. On the one hand, parallel to economic assistance, East–West relations must be substantially demilitarized. This implies a considerable reduction in military expenditure and also the gradual withdrawal of foreign troops from Central Europe. The West German Foreign Minister, Genscher, has already argued for steps in this direction: he has proposed placing upper limits on the numbers of troops stationed on foreign territory. On the other hand, the process of liberalization and democratization must be able to proceed. At the time of writing it does not look as if both these conditions will soon be satisfied, let alone that a Marshall Plan is being prepared. But Eastern Europe appears to be more interested in this approach than Western Europe. After all, the

West is in a 'privileged' position; it can get away with ignoring East Europe for some time yet. And have we not learned from history that the rich rarely feel responsible for whatever is not found in their wallets? But perhaps *common* history has preserved so much cultural unity that people from East and West will nevertheless come together and set out on this road side by side.

2

Some Lessons of the Soviet–American Detente and Bilateral Co-operation of the 1970s

Pavel Podlesnyi

The problems of the detente of the 1970s, its causes and the reasons for its failure, and the experience and lessons of that detente period have once again become a topic of active debate in political and scholarly quarters, especially in the West. The debate reflects the changes for the better that we have been witnessing in Soviet–American relations, and the activization of the overall East–West political dialogue.

The results of the Washington Summit of December 1987 and of the Moscow Summit of May 1988 are of tremendous importance. The INF Treaty between the Union of Soviet Socialist Republics and the United States of America demonstrated that it is possible to strengthen the security of the USSR, the USA and other countries not by speeding up the nuclear arms race, but by coming to agreements on the liquidation of nuclear weapons. The Summit permitted the strengthening of the political dialogue between the two countries, improvements in the political and psychological climate of Soviet–American relations, and the promotion of bilateral co-operation in the spheres of the economy, science, culture and acute global problems.

Will these events prove to be no more than another short spell of relaxation in the international situation, or do they mark the beginning of a new stage or a new detente in Soviet–American relations? Are there any reasons to speak of a second detente, and if so, what are these reasons? What might be the possible general outline of the new detente, and in what ways would it be distinguished from the detente of the 1970s? And, finally, a broader philosophical question should be posed: whether detente is a norm in present-day international relations, or an aberration, a deviation from the major course of world development in the late twentieth century. These complex questions cannot easily be answered. Methodologically, it seems wise first to note the main factors that made possible a significant easing of international tension in the 1970s (essentially in the first half of the decade) and conditioned the development of considerable co-operation in many spheres of East–West relations.

The end of the 1960s marked a new period in the development of international relations. This period was characterized: first, by the Soviet ascent to a rough nuclear parity with the United States, by the general consolidation of economic and political power of the socialist countries and by their increased influence on world development; second, by the restoration of powerful centres of capitalism, such as Western Europe and Japan, and by the increased inclination of some Western countries, primarily France and the FRG, to pursue foreign policies more appropriate to their national interests; third, by changes within the socialist community – China drifted away from close co-operation with the USSR, and the member countries of the Warsaw Treaty Organization acquired an increasingly independent political role after the mid 1950s; fourth, by the transformation of the absolute majority of former colonies into independent states. Such profound qualitative changes in the world arena could not be ignored by any state.

The Soviet response to the new situation in the system of international relations was unequivocal: in these conditions, detente was considered the only reasonable basis for the promotion of normal relations between states belonging to different social systems. More specifically, I would argue, detente was viewed in the Soviet Union as a framework for the realization of hopes regarding the curbing of the arms race; the consolidation of the territorial and political realities of the post-war period in Europe; the creation of a normal international environment for the USSR on its Eastern, as well as Western frontiers; and the use of the results of mutually beneficial and equitable economic and scientific–technological co-operation with capitalist countries to accelerate the USSR's economic development. These aims were quite consistent with the interests of other states, and with the aim of reducing the risk of nuclear war and strengthening international security.

The United States' response to the new realities of the world proved rather controversial. The concept of the so-called 'multipolar world', put forward by the Nixon administration, followed in many ways from the intention to play the 'China card' against the USSR. In other words, in practice this concept was based on the old 'bipolar' idea of Soviet–American rivalry. The revision of the bipolar model turned out to be shallow and misleading. The scale of the manoeuvre, conceived by the United States as a means of adaptation to new conditions, was too limited, and to some extent played into the hands of those who spoke for the restoration of the Cold War. The process of this restoration took some time and was marked by zigzags in policy. This can be illustrated by the inconsistency in the policies of the Nixon administration and was further evident in the course of the Ford administration, which noticeably alienated itself from detente. In its initial period the Carter administration tried to face up to the new realities and exercise a more flexible policy in the 'Third World', and to take a better and more balanced account of new factors in the world economy such as the diminishing US role. All this, however, was accompanied by attempts to combine negotiations with enhanced pressure on the Soviet Union in the style of bipolar confrontation. In the final analysis, liberal reformism was absorbed by anti-Sovietism and militarism.

The 1970s experience of detente, particularly in the relations between the USSR and the USA, allows us to draw up some conclusions as pointers to the future:

1.   American leaders were not really ready to accept the Soviet Union as an equal partner (though formally and juridically such equality was fixed by a number of well-known agreements concluded between the two countries) or to perform a fundamental and all-round reconstruction of US–Soviet relations. The United States was more or less inclined to recognize the Soviet Union's equal status only in the military-strategic sphere – not giving up, even in the years of detente, attempts to gain certain advantages in this respect. It is quite obvious that a basis for a serious shift in US military strategy towards greater toughness and towards the assumption of the possibility of waging a nuclear war was laid down in the years of detente by such manifestations as the 'Schlesinger doctrine' and Carter's 'PD-59'. The approach taken by official Washington to the development of relations with the Soviet Union did not exclude the exertion of military pressure, including the threat to use strategic weapons. One has only to remember the US nuclear alert in connection with the flare-up of hostilities in the Middle East in October 1973.

As for other spheres of bilateral relations – political, trade and economic contracts, and so on – the course taken by the United States proved that its leaders were thinking in categories of superiority. It is no accident that practically from the very beginning of detente, American ruling circles began to put forward different conditions for the positive development of relations with the Soviet Union in all these spheres, striving to find opportunities for exerting an active influence on Soviet foreign and perhaps, as during Carter's administration, even domestic policy.

2.   At the same time (particularly in the context of the domestic crisis America had to face in the late 1960s) the US leaders allowed for a possibility that in time, the Soviet Union would be able substantially to reduce its lag behind the United States in terms of military and economic power and political influence in the world. It was for this reason that the Nixon administration demonstrated a certain preparedness to build its relations with the USSR while taking into consideration the balance of forces between the two powers that had evolved by the early 1970s, in order to avoid negotiating with the USSR from patently worse positions in the future.

3.   In so doing the Nixon administration sought to obtain Soviet 'consent' to a status quo which was advantageous to the United States in the non-socialist world, and especially in the developing countries, in return for the recognition (albeit with reservations) of military–strategic parity and consideration for the Soviet Union's legitimate security interests in some regions of the world. The US leaders responded in a hostile manner to such events in the developing world as the involvement of Cuban armed forces in the civil war in Angola, Soviet military aid to Ethiopia in the latter's conflict with Somalia, the continuation of Soviet weapons deliveries to Cuba, Vietnam, and so forth. Since at that time the United States was compelled for domestic reasons to refrain from active and direct military–political interference in the affairs of developing countries, the nature of the USSR's relations with national liberation movements caused particular irritation in US ruling circles. The above-mentioned actions were viewed by Washington as Soviet attempts to use normalization of bilateral relations as a cover-up for gaining new advantages in the continuing rivalry of the two social systems on the international scene. One should also note the widespread American conviction that the new shifts in the world balance of forces which might be unfavourable for the United States would take place first and foremost in the developing world. The USA displayed particular nervousness with regard to the revolution in Iran in 1978–79, though Washington's support for the Shah's regime had been one of the major contributory causes of this revolution. In many American and Western European studies on the detente of the 1970s, Soviet Third World policy is characterized as the main cause of its failure.

In retrospect, one can say that the problem of the interconnection between the central (military–strategic) aspects of detente and its regional aspects could probably have been approached more flexibly. Besides, more consideration should have been given to the fact that events in different regions of the world exert a significant influence on the state of Soviet–American relations in any particular period. This is certainly one of the lessons of the 1970s which both sides should bear in mind.

At the same time, it would be wrong to ignore (as is often done in the West) the very complex combination of circumstances which actually brought about the failure of detente.

The first serious blow to detente was actually dealt by the 1974 decision of the US Congress to impose discriminatory restrictions on American trade with the USSR, a decision which could be interpreted in no other way than as a bold and unceremonious interference in the Soviet Union's internal affairs. These measures not only blocked the prospects for broad and long-term economic and scientific–technological co-operation between the two countries, but also caused serious doubts in Moscow about America's true intentions towards the Soviet Union. Today, even among US congressmen, there is a wide recognition that discriminatory trade policies proved detrimental to the interests of the United States. It can be said without exaggeration that Soviet–American detente never recovered from this blow.

Besides, the course pursued in that period by the US side in the realm of international politics can hardly be viewed as exemplary. The United States made energetic efforts to undermine Soviet positions in the Middle East, particularly in Egypt, fanned up anti-Soviet feeling in Eastern Europe, tried to play the 'China card' for the sake of pressurizing the Soviet Union politically and psychologically, organized a military *coup d'état* in Chile, and so on. All these developments influenced negatively the climate of Soviet–American relations, and gave rise to additional concern in the USSR over American policy.

As for the so-called Soviet 'gains' in the 'Third World' in the 1970s, these never presented any real threat to US world interests. Nevertheless, in the years of the Reagan administration these 'gains' were used as a pretext for US interference in developments in different regions of the world, with the aim of complicating the USSR's geopolitical position and destabilizing the situation in a number of developing countries.

4.   It should also be noted that the shift from detente to confrontation in US policy towards the Soviet Union in the late 1970s–early 1980s was partly connected with the domestic situation in the USSR, where phenomena of stagnation had been accumulating since the mid 1970s. Characterizing this state of affairs, Mikhail Gorbachev has written:

> An unbiased honest approach brought us to the inexorable conclusion: the country was in a pre-crisis situation. The conclusion was made at the Plenary Meeting of the CPSU Central Committee, which was held in April 1985 and marked a turn to a new strategic course, to perestroika, and formulated conceptual guidelines for such a course.[1]

One result of these complexities on the Soviet domestic scene was the aspiration of the American side to use combined economic, political, psychological and military pressure on the Soviet Union as a means of weakening its international position and internal social system, seeking to ensure a permanent economic and technological lag on the part of the USSR. At the same time internal problems in the USSR were used to portray it as the cause of all evil and misfortune in the world. One must also admit that elements of dogmatism in Soviet foreign policy, and its inadequate response to profound changes in the international system, also played a negative role.

5. It is necessary to point out that one of the most important factors which had prompted the changes for the better in US policy towards the USSR in the 1970s was the active development of relations between the USSR and the leading Western European countries, in particular the Soviet Union's relations with the FRG and France – the first countries to embark on the road of detente. In initiating its own detente policy towards the Soviet Union, however, Washington wished to maintain control and the development of relations between East and West as a whole, blocking independent Western European contracts with the USSR which could complicate US policy. These attempts did not bring the USA the desired results. Attempts to discipline US allies in the 1980s by unleashing a new round of the nuclear arms race on the European continent were not wholly successful. The events of the 1980s showed how difficult and politically expensive were the attempts to deploy new American nuclear missiles on the territory of some Western European countries.

One cannot help mentioning at this point that as the real reasons for NATO's deployment decision are being revealed, many well-informed politicians have begun at last to recognize the obvious truth: the decision to station the American Pershing II and cruise missiles in Western Europe was in no way a reply to the Soviet deployment of SS-20s (as it was depicted at that time), but was a product of NATO's strategic calculation to build up the threat to the East. Collaborating as co-authors for the first time, former President Richard Nixon and former Secretary of State in the Nixon and Ford administrations Henry Kissinger wrote recently in the *Los Angeles Times*:

> It is regrettable that in the 1970s the deployment of these weapons was justified solely on the grounds that they were needed to balance the new Soviet SS-20 missiles and that the Western statesmen said a withdrawal of the SS-20s would permit us to withdraw our missiles as well. In fact these missiles were not needed to offset their equivalents. Their real function was to discourage Soviet nuclear blackmail of Europe by whatever weapon from whatever

location and to raise the risk of nuclear retaliation by NATO to Soviet conventional attack. They close a gap in deterrence caused by the apocalyptic nature of strategic nuclear war. . . . In retrospect, NATO should not have offered the zero option in the late 1970s.[2]

General Bernard Rogers, Allied Supreme Commander in Europe until July 1987, in fact recognized in his numerous speeches that even after President Reagan officially proposed the Zero Option in 1981, NATO's Supreme Command never worked out, even by way of formality, any plans that could explain how the alliance would maintain its defence if both sides gave up their INF forces. This is convincing evidence of the deception of the public of NATO countries by their governments. On the surface they played the role of peacekeepers, champions of detente, but in reality their only concern was the speeding-up of the nuclear arms race.

But in spite of all this, the United States did not succeed in completely destroying the structure of European detente which was created in the 1970s. This is one of the key positive lessons of detente.

6.   Also important were specific features of the American political system, in which the executive power plays a tremendous, though not necessarily decisive, role. Other institutions, such as Congress, the media, and different lobbying groups and public organizations, also exert a significant political influence. As the experience of detente in the early 1970s showed, attempts to decide any problem of importance in US–Soviet relations inevitably caused the active involvement of all these influential forces, which in many cases resulted in considerable, and sometimes even decisive, alterations in US positions. The policy of detente was associated in the United States with certain political figures. This is why the discrediting of these figures in the eyes of the American public, which occurred as a result of Watergate in the mid 1970s, affected foreign policy too.

7.   The experience of the 1970s offers another conclusion: the achievement of broad and complex accords, especially of strategic arms agreements, is viewed with suspicion by US ruling circles, demands a lot of time, and faces determined resistance from the opponents of detente. In addition, the scale and speed of the American military build-up make the task of elaborating far-reaching Soviet–American agreements very difficult.

8.   Another far from easy task is the formation of a stable consensus within the US ruling elite on a broad spectrum of questions concerning US–Soviet relations which involve the relaxation of tension. The difficulty

of forming such a consensus means that US policy towards the USSR
bears, and will probably continue to bear, the hallmarks of instability and ambiguity. It is evident that for a substantial part of the US
establishment any significant detente in relations with the USSR is virtually unacceptable. The resistance of the right and extreme right of the
American political spectrum to the detente of the 1970s proved much
more substantial and stubborn than one could have expected. The opponents of detente invented one pretext after another to hamper the US–
Soviet detente process and to return the USA once again to the Cold
War policies of the past. The forces opposing US–Soviet *rapprochement*
employ a whole set of anti-Soviet stereotypes and make tremendous
efforts to ensure that they are preserved in the American public mind.

9.   The experience of the 1970s also makes it difficult to see any bright
prospects for intergovernmental co-operation between the Soviet Union
and the United States in the economy, science, and technology. The
American establishment is virtually unanimous in its view that attitudes
towards developing relations with the USSR in these spheres, excluding
those where particular US interests are obvious, should be formed by
political considerations. All US administrations of the 1970s, whether
Republican or Democrat, linked possibilities for co-operation to
demands for changes in Soviet foreign and, in the case of Carter,
domestic policy.

However, trade, scientific and cultural contacts have an important
role to play in the formation of the material and sociopolitical foundations of detente, in the creation of a new public psychology and a
culture of international contacts in conditions of peaceful coexistence.
An analysis of the 1970s demonstrates that one of the major factors
which pushed US policy towards a tougher attitude to the USSR was the
failure of both countries to bring co-operation in the above-mentioned
spheres to levels which would have challenged the fundamental Cold
War stereotypes in American public opinion. The preservation of these
stereotypes, albeit in a weakened form, created an atmosphere which
favoured the restoration of anti-detente trends in the United States and
became one of the contributing factors in the consolidation of the
positions of opponents to detente in the second half of the 1970s.

Now it would also be proper to address at least some of the lessons of
the confrontation of the early 1980s, and to compare the combination of
factors that conditioned detente in the early 1970s with the combination
that has prompted the US side to improve relations with the Soviet
Union in the second half of the 1980s.

1.   First of all, it should be noted that the major qualitative factor of present-day international life – broad military–strategic parity between the United States and the Soviet Union – is still operative. The military build-up undertaken by the Reagan administration has not brought the American side the desired results, and has not led to the restoration of a US position of strength *vis-à-vis* the Soviet Union. Evaluating the principal significance of this factor, Alexander Yakovlev, Secretary of the CPSU Central Committee, has pointed out:

> Strategic parity, virtually wrested from history by the Soviet Union, creates new conditions and thus shapes a new psychology, allowing a new look to be taken at the world. This has allowed the USSR to depart from the policy of forced, sometimes urgent searches for responses to the military–technological challenge of the West, and to embark on the road of the purposeful cultivation of the conditions for social progress. An utterly new era has arrived, in which movement to a nuclear-free and non-violent world is a quite realistic alternative. And we see that the New Thinking is forcing its way through the piles of prejudice left by the era of wars and weapons.[3]

Thus one can agree with the opinion voiced by some American experts, to the effect that in the 1980s the futility of bargaining for the attainment of decisive advantages in the military competition between the two sides has once again been demonstrated and the appropriate conclusions have been drawn about the need for the reduction of military potentials to the levels of reasonable sufficiency. 'The first half of the 1980s,' wrote Mandelbaum and Talbott in their last book,

> and the policies that both sides pursued in that period, also showed that neither was likely to gain a decisive advantage over the other. By agreeing to meet on a regular basis and to seek diplomatic accommodation on some of the issues that divided them, the two leaders were implicitly acknowledging the limits of their possibilities to get their way unilaterally. For both men, this was a lesson that took some time to learn.[4]

2.   Economic factors also have their specific and increasingly significant role to play as imperatives of detente. The Soviet leaders openly acknowledge that they view the lessening of international tension and reduction of armaments as an important condition for the acceleration of the country's economic and social development, and for the overall success of perestroika. The events of the past few years indicate that the United States is compelled to limit its military budget, since it is incapable of financing all the military programmes pushed through by the Pentagon.

3.　Another lesson of the 1980s is the revelation of the possible limits of Soviet–American confrontation. In spite of the fact that the relations between the USSR and the USA were complicated and tense, even the Reagan administration, despite its conservatism, exercised caution, not risking direct military confrontation with the Soviet Union. By the mid 1980s the administration had come to realize that the United States could not do without a certain level of interaction with the USSR, primarily for the sake of reducing the danger of nuclear conflict.

At the same time, today's international situation is marked by some new features which were either completely absent in the late 1960s to early 1970s, or were not as obvious then as they are now.

First, a new major factor has emerged on the international scene: the reconstruction of USSR domestic and foreign policies. The flexible and constructive position of the Soviet Union towards world affairs disrupts Western 'position-of-strength' approaches to the USSR, facilitates the resolution of complicated problems of security and disarmament, consolidates Soviet international prestige, and weakens the effect of various allegations about a 'Soviet military threat'.

Secondly, attempts by US strategists to realize their plans for the creation of a global anti-Soviet coalition of states have met with mounting difficulties. They have been weakened by the growing problems in America's relations with her allies, as well as by the improvement, by comparison with the early 1970s, of the Soviet Union's relations with China. William Hyland has characterized this dilemma very accurately:

> A successful alliance policy cannot ignore the fact that the industrial democracies will not support a foreign policy that does not include an effort at detente with the Soviet Union. Our Western allies and Japan obviously want both containment and coexistence. This may even be the basis on which the Chinese are prepared to join with the United States. In practice this means that the United States has to engage in negotiations with Moscow, including arms-control arrangements, not only for the sake of our alliances, but because it is also in our own self-interest.[5]

Thirdly, the threat of nuclear proliferation, leading to an expansion of the arms race, destabilization of the military–political situation and of the global economic mechanism, is steadily growing. This threat is intensified by the increasing number of regional conflicts, involving more and more countries.

Finally, a new and powerful factor in world politics is the growing influence of world public opinion, and the greater realization, by the peoples of the world, of the dangers of nuclear war and other global problems which threaten the survival of humanity.

The preceding discussion gives us ample reason to conclude that in the contemporary world, the imperatives which demand urgent measures to reduce world tensions are gaining momentum. They testify that detente and broad international co-operation are a natural state of present-day international life. The realities mentioned above – and, more precisely, the combination of these realities – have laid the basis for the positive changes in Soviet–American relations that we have been witnessing recently, though it is still too early to speak of a major breakthrough in the relationship between the two countries. In order to achieve such a breakthrough important new steps are necessary in the sphere of radical arms reductions, as well as the promotion of co-operation in other spheres of Soviet–American relations and in the consolidation of confidence and mutual understanding between the USSR and the USA.

Notes

1. M.S. Gorbachev, *Reconstruction and New Thinking for Our Country and for the Whole World*, Moscow, 1987, pp. 18–19.

2. *Los Angeles Times*, 26 April 1987.

3. *Pravda*, 4 November 1987.

4. M. Mandelbaum and S. Talbott, *Reagan and Gorbachev*, New York 1987, pp. 182–3.

5. *Foreign Affairs*, vol. 66, no. 1, Autumn 1987, pp. 15–16.

3

The Role of Governments, Social Organizations and Peace Movements in the New German and European Detente Process

Egbert Jahn

From Detente to Detente

Since the Second World War, the East–West conflict has manifested itself in two forms which have characterized different periods in East–West relations since 1947. The Cold War (1947–62) had its roots in tensions which existed from 1944 onwards and consisted of repeated episodes of high tension like the Berlin crises, and limited East–West wars like the Korean War. A policy of containment, limited roll-back efforts, brinkmanship, and war threats ran the risk of a major East–West war while trying to avoid it as far as possible. In that period such a war still seemed to be a rational option, at least for the United States of America, in a situation in which there was assumed to be a severe challenge to perceived national security interests. The Cold War period was not one of continuous high tension, as it also contained various episodes when tension was considerably reduced, as in the years 1955–57, which served as preludes to future detente. At the end of the Cold War the East–West borders in Europe and East Asia had hardly moved, but the political and socioeconomic systems behind those borders had been consolidated most efficiently by a combination of carrot and stick, according to the respective national conditions for liberal democracy in the West and communism in the East.

The Cuban Missile Crisis of October 1962 marked a dramatic end to the Cold War and paved the way for a new period in the East–West conflict: the detente period. With the build-up of a Soviet inter-continental nuclear force in the early 1960s, the United States lost its military invulnerability. After that turning point in history, no state could guarantee its security by national or multinational means alone.

Since that time, international political means have been an indispensable instrument for the prevention of war. The Test Ban Treaty, the establishment of the 'hot line' and the delivery of American grain to the Soviet Union in 1963 started a period of East–West detente in which a growing network of governmental and non-governmental political, economic and cultural East–West contacts reduced considerably the likelihood of a major war. At the same time the quantitative and, moreover, qualitative arms race went on and was moderated only to a very limited extent by arms control. Detente was never a unilinear process of continuous reductions in tension. Even limited East–West wars like the Vietnam War, and various military interventions, occurred in the period of detente. Episodes of rapidly rising tension, as after the Soviet intervention in Czechoslovakia or in the Middle East in October 1973, demonstrated the fragility of detente as a form of East–West conflict. But these limited confrontations never took precedence over the fundamental, common East–West interest in preventing a major war.

In the eyes of many analysts, the non-ratification of SALT II, the Soviet military intervention in Afghanistan, the Polish crisis, and the NATO double-track decision on the deployment of new intermediate-range missiles served to bring to an end the 1963–79 detente period. Indeed, Europe and the world faced several years of severe tension and the disruption of many promising arms-control and detente initiatives. Cold War rhetoric was revived. But the so-called Second Cold War remained largely rhetorical and symbolic in the early 1980s. Tension never reached a level at which a major East–West war was a serious possibility, by contrast with the real Cold War of 1947–62. In the real Cold War, both major powers participated in the Olympic Games as a symbol of continuous international co-operation. In the caricature period of the Second Cold War, confrontation was demonstrated on the occasion of the Olympic Games and in some other fields where little harm could be done to the basic common interest in East–West war-prevention, and the rhetoric of detente declined, but factual detente did not end.

Detente went into a period of serious crisis but its basic fundamentals, the interest in war-prevention and a balanced and controlled amnesty, were never threatened: for example, East–West economic relations did not encounter any serious political interference. The early 1980s can be described as a short period of minimum detente (1980–84) during which the prospects for further reductions in tension temporarily declined. The revival of the detente process began with the resumption of arms-control talks between the major powers and the completion of the Madrid CSCE conference, and its first major success was the signature of the INF Treaty. But the new detente will not be just a continuation of the old detente of the 1960s and 1970s. Some basic conditions have changed and the new conditions require not only new efforts for detente, but a new kind of detente.

Weaknesses and Contradictions of the Old Detente

Detente in the 1960s and 1970s rested on some common elements in Eastern and Western detente policies, but the two policies nevertheless had incompatible long-term goals. The incompatibility contributed to the crisis of detente in the early 1980s. In addition, detente policies were conceived only as complementary policies to the basic policies of defence and deterrence – that is to say, defence policy was thought of as the central pillar of national and alliance security and foreign policy, while detente policy was interpreted as a flexible and optional pillar. In other words, military policy was not yet seen as an inherent part of detente policy. In fact, detente policy had only a slight influence on the development of the arms race. Its main concern was with the non-use of armaments, not with disarmament, and hardly at all with the prevention of arms build-up.

Old detente policies promoted the hope that disarmament would follow in a second phase, after the initial phase of political detente and economic, cultural and humanitarian co-operation. Accordingly, in the late seventies the demand for 'military detente in addition to political detente' was raised, underlining the difference and the separability in principle of detente and military policies.

East–West detente in the 1960s, and especially in the 1970s, dealt with many non-military problems which had no direct impact on the arms race. The core of the European detente process was the far-reaching settlement of territorial questions in Central Europe and Germany, although a final legal settlement in the distant future was left open. The GDR was recognized as a separate sovereign state by the West, and in 1973 both German states became members of the United Nations. The borders of the Central European states were legally accepted in several treaties between the Federal Republic of Germany and the Soviet Union, Poland, Czechoslovakia, and the German Democratic Republic. The status of West Berlin was consolidated by the Four Powers Agreement, which removed a major focus of the Cold War. The whole network of bilateral and multilateral treaties that were the precondition of the Final Act of the Conference on Security and Co-operation in Europe (signed on 1 August 1975) did not seek to change the basic legal positions of 'Germany as a whole' (in the boundaries of 1937) and the positions of the four World War II allies in and in relation to that 'Germany'. In fact, they created new legal conditions for a transitional period until the German Question could finally be settled in a 'peace treaty with Germany', though there was no guarantee that this would ever be concluded. Thus the detente process in Europe deepened and consolidated the division of the German Reich into several states, at least for the foreseeable future. At the same time, detente created the conditions for the reconstruction of many types of communication among the Germans as well as among the Europeans on both sides of the East–West border, which helped in many respects to overcome the division. The future development of the German Question, which is still technically open, remains a central element in future European detente and peace politics.

The old detente was also a continuation of the Cold War by more peaceful means. As a form of East–West conflict, detente served the same long-term goals as the Cold War: the destruction of the opposing social system.

The Eastern (communist-socialist) system rests, like the Western (liberal-democratic capitalist) system, on a universal concept that conceives as transitional the geographical limitation of its implementation in the Eastern and Western world respectively. Both concepts, and the policies based on them, assume that the population currently subjected to the other system will, sometime in the near or distant future, liberate itself from the yoke of capitalist or communist minority rule, thus creating a lasting communist-socialist or liberal-democratic European and world peace order. Both universalistic concepts are based on the same hope and expectation of a historical process that consists in the accumulation of national (revolutionary or evolutionary) acts of self-determination and emancipation in the liberal-democratic or communist-socialist sense.

But only in pure theory is self-determination seen as an act in an isolated, 'independent' national area, not determined or decisively influenced by the outside world. The actual policies which have been based on the liberal-democratic or communist-socialist concepts reflect the international – mostly asymmetrical – interdependencies of the modern world and of politics. They do not simply rely on the truth of their prognosis of the sociopolitical development in other countries, but also contain an element of active interference in the historical process in those other states. This mutual interference can easily be rationalized as an answer to the interference of the other side where the original missionary impetus of democratic liberalism and communism has been lost, and where aggression must be legitimized as defence. Democratic liberalism and communism as universalistic political concepts are therefore, in practice, intermingled in many ways with imperial traditions involving a national sense of mission and interventionism. In extreme cases, the universalistic concept is simply reduced to an ideological or even propaganda screen for imperial nationalism. Thus great-power interests are pursued under the pretext of supporting weak liberal democracy or communism in a state which has received the 'help' of a major liberal-democratic or communist power. In most cases of international support and interference, however, true universalistic convictions are inseparably mixed with national motivations and specific social and personal interests in acts of international liberal-democratic or communist solidarity.

No matter how strong this imperial-national distortion of universalistic policies may be, there is a fundamental difference between traditional imperialism and colonialism on the one hand and imperial-national universalism on the other. Traditional imperialism and colonialism were mainly motivated by national or subnational interests and intentions, even if they contained a worldwide conception of the 'true interests' of other peoples. They involved conquest, annexation, and direct or sometimes indirect political rule by foreign powers. Modern liberal-democratic and communist expansion predominantly rest on indirect methods of rule and require, therefore, a minimum national social and political background for democratic liberalism and communism within the dominated country. As a rule, the goal is not to conquer, occupy and annex foreign territories and peoples but to place allies within the respective states in the dominant positions within those societies, if necessary by a transformation of the societal structure. Indirect domination by penetration, not direct domination, is the goal of interference and intervention, even if transitional occupation and domination may last for long periods in some individual cases.

In both systems, legitimacy can be gained only by national acceptance or, at least, by the tolerance of national ruling elites and social classes. As a rule, the fundamental political strength of the Western liberal-democratic system in Europe rests on its legitimacy in terms of popular acceptance, while the weakness of the Eastern system is still largely caused by majority indifference or rejection. Even if this kind of legitimacy is extremely weak in some historical situations, there are much more substantial obstacles to expansion by penetration than to expansion by conquest. Particularly in times of world peace, in the sense of the absence of world war, penetration by violent means is connected with profound social and political transformations in the countries concerned, and these seldom occur without violent unrest or even civil war.

Fundamental changes in the military power structure of the international system in the post-war world are, therefore, almost completely dependent on domestic developments and sociopolitical struggles, not on opportunities for attack or aggression caused by military imbalances. The main problem in the East–West conflict is not traditional aggression, conquest or annexation but political, economic and military interference and intervention in unstable societies. The instability of many Western socioeconomic and political regimes in the Third World and of many Eastern regimes in the Second World, including Eastern Europe, is the basic problem of the East–West conflict, not just an unbalanced military order in the world and its subregions.

Socioeconomic and political instability create incentives and opportunities for defensive interventionism in order to maintain the existent liberal-capitalist or statist-communist system, or for offensive interventionism in favour of a transformation of the existing system in cases of sociopolitical instability.

Thus the problem of creating a new and stable detente can be tackled from two sides: from the need to stabilize sociopolitical structures to avoid creating pretexts for intervention, and from the need to reduce the great powers' preparedness to carry out interventions.

Elements of Detente

Europe has not seen many wars or major military actions since 1945; this is usually interpreted as a consequence of its military alliance and nuclear-deterrence system. But if nuclear deterrence were really a decisive and reliable way of preventing war, one should not hesitate to arm with nuclear weapons all states in insecure areas which are threatened by conventional wars. Although one cannot deny that nuclear weapons have had a considerable moderating effect on the crisis behaviour and the foreign policy of the major nuclear powers, and although the Soviet ability to destroy the United States was an important precondition for a change of American foreign policy in favour of detente, one cannot reduce the complex causes of war-prevention and detente to the single factor of nuclear deterrence.

Another important condition of detente in Europe was the relative stability of the socioeconomic and political systems in all European countries, with a few exceptions, and the high degree of international hegemonial interdependence between Eastern and Western Europe. During the Cold War there were still widespread illusions in both East and West about the instability of the opposing system. Many communists still dreamed of revolutionary situations in the West in the near future, and many liberal democrats cherished corresponding dreams that the near-bankruptcy of the socioeconomic and political systems in the

East would result in peoples' upheavals. A foreign policy of military and moral superiority was seen as a favourable external condition for the anticipated dramatic domestic transformations in the other system – that is, for the roll-back of capitalism or communism respectively.

Cynical realists may not really have shared these universalistic expectations in the late 1940s and 1950s, and may just have used them for domestic purposes such as the consolidation of their own rule *vis-à-vis* the domestic political opposition. However, propaganda works only if many people, including even some of the propagandists themselves, believe in its truth. In Germany the expectation of a breakdown of the communist regime in the East or of the capitalist system in the West was and still is combined with the perspective of a unified liberal-democratic or communist *'Neues Deutschland'*. (The relatively widespread hope that Germany could remain undivided by adopting a democratic-socialist system as a tolerable alternative both to Western capitalism and Eastern communism had already been almost eradicated by the polarizing and suppressive effects of the Cold War.) The 'reunification of Germany in freedom' – that is to say, under liberal-democratic and capitalist conditions – is still the official goal of all established West German political parties (all, that is, except the Greens), although there is growing doubt as to the credibility of this perspective.

At the end of the Cold War, these expectations of an imminent breakdown of the communist or the capitalist system gradually disappeared. Both systems demonstrated their legitimacy through their acceptance by the overwhelming majority of the people; stability was guaranteed by severe military and police power, if necessary, under the assistance of allied states, as in Greece, the GDR, and later in Czechoslovakia. The building of the Berlin Wall in August 1961 gave the clear signal that even a gradual erosion of the Eastern system by emigration could be stopped by violent means.

The decline of illusions about radical systemic change and the consolidation and stabilization of the two social systems in Europe – either by legitimacy through efficiency or repression during the Cold War – was a very important precondition of detente in addition to the nuclear military stalemate. The offensive sociopolitical tactics – and, more importantly, the strategies – had to be changed. The new strategy of East–West detente was a policy of cautious and limited East–West cooperation between states and, to some extent, also between social organizations and individuals under strong state observation, as a precondition for substantial change. Detente and co-operation were justified mainly as a means for securing interstate peace, but at the same time detente has always been seen as a condition for a gradual peaceful change in the opposing system, whether or not this has been stated openly.

In the East, this strategy carried the label 'peaceful coexistence', under which communists stressed the necessity of a continuation of the revolutionary class struggle – if possible by more peaceful means – in the transitional historical period of detente between capitalist and socialist states. After 1956, detente and 'peaceful coexistence' were no longer seen as a transitional period between two major interstate and especially world wars, but as one which paved the way for a peace which would be possible after the final extinction of the capitalist system by more or less peaceful social revolutions led by Communist parties.

In the West, the new strategy for East–West conflict under conditions of detente carried names like 'change through *rapprochement*'. Peaceful change, which was mainly seen as occurring in the Eastern societies, envisaged a gradual liberalization of the Eastern societies in the Western sense of democratic liberalism. For many leftist democrats that meant above all a liberalization of the one-party political system, in the sense of a final historical creation of democratic socialism that is, not liberalization of the economic system in the capitalist sense; for many Western liberals and conservatives it meant above all liberalization of the economic system according to the capitalist experience and then, perhaps in the more distant future, the democratization of the political system and the abolition of the one-party system. Usually the final steps of the future liberalization of the Eastern societies, as conceived in the detente strategies of Western political parties and social organizations, were not spelled out; they were either concealed under general labels like 'realization of human rights', or simply not thought through because attention was focused more pragmatically on the immediate future.

During the detente period of the 1960s and 1970s the political spectrum in Eastern and Western societies changed considerably, and there were also substantial shifts in the patterns of East–West party relations which were connected with this phenomenon.

During the Cold War, the political spectrum in the East was restricted to a more or less monolithic Communist Party. This was due to a dominant state conducting a confrontation policy towards all established political parties and supporting the Western Communist parties and the more or less pro-communist, or at least pro-Soviet, peace movement, in accordance with the restrictions of the Cold War. In the West, the Cold War marginalized all independent liberal and socialist political options, isolated or suppressed Communist parties, and exerted strong pressures for uniformity on established political positions towards the East. The established Western political parties saw in the suppressed Eastern dissidents the heralds of future liberal-democratic movements and upheavals in the East. Detente, however, allowed space for a new, albeit limited, pluralization of the political spectrum in the West and a hidden differentiation of the political spectrum in the East. International detente was, to a certain extent, accompanied by domestic detente. However, limits were set to permissible domestic change in an attempt to avoid destabilizing effects on international detente.

The new detente period has seen in the West a fierce and open struggle between the proponents of detente and those of traditional containment and roll-back strategies, and later the beginning of a public debate on alternative security policies, arms control and disarmament, and social and political reforms. In the East, on the other hand, open political struggles between reform communists and traditional communists have remained the exception. Behind the screens of public unanimity, however, there has developed a process of political differentiation between wavering currents in favour of the status quo (in domestic as well as in international relations, and not always in harmony with each other) or of gradual and cautious reforms which are contrasted with the overly radical and rapid Czechoslovak reform communism of the late 1960s.

The New Sociopolitical East–West Formations

The Western liberal, social-democratic and liberal-conservative political forces have on occasion combined strategies of domestic reform and liberalization with strategies of detente, and have created a new and limited network of co-operation with the detente-orientated and often reformist wings of the Eastern Communist parties. A growing understanding between the reformist, enlightened establishments in Eastern and Western societies has created a new liberal-democratic and reformist-communist establishment internationalism, although this understanding may still be cautious and limited. At the same time, Western right-wing conservatives have tried to continue their antagonistic collaboration with the communist conservatives in the East by trying to prevent and then to limit East–West detente and co-operation, and by using all negative characteristics of the opposing system (for example the military intervention in Czechoslovakia, or the West German *Berufsverbote* and large-scale unemployment in the West) as instruments against the dominant detente politics of the 1960s and 1970s. The Western and Eastern right-wing conservatives have continued to see their main allies not in the reformist and detente-orientated elements of the establishment on the other side but, at least rhetorically, in the radical opposition fighting for a complete change in society. Power-political realism, stressing the importance of military power, has led to the abandonment of the remnants of universal thinking in these circles, and to the limitation of thinking to pure nationalism or alliance multinationalism.

In both East and West there has emerged simultaneously a new political force which considers the cautious and gradual detente and reform policies of the left or liberal wing of the Eastern and Western establishments too reluctant and moderate to deal adequately with the old and new problems of political repression, economic and social justice, war-prevention and disarmament, Third World development, and ecological catastrophe. At the same time, this new political anti-establishment movement has gradually emancipated itself from the traditions of communist unconditional system-opposition in the West and anti-communist unconditional system-opposition in the East. It has done this by formulating radical socioeconomic, ecological and political alternatives within or at least on the basis of the existing systems and by clearly distancing itself from civil war and other violent strategies, thus giving up the main objectives of the traditional radical system-oppositions in the West and in the East. Thus the New Left and the student and protest movement of the late 1960s proved a transitional intellectual and political impetus which prepared the way for a more radical departure from traditional patterns of left–right and also East–West politics.

The result of this process was a new East–West peace, ecological, women's and human- and civil-rights movement which contrasted not only with traditional militant oppositions in East and West, but also with each of the conservative, reformist, and detente-orientated parts of the Eastern and Western establishments. During the late detente period in the second half of the 1970s, a new East–West internationalism which transcended the traditional communist or liberal-democratic lines of solidarity was created. This alternative internationalism, in restricted opposition to the reformist establishment internationalism, became an important political factor in the crisis of detente in the early 1980s. Those parts of the Old and ageing New Left in the West which did not merge with the 'new social movements', and those parts of the unconditional anti-communist opposition in the East which did not merge with the new civil-rights and peace movements, either died out or lived on as irrelevant political fossils on the fringes of their societies.

At the same time, changes could be seen among the Eastern and Western conservatives who had opposed earlier detente policies. Only the most inflexible members of the right wing retained their unconditional anti-detente positions. The moderate wing of communist and liberal-democratic conservatism had strongly opposed the detente policies of the 1970s (much more effectively in the West than in the East) and had introduced a new policy of limited confrontation, though this never developed as a consistent strategy. They had often exorcized the word detente and revived memories of the Cold War in rhetoric, and sometimes also in practice, but they now adopted, silently and gradually, the basic elements of factual detente and arms-control politics in the 1980s.

The short minimum-detente period (1980–84) came to an end when Western neo-conservatism began to support more openly new initiatives for East–West co-operation. This occurred under the pressure of various problems and the new strength of the moderate liberal-reformist and explicitly pro-detente political forces, and of the new social movements. At the same time, the conflict between the communist reformers and conservatives in domestic and foreign affairs, which had been evolving behind the scenes for some time, broke out openly in the Soviet Union and in some other East European countries. The first moves towards domestic 'restructuring' and international 'new thinking' in the Soviet Union also produced some changes in Western conservatism and enabled the first new steps in the reduction of tension to be taken in the second half of the 1980s.

The growing discrepancy between the strength and the orientation of the three or four main currents in the Eastern and Western political spectrum are of considerable importance. Since the late 1970s, the general tendency has been a rapid weakening of liberal-democratic and communist universalism and a corresponding rise of various kinds of nationalism in both East and West. This reinforces the centrifugal tendencies within NATO and the WTO, although frequent talk of a decisive crisis of the military alliances mainly consists in the usual exaggerations of real trends.

Polices have been increasingly justified in the name of national interests and values, instead of universal interests and values. This is especially true for economic and security policies. The main issue in debates on security politics has been the different national security interests of France, the United States, Britain, West Germany, and so on, not the common security interests of all liberal-democratic capitalist societies. Correspondingly, we find an extending debate on the national security interests of Romania, Poland, the Soviet Union, East Germany, Hungary, and so on, in the East, and less on the common security interests of all communist-socialist societies. 'Common security' is often a label used to identify the security interests of some smaller nations on the East–West border in contrast to those of the 'superpowers', rather than the security interests of all nations.

In the economic field we also find growing national and regional discrepancies favouring debates on degrees of national or regional protectionism in the United States, Japan and Western Europe. Various degrees of economic reformism in the Eastern economies favour different national economic strategies within Comecon and towards the non-socialist economies.

But this growing concern for national interests, often praised as a process of de-ideologization, is still limited and restricted by a pragmatic attitude to the existing alliances and dependencies, as well as to the new forms of East–West internationalism. Only the nationalisms on the right wing and in some parts of the peace movement are revolutionary in the sense that they want to restructure the existing international system completely by some radical national measures. The prevailing pattern seems to be that limited and nationally justified East–West internationalism – on both the establishment and the alternative level – has been posed against traditional Eastern and Western universalism.

The Decline of Universalism and the Rise of Limited Nationalism and East–West Internationalism

There are numerous reasons for the decline of liberal-democratic capitalist and communist-socialist universalism in the detente period, and especially since the crisis of detente in the early 1980s.

After a short period of liberal-democratic and communist universalism from 1917 to 1923, both universalisms found 'national' incarnations and bulwarks of state and international power in the United States of America and the Union of Soviet Socialist Republics. These 'national' incarnations were in fact continental and polyethnic, but they prevailed in international relations for many decades. The strength of universalism did not rest on the military and economic power of the two continental states alone, but also on the decline of traditional, mainly European, nationalism and great-power politics. In two world wars, the ideology of balance-of-power politics, of colonial empires, and of national interests and spheres of interest had broken down. In 1945, not only were the politics of National Socialism in ruins but so were the politics of any integral nationalism, in material as well as in moral terms. The United States and the Soviet Union represented not only victorious state power but also the moral superiority and the associated hopes of universalistic policies.

But the moral superiority of liberal-democratic and communist universalism has gradually eroded from decade to decade. The stalemate of the East–West conflict during the Cold War not only suffocated the far-reaching hopes of liberal-democratic or communist world peace and world unity, but also resulted in the *de facto* regionalization, militarization, and attrition of the humanistic ideals and promises once held out by the liberal-democratic and communist semi-worlds. Highly militarized blocs, not world peace, were the result of the competition between the two humanistic universalisms. The practice of many traits of traditional power politics by the new world powers, liberal-democratic and communist 'neo-imperialism', 'neo-colonialism' and nuclear 'militarism', gradually destroyed the moral superiority of the United States and the Soviet Union.

The American- and Soviet-based universalisms declined further as a result of the successful, although in most cases enforced, liquidation of the European colonial heritage; of the capitalist economic recovery and liberal-democratic political consolidation of Western Europe and Japan; of the economic recovery of Central Europe and China; and of the growing consciousness of these regions' national and sometimes democratic traditions. In practice, the assumed liberal-democratic and communist internationalism more and more proved to be hegemonial universalisms, with elements of true internationalism but combined with strong elements of American and Soviet national messianism and interventionism. Non-Americans and non-Soviets learned to understand modern US- and Soviet-based internationalism as hegemonial interventionism. The differences between the USA's interventionism – primarily economic though also military in the last resort – and that of the USSR, which was primarily of a military and policing nature, were soon regarded as negligible, and no longer as differences in principle between the behaviour of different 'superpowers'. This development provided a decisive impetus for anti-superpower, nationalist ideologies of all kinds of political persuasions, traditional leftist as well as rightist.

The reformist version of anti-superpower nationalism seeks an equilibrium between reforms of the existing military and economic alliances (in the sense of strengthening the role of the smaller and weaker nations) and the development of pragmatic, cautious East–West establishment internationalism. The more radical alternative version of the anti-superpower nationalism, in the peace movement and the moderate leftist parties or party wings, works in favour of a dissolution of the military alliances and a more self-reliant, locally and regionally based world economy which ignores East–West borders, combined with a new anti-establishment East–West internationalism and with 'detente-from-below' policies. In this respect one cannot compare this modern nationalism and regionalism with pre-1945 nationalism. This alternative East–West internationalism takes up many aspects of earlier democratic socialist theories which were developed in the 1920s and 1930s against the social democratic/communist polarization, and then again in the late 1940s and 1950s against the Cold War polarization. These ideas were reformulated and augmented in the convergence theories of the detente period.

Where the new internationalism differs from the innumerable past concepts of a 'Third Way', from liberal-democratic capitalism and from communist-socialist statism, is in the absence of – and even non-interest in – any comprehensive political concept and theory. Viewed positively, this surprising openness and tolerance towards all kinds of alternative experiments is a fundamental break with the established and discredited forms of capitalism and communism.

Its approach to sociopolitical questions – atheoretical, even anti-theoretical, pragmatic and yet utopian – is a reaction against the failure of all the more or less dogmatic past theories and political concepts of a 'Third Way'. It is also a reaction to the growing loss of credibility, help-lessness, and offensive drive of the dominant liberal-democratic capi-talist and communist-socialist statist socioeconomic and political theories and political concepts, confronted as they are with the burning old and new problems of Eastern and Western societies. Thus the socio-political boundaries between the various political parties, party factions, and social movements within states and across the national and even the East–West borders have become much more undogmatic and flexible in the 1980s than they were in earlier decades of this and the last century.

The 'bloc universalism' of the Cold War and the old detente is now being challenged simultaneously by limited nationalisms and limited East–West internationalisms. Limited nationalism may be a forerunner of regressive full-scale nationalism, with a strong drive towards autarchic economic and security policies, even if this trend is bound to fail. Its failure, moreover, may have catastrophic consequences. On the other hand, it may also be a historical precondition for a new East–West inter-nationalism, or rather for many new East–West internationalisms at the same time, because we seem to be facing at least three main currents of a new East–West internationalism: partly competing, partly comple-menting each other in the historical process.

The first of these three main currents is the conservative minimum-detente current, which is mainly a political and administrative extra-polation of the approach followed by earlier innovative detente policies but with few new initiatives and some regressive setbacks similar to those seen in the earlier minimum-detente period.

A second main current is the reformist establishment current of Western liberals, social-democrats, some liberal-conservatives and Eastern reform communists, who are all politically rather weak at present. They have been trying to promote new initiatives for East–West co-operation, especially in the field of security politics – for example, under the label 'common security' and 'non-provocative or non-offensive defence' – in the hope that these concepts can be put into practice in periods of government responsibility in the near future.

The third main current consists of the new social movements, of some leftist parties and party factions, and above all of the peace movement with its many competing and co-operating organizations and circles. They formulate policies with a very low probability of being adopted by governments within the coming decades. Nevertheless, they exert some pressure on – and offer innovative potential for – established politics on single issues through a process of political diffusion from the activities of minorities to the attitudes of societal majorities and the decisions of parliaments, bureaucracies and governments. A similar process has been at work in the area of ecological initiatives. The historical function of the peace movement and the new social movements does not seem comparable with the original goals of the labour movement, which aimed at the creation of new social and political elites to occupy government positions in three, four or more generations. The function of the new movements seems to be to produce innovative ideas and political concepts which may in some cases have a chance of being adopted by ruling elites, albeit in a restricted or distorted form.

All three main currents have a certain function in the process of East–West relations, and none of them is likely to disappear for ever within the next decades. A comprehensive analysis of East–West relations and East–West detente, therefore, has to take into account the activities and relevance of all these political forces.

These currents are represented not only by political parties, factions, and movements but also by the activities of the large and smaller social organizations like corporations, trade unions, churches, and various associations. These organizations sometimes have an important impact on East–West relations, in two main ways. On the one hand, they may develop and influence societal and governmental attitudes in favour of detente. It was in this way, for example, that the German and Polish churches influenced the European situation after National Socialism and in the Cold War. Their process of rethinking led to a considerable change in the attitudes of the West and East German and Polish peoples in favour of the later governmental Ost- and Westpolitik. Before governments or established parties dare to elaborate and express new political ideas, established social organizations may develop or take them up from individual or minority initiatives. Social organizations, therefore, even if they have no specific political goal, have an important function within the political process of societies. This is especially true for those societies where social organizations may express non-governmental political ideas.

On the other hand, the social organizations may develop their own subgovernmental East–West relations with specific characteristics and with a certain political effect and weight in favour of detente. This autonomous East–West co-operation between social organizations is not entirely independent, in the sense that it is dependent on general political permission and on political limitations defined by the state authority. But within the legal and political limits of governmental decisions – and sometimes they are even transcended – social organizations have a certain room for manoeuvre in which they can develop their own autonomous activities in favour of detente. Equally, of course, they may sabotage detente. East–West politics are no longer a monopoly of governments.

Problems of a New Detente

The old problems of East–West relations that contributed to the crisis of detente in the early 1980s also constitute the main problems of any new detente which might be more than the extrapolation and administration of minimum detente. Potentially, a new detente could be a qualitatively new attempt to reduce fundamental tensions in East–West relations and to put them on a more co-operative, stable and secure basis.

The military problems of controlling and reducing armaments and the threat of war are still central. Over a long period of time, the political debate and diplomatic negotiations on military detente have concentrated on proposals for arms control and disarmament, but the possibility of achieving real results in that field was rather limited so long as no changes in military doctrines and strategies were involved. Reductions in troops and arms are possible only on condition that the military doctrines and strategies are changed, and they also involve a certain amount of transarmament. The basic conditions for such a rethinking of military policies in the minds of majorities in the societies concerned, and their establishments, were created during the previous phases of detente. The first step was the delegitimation of aggressive war. The second was the abolition of the idea that even a defensive war could end with a full-scale victory over the aggressor. The practical implication was that an arms build-up could no longer be justified in order to gain superiority over the potential enemy, but had to be legitimized and practically limited by the concept of military parity. The next step would be the acceptance of those kinds of military doctrines which foresee military defence only on one's own or allied territory. Such military doctrines would involve a substantial reduction of offensive military capabilities for invasions and interventions and would include concepts for ending wars by compromise rather than victory. Since these kinds of military doctrine are based on a readiness to make civilians of one's own country the only likely victims of a war, it is probable that they have a chance of implementation only if they are introduced simultaneously on both sides of the East–West divide.

The problem of preventing military aggression and intervention cannot be completely solved by military–technical means, because a certain degree of military mobility will remain part of defence and counteroffensive capabilities for regaining lost territory. This military mobility is likely to have some potential for limited aggression. Political means, the reduction of the readiness, willingness and intention to wage war, must be added to the reduction of offensive military capabilities. And to a certain extent, this reduction of aggression and the readiness to intervene can be supported by a reduction in the circumstances which seem likely to provoke military intervention in the societies which at present appear to be potential victims of future military interventions.

In the earlier history of the East–West conflict, any fundamental sociopolitical change in a state also meant an exchange of foreign allies and opponents. Communist or socialist revolutions involved some sort of alliance with the Soviet Union or neutralism. Reformist or other forms of national communism implied neutralism or some kind of military co-operation with liberal-democratic capitalist nations. Thus any sociopolitical change was not only a matter of national self-determination but also of international power relations and of the national security of the neighbouring nations.

The East–West conflict cannot be terminated by the mutual acceptance of the sociopolitical division of Europe and the world according to a modern principle of *cuius regio, eius religio*, which means that he who rules determines the room available for changing or preserving the existing sociopolitical order. Even if pragmatic, 'deideologized' government in East and West clandestinely made agreements on the repressive stabilization of the sociopolitical status quo, public opinion and large societal majorities or minorities would hardly give up any political concern for the fate of liberals, democrats and reform-communists in the East, or for the fate of communists and socialists in the West who rebelled against the sociopolitical status quo. And states cannot preserve or create sociopolitical consensus in favour of the existing sociopolitical system under all conditions and for all time. If splits within societies on important sociopolitical issues, and even on the question of preservation or change of the socioeconomic and political system, cannot be prevented by a system of external and, if necessary, repressive peaceful coexistence, a realistic view of the future of Europe must combine the probability of sociopolitical change and conflict with the possibility of a kind of international politics which can prevent war.

The Rise of a Civilized East–West Conflict Culture

Such a perspective is inconceivable as one of peace resulting in the
abolition and absence of East–West conflict. It is possible only as a
perspective of peace as a civilized and gradually demilitarized conflict in
which liberal democrats and capitalists will continue to support the
expansion of liberal democracy and capitalism, and communists will
continue to support communist socialism. The essence of a civilized
East–West conflict culture will not rest on a futile attempt to attain a
consensus on the fundamental sociopolitical questions but will involve a
certain consensus on the kinds of political and military means which are
acceptable as ways of preserving or changing the existing sociopolitical
order.

The 'civilization' of the East–West conflict can be enforced and
promoted by two different developments: first, mutual deterrence at the
lowest possible level and the non-use of weapons of mass destruction,
which would make deterrence gradually irrelevant and then superfluous,
together with the growing experience of the irrational character of international and civil wars as ways of solving sociopolitical questions and the
problem of national security; secondly, probable and potential political
learning processes within societies which are geared towards solving
problems not only by the successful implementation of power but also
by compromise-building, in which given interests are modified in a
peaceful competition and conflict with opposing interests. Thus not only
the goals, but the very character of politics gradually changes in the
process of civilization.

A civilized conflict culture does not rest on compromises and consensus alone and on the illusion of abolishing all power relations. A
civilized conflict culture rests on the assumption that totally antagonistic
conflicts can be reduced to limited, civilized conflicts in which the
parties fight for power in the sense of moderate domination, influence,
preponderance and hegemony, but not for life and death. The political
thinking of *kto-kogo* (who dominates, defeats, or kills whom) can be
replaced only gradually by a political thinking in terms of compromise
and co-operation. The condition of such a civilized conflict culture is
that all sociopolitical parties in international society should realize what
they stand to lose: life and the perspective of a human future.

Such a civilized conflict structure has only begun to be introduced
into history. It can be promoted further only by gradual societal learning
processes, which may not exclude even limited catastrophes and relapses
into modern barbarism with scientific–technical means. There will
remain an open historical question as to the extent to which societies are
able to base all human relations on non-violence, or to which minimum

violence will be seen as indispensable in future Western and Eastern societies.

What methods and possibilities are available for the deliberate and intentional development of a civilized East–West conflict culture? Most probably, nuclear deterrence and national military defence readiness will not disappear in the next decades; therefore, most attention should be devoted to the non-use of existing military means in order to change the existing domestic and international systems. That involves a clear separation of the problems of sociopolitical self-determination and national security policies. The margin for sociopolitical change can be enlarged only if the international military power structure is not threatened by the consequences of these changes. Sociopolitical oppositions in the West have to learn, and have partly learned already, that they may not challenge the membership of their country in NATO or their neutral status. And sociopolitical oppositions in the East may not challenge the membership of their country in the WTO or their neutral status as adopted earlier by Yugoslavia and Albania. On the other hand, NATO and WTO establishments still have to learn that growing tolerance of sociopolitical diversity and pluralism within the alliance is no threat to multinational security but a condition for the stability of the alliances, for the East–West order, and for the flexible adaptation of the two social systems.

In both systems, sociopolitical oppositions still have to learn how to integrate the ruling elites into the transformation process of their society, at least to a certain extent, even if they have used or misused their power for illegal repression and violence. This perspective can be developed only within the framework of policies of non-violent resistance.

It should, however, be taken into consideration that non-violent resistance and the avoidance of violent revolutions or counter-revolutions can hardly be successful if these activities are unilaterally supported by sociopolitical oppositions alone. Western and Eastern establishments must be prepared to use only limited violence and to show a certain degree of respect for legal non-violent resistance. The successful avoidance of lethal means in the recent vehement sociopolitical struggles in Poland is a promising indicator for developments in the direction of a civilized conflict structure in Europe. Certainly Solidarity suffered a serious defeat for the time being, but not in all respects and not for ever. The ability of the Soviet Union and the Warsaw Treaty Organization to avoid a military intervention in Poland and to use massive repression short of foreign military means certainly does not meet the requirements of civilized or even non-violent conflict behaviour, but is already an important step towards overcoming the traditions of the bloody and military interventions which took place in the Hungarian and Czechoslovakian sociopolitical crises of 1956 and 1968.

Of course, American economic pressure on the Sandinistas and the military–financial and military–technical support for the Contras in Nicaragua cannot be considered an example of civilized East–West conflict behaviour either. Nevertheless, restraints which have operated within American society against the use of massive and open military power in the struggle against the Sandinistas are important in terms of a further civilization of American foreign policy, and they should not be ignored.

A certain moderation in the goals sought seems to be a precondition for the moderation of the means used. If victory means political victory and not extermination of the opponent as an absolute enemy, a higher probability of moderated conflict behaviour can be assumed. The relative affluence of modern European societies, both East and West, and the relatively high level of socioeconomic security against death from starvation, socially conditioned diseases and other forms of extreme social injustice are additional important conditions for the civilization of conflict behaviour in present-day Europe. The development of a civilized conflict culture in East–West Europe would constitute a new stage in the historical process.

Economic boycott, as distinct from economic non-cooperation as a non-violent strategy, must be seen as a continuation of war by less violent but still violent means, which aims at the extermination of the enemy instead of his transformation into an equal partner and opponent.

The optimal condition for the development of a civilized conflict culture in a society is a limited conflict and, at the same time, co-operation between a reformist establishment and a non-violent social movement where the struggle does not concern the basic necessity and direction of sociopolitical change, but only the historical speed and intensity of that change. In this case, reform from above and non-violent reform from below may be complementary, although they are also necessarily antagonistic factors in the historical process of civilization. Peace is not a monopoly of peace movements or governments. Peace requires civilized conflicts between establishments and social movements without attempts to exterminate the governments, the social movements, or the intermediary social organizations.

If conflict is a condition of modern society and its development, then the abolition of all conflict means the absence of peace and a historically futile attempt to produce the illusion of peace by a transitional repression of conflict.

The Future of East and West Germany in European Detente

National conflicts have a specific sociopolitical dimension on both the domestic and the international level. National self-determination does not mean only sociopolitical self-determination within the boundaries of a given state, but also a process of societal self-determination which decides who belongs to a nation and between which borders.

The German Question is still the most delicate national question in Europe, although there are many other dangerous national questions provoking violence and even war – as in Northern Ireland, Cyprus, the Basque region, and Transylvania. The division of the German people into several states has a sociopolitical as well as a national dimension. Germany is not divided only because the East–West border happens to run through it, but also because the interests of many non-German nations have been seen to consist in preventing any kind of all-German national state in the centre of Europe. After the experience of German imperialism in two forms, the more traditional Wilhelminian and the National Socialist, neighbouring nations feared even a liberal-democratic or a communist all-German nation-state. Thus the allied victors in two world wars used a combination of violence and incentives to separate the Germans in Austria from the Germans in the German Reich by supporting the building of a separate Austrian nation.

Nowadays, most Germans accept the existence of a separate Austrian nation as well as the definite loss of those territories in the East which were formerly settled by Germans and which belonged to either the Habsburg or the Hohenzollern monarchies before 1914. Consequently, the meaning of the term 'Germany' is reduced to the territory of the two German states and Berlin. The division of Europe also guarantees the division of Germany and the Soviet and American control of the two German states. The moral breakdown of German nationalism contributed to the fact that the West German liberal-democratic establishment, supported by the majority of the population, and the East German communist establishment, supported by a minority of the population, served as twin spearheads of the Cold War during the late 1940s and the 1950s, and also in a more moderate way in the 1960s. Even competitive detente during the 1970s and the long tradition of social-democratic–communist antagonism helped to guarantee the neutralization of potential German power by the East–West conflict.

But do the German neighbours need a certain degree of East–West tension in order to keep the Germans in opposing military–political camps? Does detente contain the threat of a German 'reunification' for the neighbours of Germany, even in the limited boundaries of the FRG and the GDR? And would a more radical detente, including a with-

drawal of American and Soviet troops from Central Europe, lead to a
new German territorial revisionism *vis-à-vis* Poland, the Soviet Union
and Czechoslovakia, and to a revival of German nationalism in Austria?
The Hungaro–French author of the 'History of the People's
Democracies', François Fejtö, has posed the crucial question on the
future of Europe:

> Germany remains the decisive question for Eastern and Western Europe. The
> integration of the whole of Germany into the Soviet sphere of influence would
> be just as unacceptable from the point of view of security for Western Europe
> as it would for the USA. On the other side, the rebirth of German militarism
> and revanchism brings with it a danger which is as feared by the Danubian
> peoples as it is by the Soviet Union, and which is not comforting to Western
> Europeans either. Does Europe really only have a choice between three kinds
> of hegemony: one German–Russian, one German–American, and one simply
> German? Is it possible to envisage a viable German state which has come to
> its senses, which is capable of defending its independence but has renounced
> any claim to hegemony? Is the idea of a European and socialist Germany
> really a utopia? If so, then the Eastern European states' prospects of peace
> and independence can only be judged pessimistically. In that case the division
> and partition of Germany necessarily involves the division and partition of the
> continent, and indeed its Balkanization. These circumstances then make the
> two separate parts of Europe into the satellites of the great foreign powers,
> and are together preparing the way for the return of German nationalism.
> (François Fejtö, *Geschichte der Volksdemokratien*, Vienna 1972, vol. 2,
> p. 463)

Even the very moderate continuation of German–German detente by
West German Christian Democrats and East German Communists in
the mid 1980s raised anxious fears of an all-German understanding
which might go too far. The rise of a relatively strong peace movement
in West and East Germany, opposing the American and the Soviet
missiles in Central Europe and talking of (East and West) Germany as
the most probable limited war theatre in a military confrontation
between the two superpowers, even intensified this fear. For many non-
German Europeans, German pacifism and neutralism suddenly became
a more severe threat to European security than German military policies
embedded in NATO and the WTO. Would the common SPD/SED
declaration on 'the conflict of ideologies and common security', in which
both parties claim the common humanistic heritage of Europe, serve as
a further step to the reunification of the social-democratic/communist
and Western/Eastern Labour parties in some decades' time? And are
West German social democrats, who have begun to talk of Central
European historical traditions, preparing the separation of West

Germany from Western Europe and of East Germany from Eastern Europe in order to restore a politically and militarily strong and German-dominated Central Europe, or even a wider Europe dominated by its central power under conditions of long-lasting detente?

These questions are not absurd if they are considered in terms of a period of several decades. Detente served to increase the role of the German states in Europe and still does, and it assists German–German co-operation. But that fact does not lead to the conclusion that a higher degree of East–West tension could contain German nationalism and restore the Cold War antagonism between West German Christian Democrats and East German Communists.

An answer to the fears of the German neighbours could consist of the following arguments. German militarism and imperialism were not rooted in a biologically determined German nature or national character, but in specific historical circumstances that did not allow the development of a 'normal' German nation-state and nationalism. The defeat of two attempts to gain the position of a modern world power has probably terminated all serious mental aspirations to create a German world power. The material conditions of economic, territorial and demographic potential, and growing interdependence of the world market, have even destroyed the conditions which might have provided a basis for illusions concerning a quasi-autarchic German Central European empire. The present economic strength of the two German states would be destroyed by any autarchy policy. In addition, the unification of the two German armies would under no circumstances increase either the national security or the political power of an all-German nation-state. The two German states are much more influential in Europe than a potential united and isolated Germany would be. Such a united Germany would be surrounded by suspicious neighbour-states if they could not prevent the unification of the two states without waging war.

As long as there is a considerable difference between the two social systems, the peaceful unification of two semi-states with different sociopolitical systems within one state cannot be imagined. A peacefully united Germany with one sociopolitical system would presuppose a peaceful elimination of the liberal-democratic capitalist system in West Germany or a peaceful elimination of the communist-socialist system in East Germany. For neither of these developments can even hypothetical scenarios be foreseen.

A united German state could, therefore, be created only by risking a European or world war, and such a war would risk at least the existence of the Germans as a people. Thus a 'reunification of Germany' under the conditions of two vital social systems in Europe is not a historical option.

A nation-state traditionally has many functions of a nation: for example, the protection of a national language and culture, of the socio-political system or of religious traditions. But many of these functions are not threatened by the existence of two states within the same nation.

In the nineteenth century and the first half of the twentieth, another crucial central function of the nation-state was to guarantee national security – security against other nations – and also the security of nationals against being used in various 'brother states' of the same nation by the state authorities.

In the nuclear age, national security cannot be guaranteed by national means. One united German state could not secure the existence of the Germans in any better way than two German states. Nowadays, German security is dependent on European and intercontinental East–West security. This makes the overcoming of the division of Germany an inseparable part of the process of uniting Eastern and Western Europe. The Germans have only the options of playing the role of a rearguard, of a rank-and-file participant, or of an avant-garde in the process of detente; an isolated German–German Cold War or a unification of the German states is not possible. Only a dissolution of both East and West into many independent nationalisms could restore a German national-ism which would again be opposed both to Western liberal-democratic capitalism and to Eastern communist socialism. The re-emergence of a strong German nationalism is likely only if nationalism regains a decisive influence on the non-German nations in Europe.

The alternative to the dissolution of the Eastern and Western poli-tical, economic and military associations into national entities is growing co-operation between East and West on the bilateral and multilateral levels. This means the overcoming of the bloc confrontation – not by bloc dissolution but by a process of gradual East–West integration whereby sociopolitical differences will lose their importance without disappearing completely and the question of German unification would be a rather irrelevant European administrative question, like the former historical unification or separation of Baden and Württemberg. It is not the unification of the German states that is important but the unification of the German nation, divided into liberal-democrats in the West and communists in the East. If German–German communication and inte-gration achieves the intensity of Austrian–West German communication in all non-military areas of life under conditions of successful East–West detente, the unification of the German armies and states is no longer a political issue. The division of Germany is relevant only as long as civil or interstate war seems to be a historical option in Europe. If one excludes the options of civil or interstate war, the division of Germany also loses its fundamental political importance and becomes a domestic regional self-determination issue in Europe, like the case of Bavaria and Austria. Then the main issue would be not the absence of a united nation-state but the lack of regional self-determination in historically given borders.

This perspective of a new and lasting detente that promotes the civilization of the East–West conflict can overcome the futile old debate between the two traditional positions: one making detente and peace a precondition of German reunification, the other making German reunification a precondition of reliable detente and peace. The recognition of the East–West border in Germany as well as in Europe is the precondition for its permanent and intensive transcendence, until this border loses its political character and acquires a mere administrative significance.

4

A New Form of Detente: For a Relaxation of Tension with a Democratic Future

Jaroslav Šabata

Jimmy Carter's administration ceased to use the word 'detente' at the end of the 1970s. This signalled a deep crisis for the Helsinki process and a crisis for a whole conglomerate of prerequisites on which this policy in its original form rested. The absence of the word 'detente' from current political speeches shows us that the present atmosphere of international relaxation of tension is radically different from the period of 'detente'. The current relaxation in the international arena has a new political content. It has new prospects. It is an altogether *new form of detente.*

The expression 'our common European house' sums up very well the new dimensions of this relaxation of tension. 'Our common European house' is a good expression: it emphasises what our *divided* continent has in common. Nevertheless, it is not clear exactly what this expression conveys. It is unclear whether the fact that our continent *is* divided is being properly taken into consideration. Willy Brandt says that the Germans must rid themselves of the delusion that the two Germanies will be soon reunited. Mikhail Gorbachev has said that history will decide what the fate of Germany will be in a hundred years' time.[1] Does this mean that Europe will continue to be divided for forty or even one hundred years longer?

Progress continues at a snail's pace. But a civilization which functions as a potentially self-destructive system defines even the factor of time in a completely new way. In fact, time becomes a key to unlocking the meaning of all political events. Is the post-war division of our continent a natural state for Europe, which will remain unchanged for generations to come? Or is it a grandiose but makeshift solution which is now coming to the end of its natural life? Let me put this question in another

way: what are the 'final goals' of the two separate processes of integration currently under way in the two parts of the divided Europe? Will
the two European blocs be forever developing as totally opposed and
incompatible political alignments? Or should the two integration
processes eventually merge to produce a united continent?

These questions define the 'European problem' at the end of the
twentieth century. This is not merely a regional issue. Its catastrophic
background is more serious and more subtle. Europe has been brutally
torn in half. The division of Europe has paralysed the whole world
community. It has deprived it of its ability effectively to tackle the
apocalyptic dangers which threaten our civilization. This is what makes
the 'European problem' a major issue of universal relevance.

Of course, life in the two parts of the divided Europe is being
governed by strategies which reinforce this division of the continent.
Each of these two strategies has its own history and its idiosyncrasies.
The East European strategy is now undergoing a thorough re-
examination: we are told it is no longer possible to continue in the old
ways. The East European system is to be reformed. A struggle is
currently going on as to what guise this reform should take. Should it be
a profound, radical and democratic reform (in fact a U-turn) or should
it be only a reform carried out by the bureaucratic *apparat*?[2] It becomes
more and more evident that the ongoing struggle will determine whether
Europe as a whole might be able to follow the path of a democratic
unity 'in diversity' or whether it will remain in the straitjacket of its
current schism.

There are more and more signs that Eastern Europe just might go for
deep structural reform. This is certainly the path the Central European
nations and the Estonians, Lithuanians and Latvians would like to
choose. 'All the problems dogging Soviet society', wrote a Soviet
commentator about the situation in the Baltic countries, 'are amplified
here by the national issue'.[3] But classic Marxist theory fails to convey the
meaning of what is going on in these countries. Rather, it reflects the
Russians' embarrassment that the political struggle of the Baltic nations
(and the nations of Central Europe) is an attempt by these nations to do
away with the bureaucratic constraints of the Soviet Empire, the most
sophisticated (because quasi-internationalist) superpower structure
Europe has ever known.[4]

The epoch-making importance of the events we are currently
witnessing will become apparent if we return to their origins – if we go
back to the times *before* the October Revolution. If we delve deep
enough, we will discover a strangely comprehensible arena, an arena in
which representatives of European democratic, liberal and socialist
groupings weighed up the project of a unified democratic Europe – the

project of the United States of Europe. It is beyond doubt that these thinkers and politicians were considerably influenced by the American example. Nevertheless, the deepest intellectual and spiritual inspiration from which the idea of a United Europe had sprung came from the universalist approach. Modern European thinkers had reworked this approach in the spirit of democracy.[5]

It is very important to realise that the idea of a united Europe has very deep roots. Even the Russian Bolsheviks were carried away by the idea of the United States of Europe. This was primarily due to developments in the years leading up to the Russian Revolution. In the conflagration of the First World War, in a large territory to the east of the Rhine, a very disparate opposition made up of members of miscellaneous social strata, rose against the establishments of the three Great Powers involved in the War, the Russian, Prussian and the Austro–Hungarian monarchies. As the non-legitimacy of these three survivals of semi-feudal Europe became apparent, the non-legitimacy of the modern superpower principle, the principle of the inequality of nations, was also revealed. Europe had been governed according to this principle from time immemorial up to the First World War. During the First World War, it became clear that this principle was no longer tenable.

But the times had not matured sufficiently to make it possible to forge a congruous and lasting political alliance of democratic and peace-loving forces, which would find a way out of the traditional structures of dominance and subjugation. The Russian revolutionary Social Democrats went their own way. They accepted the idea of the United States of Europe only to reject it later and to adopt the strategy of a world proletarian revolution instead. They came to believe that a proletarian revolution would take a direct route to the free unification of the whole world: 'Workers of the Whole World, Unite!' They believed the revolution would bring a United States of the World in its wake.[6] When we examine the last stages of the process during which the vision of a free, socialist union of all nations eventually died, its demise seems almost inevitable. Yet we should not forget that the power of the Russian Bolsheviks did not crumble under an onslaught from the outside. They narrowed their power base far too much – and their reactionary past has caught up with them. Their system has collapsed in on itself.

We will be able to understand a great deal if we realize that Russian revolutionaries behaved like members of a large nation – like citizens of a very self-confident nation. Lenin wrote of the national pride of the Great Russians. He quite naturally believed that it was going to be large countries that would decide whether the revolution prevailed worldwide. He counted on the Germans. He did not take small nations seriously, even though he also spoke to them. Much of what had determined the thinking of Lenin's teachers survived in his own views. Along with Marx and Engels, Lenin was convinced that small Slavonic nations were the vanguard of that strongest bastion of European reaction, Russian tsarism. Therefore they had to be crushed . . .[7]

It is no wonder that the idea of the United Nations of Europe came to take root particularly in the environment of 'small' nations, European nations in the area 'between Germany and Russia'. The first Czecho-slovak President – philosopher Tomáš Garrigue Masaryk, the man who helped to destroy Austria–Hungary – was present at the birth of the Democratic Union of Central European Nations, an emigré organisation founded in the USA in 1918. For Masaryk, the idea of a United Europe was not utopian. It was a sensible, rational solution which would sooner or later be implemented in practice. Masaryk's map of the zone of small nations between Germany and Russia (if we are to count Poland among small nations, Masaryk would remark) included even the Lithuanians, Latvians and Estonians in the Baltic.

Masaryk's important memorandum from the end of the First World War, entitled 'The New Europe (A Slavonic Standpoint)' is still today a remarkable testimony as to how European political thinking worked its way towards an understanding of the demands of the new era at a time when a crisis had already broken out at one of its extremes. Masaryk addressed his memorandum to the Peace Congress. He concentrated on trying to work out ways in which Eastern Europe (and therefore Europe as a whole) could be reorganized along democratic lines; on ways in which the political freedom of all nations could be ensured; and on a political restructuring of the European continent that would protect smaller European nations against Pan-German expansion. 'History is working its way towards a more unified organization of the whole of mankind', Masaryk repeated in a number of variations.

Masaryk's hopes, which were placed in the first instrument of Euro-pean unification, the inter-war League of Nations, remained unfulfilled. It is now obvious that Masaryk did not fully understand the profound crisis within the Great Power establishments, in particular the crisis within their ruling structures in the colonies. But without our inter-war experiences with a European and world security system it would have been impossible to imagine mankind's journey from the Atlantic Charter and the UN Charter to the current form of the United Nations Organ-ization, and of course to Helsinki.

If we understand the two World Wars as two parts of a single, major event – as a modern Thirty Years War, the way Winston Churchill and others saw it – it becomes evident how well Masaryk was able to grasp the meaning of the difference between American and Prussian types of

capitalism – between the democratic and the non-democratic evolution
of capitalism. Lenin knew a great deal about this distinction, but on the
whole, Russian Bolsheviks were not at all aware of its importance. Stalin
was totally ignorant of the distinction – although, in the end, he became
one of the three members of an anti-fascist coalition alongside Churchill
and Roosevelt. His ignorance explains a great deal: not only Stalin's
pact and his treaty with Hitler on the eve of the war and in the first
stages of the war, but also the overall strategy of Stalinist Russia, which
eventually led to the Brezhnevite bureaucratic and militaristic structures
of 'really existing' socialism. Stalin's ignorance of this distinction
explains why he felt the need to annex the Baltic countries. It explains
the arrogant attitude of the Soviets to the Polish issue. It explains all
those steps taken by the Soviets in Central Europe during the first post-
war years which prevented the Central European popular governments
from introducing democracy in their countries.

On the other hand, Masaryk believed that since the times of the
American and French Revolutions, Mankind had been moving towards
an epoch-making democratic revolution. According to Masaryk, in
modern times, the focal point of political decision-making was gradually
shifting towards the grassroots of society. Masaryk's pupil, the second
Czechoslovak president Edward Beneš expressed this belief in his
concept of a 'socializing democracy'.[8]

If we take Masaryk's views to their logical conclusions, we move into
the inner world of the Cold War. These days, many people feel that the
Cold War was an absurd development. Many of our contemporaries
believe that the Cold War 'need not have taken place at all' if it had not
been for human imperfection and for ideological prejudices, if the deeds
of politicians had been in line with their words and with the international
treaties they had signed on behalf of their countries.[9] But this view
makes it difficult for us to understand the origins of the Cold War. In the
actual historical context of the first post-war years, genuine democracy
played a considerably less important role than decision-making based on
the superpower principle. This feels particularly true if we look at those
years through the eyes of the nations of our part of Europe. The main
protagonists who took part in the negotiations which determined the
new post-war status quo in Europe all made decisions based exclusively
on the superpower principle. The fact that they were at the same time
irreconcilable adversaries only underlined the fatefulness of the events
of that time. It is irrelevant whether, for instance, President Roosevelt
sincerely believed all he said and wrote. In his view, post-war peace was
to be neither an American peace, nor a Russian peace, nor any other
national peace. It should have been a universal peace, based on the co-
operation of all nations. He probably fully believed all this (just as he

had been undoubtedly fully convinced he was acting in the interests of peace when he told Czechoslovak President Beneš in 1938 to do all he could to avert a conflict with Hitler and a war with Germany). Be that as it may, Roosevelt was unable to prevent the post-war peace from becoming a peace of the large nations – an American and Soviet peace – just as President Wilson in 1918, despite his diplomatic idealism, had been unable to prevent his concept of the League of Nations from becoming a trap for the sovereignty not only of Czechoslovakia but of several other countries as well.

So – as we go through all those well known post-war events and through the whole pile of misunderstandings (some genuine, some less so) – we have to conclude that not even after Fascism was defeated were the Europeans ready to join forces. The deep chasm which had divided them at the end of the First World War reappeared in an even more dangerous form. Europe became the scene of a confrontation unparalleled in peacetime. Nowadays, our continent is more replete with military hardware than it likes to think: in its Eastern half this is doubly so.

But a new great opportunity on the winding road towards a future European unification has been born out of the very absurdity of this situation. 'The threat of Communism' from the East has accelerated the process of overcoming nationalist antagonisms in Western Europe; Soviet rule has brought about, if nothing else, at least a new historical and psychological awareness in the eastern half of the European continent. This change has gone perhaps the furthest in Central Europe: the Poles and the Hungarians, the Germans, the Czechs and the Slovaks, as well as the Austrians, feel now much closer to one another than was the case in the inter-war years. So the division of Europe has not had merely negative consequences. Paradoxically, it has accelerated those processes which may lead towards a deeper political and economic integration of the whole continent. The great epoch which began at the crossroads of the First World War is slowly but surely coming to an end. The inclination of Eastern European nations towards a democratic way, towards a democratic variant of perestroika, has created a new historical and political situation; not just for Eastern Europe, but for Europe as a whole. Although Gorbachev's statement that perestroika with all its international consequences demolishes the concept of the Soviet threat and that militarism thus loses all political justification[10] certainly requires many clarifications and additions, there is no doubt that in principle it is valid.

Thus the epoch-making democratic revolution, whose origins lie in the distant past, has reached an extraordinary watershed. The contemporary crisis has assumed totally new proportions. There are serious problems everywhere, in all countries, in all relationships. People are becoming ever more aware of the serious threat to our civilization. Ever more frequently people speak of the need to create a new, more sophisticated civilization.[11] So far, most ordinary people do not find this kind of talk very relevant or inspiring. Nevertheless, the overall atmosphere is already charged with inarticulate tension. This is a sign that people are indeed searching for new firm ground. The Czech philosopher Radim Palouš speaks of a transition from one epoch to another. He speaks of the temporary situation which separates the 'Euro-age' (which comprises all the European ages, not just the New Age) from the 'World Age'. The new 'World Age' to come will pay due attention not only to Man but to the Natural World as well.[12]

However, the outcome of the great struggle with the forces which do not accept the inevitability of change is as yet uncertain. Compromise rules supreme. Left-wing thinking tends to succumb to a 'historical compromise' because it has to contend with many by-products of the disintegration of the original vision (according to which all nations were due to be united in freedom under socialism). The persistent tendency of socialists to succumb to the idea of a siege mentality, whether this be on a small scale ('national Communism') or on a large scale ('socialist integration'), creates within them the unconscious urge to revive the philosophy by which the final aim of the movement remains unchanged while the ways and means to achieve it may vary. If the going gets tough, the fighters are allowed to retreat and re-group: having gathered renewed strength, they go on the offensive again; attacking the right, the World of Capital, Imperialism, and so on. But the intellectual volte-face, the product of inner developments which have occurred within twentieth-century philosophy, transforms the very image and concept of our 'final goal'. The traditional, non-reflective, uncritical point of view tells us that we should work towards an established, already-existing goal. But if we analyse the situation critically, we realize that we should actually be seeking an as yet unknown goal. The unknown meaning of this goal will only become apparent in the course of the development of a *pluralist* society. Our movement towards the principle of plurality will revive the great universalist approach: the striving for a united, free, democratic community of nations; a community based on a unity in spiritual, political and economic diversity, on a unity in multiplicity within each nation and also in relations between nations.

In the light of this universal pluralism, the very essence of traditional ideas about what constitutes left-wing evolution and right-wing evolution undergoes a transformation. If we believe that socialism equals common ownership of the means of production,[13] then a move towards pluralism will be seen as a step backwards – or at least as a far-reaching compromise which must sooner or later be reassessed. But a tolerant

attitude which provides freedom of all conceivable forms of ownership is
not a compromise. It is a truly revolutionary unifying principle of civilizational development. Our civilization finds itself in a crisis. This is why it
is forced to look for new solutions to old problems. It is true that the
concrete shape of things often remains unclear. However, the concrete
shape of things is not born of speculation but of economic and political
practice. Such a practice must be democratic. It must be democratic
enough to be able to return the relationship of Man and the Natural
World to a proper balance and to ensure that it will remain in balance in
future.

However, this unifying principle of civilizational development is being
threatened by a compromise, a retrograde compromise. Such a compromise is being sought by members of official establishments, by all
those who wish to retain the status quo. It is a strange paradox of our
times that the 'power centres' of the West (to use Henry Kissinger's
terminology[14]) which are seen as a combined adversary by the Eastern
Bloc, may actually act to save the East European 'bureaucracy' which is
now being threatened by 'expatriation' (this is the most radical
expression coined by the thinkers behind the democratic variant of
perestroika). The power centres in the East and in the West may well
limit themselves to structural changes that are in line with current superpower games. The basic pattern of these games has been familiar to all
of us since the foundation of the United Nations. They are often demonstrated in the UN Security Council. It is true that since the end of the
Second World War, smaller nations have played an increasingly greater
role in the United Nations. Nevertheless, the basic structure of this
organization has changed little. A truly democratic restructuring of the
United Nations is not envisaged . . .

Perhaps we can find some consolation in a historical compromise if it
is eventually made by the largest power centres of the world. After all,
we must bear in mind that it is impossible to go against the natural flow
of things. Any great revolutionary change or transformation must surely
be given time to mature. Each such change has to go through all its
natural intermediate stages if it is to become truly irrevocable. Perhaps
we will have to come to terms with the fact that Germany and Europe
will not be reunited along democratic lines in the near future. Indeed, it
is easily imaginable that 'new political thinking' in Eastern Europe might
get bogged down in attitudes of liberal pacifism, that it will be diluted
and made ineffective.

Nevertheless, let us stick to the hope which tells us that the future is
open. 'New political thinking' is also open. If the Soviets now say that
'peaceful coexistence is not a form of class struggle',[15] this may mean
that the Soviet Bloc will in future attempt to conclude treaties with its

largest potential partners along the lines of least resistance. However, it is not out of the question that the Soviet Bloc might at the same time undertake steps to offer genuine co-operation to the world public as a whole, thus contributing to a *democratic* change in international relations.

The idea of a 'European Reykjavik'[16] – that is, the idea of a summit meeting to be attended by representatives of all countries participating in the Helsinki process – has been born of a desire to break out of the vicious circle of the current talks on conventional troop and arms reduction and to 'ensure we move from words to action in the area of conventional arms'.[17] The reasoning which has led to this proposal seems clear: Gorbachev's meeting with Reagan at Reykjavik brought about some progress in the field of nuclear disarmament. But this has brought into sharp focus the problems relating to the sphere of conventional arms. The West European elite has been in the grip of an anxiety: what if the American–Soviet negotiations lead to the weakening of the defences of Western Europe?

At this stage, the preparation of the mandate for the talks on conventional arms and troop reduction is nearing completion. The negotiations themselves will start in 1989. The basic consensus of twenty-three Warsaw Pact and NATO countries is probably the result of efforts made by the Warsaw Pact countries to assure the West that a state of 'true military balance' is reached before 'symmetrical arms and troop reduction' takes place. Undoubtedly, Gorbachev's speech to the United Nations in December 1988 has underlined this assurance.

However, the history of the Vienna talks on disarmament in Central Europe does not give cause for optimism. The reason why these talks have been so unsuccessful lies beyond the realm of military security. The vicious circle out of which the Vienna talks have been unable to break is obviously of a military and political nature. Representatives of important Western peace movements are trying to argue that a successful model of detente will require a fundamental Soviet initiative.[18] Before anything else can happen, the Soviets must withdraw their troops from East Germany as well as from other countries. It is necessary to understand this step as an act designed to pave the way for structural political change. After all, the Soviet Union keeps nineteen army divisions in East Germany. The disastrous political state of Central Europe is common knowledge.[19] Is this not a situation which calls for a unilateral initiative from the East? To what extent is Gorbachev's latest move such an initiative?

In many respects it is quite understandable that influential political circles in the West still regard Eastern Europe with suspicion. I am not trying to deny there may be an element of illegitimate distrust in this

suspicion. It is undoubtedly true that to a certain extent the thinking of
the West is influenced by the pressure of the military–industrial complex,
by the NATO tradition of bargaining from a position of strength as well
as by other considerations. But this does not alter the basic fact that the
mixture of differing motives behind the West European security policy
produces an efficient overall strategy which makes Western Europe
'self-sufficient' and which at the same time reinforces the split between
East and West. A precondition for abandoning the rigid West European
defence doctrine is a strong impulse from the East. In short, Eastern
Europe must help Western Europe in this respect.

What does 'new political thinking' have to say in this connection?
When Gorbachev stated that perestroika removed the fear of a Soviet
threat (Gorbachev naturally put the expression 'Soviet threat' in
inverted commas) and that militarism has thus lost all political justification, he was implying that he was aware Eastern Europe had a
certain amount of moral and political responsibility for the present state
of the arms race. There is evidence that Soviet foreign policy is now
being critically examined. It has been mentioned officially in the Soviet
Union that in the past, Soviet foreign policy did not always try hard
enough to tackle international problems by political means.[20] Unofficial
Soviet texts and statements imply, moreover, that there is a possibility
the Soviet Union might abandon its time-honoured habit of dealing with
disarmament from a pacifist – or rather, quasi-pacifist – point of view.
This traditional view-point ignores the fact that arms are often stock-
piled as a consequence of the existence of unresolved political problems
– not the other way about.[21]

The Soviet insistence on interpreting the Helsinki Final Act 'in a
complex way' shows very well that there have been changes in Soviet
thinking on the disarmament issue. However, this demand is not new: it
is reminiscent of Gromyko's line of argument. Gromyko persistently
rejected Western criticism of infringements of human rights by the
Warsaw Pact countries. He argued that the West was taking a single
issue out of the 'complex' of all the other issues of the Helsinki process
and that, moreover, it was interfering in the internal affairs of sovereign
states. But on the twelfth anniversary of Helsinki, Soviet Deputy Foreign
Minister Anatoly Kovalyev said that the East had also misinterpreted
the Helsinki Final Act. In his view, the West was sidestepping the issue
of disarmament and concentrating one-sidedly on the human rights
issue, while the East was concentrating one-sidedly on the issue of disarmament. The connection between the issue of disarmament and the
issues of human rights and democracy had not been recognized by the
East Europeans. Although this statement was not particularly profound,
it was nevertheless encouraging also to hear from Kovalyev that the

Helsinki Final Act served as a model for Soviet 'new political thinking'. However, since then, several colleagues of Kovalyev's have assured their clients in Prague and elsewhere that the aim of 'new political thinking' is not to threaten the existing, well-established order. They emphasized that 'new political thinking' does not imply that the 'socialist concept of civil rights' would be abandoned in favour of the 'bourgeois democratic concept'. Towards the end of last winter, at the time when the anti-perestroika manifesto by Nina Andreieva was published in Moscow, Anatoly Adamishin repeated these views before the Czechoslovak public.[22] He was of course able to draw inspiration from a speech by Mikhail Gorbachev on the 'ideology of restructuring' given at the February 1988 meeting of the Central Committee of the Soviet Communist Party. This was a passionately pro-reform speech (it fended off an offensive by the bureaucratic right wing on the eve of a Party conference), nevertheless it proclaimed the readiness of the Soviet and East European authorities to fight subversion by 'foreign anti-socialist centres' – in line with the infamous ideological tenet according to which the class struggle becomes the fiercer the more successful the communist state. (Is this tenet also supposed to apply to perestroika?[23]) As has been shown in Czechoslovakia, where independent demonstrations have been ruthlessly suppressed by the authorities recently and where independent activists suffer continuing repression, the directive about 'fighting foreign subversion' is being implemented with ardour in Prague.[24]

The new Soviet policy therefore has its limits. It is imperative that we should be fully aware of its contradictory and incomplete nature. This of course means that the question remains open whether Eastern Europe will help the West. Discussions on the withdrawal of Soviet troops from Central Europe and on the possible consequences of the withdrawal of all foreign troops from Europe are currently in progress.

Mikhail Gorbachev has announced significant unilateral cuts in Soviet troops and tanks in Central Europe. Nevertheless, further progress is likely to occur only in the framework of negotiations.[25] The Soviet Union is willing to discuss, 'on the basis of mutuality', the presence of its troops on the territory of its 'allies' – naturally, after prior agreement with them and taking their views on the matter into consideration.[26]

Are Gorbachev's latest steps enough to provide an impetus for disarmament, to encourage the disarmament talks? Further reductions do require an atmosphere of trust. This should be done through the democratization of international relations. That is the aim of a European Reykjavik and a European round-table discussion involving all political parties, regardless of ideology.

The strong impulse – which is what these meetings are currently expected to provide for the disarmament talks – cannot be ensured by merely enlarging the traditional negotiating teams of the Helsinki process. There are expectations that the involvement of representatives from all European political parties in the Helsinki process will bring the attention of the European public to the large pan-European issues. This, it is hoped, will lead negotiations out of the current blind alley in which they find themselves. However, it is the agenda of these meetings that will decide whether they will be successful. What should be on their agenda? It is expected that the meetings, quite logically, will discuss disarmament. But it has been also indirectly admitted that the other great issue – co-operation in the sphere of human rights and the development of the so-called 'human dimension' of the pan-European process – will be discussed as well. It has been stated that European politicians should meet 'freely to discuss *all aspects* of European affairs, including the issues of arms reduction and the overall de-militarization of the continent'[27] [author's emphasis]. In comparison with earlier versions of the proposal for a European round-table meeting, this represents progress. There was a time when Soviet representative Yegor Ligachev spoke of a European round-table meeting which was merely to discuss security issues.

But the European 'man in the street' will naturally ask: will a free discussion of all aspects of European affairs be at all possible if these are to be official debating forums? The sceptical attitude of the man in the street (particularly if he lives in Eastern Europe) is based on his experience that the views of ordinary people do not penetrate sufficiently into the sphere of official politics. People feel that official international negotiations about averting the threat of nuclear and ecological catastrophe and averting the threat of war are conducted in a deplorably inconsequential manner. They feel that it is those at the top who should answer for this state of affairs.

But a politician like Gorbachev may consider the problem from a different point of view. He may conclude that the European public has not realised how horrifying even a conventional war would be in Europe. He may feel that the European public is not aware that the destructiveness of a conventional war, which would destroy nuclear power plants (and Chernobyl has shown what that means), would not differ too much from the destructiveness of a nuclear war. (Mikhail Gorbachev spoke about this in Poland.) The politician may consider himself able to wake up the European public and to channel its attention in a direction which might be favourable to his concept of the European issue – a concept of the common European house. On the other hand, the politician may conclude that the vicious circle of fruitless disarmament talks cannot be broken and that most Europeans (East Europeans in particular) will react to a new wave of peace rhetoric with a resigned shrug of the shoulders.

People on a grassroots level know full well that the crux of the problem is embodied in the attitudes of professional politicians. Professional international politics is not governed by moral considerations or by an awareness of what real life is like outside the corridors of power.

This does not mean that the man in the street would not welcome talks during which the numbers of weapons on both sides would be counted, during which the discrepancy in these numbers would be corrected and during which arms and troops would be proportionately cut on both sides to the lowest possible levels. Unfortunately, there is a real danger that 'the pace of the negotiations will lag behind the pace of the times, behind what is achievable and behind the demands, dictated to us by all nations and by our common sense', as Mikhail Gorbachev said in an interview in *Der Spiegel* magazine. Thus we are forced to come back to the proposal that European, American and Canadian politicians from all shades of the political spectrum should sit down to a round table to discuss disarmament and all other European issues. We must wish such a meeting success. Unfortunately, the public is sceptical because it has heard far too much rhetoric and seen very little action.

The negative attitude of ordinary people would change if they could suddenly realize that they themselves were able actively and effectively to contribute to the European peace process. This is why the plan was born to set up a 'European Peace Parliament', or European Assembly for Peace and Democracy, as a permanent forum for spokespersons of those sections of the international community who are aware that a war on this continent would mean destruction on an apocalyptic scale. This European forum would strive to articulate what political parties and governments are not saying or what they are not as yet able to say. Somebody has to express the truths which come 'ahead of their time'. Those truths prevail whose time has come. But they are prepared long in advance: they come to maturity outside the limelight.

The European Peace Parliament will in no way detract from the importance of existing representative bodies (such as the European Parliament) or from the importance of the Helsinki process as a political process conducted through the channels of international diplomacy. The European Peace Parliament will support all positive aspects of the pan-European process from the grassroots. It will look for the right direction in the complex undergrowth of relations between disarmament and the development of democratic political structures. (This 'parliament' will be called the European Assembly for Peace and Democracy.)

The idea to found a European Peace Parliament was first voiced by

Birgit Euwe-Koch from West Berlin at a meeting of peace activists from East and West in Benešov near Prague, Czechoslovakia, in May 1988.[28] The moment the idea was formulated a political problem emerged for which the official peace committees of the Warsaw Pact countries were evidently unprepared: should East European 'dissidents' be able to take part in the discussions of the proposed independent peace parliament?[29] As a result, further work on this project has been done exclusively by independent peace campaigners from both East and West.[30]

Born of the crisis in the Helsinki process, the alliance of the independent West European peace movements and East European unofficial civil initiative groups represents an important contribution to attempts to resolve the European issue. Without this alliance it would be impossible to imagine how the division of Europe could ever be overcome. There is a serious reason for this. During the period of people's greatest anxiety regarding the fate of detente and of Helsinki, it was felt that the world was in a situation which was very similar to that on the eve of the First or the Second World War. The anxiety produced an appeal to all supporters of peace and democracy to meet round a single negotiating table. The emphasis of the appeal was on the word 'everybody'. Thus even East European independents, who up to that point had been excluded, were invited. It was felt that these people in particular should be given a chance to take part in discussions on issues of peace. It was realized that peace and freedom were inseparable.[31]

Any attempt to organize a European round-table discussion which would sidestep the issue of the East European oppressed would be a mockery of the very idea of the round-table discussion. Such a discussion would lose all political meaning. Even if it were to be attended by all major European parties, it would fail to fulfil its objective if it avoided the issue of human rights in Eastern Europe. A pan-European debate has a chance of succeeding only if it is clear from the very outset that the human rights issue will be included.

A great deal has been achieved by detente, often due to the courage and initiative of German politicians.[32] But it is impossible to build on these achievements using methods and approaches derived from the first stage of European detente. We will only progress further if we understand detente in terms of a democratic revolution. A 'new detente' should be seen as the beginning of a process leading eventually to full democracy throughout a unified Europe.

What this means in practice is that people must get rid of the fears similar to those which accompanied our first insecure steps away from the Cold War. Now, as then, people are often afraid that 'Gorbachev might be deposed', that his reforms might be reversed and that the current relaxation in international relations might come to an end if they do not proceed with enough caution. Although people in the West often sympathize with the internal critics of communist regimes, they are reluctant to give them their unqualified support for fear that this might 'offend' their official East European contacts and destroy their rapport with these officials. This deplorable aspect of the policy of detente has made many people totally disillusioned with detente as such. Currently, the policy of detente is undergoing a serious test: the proposed Polish round-table debate between representatives of the government and of the Solidarity trade union. The European public should follow Polish developments very closely indeed. If it turns out to be impossible for a round-table debate between representatives of the government and the opposition to take place in Poland, this hardly bodes well for a meaningful pan-European round-table debate.

Europe should not forget this, if it is genuinely interested in thinking of its future. Some three times this century – at the ends of the two World Wars and in 1975, when the first round of detente culminated in Helsinki – it has seemed that Europe might set out along the path towards unification in the spirit of peace and democracy. Later, it has always turned out that history is more complicated. However, this does not mean that because of our past disillusionments we should become so cautious as to lose our ability to see things from a democratic point of view. In spite of our past disappointments, it remains a fact that since the beginning of the great European crisis, Europe has been trying to free itself of its imperialist past. Europe has been gathering strength for the creation of a consensus of such breadth, depth and weight as is necessary for the erection of a durable common European house.

In August 1968, after the Soviet invasion of Czechoslovakia, one of the Czechoslovak communists, deeply wounded, reproached the Soviet leader Leonid Brezhnev saying that the Russians had done great harm to the Communist cause and that they had destroyed any chance of possible future European detente. Brezhnev replied, with an air of great superiority: 'You are wrong. We have done exactly what was necessary for our cause and for the cause of peace to enable us to sit down to the negotiating table with the Americans. In two or three years' time you will see that we were right.'

Brezhnev's reply was imbued with the spirit of the legendary statement ascribed to Bismarck, the 'Iron Chancellor of Prussia': 'He who rules Bohemia rules Europe.' The spirit of this statement is still with us. In a way, Brezhnev was right. His leadership had not spoiled the chances for detente – neither in 1968 nor later when the Russians behaved even more reprehensibly. Although the Russians' behaviour often posed a serious threat to detente, it never quite destroyed it. The Russians managed to persuade people that a democratic and just peace was a luxury which mankind was going to have to abandon if it did not wish to threaten detente.

Europe is only just starting to learn to distinguish between a detente without a future and a detente with a future. But it is learning fast. The democratic reconstruction of Europe's eastern half – a task of whose great pan-European and indeed universal importance Tomáš Garrigue Masaryk spoke seventy years ago – has entered a new stage. It is up to Europe as a whole to understand the spirit of the times. If people are looking for visible signs that point to a future democratic united Europe, there is one which is quite eloquent: it has been decided that Prague should become the permanent seat of the European Assembly for Peace and Democracy.[33] He who rules Bohemia . . .

A reply to those who might object that I am devoting far too much attention to the problems of Central Europe: Europe ruled the world for centuries, often depriving people of freedom. It now has a duty to the world community to free itself of the gigantic yoke of the power blocs because this yoke continues to oppress the world. It is a geographical fact that Central Europe is of major strategic importance. What happens in Central Europe has always had rather serious repercussions for the whole of the continent.

Brno, Czechoslovakia, November 1988

Notes

1. The German issue was brought to the fore by Chancellor Helmut Kohl's trip to Moscow at the end of October 1988 and by Mikhail Gorbachev's planned visit to Bonn. During the visit of President Richard von Weizsäcker to Russia in the summer of 1987 Mikhail Gorbachev said that what has come to pass in Germany must be left to history. In his view, this concerned also the issue of German nationhood and the issue of German reunification: 'There exist two German states with two different social systems. . . . Historical forces will decide what the situation will be like in a hundred years. For the time being, it is necessary to work within existing realities and not to preoccupy oneself with inflammatory speculation.' This statement (re-affirmed in an interview with Gorbachev in *Der Spiegel* during October 1988) however does not make it clear whether Mikhail Gorbachev really believes in the theory of two German *nations* (the question of the reunification of the two Germanies is no longer relevant for adherents to this theory). Whatever his views on the matter, his current attitude suggests he sympathises with adherents to the theory of two separate German nations.

2. In his article entitled 'A Time of Decisive Action', published in the *New Times* 44, 1988, Professor Gavril Popov formulates his theory concerning two varieties of perestroika. In the 'apparat' variety, social changes are implemented 'by the old existing *apparat*'. In the 'popular and democratic' variety of perestroika, social changes come from the grassroots. The former variety protects the *apparat*, the latter sweeps it aside as a large

storm clears the air, creating a new apparat in its place. The 'apparat' variety of perestroika
frustrates the genuine activity of the masses, the 'popular and democratic' variety makes
room for it. The 'apparat' variety delays restructuring. The bureaucrats would wish to make
it last for decades ('in the end, the price of such delays is high'). The 'popular and
democratic variety' introduces decisive and speedy change: 'The expense and the difficulties are enormous, but the effect comes quickly because the most radical economic solutions are being implemented immediately, without interim stages and compromises.' The
'apparat' variety is reminiscent of the Prussian way to capitalism, the 'popular and democratic' variety is like the American way to capitalism. This theory of the contradiction
between a democratic and a bureaucratic form of perestroika poses a number of questions.
Our experiences with the 'extremist left-wing tendency' (the Chinese Cultural Revolution,
etc.) show that these questions are rather serious.

Professor Popov further develops Gorbachev's theory which sees restructuring in terms
of a revolution from above which merges with a revolution from the grassroots (cf. Mikhail
Gorbachev, *Perestroika: New Thinking for Our Country and the World*, Czech translation,
pp. 42ff., Svoboda, Prague, 1987). Popov has based his article on official Soviet teaching
according to which perestroika may assume a radical guise or a moderate guise. It is
interesting to note that the connection between the thinking of people like Popov (i.e., the
most radical theoreticians of democratic restructuring) and current official Soviet political
thinking is relatively loose.

3. Leonid Mlechin, 'A Popular Front: What For and Against Whom?', *The New
Times*, 43, 1988.

4. Leonid Mlechin (ibid.) sees the latest developments in the Baltic as a political
struggle in which whole societies within the Baltic countries have become passionately
involved. The struggle has become the main preoccupation of the lives of the citizens of the
Baltic states: 'Many of the views of the initiators of the three Baltic movements [for
instance the complaints of Russification] used to be regarded as straightforward "dissident
views".' According to Mlechin, after 1985, organizations with aims similar to those of the
Baltic movements were founded throughout the Soviet Union. None of these new organizations, however, has to date managed to attract numbers of supporters large enough to
make itself felt on the internal Soviet political scene. In other words, the situation in the
three Baltic states is exceptional in the Soviet Union. The population of the Baltic states no
longer trusts official ruling structures. People expect nothing from the government. People
place their hope in the new Popular Front movements, which have been born recently of
the nationwide dissatisfaction with the status quo. This is a very unusual situation, Mlechin
concludes. For some unknown reason leading Soviet Communist Party newspapers have to
date failed to subject it to a proper critical analysis. Yet it is necessary to analyse the situation properly because the course of events in the Baltic could take a turn which could be
dangerous for the Soviet Union as a whole.

5. Of seminal importance are Immanuel Kant's theories of 'eternal peace', dating
from 1795, and schemes for a restructuring of Europe into a free federation of nations
which indirectly develop Kant's ideas (for instance, Saint-Simon's scheme from 1814).
Also important are the 'nationalist' theories by Konstantin Frantz and his followers (F.W.
Foerster and others), who wished to create a 'universalist European federation' of which
Germany would form the centre. These thinkers were strongly against Bismarck and
Wilhelm.

6. Cf. Vladimir Ilyich Lenin, 'On the slogan "the United States of Europe"',*Social-
Demokrat* no. 44, 23 August 1915: 'The United States of the World (not of Europe) is the
only state form of the unification of nations in freedom which we associate with socialism –
until the victory of Communism makes all states, even democratic ones, wither away.' But
it is quite remarkable that Lenin regarded the call for the creation of a United States of
Europe as quite correct in terms of practical politics because, as he saw it, it encouraged
political change 'in a truly democratic direction'. This is why in his view a proposal to
created a United States of Europe would 'in no way weaken people's resolve to carry out a
socialist revolution'. The question remains why Lenin eventually abandoned the idea of a
United States of Europe. His own reasoning, namely that the economic structures of these
European United States would have been 'incorrect' (in Lenin's view, a United States of

Europe would be little more than an agreement by European capitalists on how to divide up the colonies among themselves, on how to protect these colonies from Japan and America and on how to suppress socialism) does not explain why Lenin did not opt for a 'popular democratic' alternative of European United States. Surely, if we follow Lenin's logic, a democratic revolution carried out under conditions of late capitalism need not have produced a 'bourgeois capitalist' status quo. It could have given power to a 'revolutionary democratic dictatorship of the workers and peasants'. Such a dictatorship could then have developed peacefully towards socialism. Czechoslovak Communists indirectly pointed to this alternative during the Second World War when they critically assessed, (in 'Leninist' spirit), the mistakes the Czechoslovak Marxist left made when attempting to deal with 'Masaryk's' national and democratic revolution of 1917–20. In undertaking this critical assessment of the past, Czechoslovak Communists were trying to define their wartime and post-war strategy. They came to formulate the theory of a 'specific Czechoslovak road to socialism, without the dictatorship of the proletariat and without the Soviets' (1946). The scheme however collapsed under the external and internal pressures of Stalinism. The post-war generation of Czechoslovak Communists tried to resurrect it in the 1950s and 1960s.

7. Marxists do not like to grasp this particularly stinging-nettle. Marx's and Engels's hatred of small Slavonic nations is usually dismissed by saying that their attitude was due to their youth and immaturity in 1848. This is factually incorrect. In 1882, only one year before Marx's death, Engels repeated his 'anti-Slavonic' views in a letter to Bernstein and elsewhere. With the geniality of an older friend, Engels corrected Bernstein's views by making a little confession to him: 'Originally, all of us who have gone through the liberal and the radical stages felt sympathy with all the "oppressed" [sic] nations. I know how much time and study it has taken me to get rid of this sympathy, thoroughly and once and for all.' (From Engels's letter to Bernstein, dated 22 February 1882.) Engels freed himself of his feelings of sympathy for oppressed nations through the idea that the whole of mankind would be liberated only when the proletariat is liberated:

> 'We have to work together towards the liberation of the West European proletariat. *Everything else should be subordinate to this aim* [author's emphasis]. No matter how interesting the Balkan Slavs may be, if their desire to be free clashes with the interests of the proletariat, I lose interest in them. . . . Those who have done nothing as yet for Europe and its [progressive] development, indeed, those who are an impediment to this development, must be at least as patient as our proletarians.' [Ibid.]

It would be possible to prove by further quotes that these were not off-the-cuff, marginal statements. They were manifestations of a self-contained, well-thought-out intellectual argument, based on the conviction that such an attitude was right and proper if the full emancipation of Man was to be achieved. Lenin basically took over this attitude from Marx and Engels without revision. Although in a polemic with Polish Marxists, Lenin passionately defended the principle of the self-determination of nations (he even quoted Marx's statement 'a nation which oppresses other nations cannot be free'), he nevertheless argued that Marx and Engels were justified in being against the national revival of the Czechs and the Southern Slavs [the modern 'Yugoslavs' – Tr.]. This was, he said, at a time when tsarist Russia in an alliance with France was threatening to wage a war on Germany. Germany was not at that point 'imperialist': it was an independent state (it remained one until 1890). The small Slavonic nations were 'reactionary nations'. They were the 'vanguard of tsarism'. (V.I. Lenin, *Works*, Czech edition, vol. 22, pp. 365–9.) Most important of all was Lenin's conclusion. Lenin argued that the voicing of 'democratic demands, including self-determination' (i.e. the right to self-determination for small nations) could not be 'absolute'. These demands had to be seen as 'part and parcel of a *universal* movement' towards emancipation. If a particular part of this 'movement' came into conflict with the whole, then it was necessary to '*repudiate it*' (Ibid.) [author's emphasis]. This need to 'repudiate' small Slavonic nations was in full accord with Engels's statement 'I am totally uninterested in small nations if their [liberation] movements are not in line with the aims of the pro-letariat.' It is extremely important to realize that Lenin (at least the Lenin of the wartime years) did not actually regard individual national democratic movements as parts of one general, universal democratic movement (as was customary throughout the nineteenth century), but saw them as parts of a universal *socialist* movement. Lenin took to extremes the tenet that everything must be subordinate to the aims of the proletarian movement. Thus the stipulation that all democratic demands should be subordinate to 'proletarian and socialist' principles lent considerable weight to the anti-democratic tendency which eventually prevailed in the Bolshevik movement. As a result, the Bolshevik movement gradually moved away from the democratic mainstream of European political thinking. Later, Stalinism transformed Bolshevism into the very negation of its original revolutionary idea: a utopian Communist vision had turned into a totalitarian fiction which provided a theoretical explanation for why people had to live in a world of Stalinist make-believe.

Gorbachev's attempts to revise the official Soviet ideology are now nearing this important problem. Nevertheless, the crux of the matter has not as yet been reached. At a meeting of Communist parties in Prague, Anatoly Dobrynin (still as Secretary to the Central Committee of the Soviet Communist Party, see *Rudé Právo*, 13 April 1988) said that Marxists used to believe that class oppression would have to be liquidated *first* before the universal problems of mankind could be tackled. He added that these days it was no longer possible to rely on the class struggle alone. In carrying on with the class struggle, one must arm oneself with 'universal, humanist slogans'; one must deal with 'universal, humanist tasks'.

Of course, this is somewhat superficial: Mr Dobrynin expects that the (proletarian and socialist?) 'class struggle' will be won if the Soviets 'arm themselves with universal, humanist slogans'. Naturally, one of the most important of these 'slogans' will be 'peace'. The classic Marxist–Leninist hypostasis of the 'proletarian socialist class struggle' which marches on from the aims of today to the aims of tomorrow in the name of the final goal (Communism) is seen here as an unchangeable constant. The 'universal, humanist demands of mankind' are little more than external appendages to this constant. Thus one becomes rather suspicious that people's democratic demands are in fact to be merely used by Soviet Marxists in the form of 'slogans' in order to help them further their own political ends (the 'proletarian class struggle'). Thus, the 'universal humanist demands' are reduced to nothing more than mere material for use in the construction of political traps.

8. Masaryk is often compared to the American President Woodrow Wilson. However, Masaryk's thinking was much more 'left-wing' and 'European' (Masaryk regarded Marx – alongside Plato, Vico and Comte – as one of his teachers). Although Masaryk did not reject Woodrow Wilson's view that a reformed and humane capitalism could become an economic weapon of 'evolutionary democracy', he nevertheless relativized this view (for example, in Masaryk's first presidential address). According to Edward Beneš

Masaryk took good heed of the fact that the 1848 Revolution contained the first nuclei of future social upheavals. He was trying to understand exactly what these revolutionary tendencies were aiming at. He was trying to grasp the meaning and the evolutionary paths of modern capitalism and nineteenth-century socialism. He wished to be able to choose from all this what was or what could be relevant for our society, our nation, Europe and a world where democracy is on the ascendant. He came to the conclusion that after the victory of the Third Estate in the last century and after the full establishment of national cultures and states in Europe, the Fourth Estate [workers, peasants, blue- and white-collar low- and medium-rank employees] was beginning to demand its share of power in each European nation. He understood this to be the most burning political and social issue of the nineteenth century. He realised that this issue had been formulated most succinctly by the Great War of 1914 (setting aside the rivalry of the Great Powers in that war). Masaryk understood that in this sense, European society was experiencing a major existential struggle: that *in Europe the old bourgeois democracy was being transformed into a higher, more profound form of democracy, a humanitarian democracy.* [Beneš's speech over the coffin of Tomáš Garrigue Masaryk on 21 September 1937.]

9. This is a summary of the beginning of an article by Lev Bezymensky and Valentin

Falin entitled 'Who started the "Cold War"?' published in *Pravda* on 29 August 1988. The
article continues:

> It is possible to make quite a reliable forecast: once our civilisation has freed itself of
> arrogant myths, everybody will agree that the 'Cold War' – one of the saddest chapters
> of twentieth-century history – was primarily a product of human imperfection and ideo-
> logical prejudice. It need not have taken place at all. It would not have come to pass if
> people's deeds and the actions of states had at all times and in every aspect corre-
> sponded to their declarations.

Professor J. Gaddis, Head of the Modern History Institute at Ohio University published a
critical reaction to this article in *Pravda* on 31 October 1988. He stressed that both the
Soviet Union and the United States were to be held responsible for the Cold War. In his
view, both countries tried to ensure their own security one-sidedly. They failed to work
together. A commentary by Soviet historian O. Rzheshevsky agreed that the Soviet Union
was partially to blame for the origins of the Cold War, but on the whole he reiterated
Bezymensky's and Falin's position. According to Rzheshevsky, extremist circles in the
United States and in other capitalist countries supported the idea of foreign political expansion and a hard-line policy vis-à-vis 'revolutionary–democratic' forces and forces of
'national liberation' in the world, and so on.
      To date, the Soviets have simply failed to analyse the relationship between the United
States and the Soviet Union in terms of a relationship of two differing superpower structures. They have failed to define the laws of this relationship with regard to its peculiarities
(in particular, the fact that capitalism had evolved along a democratic path in the United
States while existing Soviet social structures are undemocratic). The labels 'extremist
circles' and 'revolutionary–democratic' forces and forces of 'national liberation' have been
employed by the Soviet writers in a way which shows that their meaning is derived from an
official interpretation which originated in a much more orthodox era. In no way do these
authors explain that these labels have now become mere 'ideological prejudices' or how this
has come to pass. They have failed to acknowledge that the Soviet Union has never stood
outside the 'traditional structures of supremacy and subjugation', but formed a specific part
of them. This is a fairly widespread attitude among Soviet 'progressivists'. In a polemic
between Fyodor Burlatsky and Mient Jan Faber, published in *Literaturnaya Gazeta* on 23
September 1987, it is admitted that the Soviet Union made mistakes in the past: it was
besieged by 'traditional' (i.e. imperialist) establishments which were out to destroy it. This
is why, with the best of intentions, the Soviet Union was unable to 'keep its hands clean'.
Thus it is being silently accepted that the seamy side of Soviet official policy is a product of
external factors. Nobody seems to be able to admit that the 'dirt' might have something to
do with the nature of the Soviet system itself. Everybody seems to accept at face value that
the nature of the Soviet system is benign and 'peace-loving'. Mient Jan Faber (to whose
article Fyodor Burlatsky reacts in *Literaturnaya Gazeta*) argued that it was necessary to
search for a common language in order to be able to initiate a political dialogue. Once
found, the common language would stimulate the humanization and democratization of
European society as whole. In connection with this argument, Faber returned to the
Czechoslovak issue and the Polish issue. He said that it was going to be necessary to
resume the implementation of reforms both in Czechoslovakia and in Poland. Fyodor
Burlatsky rejected Mient Jan Faber's attempts, as he saw it, to deflect people's attention
towards issues which were the affairs of individual countries. Burlatsky demanded that
people should concentrate on the fundamental and common aim of all peace movements,
that is, disarmament. With regard to Poland and Czechoslovakia, Faber was wrong, in
Burlatsky's view, to ignore the reforms currently under way in these countries. As far as
Faber's assessment of the suppression of the Prague Spring in 1968 and of the Solidarity
trade union in 1981 was concerned, according to Burlatsky the problem was that Faber
ignored the 'external anti-socialist pressures' exerted on these countries in the 'crisis years'.
The inability of the Soviet reformers to understand that the suppression of both the
Czechoslovak and the Polish reform movements by the Soviet authorities was extremely
undemocratic; the inability to see that the policy of exerting brutal pressure on one's 'allies'

is anti-democratic, as is Soviet support for the conservative bureaucratic *apparat* in the Warsaw Pact countries; shows that Soviet reformers have fallen victim to a special case of 'false' ideological consciousness. To quote Marx, 'false' ideological consciousness is said to affect the thinking of such a social stratum or class as has elevated itself above society (and above other nations!). I am sure that not all members of the Soviet ruling class are 'inactive spineless creatures with Party cards' (to quote Boris Yeltsin). Some members of the Soviet ruling hierarchy have travelled a long way towards understanding the nature of Soviet bureaucracy. But no matter how important their critical awareness of the bureaucratic phenomenon might be to future progress, it is not enough, because it shies away from an objective analysis of the superpower, hegemonist nature of the Soviet establishment. The idea that the Soviet Union is a truly free union of equal nations and that it has even developed into a 'unique association of "socialist" nations' (a concept used by Gorbachev in his book *Perestroika* as late as summer 1987) is so far removed from reality that any attempt to formulate a really strong political strategy on its basis, a strategy which could do away with the division of the world into two unfriendly alliances, must surely fail. The Soviet Union has yet to tackle the task of transforming itself into a democratic federation: the Warsaw Pact will also required restructuring along democratic lines (this is why a declaration issued by the Polish–Czechoslovak Solidarity group on 9 July 1988 demanded that a totally new treaty be negotiated). In recent times, it has sometimes seemed as though the Soviet Union might embark on the road towards thorough reform. However, at the same time (see, for instance, how the Soviet leadership reacts to developments in the Baltic) there is still a tendency to stick to obsolete superpower attitudes. Soviet conservatives see the old 'superpower' policies as 'internationalist'. However, they are only 'internationalist' in so far as they condemn authentic movements for national liberation as 'nationalist'.

10. Mikhail Gorbachev speaking during a meeting of left-wing parties on 4 November 1987.

11. Although this may seem strange, the concept of a 'civilization of love', coined by Pope Paul VI in the 1960s, and the recent demand to create a 'higher category of civilization' (Eduard Shevarnadze) are quite closely related to each other. The idea that a new great dialogue could be initiated between the Catholic world and the Communist world is not as extravagant as it may have seemed when it was formulated by Graham Greene at a peace meeting in Moscow in February 1987.

12. Radim Palouš, *The Year 1969: a Hypothesis of the End of the 'Euro-age' and the Beginning of the 'World Age'*, Samizdat, Prague 1985.

13. The programmatic principle which equated socialism with 'common ownership of the means of production' (Lenin's expression from the spring of 1917) was of course the conceptual springboard for the Russian October Revolution. Alexander Yakovlev is right (for instance, in his Prague speech, printed in *Rudé Právo* on 16 November 1988) to interpret Lenin's critical self-reflection after the revolution as a fundamental break with the traditional social-democratic dogma which saw socialism as a *non-economic formation based on a single form of ownership*. Yakovlev argues that it is necessary to go back to that break. But surely that is not enough: the real essence of the traditional social democratic dogma still escapes Yakovlev. The way he interprets it is only how that dogma is seen from a traditional Marxist socialist point of view. The real essence of traditional social-democratic thinking is the idea that political rule over people should be transformed into a non-political management of public affairs and manufacturing processes. This Saint-Simonesque idea is closely related to the argument about the withering away of the state (the democratic state not excepted). This argument played a very important role in original Bolshevik thinking (Lenin had taken it over from Marx). This explains why Bolshevism had its strong (democratic) and its weak (utopian) points. Original Bolshevik thinking (Lenin started to revise it but he himself was unable to complete the revision) succumbed to the Stalinist tendency because it proved unable to repudiate swiftly enough its utopian (Saint-Simonesque) concept of history. Stalin the 'realist' successfully attacked this Achilles heel of original Bolshevism.

14. See the interview with Henry Kissinger, entitled 'The USSR – The USA: Confrontation or Co-operation?', in *Questions of Peace and Socialism* no. 2, 1988. When

asked what the geo-political future of the world might be at the beginning of the twenty-first century, Kissinger said that there will probably exist five or six power centres. Each of these will try to play an ever more important role in its own region and possibly also beyond. Although the Soviet Union and the United States will still probably be the strongest states, there will be several other countries with a swiftly growing potential. Japan, which at the beginning of the next century will have considerable (and growing) military strength, China, where of course everything depends on whether the reforms will be successful, maybe also India and perhaps also the countries of Western Europe which might unite. According to Henry Kissinger, the West European countries should unite not only economically and politically, but also militarily. It is up to the Europeans themselves to decide whether they wish to unite on the basis of a neutralist policy or on the basis of an independent defence policy.

It follows from all this that global competition between the United States and the Soviet Union will cease to be relevant. This is why both countries need to initiate a fundamental *political* dialogue which would reduce Soviet–American competition. Not much hope can be placed in a superpower dialogue on disarmament. ('I think a world without nuclear weapons is an unattainable goal. I hope that as realists the Soviet leaders are fully aware of this)'. A political dialogue is necessary if for no other reason than the fact that, in a world where the balance of power is changing and where inner structural changes are taking place, one needs to know where one is headed. It is necessary to work out a common theory of where we are going. This is particularly important because the West will soon plunge into a deep economic crisis in which the mistakes of past decades will be clearly revealed. A consistent leadership with a broad vision will be needed in the West to revive people's trust in the future and to give them a proper sense of orientation. This task should not be simplified. As an American poet has written:

> We shall not cease from exploration
> And the end of our exploring
> Will be to arrive where we started
> And know the place for the first time.

[T.S. Eliot, 'Little Gidding' from *Four Quartets*.]

15. See the new edition of the Programme of the Soviet Communist Party (in *The Documents of the Twenty-Seventh Congress of the Soviet Communist Party*, 1986).

16. It was Mikhail Gorbachev who first raised the possibility of holding a 'European Reykjavik'. He did so in his speech in the Polish Parliament on 1 July 1988. Subsequently, some Western commentators warned that the aim of this proposal was to isolate the United States. However, the Soviets replied to this criticism by saying that naturally the United States and Canada would also be invited to participate in the proposed meeting.

The proposal to hold a European round-table meeting has been under discussion for some time now. Originally, it was intended to hold a meeting of left-wing parties. In mid-November 1988, Czechoslovak journalists questioned Alexander Yakovlev about this during his visit to Czechoslovakia. Yakovlev implied that the round-table meeting should not only be limited to left-wing participants. ('Speaking of a forum of left-wing forces, frankly, I am not quite convinced whether we should place special emphasis on whether or not a party is left wing.') At the end of October 1988, Mikhail Gorbachev mooted a meeting of political parties across *the whole ideological spectrum*'. (See the interview Gorbachev granted to *Der Spiegel*.)

17. See the interview in *Der Spiegel*, and *Rudé Právo* of 25 October 1988.

18. Mary Kaldor and Mient Jan Faber, 'A Model of Detente', *Ogonyok*, July 1987.

19. The document by Kaldor and Faber states:

'If American political influence in Western Europe is inseparably connected with the ideology of nuclear deterrence, Soviet influence in Central Europe is based on the presence there of Soviet conventional forces. . . . There exist proposals tabled by the Warsaw Pact countries for cuts in conventional arms. But in our view, protracted talks based on the absurd concept of balance on a lower level can produce nothing but a re-confirmation of the status quo. If however, a seriously meant proposal was tabled to withdraw conventional forces from Eastern Europe, in particular from East Germany, such a proposal would be a challenge to the political structures which stand in the back-ground. . . . Such a proposal could contribute to Western discussions on the political future of Europe. We believe that without a contribution by the Eastern half of our continent the present confusion of minds in Western Europe will start a new European arms race in conventional weapons. At the same time, the number of British and French nuclear arms will be increased. If we are to rid ourselves of the East–West confrontation and of continuing militarization, Eastern Europe must help Western Europe.

At the moment, apparently, it would be difficult to contemplate the withdrawal of Soviet troops from Central Europe due to the current internal political situation in indi-vidual Central European countries and due to the different speeds at which Gorbachevian reforms are being implemented in each of these countries. Some Soviet observers have said off the record that under current circumstances it is probably a good idea to keep Soviet troops in Czechoslovakia and East Germany. . .

20. Even Mikhail Gorbachev's report to the Soviet Communist Party Conference in June 1988 contained a critical mention of past Soviet foreign policy. Apparently it did not avail itself of all the possibilities for solving various questions and conflicts by political means. However, in a text published on the occasion of the twentieth anniversary of the Warsaw Pact invasion of Czechoslovakia on 21 August 1968, a commentator of the Soviet news agency (TASS) stressed that in the Czechoslovak case, all political means had been exhausted. He obviously did this in order to prevent the reinterpretation of the 1968 Soviet intervention in Czechoslovakia.

21. In a discussion on the evolution of the policy of peaceful coexistence, which took place in the autumn of 1987, Professor Vyacheslav Dashichev said that there was a tendency to regard military questions as more important than political questions: 'We are trying hard to do away with the military consequences of political disagreements. But surely, it is much more important to find a way of solving *political and ideological* disagree-ments!' In the interview from which I am quoting (published in *New Times* 44, 1988), Alexander Bovin objected: 'I don't quite agree with this. If current political disagreements are not to be tackled militarily, we must do away with arms. Would that not open the way towards [a non-military] solution of political problems?' There is no doubt that Alexander Bovin's attitude is a manifestation of the traditional philosophical background to the Soviet disarmament strategy. This strategy sees the disarmament issue as a key issue in world politics, as the 'main link' which, if tackled, will lead to the solution of all problems. The conservative view maintaining that the stockpiling of arms is a consequence of a lack of trust between nations and not the other way about, and that it is therefore first necessary to introduce trust rather than to disarm, is conceptually stronger and – by the way – more 'Marxist'. Anyway, it is self-evident that there is a direct connection between the 'pacifist' philosophy of Soviet disarmament policy and the incredibly meagre results of all dis-armament negotiations since the end of the Second World War.

22. Anatoly Adamishin says in an interview published in *Rudé Právo* on 16 March 1988 that current Soviet foreign policy places the human rights issue on a par with military, political, economic and ecological issues. He adds that this is a policy common to all the socialist [i.e. East European] countries. This common policy is designed to strive for the creation of a complex system of international security. International co-operation must be 'complex'. It must include the 'humanitarian issues'. These issues are not mere appendages. They are equal to all the other components of co-operation. The proposal tabled by the Czechoslovak Communist Party General Secretary Miloš Jakeš to create a zone of trust, co-operation and good neighbourly relations at the point of contact between the Warsaw Pact and the NATO countries is said by Adamishin to be a good example of the proper understanding of this principle.

In Anatoly Adamishin's interpretation, the concept of human rights (or rather the concept of civil and political rights) has been narrowed to such an extent as to make it impossible to associate it with the struggle for profound democratic political reforms in East European countries. Adamishin emphasizes that with regard to the interpretation of the human rights issue, there are no problems in relations between 'socialist' countries. The relations between these countries and the West are a different matter, he continues. The West adheres to a 'bourgeois' concept of human rights. But this is exactly that point of view which has made the Helsinki Final Act function as though it existed in two independent, mutually incompatible versions, as Adamishin's colleague Anatoly Kovalyev has complained, admitting at the same time that the Soviets were also partially to blame for this (see the press conference held on 15 August 1988 to mark the twelfth anniversary of Helsinki).

23. In his speech, Mikhail Gorbachev said that 'reactionary and extreme anti-Soviet forces were becoming more active'. These forces were consolidating their positions. They were now trying hard to transfer the ideological struggle connected with the issues of perestroika and disarmament into the socialist countries. They were spreading provocative fabrications; according to which a fierce struggle was going on in Soviet society and the Soviet leadership, and the opposition against perestroika and current Soviet foreign policy was growing. Connected with this was the statement that

> anti-socialist centres are active not only against the Soviet Union. They are speedily working out new methods of subversion which are aimed at the other socialist countries where the dynamic process of further improvements in socialism are currently also underway. These centres are researching particular approaches to suit each of the socialist countries in order to be able to subvert them more successfully by taking their individual national peculiarities into consideration. [*Rudé Právo* 19 February 1988]

However, this statement must be seen in its context which emphasizes the need to restructure the Soviet political system and to establish democratic control. The meaning of this statement can only be fully understood if we compare it to the speech by Yegor Ligachev on the restructuring of education and on bringing up the young, which preceded Gorbachev's speech:

> Some individuals are hysterically shouting over the historical legacy of the Soviet epoch. They are even saying that we have not built the right kind of socialism. But the Soviet people will not impassively look on while their socialist achievements are being destroyed. Our young people should draw a serious historical lesson: they must take over the fidelity to socialism and to its excellent results of the older generations.

24. As part of a campaign against the Czechoslovak democratic opposition, on 4 November 1988, on its front page, *Rudé Právo* published a 'reader's letter' entitled 'What were the American diplomats doing there?' The letter maintains that it is obvious from the course of the 'provocations which took place in the centre of Prague on 28 October' that the independent demonstration had taken place 'at American instigation'. The letter further maintains that instructions on how to organize the demonstration were given by American Deputy Secretary of State, John Whitehead, during his meeting in Prague with ten Czechoslovak citizens who 'have been basically carrying out the instructions of their foreign paymasters for years and not without rewards'. The independent demonstration which took place in Czechoslovakia on 21 August and a number of other activities pursued by an awakening Czechoslovak civil society are being officially assessed in similar terms. This is why exceptionally extensive police action (unprecedented in recent years) was taken against independent Czechoslovak activists on the eve of the seventieth anniversary of the foundation of the Czechoslovak Republic on 28 October 1988. Extensive police action was also taken in connection with the publication of the political manifesto 'Democracy for All' issued by the Movement for Civil Freedom on 15 October 1988.

25. See the interview with Mikhail Gorbachev in *Der Spiegel* and *Rudé Právo*.

26. Ibid.

27. Ibid.

28. The meeting was organized by the official Czechoslovak Peace Committee. It was

attended by peace activists from sixteen East and West European countries. The meeting was a follow-up to a consultative discussion which took place in Dobříš near Prague in the spring of 1987. This discussion was attended – after a long hiatus – by representatives of Western independent peace movements from Holland, Belgium, Denmark and West Germany. The 1987 meeting was also attended by representatives of official peace committees from the Soviet Union, Czechoslovakia and East Germany. Soviet representatives spoke of the inseparability of the questions of peace and democracy. This was welcomed by the Western participants at the meeting. An article by the Deputy Chairman of the official Czechoslovak Peace Committee which assessed the meeting, ends with a quotation from a speech by Jan Ter Laak, a representative of Pax Christi Nederlands: 'There is a broad consensus. We have a chance to create unity between the peace movement in East and West.' (*Rudé Právo* 28 April 1987.)

29. Two Charter 77 signatories (Rudolf Battěk and myself) were able to take part in the Benešov talks. We had been invited by representatives of the Dutch and West German peace movements. In Czechoslovakia, this was an unprecedented development. It followed from the contribution of two independent activists to the discussion that the question of the participation of East European 'independents' in the work of the European Peace Parliament emerged quite naturally.

30. The basic outlines of the project were worked out during the international peace seminar Prague 88 in mid-June 1988. The seminar was organized by a group of independent Czechoslovak peace activists (the Independent Peace Association) under the auspices of Charter 77. Thirty-five foreign guests took part. After the Czechoslovak police broke up the seminar, the foreigners were expelled from Czechoslovakia. The delegates of the END Congress held in Lund, Sweden, in July 1988; the participants of the peace seminar in Cracow, Poland, in August 1988; and the participants of the seminar held by the Network for East–West Dialogue in Nijmwegen in September 1988 have all reacted positively to the Prague proposal. The project is assuming ever more concrete features.

31. Ideas formulated by European Nuclear Disarmament (END) – in particular the call to act 'as though Europe were not divided' (the 1980 Russell Peace Committee Appeal) – became the point of departure for co-operation between the Western peace movements and an important section of the East European independent movement. The 1982 Budapest lecture by E.P. Thompson provides particularly symbolic evidence of the beginning of this co-operation. The 1982 IKV appeal entitled 'Europe to the Europeans' was a remarkable contribution to the strengthening of 'pan-European consciousness'. Richard Coudenhove-Calergi's old concept of 'Pan-Europe' was given a completely new interpretation in this document. The document had been published even before the crisis within the Western peace movements which was brought about by the failure of their campaign against the installation of Euromissiles in 1983. The IKV appeal was based on the principle of solidarity with the East European movement for the emancipation of civil society. The conclusions it had drawn from the Polish crisis were of major importance for the gradual formulation by the peace movements of a more comprehensive political philosophy. The 1985 Prague Appeal set out to help this development. The Prague Appeal was followed by the call in October 1986 for the 'full implementation of the Helsinki Final Act' (the Vienna Memorandum). This document, signed by hundreds of citizens from East and West, provides a natural starting point for the creation of a philosophical framework for the European Assembly for Peace and Democracy.

32. A European democratic policy with regard to the German question would not be possible at all without the achievements of the German 'Ostpolitik'. It is clear that such a democratic policy must use as a basis all the achievements of detente. The achievements of Helsinki are extremely important in this respect. This concerns both the territorial status quo (unchangeability of state borders) and the political status quo, if this is understood to mean an acknowledgement of the legitimacy of the German Democratic Republic (but not of the bureaucratic and militarist ruling structures of 'really existing socialism'). Thus extreme nationalist demands – calling for the re-creation of a Germany with borders on the Oder and the Neisse and a revision of the expulsion of the German minority from Czechoslovakia at the end of the Second World War, as well as calls for the (forcible) reunification of the two German states – must be rejected. We can interpret Mikhail Gorbachev's

criticism of the attempts to 'erase the borders between the two sovereign German states' (*Der Spiegel* interview) in this light. But a respect for the 'German stipulation' – a position which expects the division of Germany to be overcome by *peaceful* means, and which refers to the declaration of German unity made by the German government in 1970 on the occasion of the signing of the West German treaty of co-operation with the Soviet Union, a declaration re-stated at Helsinki – is also an extremely important, indeed constitutive feature of European democratic policy. It is not only in the interest of Germans that the two Germanies should be reunited. It is in the interest of all Europeans. This view held by the German conservatives cannot be dismissed as nationalist: it is in fact democratic. The theory of the two German nations (a 'bourgeois' nation and a 'socialist' nation) is undemocratic. There is no doubt, as Mikhail Gorbachev says, that 'the fate of Germany is inseparably interconnected with the fate of Europe as a whole and with prospects for the building of a common European house.' The German issue cannot be taken out of the context of the two separate processes of European integration which are now underway in each half of the divided Europe. Surely though, the issue of German and European reunification cannot be dealt with by putting it off to the next century. On the contrary: any truly democratic policy of today must devise ways of implementing such diplomatic and political mechanisms which would be properly anchored in the existing official institutions, and which would gradually do away with the division of the world community into two opposing social and political systems.

A *Memorial Volume on the Peaceful Reorganization of Europe: a Peace Treaty, a German Confederation, a European Security System* by eighty German citizens (proposed and edited by Herbert Ammon and Theodor Schweisfurth, Berlin, March 1985) is a stimulating recommendation on how to tackle the German question. The proposal to revive the idea of a German confederation is perfectly legitimate. This idea used to be part of official East European foreign policy until the beginning of the 1960s. It was used for propaganda purposes. These days, however, East Germany is a politically stable state. Soviet restructuring is now offering it a chance to define its intrinsic, anti-fascist characteristics anew. East Germany could now become a truly *democratic* republic. Meanwhile anti-militarist and democratic forces in West Germany are surely strong enough to resist any possible reactionary pressure.

33. The proposal that Prague become the seat of the *European Assembly for Peace and Democracy* is a part of the project drafted by the participants of the Prague 88 peace seminar.

5

On Detente: An Interview with
Adam Michnik

A.M.   I'd like to discuss various aspects of detente. I'm interested in detente as a certain form of international politics; and in the specific view of detente held by a person from central Europe, from a state within the Yalta bloc. To put it simply: the origin of detente, as we see it, is the Yalta Agreement. It is a situation where the victorious anti-Nazi coalition divided up the world. And nothing that happened later, the whole Cold-War period, was ever in essence an infringement of the Yalta Agreement. Here one has to say that for us, people from Poland, the Yalta Agreement has a totally different significance than it does for people from Western Europe. For us the Yalta Agreement and its effect on Poland are to a certain extent the consequence of an earlier agreement, namely a consequence of the Ribbentrop–Molotov pact. And that is why in Poland people have never come to terms with this situation: have never been able to accept that Poland – the first country to openly oppose the Nazi policy of expansion – has at the end of the war, as a result of the victory of the anti-Nazi coalition, come out as a loser; with an alien government thrust upon it, with the imposition of a foreign system of government, with the status of a state of restricted sovereignty.

However, the second post-war phase of relaxation, which we can assume happened in the mid 1950s (the first being the end of the war), was a period symbolized by the spirit of Geneva – 1955, 1956; those years gave Poland a completely different set of solutions, a completely different set of consequences and therefore also different appraisals. What was seen as relaxation on an international scale resulted in a thaw in Poland's internal affairs. By thaw I mean the first, cautious attempt to return to normality. And from that moment detente, from the Polish point of view, began to be assessed as something positive. This was

because the internal consequences of changes on the international map
seemed to favour the development of intellectual activity; the widening
of a certain sphere of civil liberties; and, finally, greater room for
manoeuvre for the Polish State. How far the ruling elite of both
Communist Party and State were able to make use of this freedom, is
another matter. Nevertheless one can say that, from our point of view,
since Stalin's death, Western policy has realized, in one way or another,
a programme of peaceful coexistence, which can be described as a
tension between the concept of Cold War and the concept of detente.
What, to put it most simply, are the arguments for detente?

Take, for example, the controversy surrounding the Berlin Wall,
which was constructed in 1961. The moment the wall was erected,
German politicians were posed the following question: how can one
make this wall insignificant? Should one simply attack it, saying that the
construction of a wall in the centre of the city contravenes the hitherto
existing order? Such was the stance proposed by the Americans. It
would have been a sign of resoluteness against the gesture of Ulbricht
and the Soviet Union, but at that time, in 1961, it could not have solved
the problem – it could not have led to the dismantling of the wall. So
then the question arose: how does one respond to a situation where the
wall exists? And it was then that SPD circles came up with the following
idea: if we cannot demolish this wall, let us do everything to make this
wall penetrable, so that it becomes 'transparent', so that it won't
eternally divide one part of Germany from another, one part of Europe
from another, one part of the world from another. And this line of
thought was well-founded, it wasn't totally irrational. Furthermore, if we
are to consider, from our East European perspective, the consequences
of this idea of making the borders 'transparent', then apart from the
negative effects we must also realize the positive effects. The eastern
policy of the SPD was without doubt, particularly from the Polish point
of view, something positive. And the ultimate confirmation of the Oder–
Neisse border line (which was one of the significant consequences of the
SPD's Ostpolitik) was from the Polish point of view – in its international
status but also its domestic politics – something positive. The arrival of
Brandt in Warsaw in December 1970 was marked by his symbolic
kneeling down in front of the memorial for the heroes of the Warsaw
Ghetto and at the time – which was soon after a massive anti-semitic
campaign in Poland – this had evident appeal within Poland, this was
something good. On the other hand Brandt's visit – remember, this was
the beginning of December 1970 – occurred just before the outbreak of
the workers' revolt in Szczecin and Gdańsk. This was an extremely
important moment, because the argument which, without doubt, would
have been traditionally used – the argument that it would provide grist

to the mill for West German revanchists – could not now be used. This weapon which had been so meticulously loaded by official propaganda, whose basic aim was to prey on the anti-German complex of Poles – this weapon could not be fired for reasons of propaganda in 1970. Therefore the Communist authorities had to analyse Polish events in the Polish context and had to talk about this conflict in terms of a social conflict within the boundaries of a communist state and society. And therefore they could not present the protesting workers as a German fifth column – this was a positive by-product of the whole SPD eastern policy.

However, it would be a misunderstanding to reckon that the effects of this policy (throughout I have in mind specifically the Eastern European, or simply the Polish aspect) were positive solely because at that moment there was, so to say, an international rapprochement between Poland and the Federal Republic of Germany. This rapprochement was in essence a rapprochement of states rather than one of nations – from that moment on, the only 'partner' of the Germans in Poland was the Communist government. Poles began to feel that as a nation, as an issue, not only did they cease to exist at diplomatic conferences, they also ceased to exist in the minds of Westerners.

Q. Understandably you have restricted the subject primarily to the issue of Polish–German relations. However, this is not the only issue, even if Germany of course played an absolutely crucial role. Could you now broaden the subject to cover other West European states and the USA?

A.M. I think that it can be broadened, and the issue of Polish–German relations best illustrates this. As far as relations with other states are concerned – in the Gierek period, there occurred a change of policy. Gierek became a favourite of Western opinion. And again the effect of this was twofold because there followed an almost unprecedented devotion towards Gierek. (I don't know if there has been any other communist leader who has had such excellent publicity in the West: he was praised by President Giscard d'Estaing, Chancellor Helmut Schmidt said that he would like to have such a minister in his government, and he was very highly regarded by subsequent presidents of the United States.) In short, Gierek could count not only on his position in the international arena, which was relatively high for the leader of a satellite state, but he could also count on financial credit. The only state which in this sense is somehow 'beyond reproach' is Great Britain, which at the time showed a particular lack of interest in developments in Eastern Europe. But it is difficult for me to pay the compliment of calling something a policy when in fact it was a lack of policy. Yet even as far as Great Britain is concerned, I remember when Prime Minister Jaroszewicz visited London, which was also a specific expression of detente: the Polish police presented the British Special Branch with a list of people who were likely to threaten the safety of Prime Minister Jaroszewicz. I had the honour of being on that list. At the time I was in the United Kingdom and the British police were interested in whether I intended to throw a bomb at Prime Minister Jaroszewicz. In short, the fact that the British police blindly followed the Polish communist police is also significant from the point of view of our conversation on detente.

However let us return to the consequences which, it seems to me, were ambivalent. If we are to acknowledge that the Helsinki agreements were a result of detente; then in one sense these agreements ratified the status quo in Eastern Europe. But, in another, the 'third basket' introduced some sort of new element into this order; namely, the agreements concerning human rights which allowed certain elite circles in Eastern Europe to form the first bridge-heads for civil rights groups, and which referred to the human rights resolutions. And here lies the double significance in the whole process from the Polish point of view – I think not only Polish, but Czechoslovak, and also that of the Soviet Union. That is, on the one hand, Helsinki was virtually complete approval of what happened as a result of Yalta, as if it were a ratification of the consequences of invasion; the consequences of conquest. However, on the other hand, it was the first attempt to combat the principles of power from the perspective of the philosophy of human rights. This was at a time when Jimmy Carter was elected president of the United States, a man who, at least verbally, presented the principle of human rights at the forefront of his policies. Human rights became an ideological tool of American politics. And all this somehow confuses the picture, because Jimmy Carter was criticized both in the USA and in Western Europe. On the one hand, he was criticized for a certain lack of realism. That is, people were saying that to introduce human rights into international politics was a kind of demagogy or naiveté; that international politics must rely on hard facts. The existence of the Soviet Union is hard fact and one has to talk to them as if they were normal, civilized leaders of a normal, civilized state. And from this stance Carter's policy is criticized by, for instance, Kennan. However, there is another type of criticism of Carter's policy of developing detente: it is said that detente developed as a one-way street, a process which was only useful to the Russians. It did not stop the arrest and repression of people in Eastern Europe, their incarceration in psychiatric hospitals, and, to crown all this, detente did not hinder the Soviet invasion of Afghanistan.

In this conflict Poland holds a very specific place, because undoubtedly, from the Polish point of view, the policy of detente – both that of the European states and that of President Carter – had a strong hindering effect on the repressive instruments of power. Gierek wanted financial credit and he wanted to have the reputation of being the leader of a state which held no political prisoners. This opened up a certain amount of 'space', a certain freedom, which was built upon and filled by the Workers' Defence Committee (KOR) and the whole democratic opposition which was established in the second half of that decade. Basically speaking, the Western argument about human rights was contested and rejected on this side with the formula that this was 'interference into the internal affairs of another country'. Thus there arose a paradoxical situation: President Carter talked of the need to respect human rights in Poland or Czechoslovakia, and the Soviet press wrote that he was interfering in the internal affairs of other states; yet this line of reasoning did not regard as interference into internal affairs the sending of Soviet tanks to Budapest in 1956 or Prague in 1968. And it has to be said quite clearly that in the present world, a world where agreements are made as to the number of missiles each side possesses, one must not exclude from understandings and mutual agreements the issue of reducing, for example, the number of political prisoners. In short, people are more important than missiles. And agreements concerning people must come before agreements concerning missiles. If agreements concerning missiles are outpacing agreements concerning people, it is not because of the need to avoid war, it is simply the need to consolidate the existing order which divides Europe into one half which is totalitarian and another which is democratic.

Q.   Many people in the West (by no means only those from governing circles, but also, for instance, those in the peace movements) say that the situation has been so dramatic throughout the 1970s and 1980s – with a rapid increase in armaments production on both sides – that, regardless of the internal affairs of various states both in Europe and elsewhere, an agreement has to be reached to diminish, to slow down the process of armaments growth. They also say that, no matter how important the human rights issue might be, it is strictly a supplement to what, from their point of view, are the fundamental issues. To this they add another argument: that a reduction in expenditure on armaments increases the amount of money, or other resources which could be used to raise the standard of living, for example, of people in Eastern Europe. What do you say to these arguments?

A.M.   I think that this line of reasoning is either corrupted by naiveté or by ignorance. As far as the 'nuclear war' argument is concerned, it is

interesting to note that it is used when one talks of repression in Eastern
Europe. I've never heard anyone use the nuclear war argument when
talking about repression in Chile, or about apartheid, or about the
murdering of Communists in Indonesia – no-one has ever tried to
explain to people in Chile or Paraguay that they have to come to terms
with their lot or else there might be an atomic war, and that arms control
is more important than the process of democratic change. It is no coincidence that those people who say this are people who have never been
in prison. It seems to me that this line of reasoning, which allows other
people's freedom to be sacrificed for the sake of one's own safety, is
immoral. In reply to that, one can say that politics is not the domain of
moralists. True, yet this is also an argument which is politically unwise,
because one has to set oneself the question: what is the origin of the
conflicts which could lead to the world's annihilation? Is it the fact that
weapons exist? No! The origin of these conflicts is the fact that there
exist totalitarian systems which threaten the world and that this is
known ...

About the argument that resources used for armaments could be used
for other purposes. This is a complete misunderstanding. In Eastern
Europe, resources spent on armaments are a way of strengthening the
internal military and industrial complex. When these resources are freed
they are wasted. Gierek had a large amount of financial credit and it is
enough to take a closer look at what he did with it. The basic source of
misfortune in communist economies is not the fact that so much money
is being spent on armaments, particularly nuclear armaments, but the
fact that the money that *is* available is wasted. And I emphasize, that,
from this point of view, the reduction of armaments is both unrealistic
and will not have the desired effect. When I think about the whole
process which is now taking place, it seems as though I'm setting myself
a question about the future of the world. Because if indeed someone
thinks that he can maintain the kind of peace which we live in, the post-
Yalta system, which divides Europe into totalitarian and democratic
halves, then he is simply mistaken. Totalitarian states, if they are not
very powerful, as in the case of Albania, have something of a self-
propelling mechanism: similar to a bicycle which has to go forward, it
cannot stand still for when it stops it falls over. In other words, the
essential difference in views of detente depends more or less on the
fact that for people in Western Europe the stabilization of the existing
order is a way of maintaining peace, whereas for us the way to create a
peaceful Europe is to destabilize Stalinist totalitarianism. In other words,
every action which stabilizes Stalinist totalitarianism, whether it be
through credit or through diplomatic activity, works against peace in
Europe. This isn't the policy of detente, although that is what people call

it. It is a sort of policy of appeasement. It is a policy of constantly conceding to force – it is called concern for peace, but that is exactly how Chamberlain defined his policy. Of course, in reply to that I hear the argument that one cannot compare Hitler's Germany with any other state. To a certain extent that argument is true. Indeed these are different states. However, a certain kind of reasoning, a certain type of argumentation, a certain technique of self-deception – these indeed can be compared. I *do* make comparisons and I want to make them. When I talk of destabilizing Yalta I'm not thinking of war, far from it. It seems to me that in essence the 'better red then dead' alternative posed by the Western peace movements is not true. When I hear people say that the most valuable thing is human life and this, in addition, is equivocally supposed to be concern for my own life, I always say: well, in that case people shouldn't have defended themselves against Hitler, England should have surrendered, because every day English people were being killed by German bombs. I simply don't understand this argument. As far as the thesis that it is better to talk than shoot is concerned: one can say without a doubt that at least in the present world there are situations when it is better to stay silent than to hold talks which only serve as smoke-screens for the totalitarian policy of expansion. From this point of view one has to ask oneself the question: is that how it really is? Is that how it was in the Brezhnev era? Were Brezhnev and his colleagues, comrade Grishin and comrade Gejdar Alijev indeed the civilized leaders of a civilized state that George Kennan would have us believe? I reject this point of view. I agree with everyone who recalls that these cultured, civilized people had their party comrade Alexander Dubcek, transported out of Czechoslovakia to Moscow, manacled in a cattle-wagon, not because he wished to leave the Warsaw Pact, but because he had different ideas about internal policy. At the time, Brezhnev's neo-Stalinist policy should have been called just that by Western politicians, by Western public opinion, as today even Gorbachev and Russian public opinion call it. If at the time there could have been a better understanding of this policy, if it could have been called by its real name, then those numerous mistakes made by the West concerning Russia would not have been committed. One has to realize this. This aspect has to be remembered if one wants to understand why a politician like Ronald Reagan has such great popularity here in Poland. Poles are basically not interested in and don't know much about Ronald Reagan's internal policy, and this is not of course a good thing, for ignorance on this subject is not a virtue. However, they do know one thing: that he is the first American president in living memory to so resolutely say 'no' to the Russians. So much so that the Russians had to realize that the traditional tricks of the Brezhnev policy would no longer have any effect, that they would have to talk seriously or else there would be a serious conflict. The result of this policy is a totally new type of negotation in Soviet–American relations.

Q.   Does this also apply, for example, to Mrs Thatcher's policy, which is similarly resolute and without any misapprehensions, or, for instance, to the change in attitude among French socialists, whose president had previously stood at the helm of the nation's at one time obsessive policy towards the Soviet Union.

A.M.   Generally speaking I think that it does. However, I find myself in a difficult situation here because I understand my English friends when they say that we are only interested in what Mrs Thatcher has to say about the Soviet Union, and that we are completely indifferent to her internal policy; her war with the trade unions; the reduction of the workforce; the hard, inhumane social policy and so on. I have to say that I don't feel competent enough to comment on these subjects, although many of these arguments appeal to me emotionally, a great many indeed. Nevertheless we are talking here about a very specific issue, namely about international politics, and it sometimes happens that an internal policy which is quite repressive can be coupled with a foreign policy which is based on the correct definitions of who is a partner and who is an opponent. It seems to me that Mrs Thatcher fits such an example. The welcome given to Mrs Thatcher in Poland was the welcome given to a politician who is opposed to Soviet dominance over Europe, not one given to the opponent of trade unions, because, to tell the truth, Poles don't have much real knowledge on this subject. Some time ago in one of my interviews I attempted to compare Mrs Thatcher's non-conformism to the conformism of the TUC. Later on I received a letter from one of our British friends, who showed me how superficial my assumption was because in fact TUC leaders spoke publicly about Solidarity in Moscow. I would therefore now like to thank those TUC leaders who spoke about Solidarity and also express regret that my previous utterance was based on ignorance. Nevertheless, what I have just said does not alter the basic issue. The basic issue is that Poles and, more generally speaking, people in Eastern Europe judge the rest of the world in terms of its attitude towards their oppressors. I agree that this is a narrow view, very particular, parochial, but then again none of us would think to hold it against people in Johannesburg that they judge the rest of the world in terms of its attitude towards apartheid. Well, I am sometimes tempted to tell my West European friends that we Poles are just like the Negroes except that we are white. We want to have that degree of understanding which exists for people who, indeed with great justification, are fighting against apartheid in South Africa.

It seems to me that the whole problem of detente has taken on a new meaning in recent years, namely: how should the West, the NATO alliance, react to Gorbachev's policy? Here again we have a very interesting situation. Gorbachev's policy has virtually swept the chessboard clean. It is a kind of cancellation of the old playing positions. And the most important thing for us here in Eastern Europe – and, it seems to me, also for those in Western Europe – is this challenge set by Gorbachev, which is how to define this policy. Gorbachev has set the world a new challenge in the name of Russia, in the name of the superpower of real Communism, which dominates Eastern and Central Europe. How should we reply? Both in the West and in Eastern Europe there have appeared two types of response. On the one hand there is the response that can be defined as follows. Everything that is going on in Russia is cosmetic. Everything that is going on in Russia is a very specific, peculiar kind of game played to deceive the West. It is an effort to reverse the political trend which preserved the Brezhnev era and that of his elderly and transitory successors, and which meant that Russia was losing allies all over the world, becoming more and more an isolated country that was sinking into stagnation, unable to take new, original political initiative. And from this point of view Gorbachev is a new, significantly more intelligent version of Stalin. Such opinions can be found among observers of his policy both in Western and Eastern Europe. The second point of view is that Gorbachev is the continuation of that wonderful, interrupted work of the Twentieth Party Congress, work which really changed Communism, destalinized Communism. He is the man who gave back to socialism its human face and who, in all the world, cares most for peace.

It is not by chance that many Western opinion polls show Gorbachev to be the most popular politician in the contemporary world. To be fair, one has to say that in East Europe few people agree with this second assessment. Here in East Europe people are more distrustful and they are more likely to agree with those opinions on the subject of Gorbachev of people like Alain Besançon rather than those of people like Stephen Cohen. It seems to me that we are basically only witnessing the crystallization of the social consequences of the effect Gorbachev has had. In my opinion, both of these stereotypes which are present in Western thought are false stereotypes. What is happening in Russia is not a farce. What is happening in Russia is not a cosmetic operation; but then again, neither is it a noble gesture from the Soviet leader. It is simply a thaw which it is possible to interpret as something granted from above by the authorities. What is happening in Russia is a social process and social conflict. What is happening in Russia is the disintegration of Stalinist

Communism and the search for new forms. Gorbachev could, like
Cromwell, say: 'I know what I don't want, but what I want I don't yet
know.' At the same time we can say that there is something that Gorbachev does know. Gorbachev knows that he wants to modernize this
superpower so that it can continue to be a superpower in the future.
Gorbachev knows that if Russia doesn't modernize, then it can expect
the same fate as Turkey or Spain, which ceased to be great powers
because they were unable to respond politically and technologically to
the challenges of their times. That is why, I think, Gorbachev needs
glasnost as an instrument to realize his policy of modernization; that is
why he has resorted to glasnost.

Of course, in international terms this is obviously an attempt to
change the current trend in the West. However, if for years we have
been saying (as we, the critics of this policy, from East Europe, *have*
been saying) that Soviet foreign policy has to be related to the internal
policy; that to some extent it is a function or product of internal policy;
then we must also say that a transformed internal policy will produce a
new foreign policy. And at present one has to look at Russia as a country where Stalinism is in a state of disintegration. The conflict which
exists in Russia today has to do with this disintegration. There are forces
which are defending the system and there are forces which are encroaching on, and attacking it; that is my opinion. This is a social process
where the traditional, conservative *nomenklatura* is defending the old
order, the old model of government, because only the old model of
government guarantees them their privileges and social status. On the
other hand, those who are attacking this old order are a very heterogeneous group. It ranges from enlightened *apparatchiks*, who are
basically dreaming of a situation where there is perestroika without glasnost, to people who simply think of Russia as a country that in the future
will be democratic and respect laws, human rights, and so on. It seems to
me that the criterion for assessing change in Russia should be human
rights. Any development in the field of human rights deserves support
and is a factor favouring the creation of a new peaceful order in Europe
and in the whole world. Anything that sets aside development in favour
of human rights also sets aside this other prospect. This is the appropriate point of view that should be taken when considering what kind of
detente is needed today and not the question whether Gorbachev is
sincere or not; that should only interest his wife. It isn't important
whether a politician is sincere or not: a politician is always what he
pretends to be. That is why one has to take a good look at what image
Gorbachev and his team are trying to present. The problems that come
to my mind here are as follows: if the West really wants to ease relations
with Russia, then it must realize that the Soviet Union isn't just Russia.

The Soviet Union is over a dozen nations. There is no good reason why Holland, France or Great Britain could not maintain direct cultural links with countries like Lithuania, Estonia, Armenia or the Ukraine. This isn't a way of breaking up Russia, but it *is* a way of reforming the Soviet Union so that there is room for the subjectivity of other nations, because if these nations don't get to have their say by evolutionary means which can be supported by the West, then the empire will be set on fire. And then maybe peace will really be threatened. That is why all peaceful means of destalinization should be supported by the West, but the West must have its own plan; so far this plan does not exist.

The image of Armenians being murdered before the eyes of the civilized world is terrifying. Armenians today have a feeling that they are condemned to genocide, that they will be destroyed, that they will be degraded as a nation and this view is confirmed by the complete silence in the West, with public opinion following the example of governments in its reaction to what is happening in Armenia. This silence is both immoral and foolish, as is always the case when a crime is passed over in silence. There is of course overwhelming sympathy in the West for the victims of the earthquake, but it does not mean that there is political understanding. To put it most simply: the terms for peace cannot be based on the Yalta terms in their present form. (This means, those terms which were agreed by Roosevelt and Stalin, and endorsed by a helpless Churchill.) One cannot suddenly acknowledge that Stalin, who was a criminal and a mass-murderer (as Soviet newspapers now tell us), could at the same time be the architect of a fair system in Europe. This system is unfair, and it is interpreted as such. Furthermore it is a time-bomb – when it explodes everyone will be wiser and will talk about where the fault lay, but by that time it will only be like crying over spilt milk. Today is the time to talk responsibly and seriously about rejecting the Stalinist form of detente, the Stalinist form of the Yalta Agreement. This does not have to lead to the destruction of the Warsaw Pact or, more generally speaking, the Communist Bloc; but it must encourage the destruction of Stalinism within this bloc, it must lead by an evolutionary process to the creation of a new system. And now if we are to look at this evolutionary process we must be able to distinguish fact from fiction. When Mieczyslaw Rakowski is constantly telling Western ambassadors that he is trying to change the Polish United Workers' Party into an SPD one cannot just listen to what he is saying and believe him. One has to take a closer look at what he's doing. If he wants to create an SPD using Comrade Stalin's methods – that is, against the community's will, offending this community, taking away its symbols, slandering its leaders – then he isn't creating the SPD, that's not true; he is in fact doing nothing more than creating a new version of the

Communist Party of the Soviet Union, a new version of a Stalinist party in the Gorbachev era. One has to realize this. From this point of view, whenever a communist regime acts against the community it is supposed to govern, it doesn't act to ease relations because at the end of this process there is always an explosion, an explosion of dissatisfaction, a revolt. Willy Brandt's visit to Warsaw at the beginning of December 1970 was indeed symbolic; it was the greatest triumph of Gomułka's policy and two weeks later the Party Committee Building was in flames – that was the greatest catastrophe of this policy. One has to see the two things together, as an integrated entity. That is how we must look at it.

There is another thing we must realize; that just like in the West, new movements and new phenomena are being born here which no-one in their right mind can ignore. Whatever one might think about them – movements like the Greens in the German Federal Republic, or the peace movements in Great Britain – one cannot deny their existence because they are an important new element on the political map. One has to understand that one cannot look at the Central–East European political arena without recognizing independent social movements. It's not just Solidarity. And from this point of view one has to say that it is in fact the Greens and those peace movements who are looking for allies here in movements such as *Wolność i Pokój* ('Freedom and Peace') – and that is something invaluable. This is extremely significant, particularly as it forms part of the peacemaking process. It is typical of the Russians that they want to talk about reducing the number of missiles but they don't want to talk about the civil right to refuse to do military service as a means of guaranteeing peace. Why do they not want to talk about this? This is the great merit of these movements, at least here in Poland (and, I think, also in the West) – that the problem of war and the army has been interpreted as a problem concerning human rights. Furthermore, when people ask me what I think about the Western peace movements, I always answer with another question: what do those Western peace movements think of Yalta? If those movements are for a unified democratic Europe, and if they are striving for this unity without resorting to violence, then I am for them. I'm for them because I believe that there lies the future. The future does not lie exclusively in armaments. However, I also realize that unilateral disarmament in the West (as is proposed, for instance, by certain sections of the Labour Party) works essentially against peace because it would serve to encourage the most aggressive elements in the Soviet Union. The response to crisis is reform: at present there is reform, but this reform can fail and then the answer will be military aggression. A Russian dissident recalls that a certain Soviet field marshal often liked to repeat that an internal crisis can be solved by creating external pressure and a conflict which is victoriously resolved, a small victorious war. That is why the criterion for judging detente is the issue of human rights.

What I have just said about Russia is equally applicable to all the other people's democracies. This is very important because a great power like the United States can be fooled by the declarations of Nicolas Ceaucescu (and this was happening for years!) who is a kind of Bokassa or Idi Amin of Eastern Europe. Just because he used anti-Soviet rhetoric, he had practically total approval for all those excesses in his internal policy – and that is how it was for many years.

No! It has to be said here, and this must be a long-term policy: that anything that contravenes human rights and ipso facto the Helsinki Agreements, must be stigmatized. There can be no other way. Detente is an instrument of policy, it is not an end in itself. The ultimate end, if I'm not mistaken, is a world without conquest or suppression, because conquest and suppression are the source of wars. The detente worth fighting for, as Bukovski was saying years ago, is detente with a human face.

PART II
Geopolitics and Demilitarization

6

The Superpowers and a Sustainable Detente for Europe

Richard Falk

> I believe that people coming after us will marvel that on the one hand we
> accumulated more and more information, while on the other, we made no
> attempt at all to use it to improve our lives . . .
>
> (Doris Lessing, *Prisons We Choose to Live Inside*, New York 1987)

To consider what a suitable detente for Europe implies for the 1990s is
the structuring idea of this chapter. Such an inquiry proceeds by way of
investigating shifts in geopolitical encounter on the part of the two
superpowers, and what these shifts imply for the near future of Europe.
In one sense, the 1990s give countries in both halves of Europe a chance
of recovering a measure of their autonomy as independent states and an
attractive option to move beyond the divisions of the post-war world in
the direction of regional identity. But less appealing scenarios are also
plausible in reaction to reduced superpower roles in Europe. These
include a post-1992 reconfiguring of divided Europe in a manner that
ensures the resumption of tension and risk, although in a more Euro-
peanized form than in the decades after World War II.

'Texts' to Ponder

Perhaps we can be led to think more helpfully by considering some
unexpected lines of recent commentary that disclose tensions in the
ranks of the United States foreign-policy establishment. Samuel P.
Huntington, a stalwart figure renowned for his principled conservative
stands has, of all things, attacked Ronald Reagan from the right.
Regarding issues of nuclear-weapon policy and superpower relations as

central elements of American foreign policy, Huntington writes:

> [o]n these issues, the Reagan administration seems not to have moved from
> the radical right to the pragmatic centre but rather to have flipped across the
> entire length of the continuum from one extreme to the other.

And a little further on: 'the naiveté concerning the Soviets that President
Carter abandoned in 1979 President Reagan appeared to embrace in
1987.'[1] Huntington is especially disturbed by Reagan's alleged reversal
of attitudes towards arms-control agreements with the Soviet Union,
supposedly shifting from harsh critic to ardent exponent, and by what he
calls Reagan's 'nuclear aversion',[2] which he feels was irresponsibly manifested both by the *presentation* (*not the programme*) of the Strategic
Defense Initiative as rendering nuclear weapons obsolete and at the
Reykjavik mini-Summit in 1986 when Reagan appeared to join
Gorbachev in endorsing a proposal to eliminate all strategic weapons
and, by some accounts, all nuclear weapons within discrete and relatively short time periods.

Huntington augments these arguments by scorning the INF Treaty,
implying that it produces a major shift in the European strategic balance
that works in the Soviet favour. He dismisses the asymmetrical obligations of the formal treaty (the Soviets' willingness to destroy three
times as many missiles as the United States) and offers an asymmetrical
interpretation of his own that moves in the opposite direction: 'The
Soviet Union does not need nuclear weapons to conquer Western
Europe; NATO does need them to deter and to defeat a Soviet attack.'[3]

This attack on Reagan's moves towards moderation in East–West
relations is not an isolated diatribe. Such familiar centrists as Stanley
Hoffmann, Joseph Nye, Cyrus Vance, and the somewhat more conservative James Schlesinger have registered similar criticisms of
Reagan's nuclear aversion, although generally accepting the desirability
of the INF agreement from the dual perspectives of managing the arms
race and containing Western European dissent.

But there is another line of attack on those within the foreign-policy
elite suspected of harbouring secret feelings of animosity towards the
bomb. It is to label as far-out thinking comparatively mild repudiations
of the nuclear option, such as proposals for no first use of nuclear
weapons. Kissinger and Vance, collaborating across party lines on a
major article on foreign policy, express their views as follows:

> It is no service to the alliance to engage in speculation about extreme pro-
> posals or fanciful notions – such as complete denuclearization of Europe, the
> total elimination of all ballistic missiles, pledges against the first use of nuclear
> weapons or exaggerated claims SDI will provide an impenetrable shield.[4]

This article was featured in *Foreign Affairs* as establishing common ground for the post-Reagan years, and in such a passage the obvious targets of their comments were, as with Huntington, the allegedly nuclear-averse latter Reagan years, as well as such prominent liberal/moderate figures as George Kennan, Robert McNamara, McGeorge Bundy and Gerard C. Smith, the joint authors of a no-first-use proposal for Europe that had been promoted a few years earlier.[5] Incidentally, also, the influential Pentagon bipartisan commission that issued *Discriminate Deterrence* operates within the four corners of this nuclearist consensus.

Decoding both what is affirmed and what is negated suggests the following lines of policy:

- the United States government remains unconditionally committed to nuclear weaponry as a foreign-policy option; those who oppose such a commitment, even if they are card-carrying realists of the highest reputation, are derided as extremists or utopians;

- the Cold War rivalry is postulated as a constant for the indefinite future, and there is an evident refusal to assess whether Gorbachev's 'new thinking' offers genuine opportunities for a more moderate phase of international relations;

- the implications for Europe are to freeze the post-war experience as far as possible, but in any event to encourage a perpetuation of a divided and militarized Europe.

But the text may be overshadowed by an unacknowledged subtext: namely, an obsessive insistence, come what may, on sustaining the psychopolitical foundation of post-war United States imperialism, thereby rejecting the claim that the new priority of US foreign policy was how to manage a condition of imperial decline, a view most fully developed in Paul Kennedy's best-selling *The Rise and the Fall of the Great Powers*.[6] Until the imperial-decline hypothesis found an elite audience, there was relatively little tension within the US foreign-policy establishment.

Those who support a strategy of imperial continuity needed to do two things: (1) show the inconclusiveness of the application to the United States of either indicators of relative decline or of historical analogies drawn from earlier instances of imperial decline; (2) establish the instruments for imperial continuity under conditions of fiscal constraint.

Huntington, it should be recalled, orientates his whole argument around overcoming the so-called Lippmann Gap between commitments and capabilities which, some contend, has been rendering US foreign policy ineffectual. In such a policy setting, sustaining strategic advantages and avoiding waste become crucial. Concretely, the nuclear option gives the USA an edge and SDI as gateway to a post-nuclear world is a potentially expensive delusion, but not SDI in its geopolitical role of leading the way to the militarization of space.[7]

The imperial-continuity school is infatuated with devising a grand strategy by which the means and ends of US foreign policy can be brought into balance. If such is the priority, then those whose main concern is to improve the safety of the world are dangerously off-course, and even on the issue of peace they have missed the main message of the post-war world – peace through military strength and readiness, but more than this, a stable peace built on the foundation of nuclearism. In this regard, such unlikely bedfellows as Reagan (since Reykjavik), McNamara and Kennan misread history and misconstrue the American circumstance in the current world. They are preoccupied with the flaws in the world political structure in the nuclear age, and they thus seek an agenda of reforms that corresponds closely with the apparent programme of Gorbachev.

The Soviet debate is, of course, hidden from scrutiny to an even greater extent than the American one. There are no offsetting commentaries to decipher. Gorbachev seems to be accepting the necessity of imperial withdrawal and geopolitical accommodation as implicit in the whole idea of perestroika. Put differently, Gorbachev's Lippmann Gap is both more insistent and internal; augmenting domestic capabilities requires cutting external commitments.

It is naive to perceive Gorbachev as a Western liberal or humanist. His career and outlook seem above all to be pragmatic, to oppose any grandiose conception of the Soviet global role and to cut losses where possible. Even in his book *Perestroika*, presumably written with a Western audience mainly in mind, Gorbachev provides a standard ideological account of the Soviet role in Afghanistan:

> Afghanistan has many problems owing to its extreme backwardness, which largely stemmed from the British rule . . . as soon as progressive changes were charted imperialist quarters began to pressure Afghanistan from without. So, in keeping with the Soviet–Afghan treaty, its leaders asked the Soviet Union for help. They addressed us eleven times before we assented to introduce a limited military contingent into that country.[8]

Given the aggressive character of the Soviet intervention in Afghanistan, this passage shows us that Gorbachev could get along quite well in Orwell's world of *Nineteen Eighty-Four*! Further, it makes the agreement to get out so rapidly and unconditionally (despite some gratuitous provocations from Pakistan and the United States) reached in Paris early in 1988 even more impressive in what it suggests. To the extent that Gorbachev speaks for a unified Soviet leadership, the foreign-policy meaning of perestroika is the reduction of overseas commitments wherever possible, and without even the appearance of 'a decent interval' to cover the reality of geopolitical defeat.

This leaves the two superpowers in rather dissimilar, but not necessarily incompatible positions. The dominant US view most likely to set the boundaries of post-Reagan foreign policy for the next several years, regardless of which political party is in office, is intent on sustaining a high imperial profile, whereas the Gorbachev approach is one of withdrawal and retrenchment. In effect, the United States is being handed a blank cheque to carry on unopposed its interventionary diplomacy in most of the Third World. In some respects, such a Soviet withdrawal may cut down on the scale and incidence of political violence in the Third World, but at the probable cost of weakening the progressive side of the political ledger in struggles for control over the destinies of particular countries. This anticipation of a Soviet 'Afghanistan syndrome' far more enduring and comprehensive than the alleged 'Vietnam syndrome' is further reinforced by Gorbachev's emphasis in *Perestroika* on the European character of the Russian state, and by a variety of initiatives to cut Soviet tensions all along its borders, especially in relation to China. Of course, these steps could be interpreted differently. The Soviets might just be pausing between rounds in an ongoing fight, awaiting a favourable swing in regional and global balances once their rift with China is healed. Indeed, a restoration of Sino–Soviet friendship would be a geopolitical victory of great magnitude for Gorbachev, greatly enhancing Soviet potential diplomatic capabilities in many international arenas.

The emphasis on space as the bullring for contending hegemons is complemented by an endorsement of the Reagan doctrine of anti-'Marxist' (that is, anti-progressive) intervention in the Third World, at least where practicable. In this regard, markets, raw materials, investment climates and prestige provide sufficient grounds for US interventionary diplomacy even in the face of a virtual Soviet 'disappearance' in the context of its post-Afghanistan readjustment.

This Soviet dynamic of withdrawal is not necessarily applicable to Europe. Although glasnost is likely to spill over to establish a more vibrant atmosphere in Eastern Europe, it seems unlikely that any significant state/society restructuring of the sort implied by 'democratization' is likely to proceed. For one thing, the Soviets are faced with an escalating series of autonomy claims at home that could, if unchecked, threaten to dismember the state itself; for another the heavy reality of the Stalinist bureaucratic edifice remains, in place and deeply rooted, in both the Soviet Union and the countries of Eastern Europe.

Detente is neither altogether desirable nor very durable, so long as uncontested militarism in the West and essentially unopposed oppressiveness in the East persist unchallenged. Yet if the structuring of detente is left to the diplomacy of the superpowers such a trade-off is *the best* that can be envisioned, and although worthwhile as a stopgap, providing a geopolitical breathing spell, it is not sufficient over time. Such an arrangement is flawed, precarious, and will certainly give rise to renewed tensions in a time of crisis. Further, such a relaxation between the superpowers tends to weaken objections to ongoing US military programmes that extend the arms race to space or produce recurrent interventions in Third World countries; less hostile relations between Moscow and Washington also dilute concern about the continued subjugation of the peoples living in Eastern Europe and in many of the Soviet republics. Traditionally, also, peace activism in the West regresses to a hibernating posture as soon as Moscow and Washington act friendlier and negotiate about arms-control arrangements. Such a calm is not desirable in so far as many of the human costs of militarism, the Cold War, and the bloc system persist. It is important to appreciate the complicated character of this hopeful yet ambiguous phase in the early years of superpower relations in the post-post-war world.

The First East–West Bargain: The Cold War

The complex choreography of superpower relations since 1945 has never been convincingly scored. Most informed commentators have been caught up with the *adversary narrative* of these relations, and whether writing as apologist or revisionist their central preoccupation has been upon conflictual dimensions, especially arguments as to which side was primarily responsible for starting and sustaining the Cold War.[9] Because this conflict involved issues of fundamental ideological identity, the legitimacy of a given line of interpretation depended on remaining within the zero-sum mind-set of one or other of the antagonists as represented by their respective governing elites.

These official mind-sets were shaped in relation to Europe in particular. The Soviet Union was determined to extend its control over the countries in the East occupied during the war against Fascism, whereas the United States was as determined not to allow the large indigenous Communist parties in France and Italy to take power in either country. The two halves of Europe became 'blocs' organized around opposed alliance structures. Germany was a symbol of this post-war 'settlement' – in its division, epitomized by the Berlin Wall, and in its asymmetrical character, designed to wall East Germans in and West Germans out. In Western polemics there have been recurrent debates as to whether the arrangements at Yalta were an ill-conceived wartime concession by soft-headed Americans or whether the Soviets broke the arrangement by claiming more than they had been given.

Yalta, Potsdam – the wartime conferences – were perceived in the West at the time as ambiguous happenings, in retrospect, unduly shaped by the misleadingly expedient co-operative nexus of the anti-Fascist wartime alliance. It therefore remains possible to regard Yalta either as a bargain as well as a betrayal, or as some ambiguous combination. With the defeat of Fascism and the emergence of the United States–Soviet rivalry, post-war diplomacy was too often depicted in one-eyed fashion as resting on this basic war-threatening conflict between the two super-powers. Such a concern was natural, reflecting partly anxiety about nuclear war, partly a fear by ascendant diplomats in the West that the crucial anti-appeasement lessons of Munich must be energetically applied. The mixture of these two elements meant that 'peace' could be achieved only by 'deterrence', and credible forms of deterrence could be maintained over time only if a rival could be convincingly portrayed as menacing. The exaggeration of East–West intergovernmental conflict seems at once both inevitable and functional.

Recently, mainstream commentators have been celebrating its achievement – the longest European peace since Roman times, a period of sustained economic growth, a successful adjustment to the twin threats of nuclearism and aggression.[10] Such achievements are regarded as justifying encroachments on European sovereignty: by control over strategic matters, by economic penetration, and by the fundamental frustration of the political will of those living in the East.

What has been left virtually untouched by the historians of the period is the tacit co-operation, including mainly a series of unintended effects, that was the flip side of overt conflict, a dimension of East–West relations ever since the Cold War came to dominate our political imagination. In this regard, even the conflict that hardened into rival European alliance frameworks in the late 1940s was 'a bargain' between the superpowers, and in its own way reinforced rather than contradicted the bargains struck explicitly at the wartime conferences, especially at Yalta. Rather than constituting an arrangement in lieu of a 'peace settle-ment', it was a peace settlement brilliantly conceived and executed to avoid recurrence of general war in Europe, at least through the agency of German expansionism. Each superpower was confronted by a security need that had assumed urgency by the middle of World War II: that 'peace' meant, above all else, a set of conditions that would make World War III far less likely. Both superpowers believed that this set of

requirements depended on two factors: the containment of German
ambitions and the maintenance of military readiness.

The United States had an additional requirement: a persuasive justification for a *pre-war* military and diplomatic presence in Europe as a
means to assure the *prevention* of a third world war (thereby avoiding a
repetition of reactive entry into an ongoing general war in Europe).
The satisfaction of this requirement depended on the existence of a
threat, and the only plausible source of threat in the 1940s could have
been the Soviet Union. Without the Soviet threat, the domestic
pressures in the United States would have induced demobilization and
European withdrawal. The years 1945 to 1947 before the Cold War
took hold on the political imagination reinforce this impression,
exhibiting demobilizing, isolationist pressures with regard to the maintenance of an American presence in Europe. Such a view is also
sustained by the expectations of the public and most leaders that
American troops would be withdrawn from Europe as soon as ground
conditions in the occupied countries permitted.

The Soviet approach involved an additional requirement that
pertained only to itself: the need to extend hegemonic authority over
Eastern Europe and establish a buffer zone that would effectively extend
the reach of Soviet military capabilities beyond its frontiers, thereby
reducing the prospects of a third invasion in this century. Stalin's expansionist ambitions were undoubtedly an added element, as was the sense
that the Soviet Union deserved some 'fruits of victory', especially in the
light of the enormity of the social and human costs borne in the struggle
against Fascism.

As has become so evident, satisfaction of this Soviet security requirement has entailed suffering for the peoples of Eastern Europe, pawns in
these post-war geopolitical manoeuvres. Yet the West was not innocent.
To begin with, it acquiesced in some measure, although the extent of
Western complicity is necessarily conjectural. More than this, the West
used its hostile response to Soviet occupation policies to provide the
essential basis for perceiving the expansionist threat necessary to sustain
the US military presence in Western Europe, especially Germany, for
decades after fighting ceased in 1944.

If one conceives, just for the moment, of the Cold War as a peace
settlement, then we can appreciate how much better adapted it was to
the central mission of war-avoidance in Europe than had been the
earlier Versailles Peace Treaty. Europe has remained at peace and, as
we noted, generally prosperous. Germany has recovered from the humi-
liations of defeat and Nazism without posing a military threat of the sort
that led to the earlier breakdowns of order. Both superpowers have
avoided war, and the feared complacency associated with real peace. On

the Western side, one need only read the memoirs of George Kennan or Dean Acheson to realize how much more worried they were by the 'threat' of a strong United Nations than by the Soviet military menace. Why? Because these children of the 1930s associated war with withdrawal from Europe and military demobilization. Public pressures for 'peace' in the immediate post-war years (1945–47) created irresistible pressures towards withdrawal and demobilization. The United Nations, in such an alternative potential history of the post-war period, was supposed to provide a substitute for military capabilities and alliance diplomacy.

In fact, the Cold War as it took hold in the West managed to merge and confuse these alternative histories. The Kennan–Acheson image of peace prevailed, and produced American post-1945 dominance in virtually every diplomatic arena outside the communist camp. The United Nations, in its early stage, was effortlessly enlisted as a partisan on the Western side in the Cold War, and no longer challenged a traditional military approach to security; efforts to shape a collective security system within the UN framework were still-born for lack of motivation, and on the Soviet side outright resistance. The United Nations became, in other words, a tool of the West, culminating in the defence of South Korea (1950–53), which was American in *substance* even if it was under the auspices of the United Nations in *form*. Later, during the 1960s, the momentum of decolonization spoiled this part of the game, detaching the United Nations by stages from control by Washington and, through ironic effect, gradually enticing more constructive forms of Soviet participation.

The dubious side-effects of these arrangements involve a dependence on periodic renewals of international tension to justify superpower encroachments on European sovereign rights. By and large, these encroachments were voluntarily accepted in the West as exceedingly worthwhile, given the earlier history of intraregional warfare and the perceived Soviet threat, whereas in the East, especially after a few years, these Soviet encroachments were regarded as brutal denials of self-determination, given no more than an illusion of legitimacy through the juristic device of imposed regimes. In fact, the peoples of Eastern Europe could only be governed oppressively and could hope to recover their fundamental rights only by 'resistance' or 'liberation'. The countries of Eastern Europe truly became what the propaganda phrase of the West called 'captive nations', for once an occasion on which propaganda was descriptive of reality yet the source of cruelly and irresponsibly misleading signals, as the Hungarians found out in the course of the bloody events of 1956.

It was misleading and irresponsible because there was no Western intention to challenge Soviet hegemony in the Eastern half of Europe, and popular resistance was insufficient in the 1950s and 1960s to dislodge the imposed regimes. Western propaganda was 'irresponsible' as it implied rather pointedly a prospect of intervention on behalf of popular resistance, and thereby tempted captive peoples to revolt prematurely. There were highly persuasive reasons for ruling out intervention in Eastern Europe associated with the widespread, realistic expectation that such action could trigger World War III. In this regard, not only did the West 'sacrifice' the peoples of the East for the sake of stabilizing their post-war arrangements, they also failed to clarify the operational consequences of this arrangement and arguably contributed to several of the ill-advised early challenges directed at Soviet hegemony, especially the 1956 Hungarian uprising.

In fairness, the brutality of the Soviet approach to establishing hegemonic rule was not entirely expected, nor uniformly perceived. It was not widely appreciated what an immense burden was being placed on the peoples of these countries, who had no say whatsoever in shaping the post-war arrangements and were made to bear the full burdens of Stalinist vindictiveness. Part of the Western reaction by way of ideological aggressiveness on conditions in the East has to be explained as an expression (and deflection) of guilt, an acknowledgement of an earlier complacency. And indeed that aggressiveness complicated the lives of the peoples in the East still further. It encouraged Western militarization and an atmosphere of tension which 'justified' the Soviet security responses: hardening their occupation policies and engaging in their own reactive military build-up (a policy also encouraged by the US/NATO reliance on the nuclear option that induced Soviet compensatory efforts to threaten the occupation of Western Europe, which meant a deepening of militarization in Eastern Europe).

It has been one function of the European peace movement to develop an alternative image of Europe based on a different role for both superpowers. Essentially, it was the resistance by Western European civil society to further steps towards militarization, especially nuclearization, that encouraged a political process that has lowered tension and enlarged somewhat room for manoeuvre for opposition politics in Eastern Europe, with important variations operating from country to country. But the real breakthrough, led especially by END, was to couple its support for demilitarization in the West to intense expressions of involvement in solidarity with those struggling to obtain freedom, democracy and human rights in the East.

All these developments occurred against a background of social learning and creative adjustment by the peoples living under harsh rule in the East. In effect, resistance tactics abandoned violence and no longer sought to take over and challenge directly the formal governing structures of the state.[11] The objective was to constitute freedom in civil society by independent initiative, and to alter the political climate so greatly that it would be impossible for the state to govern in the old ways. The outcome of these struggles is by no means assured. The new style of Soviet leadership during the Gorbachev era – which above all seems to have renounced direct intervention as a policy option, at least for now – has changed the situation considerably, alleviating some *conditions* of oppression, but quite possibly stablizing its *structure*. The loosening of the atmospheres of oppression – even a variety of versions of glasnost – does not by itself bring about improved economic, social and political conditions of existence. In fact, there are new anxieties about a restabilization of conditions over the head, once again, of the East Europeans, this time by way of a bargain between Western Europe and the Soviet Union, possibly facilitated by some tactics of economic co-option.[12]

Here is the point. The peace movements of the West established a political climate that helped to produce a dramatic reversal in the militarizing momentum – namely, the INF Treaty. Moreover, in the process the political momentum temporarily strengthened the resistance prospects of the East. Of course, repressive regimes learn and adapt in their own way, and seek by a variety of means to co-opt, mute and coerce their opposition. The various struggles continue, but informed efforts in the West to expose torments in the East (and in the Soviet Union as well) are a belated but genuine way of encouraging resistance and liberation without depending on illusions of intervention and without raising risks of general war.

The related concern, to be discussed in the next section, is whether such liberating tendencies are being reinforced by the new phase of superpower relations, including its tacit dimensions and possibly unintended effects. Our concern is, especially, whether this diplomacy of the 1980s is working towards a Europe of the 1990s that will be both more 'secure' (reduced perception of risks of war) *and* more 'democratic' (increased realization of human rights and popular sovereignty). In the end, such favourable prospects depend on the substantial revitalization of civil society, a formidable undertaking in the East after decades of erosion and suppression, and difficult in the West as well, due to the co-optation of the main political parties by the outlook and practices of the national security state.

New Directions for Superpower Diplomacy

The Cold War persisted as the centrepiece of the post-1945 world but gradually assumed a more traditional shape in geopolitics, an instance of great-power imperial rivalry. It was also a structure vulnerable to various types of democratic backlash, characteristically involving the struggles for self-determination in the East and for disarmament, especially nuclear disarmament, in the West. As is so often the case with geo-political bargains between predominant states, they are struck largely at the expense of others and to obscure their illegitimacy, their terms are kept secret and implicit.

It is assumed in most discussions that detente is an easing of East–West conflict by deliberate intergovernmental and interbloc action. In this way the co-operative dimensions of the overall relationship among the superpowers are suddenly emphasized, and likewise the conflictual dimensions recede. The diplomacy of detente represents a reaction by official elites to the perceived costs and risks of Cold War diplomacy, including high anxiety levels about the onset of nuclear war. It reflects a shift in priorities by both superpowers, especially the pressure to provide reassurances and possibly resources for domestic restructuring. These two poles of detente and Cold War are both exaggerations of the actual relationship between the superpowers, which since 1945 has been based on a far more consistently mixed structure of tacit co-operation and manifest conflict.

One implication of such a characterization is that the intrabloc arrangements have hidden and suppressed patterns of state–society conflict, particularly between bloc leaders and the rest of the bloc. Such a circumstance of suppressed conflict has been obvious in the East, less so in the West – indeed, the two bloc formations are notably dissimilar in almost every respect, with the Western bloc far more closely resem-bling an alliance between independent states and the Eastern bloc an empire, albeit 'enforced' by way of regimes that accepted – indeed, depended upon – the maintenance of the bloc structure. That is, the regimes in the East were no less willing partners in alliance frameworks than their Western counterparts, and have remained more dependent on the bloc system, but they were less 'legitimate' in the eyes of their own population and of wider currents of opinion.

But our overall point pertains: both superpowers have viewed their relationship with one another through cycles of geopolitical interaction that stress one or another aspect of the abiding and mixed structure of their relationship, and thereby encourage a misleading succession of one-sided, distorting overall perceptions. There is also an evolutionary process that has over time increased the perceived relative payoffs for both superpowers of accentuating the co-operative pole of their relationship. For the Soviet Union, the Cold War pole maintained tension at a high level and/contributed to its economic isolation and backwardness, as well as diverting attention from a deteriorating domestic situation./For the United States, the Cold War pole raised fears of war, contributed to fiscal and overall economic deterioration, and precluded some opportunities for trade expansion.

The detente of the early 1970s, largely initiated and stage-managed by Washington, was ill-conceived, filled with illusions, and vulnerable to a domestic backlash. It was mainly conceived as an adjustment by the United States to defeat in Vietnam: the altered East–West relationship christened 'detente' was conceived by Nixon/Kissinger as a way to shift the domestic mood in the United States in a more hopeful direction, take advantage of the Sino–Soviet split, and restore in the West a sense of the positive character of American leadership. The Soviet Union responded formally, agreeing in these years to this moderating initiative with great fanfare, being validated as a co-superpower (despite its economic and cultural weakness), hoping for tangible gains by way of trade, cultural exchange and enhanced prestige, but not altering its basic commitment to pursue geopolitical opportunities for increased influence as they presented themselves, especially in the Third World, or loosening its hold over the bloc. The opportunism of Washington's handling of the 'China card' must also have caused normally suspicious Soviet leaders to be especially apprehensive.

The momentum of detente in the 1970s was associated with summit meetings, a stress on 'negotiations' supplanting 'confrontation', arms-control arrangements, and an affirmation of the interbloc status quo in Europe. Perhaps the most significant, enduring result of the short-lived 1970s detente was the Helsinki process that arose out of the 1975 agreement to regard existing European boundaries, including the division of Germany, as legitimate and no longer contested and, by its inclusion of Basket III, opened up state–society relations in both blocs to periodic scrutiny. In essence, a bargain in which the East was reassured about boundaries, including that of the German Democratic Republic, and the West was formally allowed to reassert its concern for the well-being of the peoples caught in the vice of communist rule in the East. Little attention was devoted to what level of accountability was agreed upon, nor was it originally expected to amount to much.

The Soviet Union and its bloc members regarded the Helsinki provisions on human rights as *pro forma*, not intended to pierce the veil of sovereign control over internal political life, whereas the United States government, in particular, came to regard Basket III as a valuable, structured opportunity to expose the inadequacies of life under communism and win points back home. As the Cold War heated up again in the late 1970s and early Reagan years, these annual sessions of scrutiny provided American politicians with occasions for ideological denunciation. These propaganda exercises did touch on some important political truths about the harshness of life in the Eastern countries, but the official motivations of the United States government seemed so closely linked to the advocacy of militarist approaches for the West that the positive side of the message, addressing the captive status of the peoples in the East, seemed secondary and somewhat hypocritical. At the same time, this renewed salience of the human costs of the bloc system helped to create a climate in which END and other European peace initiatives reversed the intergovernmental equation of human rights and militarism by linking support for the liberation of the peoples in the East with a continent-wide dynamic of demilitarization and depolarization.

The diplomacy called detente was poorly negotiated and implemented, although its failure was a product of converging domestic, regional and global forces. United States opponents of the 1970s detente, those who espoused an ideological view of post-war relations among the superpowers and those whose capitalist and bureaucratic interests were associated with militarism, successfully counterattacked.[13] But detente as a geopolitical bargain failed mainly because it was linked to a perception of imperial decline in the West, especially the United States.[14] The outcome of national revolutions in Africa and Central America, the Iranian Revolution, and especially the American humiliation during the hostage crisis of 1979–80 fostered this impression, culminating in the massive Soviet intervention in Afghanistan of December 1979.

American leaders and the mainstream public regarded these developments as expressive of bad policy rather than as indicative of a new structure of power relations producing a reduced US role in the world system; in this way, with renewed assertiveness and a commitment to restore the post-war leadership role, the perception of decline could be diminished, if not eliminated. In such an atmosphere it was all but inevitable that detente should founder, and the Cold War revive. The relative interests in underscoring conflict once again, for a time, outweighed those of emphasizing co-operation – at least for the United States, but also to a lesser extent for the right-of-centre governments that took power in the main industrial democracies.

But the experience of the late 1970s also reflected the growing obsolescence of the Cold War (bipolar) framework. With European economic recovery and Japanese economic emergence as a formidable rival, a structure of economic multipolarity was developing in the West. Furthermore, the experience of the first detente for Western Europe was more positive, generating considerable trade expansion in East–West settings and raising questions about whether European subordination to the United States continued to serve the interests of Western European countries. On the Soviet side, the claims for domestic reform required some opening of the political process, and this kind of development was not fully consistent with their post-war approach to Eastern Europe. Also, the challenge of Solidarity in Poland and the desperate stratagem of bringing in General Jaruzelski to head the government ended any illusions that the Helsinki Accords might by themselves lend *internal* legitimacy or even political stability to either the governing arrangements of particular countries or the bloc character of Eastern Europe.

Finally, subduing the Afghan resistance turned out to be a geopolitical nightmare, a Soviet Vietnam, rather than resembling such earlier brutally effective interventions in Europe as Hungary (1956) or Czechoslovakia (1968). Reaganism challenged the Soviet leadership by exerting military pressure and greatly raised tension, which was further heightened in the early 1980s by irresponsible rhetoric about the feasibility of limited nuclear war that seemed especially alarming when coupled with a renewed attack on the overall legitimacy of the Yalta consignment of East Europe to the Soviet camp.[15] In this regard the early Reagan period, by ignoring the Helsinki bargain on European boundaries, seemed to revert to early 1950s stages of Cold War thinking, but in an environment of more menacing military technology.

How these factors were actually interpreted by the Gorbachev leadership is not directly knowable at this stage, but we do know two things: that Gorbachev received a mandate from the Soviet ruling elite to embark upon domestic restructuring, and that action on this mandate seemed dependent on achieving calmer superpower relations. Furthermore, Moscow seemed far more disposed to take steps to make detente work this time around – the Kremlin had had its fill of Third World involvements, especially in the light of its troubles in Afghanistan and the heavy and continuing claims on its resources from Cuba and Ethiopia. Perestroika disposed the Soviet Union to find ways to reduce its defence burden, and the Gorbachev leadership correctly associated the recovery of Soviet international stature with a new peace offensive, a diplomacy made possible in part because it could be played off against Reagan's militarist posture and increasingly unilateralist diplomacy.

Thus quite remarkably, given its own dismal record on human rights, Moscow has seized the normative initiative in recent years by proposing a strengthened United Nations, putting forward far-reaching yet carefully framed conceptions of total nuclear disarmament and European demilitarization, and facilitating the settlement of troublesome regional conflicts. Of course, despite the dubious Soviet credentials to sponsor such constructive reforms, their intrinsic merit makes their espousal generally welcome almost regardless of source. At the same time, the fickleness and superficiality of public opinion causes some worries. There is a tendency towards love–hate attitudes in geopolitics, and the positive imagery Gorbachev has achieved (so-called Gorbomania) tends to make it seem in certain liberal circles obstructive, even reactionary, to dwell on societal inadequacies that persist in Eastern Europe and the Soviet Union. It is more important than ever for peace groups to combine responsiveness to Soviet peace initiatives with support for democratization and human rights in Eastern Europe and in the Soviet Union, including especially lending support to efforts to reconstruct civil society as a terrain for democratic politics.

To Washington, the geopolitics of co-operation again appeared favourable, but this time in a more sustainable fashion. Moscow was offering attractive bargains that included asymmetrical arms-control measures such as INF, and encouraging resolution of regional conflicts. The United States was proceeding from a position of generally renewed confidence as far as its geopolitical potency was concerned. Indeed, the United States' positive partial response to Gorbachev's initiatives were alleged to depend on sustaining cohesion in the West and reviving US claims of responsible leadership. Arresting the actualities of imperial decline for both superpowers was now seemingly understood in both Moscow and Washington as requiring the muting of East–West conflict. Indeed, the Reagan administration claimed that more forthcoming Soviet behaviour in international relations was a dividend of its earlier military build-up, geopolitical resolve and ideological robustness – in effect, that the ideological mobilization of hostile imagery in the early 1980s induced Soviet adjustments in style and behaviour that enabled the softening of the rivalry in the latter part of the decade. Unlike the Nixon initiatives that flowed from weakness, the Reagan diplomacy was allegedly based on strength and confidence, including a high degree of domestic consensus.

It is, of course, impossible to assess such claims, or various alternative counterfactuals – what if Gorbachev had chosen a confrontation strategy to avoid the 'impossibility' of the domestic agenda? What if Reagan had accepted the more ambitious Soviet proposals to demilitarize inter-national relations (abandoning SDI, trading the bases in the Philippines for Cam Ranh Bay in Vietnam, strengthening the UN's peacekeeping capacity, proceeding towards the reduction and elimination of all nuclear warheads)? It seems evident that moderation in East–West relations has been reconciled for the time being, in US government circles, with current levels of defence spending and military deployment, with offensive-minded strategic thinking, with the extension of the arms race to space, with the retention of the nuclear option, and with an affirmation of the Reagan doctrine *vis-à-vis* Third World radicalism.

And on the Soviet side there is as yet no clear indication of letting go of East Europe, or of encouraging the kind of political developments that can supersede the imposed post-war governing arrangements that have been unable to legitimate themselves in the eyes of their own peoples and continue to depend for stability on coercion, varying in degree from country to country and through time.

The 1990s seem likely to witness the uneven, often unacknowledged, yet substantial withdrawal of both superpowers from Europe. The energy for this withdrawal will stem partly from the superpowers themselves, a logical sequel to the Helsinki accommodation, but even more so from shifting priorities in both Moscow and Washington: for Moscow, a combined emphasis on perestroika, a reduced threat of territorial war, and a commitment to sustain the appearance of non-interventionary, constructive diplomacy; for Washington, the emerging primacy of geoeconomics, a shift to Pacific priorities and a consensus that post-war levels of involvement are no longer wanted or warranted. This dynamic of superpower withdrawal is likely to be abetted by European assertiveness in the West to regroup for intracapitalist rivalry; in the East to attempt one last, surely futile, effort to legitimize communism as a consensual form via a series of mini-perestroika, glasnost adaptations.

In one disturbing sense, the 1990s could turn out to be a return to the late 1950s and 1960s, but without comparable international tensions and a strong sense of superpower rivalry. In effect, the Soviet Union would revert to being a regional power while the United States would resume its role as manager of change and stability in many parts of the Third World, shifting its main geopolitical attention from Europe to the Pacific and being more conscious of fiscal constraints. Each superpower would tacitly accept this reorientation of roles. Western Europe, by its integrating momentum, could assume responsibility for its own security and work out East–West arrangements for the continent that might include new military uncertainties that could lead Moscow to be apprehensive, and tighten its grip on Eastern Europe. Alternatively, Europe as superpower might adopt a variant of equidistance diplomacy that would stabilize relations in Europe along Helsinki lines, and emphasize its rivalry with the United States and Japan for shares of the world market.

The overall situation remains ambiguous, and is possibly quite fluid. One set of possibilities involves a more-or-less definite world order bargain that ends up giving the United States a virtual blank cheque to engage in interventionary diplomacy in the Third World in exchange for calling off the Cold War. Many Third World leaders, including those associated with the Non-Aligned Movement, were quite alarmed by this turn in geopolitics. In late 1988 developments suggested that the Kremlin may have considered – at least partially and temporarily – suspending Soviet troop withdrawals from Afghanistan as of October 1988 in response to alleged violations of the Geneva Accords by Pakistan and the United States, especially regarding arms supply to the Mujahideen forces and Gorbachev's highly promoted state visit to India in November 1988. Nevertheless, the drift of Soviet foreign policy, especially in light of Bush's election as President of the United States, suggests asymmetrical relations between the superpowers and regional, ethnic, and revolutionary conflict in the Third World. Far preferable from the perspective of world order or international law would have been a geopolitical bargain between the superpowers, based on the development of a non-interventionist regime based on a code of mutual restraint, especially with respect to arms transfers and sales. Such a prospect is inconsistent with the US foreign policy establishment's continuing adherence to the premises and directives of the Reagan Doctrine – a view endorsed in *Discriminate Deterrence*, the report of the authoritative, bipartisan (Ikle/Wohlstetter) commission of national security experts.[16]

Concluding Conjectures about Sustainable Detente

This new phase in superpower relations offers some room for manoeuvre in the remaining years of this century to move in two linked desirable directions – towards demilitarization and democratization. Such prospects are almost totally dependent on a renewed dynamism for the complex processes of detente from below, building a transnational climate of opinion based on a sense of European political community that extends concerns of peoples to the problems and priorities of the region as a whole. Such a dynamic is likely to be seriously obstructed in the early 1990s by the initial impacts of deepening Western European economic integration (1992). A resurgent and refocused grass-roots radicalism will be needed to offer a vision of a different future for Europe that resists pressures towards bloc realignment and militarization, West European superpower status, reactive formations in the East. That is, a Europe without the nuclear superpowers could either move towards a reconfigured structure of regional conflict, fraught with danger and inhospitable to the extension of human rights and democracy, or it could break with this legacy of the post-war world and reconstruct regional relations along more peaceful and positive lines. The elites in both halves of Europe remain overwhelmingly committed to perpetuating 'the old ways', but in new forms, taking the shape of an adjustment to the substantial withdrawal of the superpowers.

Despite this altered configuration, a sustainable detente *for Europe* requires democratization and demilitarization as well as the phased withdrawal of the superpowers and the muting of the Cold War.[17] The dissatisfactions of the peoples in the East will recurrently produce confrontations that expose the oppressive character of state–society relations. Such disclosures will activate hostility in the West, even interventionary pressures, which in turn will stimulate an action–reaction cycle of militarization. The avoidance of such patterns depends on transformation from below. Progress along several lines is an important sequel to superpower withdrawal: (1) an intensification of transnational support for human rights and democracy throughout Europe; (2) reduced military deployments in Europe, including forward deployment, provocative manoeuvres, non-defensive doctrines; (3) a surge of economic, political and cultural efforts to strengthen an all-European identity.

This latest variant of detente has been, in part, a response to the rise of the peace movement in Europe. The successful mobilizations in the early 1980s created great pressure on the democratic governments of Western Europe to reduce the perceived risks of nuclear war, and to break free of their subordinate state in NATO. This message was initially transmitted as an objection to the deployment of Pershing II and cruise missiles, but as that message was deflected by various social forces, it raised new questions about the political preconditions of sustainable detente. In essence, these 'discoveries' involved a growing realization in Europe that intergovernmental bargains between the two superpowers were reversible, partial, and somewhat unreliable ways to establish 'common security'. More was needed. The region itself had become a larger pawn than East Europe taken alone, but still a pawn in the bilateral diplomacy of the superpowers. Europe and Europeans were effectively excluded and, moreover, the repressive conditions in the East meant that detente was still being used – or could be used – to evade the aspirations of these populations.

Several issues and concerns remain serious:

1. This second detente was largely 'imposed' on Europe as a superpower bargain;

2. Governments in both Europes had either involuntarily or unknowingly, through the years, relinquished sovereign rights over vital sectors of public policy;

3. The attainment of human rights and democracy is integral to a

process of 'ending' the Cold War and generating a 'sustainable detente';[18]

4. Similarly, the relationship of *both* superpowers to Third World revolution needs to be premissed on joint adherence norms of non-intervention; Soviet withdrawal without United States reciprocation is neither responsible, nor altogether desirable;

5. Superpower relations need to be separated as far as possible from respective domestic debates about adjusting to imperial decline, and its psychopolitical perception;

6. The character of the superpower bargain on this rotation of the geopolitical clock appears to de-emphasize Europe as a zone of conflict, thereby providing its best opportunity for diplomatic inno-vation since 1945 by way of regional self-determination;

7. As a region, Europe (and the Europeans) must be primarily under-stood in relation to popular sovereignty, consisting of the values and aspirations of various peoples and nations for self-determination, peaceful accommodation, human rights, demilitarization, environ-mentalism and revitalized democracy (that is, tested by the substance of participation, freedom, and control, and not by the rhetoric and rituals of empty forms).

Notes

1. Huntington, 'Coping with the Lippmann Gap', *Foreign Affairs*, no. 66, 1987/88, pp. 453–77, at p. 464.

2. At p. 465; for an interesting confirmation of Reagan's 'nuclear aversion' see remarks by Brian Urquart, *A Life in Peace and War*, London 1987, p. 357.

3. p. 466; and on p. 466: 'Europe becomes less secure with the treaty than it was with the missiles.'

4. This follows the assertion that 'the United States must make unequivocally clear that NATO cannot be defended without sufficient quantities and types of both nuclear and conventional weapons, so as to deter a nuclear adversary that continues to enjoy a con-ventional superiority in some significant categories and to possess nuclear weapons stationed inside its territory capable of reaching all of Europe.' Henry Kissinger and Cyrus Vance, 'Bipartisan Objectives for American Foreign Policy', *Foreign Affairs*, no. 66, 1988, pp. 899–921, at p. 908.

5. For earlier article see Bundy and others, 'Nuclear Weapons and the Atlantic Alliance', *Foreign Affairs*, no. 60, 1982, pp. 753–68.

6. New York 1987; Kennedy's interpretation of decline is elegantly foreshadowed in Robert Gilpin's *War and Change in World Politics*, Cambridge, 1981.

7. See Zbigniew Brzezinski, 'America's New Geostrategy', *Foreign Affairs*, no. 66; 1988, pp. 680–99.

8. *Perestroika*, New York 1987, p. 177.

9. For well-balanced standard accounts see John Lewis Gaddis, *The United States and the Origins of the Cold War, 1941–1947*, New York 1972; Gaddis, *Strategies of*

Containment, New York 1982; but see also Gian Giacomo Migone, 'The Nature of Bipolarity: An Argument Against the Status Quo', in Mary Kaldor and Richard Falk, eds, *Dealignment: A New Foreign Policy Perspective*, Cambridge 1987, pp. 52–66.

10. Cf. useful variations on this familiar theme in Immanuel Wallerstein, 'European Unity and its Implications for the Interstate System', in Bjorn Hettne, ed., *Europe: Dimensions of Peace*, London 1988, pp. 27–38.

11. For exceptional discussions of this 'political learning' process see George Konrád, *Antipolitics*, London 1984; Adam Michnik, *Letters from Prison*, Berkeley, CA, 1985.

12. Cf. for example William Echikson, 'Why Poles are concerned about Soviet-German rapprochement', *Christian Science Monitor*, 25 October 1988, p. 8.

13. Well recounted in Jerry Sanders, *Peddlers of Crisis*, Boston, MA, 1983.

14. Vividly argued by 'The *Business Week* Team' in Bruce Nussbaum and others, *The Decline of U.S. Power (and what we can do about it)*, Boston, MA 1980.

15. For elaboration see Falk, 'Superseding Yalta: A Plea for Regional Self-Determination', in Kaldor and Falk, pp. 28–51.

16. For the probable course of US foreign policy in the next decade see references cited in notes 1, 4, and 7, and compare the influential report of bipartisan Ikle–Wohlstetter Commission appointed by the US Secretary of Defense, *Discriminate Deterrence* (Report of the Commission on Integrated Long-Term Strategy), Washington DC 1988.

17. The argument here supports dealignment, not rupture; the post-war framework needs to be gradually displaced and a new demilitarized framework evolved, but time is required. For fuller rationale see 'Introduction' to Kaldor and Falk, pp. 1–27.

18. Cf. argument of Richard Ullman that Cold War can end because the Soviet Union is becoming an 'ordinary state': Ullman, 'Ending The Cold War', *Foreign Policy*, no. 72; 1988, pp. 130–51.

7

The Decline of the Bipolar System, or A Second Look at the History of the Cold War*

Gian Giacomo Migone

History books have taught us to understand relations between the United States and the Soviet Union since the Second World War as a sequence of conflicts.

Of course nobody denies that there have been periods of detente, though both orthodox and revisionist historiography take for granted that tension and conflict are the prevailing features within the relationship. Agreements and dialogues are considered episodic and scrutinized with prudence, if not with scepticism. It is no coincidence that no historian has seriously challenged the expression 'Cold War' as a global description of the last forty years of international relation, in spite of the fact that every now and then somebody decrees its end. One of the foremost architects of the orthodox school, Adam Ulam, has quite accurately pointed out that revisionist historians have never revised the plot of the Cold War, but only changed the roles of the protagonists. The good guys have become bad, and vice versa.[1] Not even the so-called post-revisionists have questioned the fundamentally antagonistic nature of the relationship, but simply added what they consider to be a more balanced allocation of the responsibilities for the origins and the development of the cold war. Should anyone wonder why this sup-

*The author is heavily indebted to many friends and colleagues for criticism and stimulation in the formulation of the points of view expressed in this chapter. I am thinking of the editors and other contributors to this book, and also of many participants in discussions more distant in time and place. Let me at least mention two of them: David Calleo, who acted as a good-humoured host for a year at the School for Advanced International Studies, Washington, DC, and Stanley Hoffmann, who wrote a long letter of criticisms of an early version of this same essay. I have never thanked them properly, and am glad to have the opportunity to do so now.

posedly fundamental antagonism has not been carefully argued, but rather taken for granted (the Soviet school of thought provides no exceptions from this point of view), it should be remembered that every policy produces its own historiography. After all, the existence of a Cold War justifies a post-war settlement which, as Richard Falk has reminded us, is and remains 'illegitimate' from the viewpoint of political ideology prevailing on all sides'.[2]

Naturally, the author of this chapter also runs the risk of remaining a prisoner of a similar mechanism. Rejection of the bipolar logic, hope for a more peaceful coexistence in a world threatened by nuclear weapons, concern with a more democratic approach to foreign relations, a greater attention to the North–South relationship, and commitment to a united European continent free from the condominium of the superpowers – all are factors which can lead to a new historiography *ad usum delphini*. But this danger will shock only those who set their faith in historical objectivity and who refuse the stimuli that a renewed political perspective can offer a reading of the past.

In point of fact I have already expressed my conviction on other occasions that agreements have been at least as important as conflicts in the relationship between the superpowers – that, to be more exact, the former have been strictly complementary to the latter, to the point of forming what might temporarily be called a conflictual alliance (until we find a better expression). We should not be looking for a history of detente where dialogues and treaties claim a central position. The point is rather to show how, in each phase of negotiation as well as of conflict, there has been an area of mutual consensus, generally taken for granted (and therefore mostly left unspoken), often at the expense of third parties and in any case of such importance as to define the relationship as a whole.

Obviously all this is not meant to deny the existence of antagonism between the superpowers. The Cold War – sometimes running the risk of becoming hot – cannot be written off as a gigantic farce or a Machiavellian expedient of unprecedented dimensions, staged at the expense of lesser actors. The antagonism has been and – in spite of Gorbachev's reforms and public-relations successes – remains genuine, just as the joint interests and connivances are genuine. Precisely because their approach has been unilateral, both orthodox and revisionist historians have been successful in explaining, respectively, the defensive syndrome of paranoiac dimensions that pushed the Soviet Union to expand its power in Europe and in the world and the pursuit of a global stabilization, responsive to the expansive ambitions of the dollar on the part of the USA.

These conflictual tendencies were far stronger than any ideological controversy, however vigorous. It is therefore necessary to ask the crucial question: why has antagonism not prevailed or, at least, not taken the form of armed conflict between the superpowers? The conventional answer is that peace has prevailed not in spite of but thanks to the nuclearization of world politics and, in particular, of continental Europe. Both sides have argued that the nuclear deterrent has been necessary because the other side was likely to plan a frontal attack or invasion, as a result of some ideological imperative, that only a nuclear threat could avoid. The pre-emptive use of this capability could be stopped only by a second-strike capability which became essential to the maintenance of peace.

One of the basic points of my argument is that it has not been Mutually Assured Destruction that has kept the peace but the mutual interest of the superpowers. Or rather: not only the obvious but negative interest to avoid physical destruction, but the magnitude of the positive interests that the superpowers shared in the face of third parties. In this perspective, it is no surprise that the United States and the Soviet Union have shown considerable pragmatism and diplomatic savvy in solving their differences at the expense of others, even to the point of fighting major but peripheral wars by proxy. At the root of what became a way of thinking which moulded the post-war international system was a relatively simple fact of life: the Soviet defensive syndrome and the American quest for worldwide social and economic stabilization could only be reconciled with the partition of Germany and, consequently, of Europe, and with the sacrifice of the independence of the Eastern European population and of the hopes for radical change of the working classes of Western Europe.

If one sees the matter from this point of view, there is no longer the need, so typical of orthodox historiography, to scorn the supposed naiveté of Franklin Roosevelt and, initially, of his successor, held to be responsible for the sacrifice of Western interest to Stalin's cunning aggressiveness. We are also able to provide an answer (without resorting to purely psychological explanations) to the question that Ulam and his colleagues ask obsessively – why, in 1945, did the Americans (Roosevelt but also Douglas MacArthur) not have the sense to ally themselves firmly with Churchill against Stalin?[3] Many events proved that the United States considered its conflict of interest with the sterling area and imperial preferences as perhaps less vital (in the literal sense) but more immediately relevant than a showdown with the communist empire. The negotiations that led to the Bretton Woods agreements, the anti-colonial aggressiveness of the United States – but also less visible episodes, such as the obstinate American desire to exclude Great Britain from any role in the conquest and occupation of Japan – clearly indicate that the consolidation of American leadership within the capitalist world was considered a top priority, as long as the decline of the British Empire had not become an irreversible historical fact.[4]

Even at a later stage the wars in Indochina and Algeria, as well as the 1956 Suez crisis, demonstrated American awareness of the importance of its anti-colonial past. The revolutionary and anti-imperialist tradition, renewed by Woodrow Wilson at Versailles, encouraged newer and more sophisticated forms of penetration and control of newly independent countries, such as had already been successfully experimented with in Latin America during previous decades. All in all, a realistic appraisal of immediate and tangible interests was more important than any short-term anti-Soviet solidarity. After all, in these cases even somebody like John Foster Dulles understood that the Soviet Union would have gained from any American temptation to lend its shield to the outdated empires of its lesser European allies.

Naturally, the conflicts of interest between and within the future NATO partners were even more evident in the events that led to lasting division of the European continent. In this context, which were the considerations that governed American conduct?

In spite of everything that has been written to the contrary, on one point there is a fundamental continuity between the wartime and postwar policies of the United States. Neither Roosevelt nor Truman, before and after the watershed of the official declaration of the doctrine of containment, hesitated to protect the prevailing social and economic structure of Western Europe. Those responsible for American foreign policy did not wait for the withdrawals of the British military presence from Greece and Turkey to support those forces which, within each European country, resisted any basic change of the social and political status quo beyond the defeat of the Third Reich. There were of course disagreements concerning means, but even when this policy hampered the war effort, support of any force potentially hostile to a future European settlement congenial to American values and interest was limited to a minimum. It is significant that after the fall of Germany the American secret services enlisted the co-operation of war criminals who were willing and able to continue their struggle against the left under different circumstances. It is certainly more important that all those sectors in the European Socialist parties and union movements which tended towards neutrality and were not willing to interrupt their relationships with Communist parties, where they existed, were to be opposed in every possible way.[5] These policies developed all their strength as political and consequently financial support grew in the late forties, but they already existed *in nuce* behind the German lines.

Similar policies conducted with more brutal means by the Soviet

Union in Eastern Europe were naturally an important factor in strengthening American *resolve*, but it is important to understand that they were not causative. The links between dissenting forces and the other superpower may have provided a justification for repression, but they were not the reason for it. The division of Europe and the mutually threatening attitudes of the two blocs became factors of social and political stabilization in both East and West. We are dealing here with a parallel will of the superpowers not only to hold on to what they had conquered with so much sacrifice, but to impose or safeguard their conceptions of society and the political system. Once again, the principle *cuius regio, eius religio* governed their acts. However, their methods and timing were different.

Stalin could conduct his policies with a coherence which Western leaders lacked until they had enlisted the sort of consensus which their systems required. Even goals varied: the victors from the West would settle for more sophisticated forms of political control than those congenial to Stalinist rule. None the less, neither side could or would escape the simple fact that Stalin himself stated, in a never-too-often quoted conversation with Milovan Djilas, that the partition of Europe was not negotiated but coincided with the military presence of the victors at the end of hostilities. It should be added that those lines of demarcation were not only to become national boundaries, but also indicated the social and political criteria of reconstruction. From then on there was never any policy of roll-back on the part of the superpowers, except in the dogmatic formulations of the Soviet leadership and in the more exalted propositions of a handful of Republican politicians (among them John Foster Dulles and Ronald Reagan). There was never any lack of practical reasons for this sort of mutual appeasement (a much-abused word which in this case is appropriate). Even those who *ex post* would accuse Roosevelt of pusillanimity shared priorities dominant in 1944–46 which did not include democratic rule in Eastern Europe.

The foremost preoccupation of the American leadership at the time was, not unreasonably, to end the war as quickly as possible with a minimum number of American casualties. In particular those bent on American world leadership in future years had learned the Wilsonian lesson, fearing an isolationist reaction that would hamper what they saw as the necessary assumption of post-war responsibilities. Not even the most hardened *ante litteram* cold warrior would have been able to envisage a pre-emptive attack on Soviet lines in Central Europe, and nothing short of such an attack – certainly not greater diplomatic firmness at Yalta or elsewhere – would have had any effect. But, quite apart from these practical reasons, the United States did not make the liberation of Eastern Europe a top priority because it was not in its national interest, as then understood, to do so. It is a major mistake of many orthodox historians to believe that this was so, because undue priority was given to flimsy issues such as the universal character of the United Nations with its full Soviet participation. More important to Washington was Soviet help in the war in Japan until the atom bomb was dropped.

Nevertheless the main drift of events both at Yalta and Potsdam guaranteed two basic outcomes of the war which corresponded to very substantial American as well as Soviet interests: the elimination of Germany as a factor in the European balance of power, and a hierarchy of nations which consolidated the leadership of the emerging super-powers within their prospective spheres of influence. From the American point of view, consciously or unconsciously, the sacrifice of Eastern European countries as a *cordon sanitaire* to the historically founded Russian obsession with security was a reasonable price to pay. It would in fact turn out to strengthen American hegemony over Western Europe. Quite realistically, the Soviet Union was not perceived as the main threat to American post-war ambitions as long as it was kept out of Western Europe. It was identified as such only when it became necessary to justify a major programme of expenditure based on foreign policy, including the Marshall Plan, and the establishment of a multitude of foreign bases.

Naturally there was a price to pay for such an unwritten pact between the superpowers, but from a strictly American point of view this price was prevalently ideological.

The United States had to accept the abandonment of the Eastern European population to a communist dictatorship imposed from outside with only minority support (which varied in degree from country to country) from anti-German resistance movements. The Soviet Union once more confirmed its allegiance to the principle of socialism in one country at the expense not only of revolution, but of social and political reform elsewhere in Europe. Western Communist parties were irre-parably hampered by their fidelity to Moscow, which at the same time destroyed their credibility as national reformers and, in various instances, pursued agreements with the West over their heads. Even socialists were forced to accept the constraints imposed on internal as well as foreign policy by the hardening division of Europe that gradually emerged in the post-war period. The cleavage was not only territorial and military, but also ideological. The superpowers renounced any serious attempt to spread their values to the rest of Europe but, in so doing, also put them into an iron cast. On each side of the wall democracy became incompatible with fundamental social change and socialism with democracy.

In this way not only was the possibility of a hypothetical common ground eliminated for the foreseeable future, but the original revolutionary values of the two great powers were frozen and distorted. While military confrontation remained peculiar to Europe, the separation between democracy and social transformation became a fundamental principle which the superpowers eagerly expanded and enforced in other parts of the world. Although in this respect Soviet policy has been more subtle, it has shared a fundamental hostility to genuinely non-aligned states or movements. The United States has in various instances proved its preference for an unequivocal allegiance to the Soviet camp to any sort of independent reformism (most recently in Nicaragua). When, in such disparate places as Czechoslovakia and Chile, serious attempts were made to develop a socialist democracy in opposition to superpower domination, repression was ruthless and the passivity or even connivance of the superpower not directly concerned was equally evident.

The post-war settlement in Europe between the emerging superpowers was possible because it was not they but the European populations who were to pay the immediate price for it. This was of course particularly true for the populations of Central Europe, which had been physically decimated in the last phase of the world war. The Eastern European populations were made to renounce their sovereignty, democratic rights and individual liberties (where they had existed before the German invasion). Police states were established under foreign control. National bureaucracies, dependent on Soviet political support and military presence, ruled through centralized governments in the name of Communist parties which did not enjoy majority consensus. Even the economic relations established by Moscow were initially of an exploitative nature.

Of course, things were different in Western Europe. Political reconstruction was conducted according to principles of liberal democracy, even in the defeated states. Generous aid was granted by the United States: although it corresponded to the humanitarian feelings of many of those who provided it, it was basically an effective way of preventing radical social and political change and, above all, it was an overriding economic necessity. The American economy, to meet the needs of postwar conversion, had to expand its capital and commerce abroad. The far-sighted planners responsible for American economic foreign policy clearly understood that this could not be done without the reconstruction of European industry. The Marshall Plan became the apex of a hegemonic policy, whereby control in Europe was based primarily on meeting basic economic needs and forming a political consensus. Military presence, propaganda, and interference in the political processes of individual countries were of course important, but not decisive. It all amounted to the sort of benign limited sovereignty which,

in a later period and in a different context, has been called
Finlandization.

Both the Soviet Union and the United States came to exercise control
over their respective parts of a globally defeated Europe. As I have
already pointed out on other occasions, American control was
hegemonic because it enjoyed the support of a majority of the populations in question, who received a number of tangible benefits. Soviet
control took the form of domination because it lacked the economic
resources and the political flexibility to ensure a consensus which could
take the place of force.[6]

None the less national sovereignty in Europe, both East and West,
was severely curtailed. The establishment of military alliances justified
the permanent presence of Soviet and American troops in Europe after
the end of the post-war occupation. All European nations lost control of
their defence and security systems (France, under the leadership of
Charles de Gaulle, had to leave the military structure of NATO in order
to regain such control). The prerogatives of these curtailed forms of
independence did not include abandonment of military alliances or a
fundamental change of social and political systems. These limitations
were dramatized in the East when attempts to move beyond them were
ruthlessly repressed. In the West, the same limits were enforced with
subtler means, especially in the North Atlantic region. In the Mediterranean countries, whenever any real or potential threat to the status quo
has emerged, American intervention has been more blatant, even to the
point of supporting existing dictatorships (Franco, Salazar, Metaxas),
promoting new ones in the face of political and social change (more
recently, Greece and Turkey), or manipulating and curtailing democratic systems (Italy). Why did European nations accept a settlement
which contradicted centuries of recent history spent in the struggle for,
and celebration of, the principles of self-determination and national
independence? The obvious answer is that they had no choice. The
division of Europe and its dependence on outside control constituted
the outcome of two world wars caused by the incapacity of its components to agree upon a stable balance of power. The destruction of
Europe was not only a physical fact.

However, it should not be forgotten that the partition of Europe was
also the extension of the partition of Germany; that the impotence of
Europe was also the consequence of the impotence of Germany. It was
Germany that had twice in the same century upset the continental
balance of power, invaded peaceful neighbours, imposed alien rule and
exterminated entire populations.

A unified Germany represented a potential threat that the Soviet
Union was not ready to face in the aftermath of a German invasion of its

home soil. The existence of the Morgenthau Plan proves that the
Americans were also affected by this sort of preoccupation. Even when
it became clear that the reconstruction of the German economy was
necessary to the industrialized world as a whole, the division of
Germany permitted such a reconstruction in forms compatible with the
social systems and the security of the two superpowers. It was Germany
that, until the outcome of the Second World War was settled, had
constituted the main threat not only to the Soviet Union but also to
those other nations which, to varying degrees, suffered from the war. It
was therefore the partition of Germany that, to a considerable degree,
legitimized the post-war settlement, because it also met the aspirations
of those who were to suffer from it. It seemed to remove, once and for
all, the German threat.

This solution was all the more solid because it was not the outcome of
a treaty, like Versailles, but of a process which consolidated the
American and Soviet military presence in occupied territory. Therefore,
the integration of western and eastern Germany into separate spheres of
interest controlled by the superpowers became at the same time the
definitive elimination of a German threat and the cornerstone of the
bipolar order. What appeared as a historic achievement gave an
apparent justification to the past and future sacrifices of millions of
people. At the same time, the seeds of a future conflict of ever greater
magnitude were planted in the graveyard of the Third Reich.

It is significant that the subsequent crises over Berlin have been highly
dramatic in their emergence but stabilizing in their outcome. It is difficult to know whether Stalin seriously wanted to eliminate Berlin as a
Western outpost in East German territory. The airlift ordered by Harry
Truman made it clear that this was not going to happen. Therefore,
Berlin remained a source of political embarrassment to the Eastern bloc,
above all because it highlighted Western national well-being in stark
contract to conditions prevailing in the whole of Eastern Germany. For
this reason, the construction of the Berlin Wall was welcomed by the
Soviet Union and, at the same time, was accepted by the United States
as a solution entirely consistent with its interests: it confirmed the
division of Germany and the acceptance of the presence of Western
troops; it reinforced the Cold War rhetoric, making the symbol of the
Iron Curtain a visible fact; and it demonstrated the national and ideological weakness of Soviet rule to those in Europe still receptive to the
myth of Soviet revolution and wartime vitality. All in all, Berlin is an
excellent example of the overriding importance of unwritten agreements
concerning dramatic but short-lasting conflicts between the superpowers. Again and again, up to the time of the Kennedy administration,
the German issue was central to the co-operation of the superpowers

because, more than any other foreign-policy issue, it legitimized their global authority beyond the quadripartite arrangements immediately subsequent to the war.

The other basic legitimizing factor of the bipolar system is nuclear weaponry. Readers of contemporary history have been surprised not by the rejection of the Baruch Plan by the American government but by the very fact that it was conceived. How could the Americans even contemplate the possibility of renouncing the advantage they had achieved through the successful experimentation with and actual use of the atomic weapon, in their relationship to the Soviet Union? How does one explain the contrast between this attitude and the persevering intransigence in pursuing a non-proliferation treaty in subsequent years? But above all it should be noted that the proclamation of the Truman doctrine and even the decision to form NATO preceded (chronologically) and were all in all independent of Soviet acquisition of nuclear weapons. Although popular emotions in the United States were considerable (as the Rosenberg trial and McCarthyism indicated), government and establishment reactions were, under the circumstances, more relaxed than could have been expected, if the modification in the balance of power existing between the two superpowers is taken into consideration.

The point is that the inauguration of what was to be called the balance of terror strengthened and legitimized the post-war alignments to a decisive degree. From then on the division and limited sovereignty of the European peoples, as imposed by the post-war settlement, became the necessary sacrifice to an overriding general interest in protecting peace in a world where Mutual Assured Destruction had become a material possibility. Furthermore, if the possession of nuclear weapons shortened the distance between the superpowers, it simultaneously widened the gap between them and their respective lesser allies and satellites. From this moment on, the United States and the Soviet Union acquired a sort of politically reserved territory – the nuclear issue – to which they could claim exclusive access in the general interest of peacekeeping. Even the remnants of the wartime alliance, based on a quadrangular relationship, were swept away by the overriding interest in a direct dialogue between those who held the keys to peace or general destruction. Within the context of their respective alliances each superpower could claim a practically unchecked right to establish *de facto* extraterritorial missile bases, air and sea ports, with all the accompanying security apparatus. Even the presence of American and Soviet troops, which many years after the end of the war could have been considered an arbitrary continuation of military occupation, became in fact the necessary guarantee that the superpowers would not use European territory as a nuclear battlefield. The continued presence of these troops in Europe became an essential link between European security and the defence system of the superpowers. The occupiers had become peace hostages, while not renouncing any of the prerogatives of occupiers.

As a consequence, conflicts within the alliances (particularly within NATO, about which we have more direct information) did not arise from any desire of the lesser allies for denuclearization. On the contrary, the presence of nuclear weapons on the European continent was considered a permanent fact of life, and governments were on the whole favourable to any form of deployment which strengthened the deterrent. The change in NATO strategy from massive retaliation to flexible response met a certain amount of opposition, but not primarily because it increased the deployment of tactical nuclear weapons and opened the road to medium-range missiles. What worried European critics was that the very flexibility of the strategy would permit the possibility of a limited nuclear war confined to the European continent. This preoccupation is based on significant historical precedents. In both world wars the United States' participation was decisive, belated and confined to foreign soil. It is therefore not surprising that the USA's European allies have been partial to a strategy that requires an early involvement of American troops and a commitment of the American mainland to the principle of deterrence. However, such preoccupations have been a further incentive towards closer Atlantic and military integration, as well as an increase of nuclear weapons at all levels. Even the recent opposition of some European governments to the Gorbachev–Reagan treaty abolishing medium-range missiles belongs in part to the same logic.

The only alternatives to this general tendency have been the French independent deterrent and the activity of the peace movements, which have stressed the risk of increasing nuclear targets in Europe and advocated unilateral acts of disarmament as a viable alternative. The peace movement in the fifties was a clear extension of Soviet foreign policy, but even the credibility of the contemporary peace movement has suffered from the impossibility of developing independently on a major scale in Eastern Europe.

As long as the peace debate is confined to military aspects and does not focus on political causes and consequences of the military status quo, technical and strategic arguments prevail in the name of the principle of deterrence. It is true, as we shall see, that an excessive acceleration of the arms race and its negative effects on the economies of the superpowers permit interludes of detente based on arms control (such as the limited Test Ban Treaty of 1963, SALT I and II, the ABM Treaty) and, more recently, disarmament (the INF Treaty). It is also true that

there is a growing awareness that the dynamism and sophistication of
the arms race increase the risk of a nuclear conflict occurring by mistake.
However, such considerations are in themselves insufficient to undermine the principle of deterrence as the only possible foundation of
peace. Even disarmament agreements more important than the
Washington treaty will remain precarious as long as most people are
convinced that it is the threat of Mutual Assured Destruction that has
prevented a conflict in Europe for more than forty years. Yet as long as the
political equilibrium stemming from the Second World War remains
intact, there is no alternative to the precarious peace offered by mutual
deterrence and the superpower condominium that controls it.

It was no accident that the superpowers tacitly agreed in the past to
the post-war settlement and the confrontational build-up it has generated. As I have tried to explain in an earlier essay:

> Two kinds of international conflict exist in the world today: one could be
> called the theoretical type of conflict and the other, the actual type. A theo-
> retical conflict is that embodied in the opposition between the United States
> and the Soviet Union, between East and West. This is expressed in the desire
> of the superpowers to make the rest of the world choose sides through military
> alliances, thus reciprocally justifying the arms race. This type of conflict is
> theoretical in the sense that its logical consequence, nuclear war, has not yet
> happened, in spite of the fact that the superpowers tend to reduce every actual
> conflict to terms fitting this polarity.
>
> Actual conflicts, by contrast, arise when nations or peoples oppose the
> hierarchy based on the bipolarity of the superpowers, by pursuing inde-
> pendent policies even within the alliance system.
>
> Obviously, it is the threat posed by the theoretical conflict which permits
> the dominant powers to control the actual conflicts. It strengthens the military
> blocs; it stimulates the escalation of the arms race; it forces Third World
> nations to sacrifice autonomy for the sake of avoiding nuclear conflagration.
> This theoretical conflict is in itself a weapon to reinforce nuclear monopoly,
> limit the actual conflicts and maintain current power relationships. Although
> the actual conflicts are by no means confined to Europe, they are rooted in
> the division of Europe.[7]

If this is so, the strength of the bipolar system should not be underestimated. Not only has it ensured an – albeit precarious – nuclear
peace, but the stakes invested in it by the superpowers are truly formidable. In fact it is only within this system that the United States and
the Soviet Union could survive as such. Only a peace founded on arms
can ensure the supremacy of nations which are militarily supreme, but
have gradually been losing ground in many other ways.

Furthermore, it should be borne in mind that something more than
the position of the superpowers in the international hierarchy is at stake.

The East–West confrontation (that is, the theoretical conflict) has not only consolidated American and Soviet domination abroad but has also deeply affected the social and political structure of both countries. Recent historical scholarship has selected the Korean War as a turning point in recent American history. According to this analysis, it was this first American intervention on a large scale that made military mobilization and vast expenditure for foreign-policy purposes a permanent feature of American life. However, this would not have been possible had not the invasion of South Korea been considered as part of the East–West confrontation in accordance with parameters that had already been established with the Truman doctrine, the Marshall Plan, and the formation of NATO. In the same period (as Alan Wolfe has convincingly argued[8]) a bipartisan coalition emerged on the basis of a programme of domestic and foreign stabilization. The politics of productivity at home and abroad required social discipline, an expansive economic policy and high military and foreign expenditures.

What Dwight Eisenhower would call the military–industrial complex – as a set of links between military policy and defence contractors – was only part of the picture. The so-called Soviet threat – all the more effective because it corresponded to actual forms of Soviet domination around the world – served numerous domestic purposes: imposing a limit on what was considered legitimate social and political conflict; strengthening those sectors of private interests and government connected with national security; justifying various forms of presence and intervention abroad. Long before the existence of the imperial presidency was widely proclaimed, the so-called Cold War affected the powers of the executive, especially in its relationship to the legislative power. In other words, the theoretical conflict perpetuated a sort of national emergency which had the traditional centralizing and stabilizing effects of such occurrences. It should not be forgotten that we are dealing with a continuum rather than with a new state of affairs. The Depression, at least in its first phase after the election of Roosevelt, the advent of the Second World War first in Europe and then in the Pacific, the dramatic break with the one-time war ally (but originally a symbol of social unrest and subversion) perpetuated a condition which could be used with advantage by all those in positions of power and responsibility.

Not dissimilar were the effects of bipolarism on the Soviet regime. After the obsession with external attack on the Revolution which justified the transition from Leninism to Stalinism, the emergence of the Third Reich helped to consolidate and justify the harsh methods adopted by the Soviet dictator. After the destruction of Nazi Germany, American imperialism was badly needed as a stabilizing myth that justified the subjugation of foreign countries, vast military expenditure in a country in which people barely had what was indispensable, and the continued curtailment of any forms of individual and collective liberties and democratic rights. All in all, the continued militarization of Soviet society strengthened not only the armed forces but also the security apparatus and the *nomenklatura*, while emphasizing the need for social discipline connected with war production.

To sum up: the bipolar system provides connivance as well as a mutual threat which is essential to the perpetuation of the internal stability of each superpower as well as to their capacity to extend and consolidate their influence and control abroad. It would, however, be a mistake to assume that these goals are achieved exclusively through tension. Forty years of history have demonstrated that it is, rather, 'the alternate use of tension and detente which strengthens the privileged position of the dominant powers'.[9] Too much tension, apart from other obvious risks, could produce the impression that Moscow and Washington are not able to manage the world in a responsible manner. Too long periods of detente could destroy the foundation of the bipolar discipline which is based on emergency. In this sense detente has to be managed from above, by the same centres of power within the United States and Soviet Union that have been risking a collision in a previous phase of their relationship. Even if the effects of detente could and should be calculated and negotiated, the change from a phase of tension to one of detente has always been triggered by a particular state of distress of one superpower, to which the other responds in a positive manner, to stabilize the bipolar system while hoping to gain some further advantage.

In retrospect, Camp David in 1959 (but also the abrupt interruption of the dialogue at the Paris Summit after the U2 incident) coincided with the beginning of an internal crisis which ended with the removal of Khrushchev from the position of First Secretary of the CPSU. Likewise, detente in the seventies was a response to the United States' need to negotiate a limitation in the arms race after the defeat in Vietnam. It is no coincidence that this process culminated in the months preceding the resignation of Richard Nixon as a consequence of the Watergate crisis. The present phase of negotiations between the United States and Mikhail Gorbachev is perhaps more promising than the previous instances because it has so evidently been triggered by internal difficulties that have affected both superpowers simultaneously, as we shall see in more detail.

It should be noted that while detente produces agreements of varying substance and importance between its protagonists, it invariably strengthens (at least temporarily) their control over domestic policies and within their respective spheres of interest. Khrushchev survived politically beyond the missile crisis. Nixon was temporarily rescued from the effects of Watergate by his dialogues with Moscow and Beijing. The treaty Reagan negotiated with Gorbachev distracted American public opinion from the Irangate scandal, other foreign-policy failures and the negative effects of the budget and balance-of-payments deficits on the American economy. The very symbolism of summit meetings strengthens the two leaders in the eyes of domestic audiences and other countries who become more willing to delegate powers to them. In the subsequent crisis a similar delegation of power will be justified by the need not to rock the boat when the weather is stormy. After all, confrontation and detente are two different but complementary phases of the bipolar system.

What we have learned to call detente does not in itself imperil the *raison d'être* of the bipolar relationship. First of all, detente, just as much as confrontation, is conducted by the superpowers. Lesser allies are supposed to be content with the temporary lessening of the danger of a direct conflict. American reactions to Willy Brandt's version of detente, in the form of Ostpolitik, are eloquent in this respect.

Secondly, detente is no obstacle to internal repression within each sphere of influence. On the contrary, some of the most brutal forms of normalization have taken place in periods of detente or, at least, not in the context of East–West confrontation. The invasion of Hungary followed the 20th Congress of the CPSU. The invasion of Czechoslovakia took place when American attention was directed elsewhere. The *coup d'état* in Chile coincided with one of the high points of Soviet–American dialogue. Only the more recent normalization of Poland coincided with the verbal animosity which was typical of the first phase of the Reagan presidency. Its timing, however, was quite independent of the state of US–Soviet relations. It should be added that acts of normalization do not provoke any serious retaliation on the part of the superpower not directly concerned, which remains content with the ideological and propaganda benefits gained. Concern for repressed populations is prudent and purely verbal (in the interest of detente). It can therefore be said that a third basic ground rule of the bipolar system is not upset by detente: superpowers do not seriously try to subvert each other's spheres of influence, at least in Europe. In the post-war period the Soviet Union has discouraged any revolutionary aspirations of Communist parties in the West. Even in the Third World, Communist parties have always been very careful in their support for national liberation movements, especially in their initial phases. Soviet support comes after they have gained state power. More recently, attempts to tie international terrorism in the West to the Soviet Union have been totally unsuccessful. Likewise, Western support of dissidents in Eastern Europe has been minimal and essentially confined to the realm of propaganda.

If these basic rules do not change, either in periods of confrontation or during detente, should we conclude that the latter yields no benefits to third parties concerned? It should not be forgotten that some initiatives – again Willy Brandt's Ostpolitik – would not have been possible except in the context of detente. Furthermore, such a conclusion would underestimate the strength of detente, which is rooted in the decrease of the danger of war. Therefore, the conclusion is contradictory: detente is beneficial to peace because it lessens the risks of war as long as it lasts; it buys time. But in the long run it strengthens a system – the bipolar system – which deprives whole populations of their rights, strengthens the military alliances, has accelerated the arms race and in the long term increases the dangers to peace.

It does not necessarily follow that the present dialogue between the superpowers is simply a cyclical phase of this bipolar relationship. We are heading towards a fundamental crisis of the bipolar system which could push us beyond detente as we have known it in the past.

The international system rests upon the dominant role of the United States and the Soviet Union. Their decline, which began during the sixties, has entered a new and acute phase. It is not difficult to predict that the effects on the bipolar system as a whole are going to be devastating. The outcome is both promising and extremely dangerous. The superpowers' decline is, of course, relative. Both the United States and the Soviet Union are, in absolute terms, richer and stronger than they were at the end of the Second World War. But if we compare their strength and consequent influence to that of other parts of the world in that period with the present balance of power, we realize that a process of fundamental change has been taking place for quite some time – or, to put it in different terms, the outcome of what I have called the actual conflict is for the first time uncertain, to say the least.

The most obvious change has been economic. After the war the greater part of Europe was physically destroyed. In spite of all its institutional shortcomings and bickering over economic issues, today the European Community has a larger GNP and share of world trade than the United States. Its productivity, though inferior to Japanese standards, is higher. While Europeans have improved their competitiveness, military investments have afforded a dynamic but limited progress to American technology. The size of the balance-of-payments and budget deficits are a permanent threat to the stability of the American economy as a whole. Meanwhile the progress of the nations defeated in the war has, to a considerable extent, restored the previous economic hierarchy of nations. A dynamic process of industrialization has affected several areas of the Third World.

On the other hand the Soviet economy is stagnant, badly dependent on the import of Western technology, and burdened by the support it has to offer some of its satellites for the sake of political stability: the last remnants of a traditional form of colonialism, where political control has to be paid for instead of yielding economic benefits. The burden of military expense is even more cumbersome because the total Soviet economy is so much smaller than its American counterpart.

Naturally, this change is the net result of a long process during which the United States has lost the capacity to regulate the world economy as a whole, as was sanctioned by the Bretton Woods agreements. In the early 1970s the American government, having financed the Vietnam War by exporting inflation, ended the convertibility of the dollar and ceased to act as a regulating power of the world economy as a whole. A comprehensive history of the oil crisis has yet to be written, yet there is no doubt that its significance was not only a long-overdue assertion of power by the producers, but also a substantial weakening of those parts of the industrialized world which were consumers, without being significant producers of oil (mainly Western Europe and Japan).

This temporary advantage of the United States in relation to the countries which it by then regarded primarily as industrialized competitors was not enough to arrest the US decline. Meanwhile, the Vietnam War had transformed the policy of containment into a sort of trap which its early critics – Walter Lippmann, but also George Kennan (who soon came to feel like a sorcerer's apprentice) – had predicted from the beginning.[10] An extended and rigid interpretation of the Truman doctrine had drawn the United States into a mainland war on the Asian continent. The Wilsonian tradition, coupled with a natural tendency of American imperial interests to support subservient clients all over the world, led to what psychoanalysts call a grandiose fantasy which Democratic administrations have found it particularly hard to abandon. The Vietnam war was waged and lost on the basis of the conviction that a colonial war could be fought while exporting the American system. The combination of intransigent resistance on the part of the Vietnamese and a dramatic cleavage on the home front led to a traumatizing defeat which pre-empted any significant future use of American troops in foreign countries. The so-called Vietnam syndrome was and still is of great importance because it has nothing to do with any lack of resolve on the part of this or that administration, as the experience of the Reagan administration conclusively proved. It is not the single politician or institution, but the body politic as a whole that suffers from a sort of schizophrenia: while the majority continues to subscribe to an ideology of American primacy which frustration has made more strident, it will not foot the bill in terms of American human lives and economic sacrifices.

American foreign policy since Vietnam has been a tenacious but
fruitless search for some means of bridging this gap between fantasies
and harsh realities. Only President Carter, spurred on by the Watergate
scandal, tried to get the nation to accept the limits of American global
power during the first part of his administration. When it became clear
that Third World revolutions (Angola, Ethiopia, Mozambique,
Zimbabwe, Nicaragua) would not wait and that the Soviet Union was
eager to take advantage of American weakness, he had to change course
and was left without a policy. The way was open for a doctor who, far
from explaining to the patient the true nature of his disease, was more
than willing to provide increasing doses of morphine.

From the beginning the answer to the Vietnam syndrome provided by
the Reagan administration was first and foremost rhetorical: it was
claimed that the disappointments of American foreign policy were
caused not by the disproportion between intention and capabilities, but
rather by a lack of resolve. According to this interpretation, the Vietnam
War was lost because the United States did not dare to win. Therefore
the quest for primacy (not only containment) should not only be maintained but stepped up, and capabilities (mostly psychological and political, according to this reading of contemporary history) increased to
match the goal.

Initially, the targets of this policy were chosen with prudence. The
objective was to 'win one' in order to educate the Reagan constituency
(only 29 per cent of those who had a right to vote, but enough to
provide a 'landslide' in a country where little more than half the adult
population nowadays choose to exercise this right) to pay the price for
this renewed form of containment. This is why El Salvador suddenly
became the centrepiece of American foreign-policy strategy. When
Congress and public opinion (as well as good sense, probably located
among the military ranks of the Pentagon) would not permit the direct
American intervention necessary to affect the scales of power between
the Salvadorian military and the guerrillas, the Reagan administration
sought out (possibly produced, but we have no evidence to this effect) a
situation small enough for the American public to bear direct military
intervention. But even in Grenada it became necessary for the administration to exclude media coverage, thus setting an important precedent
as a further lesson of the Vietnam War.

As a third step of its Central American strategy, the Reagan administration embarked on a policy of support for the Nicaraguan Contras
which turned out to be politically costly on the home front and devoid of
any significant military dividends. In terms of foreign policy the only net
effect of the Central American exercise has been to make the
Sandinistas and other opposition forces in Central America more

authoritarian and, above all, more dependent on Cuban and Soviet support. Meanwhile, the Reagan administration did its best to hamper any diplomatic effort by its traditional allies in that region, be it the Contadora group or the Central American states, led by President Arias of Costa Rica. If one views the whole policy from a perspective of East–West confrontation (virtual conflict) it is so incomprehensible as to require a second look. In terms of actual conflict – where the real adversaries are no longer the Soviet Union but Western Europe, the Socialist International, progressive Catholics and Latin American independence – this policy at least begins to make sense. The immediate purpose is not to overthrow the Sandinistas but to destroy any form of government in the Western hemisphere which is genuinely non-aligned, pluralist and committed to social change. The reasons for intervention are the same ones that moved the Nixon administration to conspire against Allende, and the minimal outcome consciously or unconsciously pursued, as a lesser evil, is a second Cuba (if a second Chile is not available). At least the lesson will have been brought home that in the present phase no more appealing model outside North American influence is historically available in this part of the world.

After all, this could have been the real purpose of the Reagan doctrine (as analysed by Fred Halliday[11]). In a sense it stemmed from the Nixon doctrine, originally proclaimed to cover the American retreat from Vietnam. Both are what we call in Italian *scelte obbligate* (forced choices): if Congress and public opinion are not willing to send American boys to fight abroad, the only remedy is to get local forces to do the job. Americans have been less successful than the Soviet Union in fighting wars by proxy. The South Koreans would not have made it on their own, and the South Vietnamese never seriously tried. The Reagan doctrine has been less ambitious than the Nixon doctrine: it was not applied to full-scale wars of containment but provided support for opposition guerrillas, with the immediate purpose of not permitting the legitimate government to develop its policies in normal conditions. Therefore it has been more successful than the Nixon doctrine. The problem is that in both cases American allies lack genuine popular support. Their effort therefore becomes artificial, their methods terroristic and their character and composition have a mercenary nature. The Soviet Union has been more successful in applying the equivalents of the Nixon and Reagan doctrines because they have had better allies fighting for them. Liberation movements fighting against unpopular military or oligarchic governments make good use of external support. It is no coincidence that Afghanistan is the case in which the Reagan doctrine has been most successful, because here the roles of the superpowers are reversed.

A further problem with the Reagan doctrine is that the lack of legitimacy of its beneficiaries has been perceived also in the United States. In the case of the Nicaraguan Contras the administration was forced to use unorthodox means and distorted legal devices (so-called humanitarian aid) in order not to abandon its policies. Also from this point of view the Reagan administration invented nothing, but merely continued practices that stem from the constraints imposed on American foreign policy by the outcome of the Vietnam War and the enduring opposition of Congress and the majority of opinion to any outright use of American ground forces.

In spite of the outcome of the Church and Pike investigations in the mid seventies, the need for a greater flexibility in pursuing a global foreign policy has been such as to induce American administrations to lower the threshold of covert action and various forms of illegal intervention abroad. In the aftermath of Irangate it became apparent to a fairly wide public that these forms of intervention have generated the growth of a national security establishment, rooted in the executive, with important allies in private interest groups but with ramifications which make it similar to a parallel government with priorities and means of its own. President Reagan has been an important factor in this kind of development because he contributed a unique blend of willingness to delegate responsibility and personal rhetoric. When Reagan accused the Soviet Union of 'lying, stealing and cheating' he indirectly justified similar practices within his own government. His emphasis on anti-terrorist action served the same purpose.

In the first report of the Trilateral Commission, Samuel Huntington wrote that the conflict between American constitutional values and national security had become irreconcilable. More than a decade later, the conflict is still present. Although government illegality has increased, the guardians of the constitutional tradition have not been disarmed.

Edward Gibbon identified the decline of the Roman Empire in its incapacity to respect its own laws. A return to the law is perhaps still possible. What is probably gone for ever is the hegemonic phase of American foreign policy. When this role was first envisaged by Woodrow Wilson, and even after the Second World War, the United States identified itself with a world order and acted in a legislative and also in a jurisdictional capacity, brokering conflicts between other nations. The United Nations and its associated agencies, the International Monetary Fund, even the regional alliances after the split with the Soviet Union, were all to a great extent the products of American policy.

In these institutions the United States controlled a majority which could transform American interests into a general policy, claiming a validity *erga omnes*. To counteract this the Soviet Union had to expose its weakness by resorting to the veto power. Today, instead, the American government has abandoned UNESCO and has been condemned twice by the International Court of the Hague for its Nicaraguan activities. In the UN it is frequently faced with hostile majorities in the General Assembly, against which the US itself now has to take refuge in the veto power. The United States even has difficulty handling its own alliance system.

It should of course be noted that the capacity to legislate, settle international controversies, build and rely on international institutions are all hegemonic prerogatives which only empires at the peak of their power have been able to exercise. The trouble with American foreign policy in its present phase is that it has not been able to adapt to a new situation, of great but more limited power, perhaps because it refuses to recognize it. The Soviet Union lost its hegemonic claims the moment it settled for the Stalinist formula of socialism in one country, and ever since then it has exercised domination in different parts of the world with varying success. Domination is unilateral, and does not require the sort of internal and external consensus which hegemony claims. However, precisely as Samuel Huntington foresaw, domination can be carried out only through an institutional framework in which national security becomes the unquestioned priority of government action; something quite different from the system of checks and balances the founding fathers provided for. Some steps have been taken in this direction, from the Johnson administration on, though the Reagan administration went further than its predecessors: a *de facto* restriction of the electoral body, a foreign-policy and security apparatus running amok under the theoretical control of the presidency, some limitation of congressional authority. It is likely that this tendency reached its apex and a turning point with Irangate. However, it has never been strong enough to undermine prerogatives which are firmly embedded in the American constitution.

American opinion has been prepared to accept unilateral action abroad without too much concern about the agreement of the affected populations, but it is not prepared to give up its right, through Congress or otherwise, to control and disapprove of whatever action the executive is about to take. This limitation has proved to be, at least up until the present, an insurmountable obstacle to American foreign policy based on unilateral actions which do not have popular support in the United States.

Within these limits the Reagan administration was unable to formulate a coherent foreign policy, but rather interspersed its rhetoric with a number of specific actions. It would, however, be a mistake to attribute this policy exclusively to the Reagan presidency. Most observers agree that the most recent period of confrontation began in the second half of the Carter administration, as a result of a series of setbacks which had marked the post-Vietnam period. Setbacks in the Third World as well as Soviet initiatives (SS-20s, Afghanistan, Poland) helped to revive American aggressiveness and gave a renewed but temporary credibility to the Soviet threat. The 'loss' of Iran with the capture of the American hostages in Tehran set the stage in a suitable manner for a confrontational policy on the part of an incoming administration which needed to free itself, in the eyes of its more militant supporters, from the legacy of the Nixon–Kissinger era. What the Brezhnev doctrine did not offer, a new and more aggressive rhetoric had to supply. 'The empire of evil' and other similar expressions were supposed to prop up a bipolar policy which could not be sustained in a prolonged atmosphere of dialogue with the Soviet Union. The theorization of international terrorism lumped together any act of terrorism with the action of national liberation movements hostile to American imperial interests, under the supposed leadership of the Soviet Union.

In spite of its absurdity, such a theory again served the purpose of sustaining a bipolar interpretation of the world which strongly reminds one of the 'international communism' so popular during the fifties. The function of such simplifications, past and present, is to justify a policy of intervention against a unified enemy. As we shall see, the weakening of the proto-enemy encourages a more strident rhetoric and more hazardous theories.

Here it should be noticed that the direction of the prevailing policy has become more orientated towards the Third World and to the Middle East in particular. The intellectual climate of this radicalization, primarily directed against Third World countries, is the outcome of a political realignment concerning foreign policy in the United States. Some particularly influential sectors of opinion, centred in journalistic and academic circles close to Israel, have abandoned their traditionally moderate view of the East–West relationship. Probably as a consequence of the growth of Arab influence in the United States, the Jewish community and its intellectual allies have become convinced that American solidarity with (or rather subservience to) the Israeli government could no longer be safeguarded as a separate issue. The continuity of the pro-Israel policy required a general radicalization of American foreign policy. In a climate of greater tension the United States would have to rely on Israel as a reliable outpost of Western interests in a particularly turbulent as well as crucial area of the Third World, on the basis of what Alexander Haig called a strategic consensus between the two governments.

This development has involved the Washington government further in the Middle Eastern imbroglio but has also made it less able to formulate a coherent policy for the region as a whole. In addition, the American incapacity to undertake military operations where American lives are at stake seriously hampered the Reagan administration. The intervention in Lebanon ended dismally after the marines were forced to withdraw after a successful assault by Shiite terrorists. Current naval operations in the Persian Gulf entail similar risks. Incidentally, in both these cases the most important achievement on the part of Washington has been to destroy the Middle Eastern policy of the European Community by involving three of its governments in operations, led by the United States, which were considered hostile by most Arab countries.

Otherwise, American military activities in the Middle East – notably against Libya – have shown a tendency, typical of the post-Vietnam era (but with roots in traditional American warfare), to forgo a more permanent military presence in favour of excessive and unilateral use of military technologies. The bombing of Tripoli, preceded by manipulation of information, subsequently exposed by government sources, had no effect except to strengthen the domestic position of Colonel Qaddafi, embarrassing traditional American allies in the Mediterranean and again dramatizing the absence of a coherent and comprehensive policy. The illusion of strength, sought for domestic purposes, was clearly bought at the expense of more permanent American interests in the region.

Another important characteristic of American policy in this region has been its vulnerability to manipulation by its local allies. After the report of the Tower Commission, it is no secret that Israeli influence was important, if not decisive, in convincing the Reagan administration to trade arms for hostages with the Iranian government, having accused it of being responsible for terrorist activities. Subsequently, as Theodore Draper has convincingly claimed, the Kuwaiti government succeeded in involving the United States in naval operations, this time directed against Iran. In this manner the Washington government at first became a tool of Israeli tactics which tended to strengthen the radical component of its Muslim enemies and, subsequently, of the Arab moderates, when the Reagan administration was forced to move in the opposite direction by an outraged public opinion.

To sum up: the vicissitudes of the Reagan presidency have dramatized what was latent in past years. Not only does American hegemony belong to the past, but the occupants of the White House are finding it increasingly difficult to steer a transitional course compatible with the contradictory moods of American public opinion.[12] The internal crisis is seriously affected, if not caused, by an overextended foreign policy which has inflated the role of the executive. Watergate and Irangate are serious symptoms, but the gradual shrinkage of the electoral body and the political as well as socioeconomic exclusion of a substantial part of the population (the two Americas of which Mario Cuomo spoke at the 1984 Democratic convention) point to a situation in which the very principle of democratic government is seriously undermined. Political and cultural moods have serious effects. In the sixties the left all over the West prematurely denounced the end of democracy. Where are they now, when the disease is far more acute?

Many analysts agree that these problems cannot be tackled without structural changes that affect the public and balance-of-payments deficits. Reagan did not properly address the problem by reducing social expenditures, nor can new taxation solve it even if elected officials are willing to raise taxes in future. Military expenditures are at the root of the deficits, and these cannot be reduced without a fundamental change in foreign policy.

I have already tried to point out how the bipolar policy has deeply affected domestic policies and coalitions of interest, both East and West. Therefore, in the United States as well as in the Soviet Union, domestic conditions cannot be seriously modified without fundamental changes in foreign policy. For this reason the simultaneous decline of the super-powers gives rise to great opportunities but also to considerable danger. The international political system is at stake, and there is no clear sense of direction for a transition to any new system.

In this phase, the interdependence of the superpowers has radicalized the problems each one has had to face. From the viewpoint of the United States, the dialogue between Nixon and Brezhnev was an important factor in surviving the ordeals of the post-Vietnam and Watergate era. More fundamentally, the continued existence of a unified and potentially threatening Soviet bloc has justified and strengthened American leadership of the West. Therefore, the decline of American relative power is tied to the fragility of Soviet primacy in the Eastern bloc, which is obvious to everyone except NATO propagandists.

First of all, the ideological credibility of the Soviet Union has been constantly waning since the end of the Second World War. The combination of economic inefficiency and lack of democratic liberties typical of Soviet society has been inspiring to no one except the most inveterate Stalinists in Western countries and has at most been considered a necessary evil in the Third World. There has been no sign of genuine integration of the Eastern bloc, which has been kept from falling apart only by the Soviet capacity to apply the necessary amount of military repression. The ambiguous outcome of the Polish crisis has proved that even this Soviet capacity cannot be taken for granted.

Since what E.P. Thompson has called the digestive problems of the Soviet bloc are so evident, the military threat (of permanent importance to the existence of NATO) to Western Europe has become less and less credible. Even NATO hardliners admit in private that the classic scenario of the Red Army invading Western Europe is unlikely, when it has a hard time holding on to what it already possesses. The whole theory of Finlandization has been invented to meet this objection. The Soviet Union, with a shaky economy but militarily superior, would blackmail fat but complacent Western Europeans into concessions on political sovereignty, were the NATO nuclear and conventional umbrella to be abandoned. So goes the argument, which ignores not only George Kennan's simple objection – there is no reason to give in to a threat that cannot be carried out[13] – but also the fact that the economic weakness of the Soviet Union is more likely to push it towards reform and greater economic ties with the West, rather than infringements upon European sovereignty.

It is primarily the economic nature of the crisis that makes the Gorbachev reform movement so different from what Khrushchev attempted in the 1950s. Gorbachev had to change Soviet foreign policy and make concessions in order to start a process of disarmament, so as to be able to reallocate resources from the military to other sectors. The claim from conservatives that Gorbachev was forced into this policy by the increase in American military expenditures is an oversimplification, but with an element of truth. It is an oversimplification because a change of policy requires a coalition of interest and of power that cannot be improvised overnight.

The information we have at our disposal is limited, but from what we know and what can be conjectured, Gorbachev is supported by dynamic and more outward-looking sections of the bureaucracy and the KGB. At the same time it is not improbable that the very aggressiveness and military zeal of the Reagan administration has upset the bipolar status quo, bringing both the arms race and the tension between the opposite camps to a point at which the hand of the innovators within the Soviet system was strengthened. The advantages to the USSR which accompanied the post-Vietnam crisis had clearly come to an end. The Reagan administration would not simply return to the traditional equilibrium of the bipolar system typical of the Brezhnev era. Therefore, there were only two possibilities: either to follow Washington in an increasingly costly arms race, sustained by steadily increasing tension, or try a new policy. The latter course of action was presumably encouraged by the existence of a Western European peace movement, not strong enough to stop the installation of cruise and Pershing II missiles but capable of providing incentive and support for a less inflexible Soviet policy. This is particularly

true, as we shall see, if the purpose of Gorbachev and the Soviet
reformers is to go beyond the bipolar system and to move in the
direction of pluricentrism. In that case greater independence of Western
Europe from the United States, but also a potentially more autonomous
Eastern Europe, become a necessary condition rather than a danger.

However, for the Gorbachev strategy even to begin to be successful,
the Soviet concessions had to be acknowledged and matched by a similar willingness on the part of Washington to enter a phase of negotiation.
It is here that what the great seventeenth-century Swedish statesman,
Axel von Oxenstierna considered the essential factor of any policy
presented itself: the *occasio*, the historic opportunity. The Reagan
presidency, in order to rescue itself from the collapse of its foreign
policy, an economy in turmoil and declining success at the polls, needed
a dramatic change of policy. The fact that the Reagan administration
was not bound by conventional bipolar orthodoxy but inspired by a
more radical and sincere form of anti-communism proved a paradoxically liberating factor.

It would be a mistake to confuse *occasio* with mere opportunism.
Ronald Reagan's response cannot simply be explained by his (or his
wife's) desire to end his term of office in a more dignified manner,
though this may have been an important personal motivation. The point,
of course, is that both leaders faced parallel crises which dramatized a
decline of their relative power incompatible with their dominant roles
within the international system. In particular, they have both responded
to the need to reallocate resources invested in the military sector. The
urgency and nature of this change may be different, but its causes are
similar: the excessive load that foreign policy has imposed on the
domestic economy.[14]

Does this mean the trend is irreversible? That we are entering a phase
in which military equilibrium will consistently be pursued at a lower
level? Where detente is genuinely new in its nature and will ultimately
democratize the superpowers and liberate their clients and satellites?

These questions should be answered cautiously, for many reasons.
First of all, detente and disarmament are in themselves not incompatible
with the bipolar relationship and are therefore by definition reversible
whenever tension serves the interests of the protagonists. It is no coincidence that the setting of the Reagan–Gorbachev dialogue has been
such as to underline its exclusive nature. Therefore, an important test of
the value and durability of future negotiations will be the openness to
new participants.

A significant aspect of other episodes or phases of detente has been
the strengthening of superpower control over lesser allies. Will the
Gorbachev reforms include relationships within the Warsaw Pact and,

above all, will they stand the crucial test of upheaval in an Eastern European country, or will Gorbachev be forced to react as Khrushchev did in Hungary? On the other side, will Western European countries assume greater responsibility for their security and acquire the capacity to formulate independent policies in the rest of the world?

Thirdly, it is vitally important that changes in foreign policy are developed to the point at which they can affect domestic superpower reform. As long as the totalitarian structure of the Soviet society and political system are not seriously affected, foreign-policy trends remain fragile and, consequently, reversible. From this point of view the greater freedom of cultural debate in the Soviet Union is at least as important for peace as the scrapping of hundreds of nuclear missiles. The important distinction is between what comes from above and what develops from below and is tolerated by institutional authorities. The presence of conflict is more significant than any consensus, however appealing in its policy content. The outcome of the present trend of events is uncertain. There is no doubt, however, that should progress towards democracy prevail, nothing could be more destabilizing to the bipolar system.

Of course the situation in the United States is different. Even here, however, it is not only necessary that the mainstream of public opinion should adjust to a less belligerent mood; it is even more important that those excluded from the political system should bring their interests and views to bear. From this point of view the Jackson candidacy was an important political development, though the nature of the presidential campaign – and, above all, the incapacity of the Democrats to formulate an alternative foreign policy – indicated that there is still a long way to go.

The nature of these tests, the simple fact that they can realistically be formulated, are an indication of what is at stake. Recent developments are important not only because they suggest a halt to an arms race that seemed irreversible. The Reagan–Gorbachev dialogue was the outcome of the decline of the superpowers and the crisis of the bipolar system. As we have seen, this system has not only dominated foreign policy but affected the domestic power relationships within all countries. There are powerful ruling classes, political elites, military and civilian bureaucracies, who have a stake in bipolar policies both in the United States and the Soviet Union. Peripheral authorities owe their local power to the subordinate relationship to the superpowers. Therefore, the crisis of bipolarism does not just demand a change in foreign policy, but signifies social and political instability in many parts of the world. All this is difficult and even dangerous, but were it not, the detente we are discussing would not be new and the prospects of peace would be as frail as ever.

Notes

1. Adam B. Ulam, *The Rivals, America and Russia Since World War II*, New York 1971, p. 28.

2. Richard Falk, 'Superseding Yalta: A Plea for Regional Self-Determination in Europe', in Mary Kaldor and Richard Falk, eds, *Dealignment: A New Foreign Policy Perspective*, Oxford 1987.

3. Ulam, pp. 79–84.

4. Ibid.

5. Ronald Radosh, *American Labor and United States Foreign Policy*, New York 1979, ch. 11.

6. Gian Giacomo Migone, 'The Nature of Bipolarity: An Argument Against the Status Quo', in *Dealignment*, pp. 53–5.

7. Ibid., pp. 58–9.

8. Alan Wolfe, *America's Impasse*, New York 1981.

9. Migone, p. 57.

10. Ronald Steel, *Walter Lippmann and the American Century*, New York 1980, pp. 441–61; 'A Conversation with George Kennan', *Encounter*, 1976.

11. Fred Halliday, *Beyond Irangate: The Reagan Doctrine and the Third World*, Transnational Institute Issue Paper No. 1, 1987.

12. A symptom of this mood is the success of some recent and important books: Paul Kennedy, *The Rise and Fall of the Great Powers: Economic Change and Military Conflict from 1500 to 2000*, New York 1987; David P. Calleo, *Beyond American Hegemony: The Future of the Western Alliance*, New York 1987.

13. George Kennan, 'Mr. X. Reconsiders', *Encounter*, 1978.

14. Kennedy, pp. 438–540.

8

Soviet Foreign Policy under Gorbachev and Revolution in the Third World: An Ideological Retreat or Refinement?*

Mammo Muchie and Hans van Zon

> In the current epoch the survival of humanity is on the agenda, not the world revolution.
>
> (Y. Popov, member of the USSR Academy of Sciences, 1986)[1]

Gorbachev's new foreign policy proceeds from the idea that for all the profound contradictions of the contemporary world, and for all the radical differences between different countries, the world is interrelated, interdependent and integral:

> The reasons for this include the internationalization of world economic ties, the comprehensive scope of the scientific and technological revolution, the essentially novel role played by the mass media, the state of the earth's resources, the common environmental danger, and the crying social problems of the developing world which affect us all. The main reason, however, is the problem of human survival.[2]

> The ongoing processes have the force of an objective law; either a disaster or a joint quest for a new economic order taking into account the interests of all on an equal basis.[3]

The 'interests of humanity', in contemporary world politics, are described as transcending national, state and class boundaries and taking precedence over everything else. This all-human approach is rooted in the material foundation of a world which has become increasingly 'interconnected, integral and interdependent'. Side by side with the interdependent world is a distinct set of global problems which threaten the human race in the nuclear age with catastrophe.

*Acknowledgements: thanks to our colleagues in the department for their criticisms.

As a result of the development of this all-human approach, a new criterion has emerged for assessing the contemporary disposition of world political forces. There is said to be a new contradiction between those who understand the necessity of giving priority to the 'interests of humanity' and those who do not.

The new political thinking clearly marks a break with the old Stalinist framework of political analysis in general, and foreign-policy analysis in particular. Its other distinguishing characteristic is that it is not being codified into a new dogmatic system. In the preface to his book *Perestroika*, Gorbachev says: 'We have no universal solutions, nor do we claim that what we offer is the only truth.'

In general, two main tendencies are observable within the 'New Thinking'. The first is a vigorous advocacy of one world economy, of which the existing socialist countries should be an integral part. The fact that this world economy happens to be a capitalist one and that being involved in it may mean accepting its ground rules does not seem to worry a good number of the 'New Thinkers'. There are ample statements to support the idea that the 'New Thinking' advocates the acceptance, or at least the non-rejection, of the international-status-quo system of power relations.

The other tendency which can be observed in the 'New Thinking' is the realization that socialism is not the sum total of a number of national socialisms, including countries with a very low level of development of the forces of production. The further development of both capitalism and socialism in interaction is necessary for the realization of global socialism. In this conception, the goal of world revolution is not abandoned but is postponed until perestroika can put the Soviet Union in better order.

If this reformulation of Soviet foreign policy is to be taken seriously, what are its implications for the Third World? How will the Soviet Union perceive the world in these new circumstances? The aim of this chapter is to establish the extent to which perestroika in foreign policy represents a continuity of or a break with traditional Soviet perceptions of the Third World as the Soviet Union's 'natural ally'. We also try to explain current changes in Soviet thinking about the Third World and to assess their implications.

The Legacy of Past Thinking

Two cardinal principles of Soviet foreign policy clashed at the birth of the Soviet Union: proletarian internationalism and peaceful coexistence. The former entailed support through propaganda and material aid for the workers' movement in the developed capitalist countries and the national liberation movement in the colonies, semi-colonies and dependent countries. The latter suggested that the Soviet Union should enter into normal state-to-state relations with the capitalist and pre-capitalist world.

The left in the party stressed the difficulty of combining the two ideas. Lenin saw no difficulty. For him, proletarian internationalism was a cornerstone of Soviet foreign policy. In theory, the maintenance of normal state-to-state relations was not to be equated with Soviet approval of the domestic policies of the capitalist countries or with the suppression of revolutionary movements. However, the Soviet Union could not avoid the charge of either subversion (from the bourgeoisie) or of sacrificing the revolutionary movement (from sections of the left).

In a sense, nearly all the later concepts of foreign policy which were picked up and dropped by different Soviet leaders at different times can be said to have emerged during the brief experience of Soviet foreign policy under Lenin. Lenin was the originator of 'detente', the 'two-camps concept', the 'weak-link hypothesis' and the 'non-capitalist road'. The fundamental characteristics of world politics after the October Revolution were formulated as follows:

1. A *systemic* contradiction between socialism (represented by the USSR at the time) and capitalism (represented by the great powers);

2. A *class* contradiction between labour (the working classes in the advanced capitalist countries) and capital (the bourgeoisie in the advanced and pre-capitalist countries);

3. A *relationship of domination* caused by capitalism–imperialism, referring to the relations both between the great powers and the colonies, and between great powers and semi-colonies including the dependent and smaller capitalist countries;

4. *Interstate rivalry* (chiefly among the great powers to redivide the world or acquire sources of trade and markets).

The first three contradictions were in turn related to the concept of proletarian internationalism: the struggles for socialism, of the working-class movement, and for national liberation were considered to be inter-linked. The last contradiction, in interstate relations, fell within the realm of peaceful coexistence.

Soviet leaders sometimes classed contradiction 3 within the category of peaceful coexistence, while at other times they regarded support for national bourgeois regimes as part of the policy of proletarian internationalism (depending on whether they were perceived as enemies or friends). In countries where there was a communist movement side by side with the general anti-colonialist movement (for example China, India), Soviet leaders tended to class their relations with the former in the category of proletarian internationalism and the latter in the category of peaceful coexistence, or at least a broader version of proletarian internationalism. Often the job of reconciling support for bourgeois nationalists with the communists of a given semi-colonial country was difficult (for example Turkey, China).

Whilst the notion of separating analytically state-to-state, people-to-people and party-to-party relations is plausible, in practice it was difficult to carry through. Often in the Soviet Union, government, party and legislative personnel tended to overlap and the other side inevitably had difficulty appreciating the Soviet perspective.

When proletarian internationalism was understood in the restricted class sense, it meant general support for the national liberation movement followed by strong support for the communist movement within it. When proletarian internationalism was understood in the broader sense as support for a bloc of classes, it very often meant material and political support for the bourgeois nationalists within the national liberation movement.

In the 1920s the Indian Marxist M.N. Roy criticized Lenin's draft thesis on the national and colonial question, arguing that communist support for bourgeois nationalism in countries like India and China would prove self-defeating. Roy posed the question which has remained unresolved in Soviet foreign policy to this day: who is more reliable for advancing the interests of world socialism; Third World communists or bourgeois nationalists? This tension in the doctrine of proletarian internationalism ran like a thread through the theory and practice of Soviet foreign policy until the advent of Gorbachev as party leader.

During the period of the New Economic Policy, the foreign policy of the Soviet Union was in the hands of Stalin and Bukharin. At this time the concept of proletarian internationalism was employed in the broader sense to encompass bourgeois nationalists in an alliance with communists in the colonies and semi-colonies. The Communist parties were advised to enter into 'national democratic fronts' and 'four-class blocs' (for example with such forces as the Chinese Kuomintang, the Indian National Congress, the Sarekat Islam in Indonesia and the Wafd in Egypt).

When the USSR embarked on the twin task of accelerated industrialization and collectivization in the late 1920s, relations with the great powers became tenser. The 6th Comintern Congress reformulated the concept of proletarian internationalism in its narrower sense. It advised local Communist parties in the colonial world to break ranks with the bourgeois nationalists and embark on insurrectionary projects. In Asia, the Indochinese and Chinese Communist parties launched armed struggles in the early 1930s, and in Latin America the Brazilian Communist Party did the same. It seemed that the narrow concept of proletarian internationalism gained strength whenever the USSR reduced its application of peaceful coexistence or alliance with the great powers. From 1935 to 1939 the Comintern advocated the concept of the Popular United Front, and the pendulum swung back towards the broader concept of proletarian internationalism. From 1939 to 1941 the Comintern advised the local Communist parties to work for peace and frustrate the war preparations of the colonial powers in their countries. During the Second World War, the USSR posed as a partner of the allied camp and all the Communist parties followed its example in creating anti-Fascist patriotic fronts.

After the Second World War the USSR found new allies in Eastern Europe, China, Vietnam, and North Korea; then came the onset of the Cold War.

In 1947 the now-dissolved Comintern was succeeded by the Cominform. Andrei Zhdanov embraced the narrower concept of pro-letarian internationalism, advising Communist parties to follow insurrec-tionary policies and to fight their erstwhile bourgeois nationalist allies (for example the Chinese Communist Party v. the Kuomintang). In the Chinese case, the policy succeeded. Elsewhere Communist parties were defeated: in India, Burma, Malaysia, the Philippines and Indonesia.

After the death of Stalin, Khrushchev developed the revision of Soviet foreign policy which had been foreshadowed as early as the 19th Party Congress in 1952. He revised the theory of peaceful coexistence. It was declared in 1956 that the competition between socialist and capi-talist states would not inevitably lead to war. This revision was related to the emerging nuclear stalemate and the new stature of the Soviet Union as a world power.

The decolonization process in the Third World offered the Soviet Union new opportunities for alliances with Third World countries, the more so because many, such as Egypt, Algeria, Ghana, Guinea, Mali, Congo, Somalia, Tanzania, Syria, Iraq and Burma, tried to break with the capitalist 'model'. None of these states was governed by a Com-munist Party. Khrushchev applied a broader concept of proletarian internationalism and pleaded for many-sided co-operation with the national liberation movement. He sought a *rapprochement* with the non-aligned movement, which was founded in 1955.

The Third World acquired greater weight in Soviet foreign policy. New tools in foreign policy-making were used, such as aid projects which were often spectacular and beneficial for Third World countries. Soviet aid, which was mainly directed towards regimes which followed the non-capitalist road, changed the terms of the debate on aid to the Third World. At this time the Third World was seen as a 'natural ally'. The 1961 party programme was extremely optimistic about developments there: 'The mighty wave of national liberation sweeps the colonial system away and undermines the pillars of imperialism.' The international system was perceived to be moving rapidly towards socialism. It was foreseen that by 1980 the Soviet Union would overtake the United States in net material product.

During the second half of the 1960s economic growth figures improved after a period of slowdown and the enhanced armaments efforts under Brezhnev led, at the beginning of the 1970s, to what was regarded as strategic parity with the United States. A gradual shift of the global correlation of forces in favour of the Soviet Union was perceived, although expectations about the future of socialism ran less high than under Khrushchev.

In the course of the 1970s newly formed governments emerged in the former Portuguese colonies in Africa, in South Yemen, Indochina, Ethiopia, Afghanistan and Nicaragua, and chose a socialist orientation. Those mostly extremely backward countries found support from the Soviet Union. This wave of Third World revolutions prompted the Soviet Union to emphasize again relations with radical-left governments in the Third World, and Moscow stressed the importance of the formation of revolutionary vanguard parties on a Marxist–Leninist basis in socialist-orientated countries.

Authoritative speeches and articles during the mid 1970s gave the impression of a highly ambitious global power which considered that the tide of history had shifted decisively in its favour and was inclined to exploit this situation to its advantage. However, as the number of socialist-orientated countries and Soviet involvement in the Third World grew and economic growth in the Soviet Union slowed down, the Soviet Union's limited economic ability to influence developments in the Third World became increasingly apparent.

Gorbachev's International Programme

Gorbachev's speech at the 27th Congress (1986) did not even refer to the socialist-orientated states or revolutionary democracies, or even to national liberation movements in the Third World. This speech was characterized by minimal attention to the problems of the Third World.[4] By comparison with Brezhnev's congress speech in 1971, the terms of analysis were completely different. In 1971 Brezhnev used a militant vocabulary in describing exploitation in the Third World. Gorbachev does not analyse international relations in class terms. His international programme may be described as a programme for the survival of humanity, not as a programme for world socialism.

Current global problems, primarily that of war and peace, are considered to be so urgent that they require a common multilateral approach. The Soviet leadership now envisages an international regime comprising a strategic coalition of forces which were hitherto antagonistically opposed. Gorbachev envisages a progressive transformation of the existing world into a new worldwide international regime with different socioeconomic systems peacefully coexisting and co-operating. It is acknowledged that the conflict between capitalism and socialism cannot be reduced to the conflict between socialist and capitalist states, and that elements of socialism are also present in the 'non-socialist' world.

Gorbachev starts from the premiss that international relations must be made 'more human'.[5] The humanization of international affairs means that nation-states must commit themselves to 'rise above ideological differences'.[6] The ideological edge can be removed from inter-state relations when 'considerations for one's own national interest', followed by 'respect for other countries' interests', become the organizing principle of international life'.[7] It was in this context that the CPSU abandoned, at the 27th Congress, Khrushchev's definition of peaceful coexistence between states of different social systems as a specific form of class struggle.[8] Peaceful coexistence has become, for the CPSU, a universal value in the relations between socialist states as well.[9] The concept of proletarian internationalism, traditionally one of the theoretical foundations of Soviet foreign policy, has been set aside.

The pursuit of socialism in the (pre-)capitalist part of the world seems to be for Gorbachev merely a matter for the progressive forces in the respective nation-states; it cannot be an element in Soviet foreign policy, apart from material support for governments which are committed to socialism. Y. Primakov, Director of the Institute for World Economy and International Relations, has written that 'international relations in general cannot be the arena in which the contest between global socialism and capitalism can be decided.' He has also argued that

> a thorough change is also appropriate for the Marxist theory of class struggle – this also must find a way out of the critical situation and find ways in which a social renewal of the world in the extremely complex new situation can be found. The nuclear era necessitates that the revolutionary forces are extremely cautious in deciding to wage an armed struggle and that they categorically reject the various forms of left-extremism.[10]

G. Shakhnazarov has noted that the Marxist concept of two opposed social systems was occasionally interpreted simplistically:

> The concept of systems was virtually replaced by a concept of states belonging to different social and economic formations. As a consequence, the idea of competition inevitably acquired all the characteristics of state-to-state relations. The progress of socialism at world level was gauged chiefly by the growth of the economic power of socialist countries and by mounting crisis phenomena in this or that area of the capitalist economy. It was also judged according to the changing balance of military might. Cumulative social changes in capitalist countries were practically dismissed as 'small quantities'. This mechanistic notion of competition between the two systems was an extremely primitive reflection of reality and largely distorted it, making it difficult to see this most intricate socioeconomic process in all its aspects.[11]

This approach implies an undermining of the Stalinist notion of socialism in one country, according to which full socialism could be completed in one country and international progress towards socialism became virtually congruent with the consolidation of the Soviet Union's power. Gorbachev has abandoned the concept of the two competing and hostile world markets. He does not speak, as Brezhnev and his predecessors did, about the continuous shifting of the correlation of world forces in favour of socialism.

In the new Gorbachevian account, it seems that imperialism does not have to be converted to socialism for the two systems to be able to live together in peace in this 'interdependent' world. It seems that the revitalization of socialism is conceived in terms of interaction with the capitalist world economy, rather than in dissociation from it. Thus the Leninist framework of foreign policy in respect of the two camps, class contradictions, the domination of the many by the few and interstate rivalry has been replaced by the concept of one 'interdependent, integral and interconnected world'.

By 1986, the concept of 'interdependence' had been embraced in its entirety by the Soviet Union. If the 'New Thinking' is to be translated into practice, the communist movement in the capitalist world and the revolutionary movements in the Third World cannot expect much support from the Soviet Union. However, many authoritative 'New Thinkers' will deny that. Primakov, for example, has pointed to the documents of the 27th Party Congress, in which a sharp distinction was drawn between external assistance in creating a revolutionary situation, which is currently denied by the CPSU, and the assistance of 'revolutionary forces which rely on objective conditions in their struggle to end the national and social oppression of their peoples'.[12] The question, of course, is where the boundary line will be drawn.

Previously in Soviet foreign policy there had been continuous shifts in strategy, ranging from support for revolutionary forces and radical regimes to an emphasis on support for broad coalitions and more moderate regimes. Until the arrival of Gorbachev these shifts were accommodated within the same theoretical framework, but Gorbachev has changed the theoretical parameters of Soviet foreign policy itself. Now, the doctrine of proletarian internationalism has been pushed into the background and replaced by the doctrine of peaceful coexistence or interdependence. The break in Soviet foreign policy is not in Gorbachev's pursuit of a pragmatic course. All Soviet leaders have practised various degrees of pragmatism. In that sense, there is a foreign-policy continuity. The real break under Gorbachev consists of his setting aside the old framework of foreign-policy analysis in order to practise his own brand of pragmatism.

States of Socialist Orientation: Transition to Socialism?

Just as Soviet thinkers have dared to open a 'Pandora's box' about the nature of socialism in their own society, they have begun to question the utility of socialism in the Third World. According to R. Avakov, a famous Soviet Third World expert,

> the number of publications about problems of socialist orientation is inversely proportional with the quality of the research. Instead of analysis of the crises existing in the states of socialist orientation and other negative phenomena, including complete collapse of the economy, of domestic and foreign policy, conjuring phrases are used . . .[13]

The Soviet Third World expert Mirskii has criticized earlier optimistic Soviet analyses of developments in the Third World:

> Years passed before we understood the significance and influence of the middle classes, the intelligentsia, the bureaucracy and the army, which indeed had been understood earlier by Western scholars. And years passed before we sufficiently realized what enormous weight can be attributed to traditions and non-class-related social institutions like tribalism, the deeply rooted dividing lines in Asian and African societies according to ethnic, religious, caste and clan lines, which ultimately are laid down in a lasting system of patronage–clientele relations which push class contradictions to the background. These class contradictions are unmistakenly present but come to the fore in specific, indirect, hidden and unclear forms.[14]

> Economically these [socialist-orientated] countries remained linked with the capitalist world system. Even the most leftist and progressive regimes have

obtained most credits from the Western states towards which their foreign trade was directed. The capitalist world not only sends goods to Asia and Africa, but also actively introduces its value system. The aid of the socialist world system, its influence and example may weaken this capitalist influence, but it cannot, for the time being, neutralize it.[15]

According to W. Sheinis, the Soviet Union's experience with Egypt shows that the choice of a socialist path of development is reversible. The reasons for this lie in the domestic circumstances of developing countries:

> The preconditions of such counter-coups and degenerations are included in the fact that some negative social phenomena, such as corruption, nepotism, economic and administrative inefficiency, stagnation or low growth of living standards, the passivity of the masses, non-democratic government and similar phenomena are rooted in the existing social-economic and social-cultural structure of developing countries. The choice of a progressive orientation is in itself, taking into consideration the specific forms of political leadership in specific states and the absence of a broad proletarian class basis, not sufficient to set up a relatively reliable barrier against such phenomena.[16]

Avakov has noted the historical fact that the path of socialist orientation was primarily chosen by some of the poorest countries, and that this is in itself remarkable. The leaders of those countries opted for the model that promised the most rapid development: 'But besides the logic of the choice, which can be made under the "demonstration-effect" of socialism, there is the logic of objective conditions.' According to Avakov, the path of socialist orientation has not yet proved its superiority: 'None of the countries which have chosen this path could surpass the category of the poorest nations. The model is not attractive enough for dozens of liberated countries.'[17]

Avakov suggests that the countries of socialist orientation should not be considered as being in a transitional phase moving in the direction of socialism, but as a distinct social formation with a number of variations. In his view there are progressive, negative and even reactionary variations. He points to the terroristic regime of the Khmer Rouge in Cambodia.

Thus the old dogma of a possible non-capitalist path to socialism seems to be under question. Nevertheless it must be emphasized that the 'New Thinkers' represent a highly differentiated conglomerate of schools of thought. There are those who opt for a progressive transformation of the existing world order in the direction of socialism. Within this brand a revival of Marxist notions and approaches can be observed. Others incline towards acceptance of the existing international status quo, and envisage trying to solve global problems within the current framework of power relations.

A Re-evaluation of the Role of Capitalism in the Third World

Along with the reappraisal of socialism in the Third World there has been an increasing reluctance to present the traditional Soviet model of economic development as an alternative for the developing countries, especially after the Soviet Union introduced, in 1987, a new planning system and admitted that the traditional one did not function well. The enormous economic problems of the newly formed centrally planned economies in the Third World induced a re-evaluation of the traditional Soviet planning system as a functioning model for developing countries. An increasing number of Soviet specialists on Third World problems have been proposing another path of development. In particular, they have been pointing out the importance of the private sector in agriculture, the service sector and handicrafts. A. Butenko, for example, concludes that 'there is no other alternative for the stimulation of productivity in a peasant and crafts economy than to emulate the mixed economy model of the NEP.'[18] He also says that priority should be given to agriculture and to the traditional path of initial industrialization, based on the need for the priority growth of the food industry and light industry.[19]

Several writers seem to suggest that capitalism may be the appropriate model for Third World countries. Sheinis asserts that 'capitalist-orientated development may offer in a series of developing countries specific possibilities for elements of social progress.[20] In a recent article, he even suggests that there is no viable alternative to capitalism in the Third World. He argues that it is necessary to avoid

a one-sided evaluation of the activity of the Transnational Corporations and of the recommendations of the IMF, the World Bank and the other international organizations. It is not of course a question of the unconditional acceptance of such recommendations . . . but of a sober approach to them, a rejection of the view that the very social nature of these institutions compels them to advance plans deliberately opposed to the objective interests of the development of the world capitalist economy. If we are to be consistent in acknowledging the interdependence of the present-day world, we need to adopt a more considered view of the economic basis of that interdependence – not only the international division of labour, but also institutionalized flows of material and financial resources (which include, but are not reducible to the transfer of capital).

Sheinis warns against the identification of capitalism as such with the economic laws of modern production, which are equally binding for capitalism and for socialism.[21]

Many authors argue against breaking with the capitalist world market. Avakov has noted that 'it is not a question, as has been asserted up to recently, of letting [those Third World countries] break with the capitalist world economy, but of bringing about an equal partnership with it.'[22] Generally speaking, Soviet analysts of the Third World are now paying more attention to its differentiation and complexity. These ideas imply a break with earlier tenets concerning the laws of development of socialism and capitalism. The quotations above are not representative of Soviet publications on Third World problems, but they are characteristic of a new orientation which is coming to the fore and has been legitimized by the party leadership under Gorbachev. Even the role of the Soviet Union is sometimes analysed critically. A. Bovin wrote recently in *Izvestiya* that 'There has not been created a society which in respect to all features could have been an example, a model and an incentive in the struggle for the socialist transformation of the world.' As one of the reasons for the failure of the Communist parties in the capitalist part of the world to attract large masses, Bovin mentioned 'the failures, contradictions, crises and stagnation phenomena in the development of the Soviet Union, other countries of socialism and worldwide socialism as such'.[23]

Yet in depicting prospects for development in the Third World, even the authors most critical of former Soviet analyses remain basically optimistic. Avakov has emphasized that 'this does not mean the failure of the model of socialist orientation, and it should not lead to an excess of pessimistic conclusions about socialism's long-term prospects.'[24] K.N. Brutents, Deputy Head of the Central Committee's international department, has stressed the anti-imperialist potential of the Third World: 'The developing countries remain an enormous reservoir of socially inflammable and anti-imperialist sentiment, whose objective basis does not narrow or weaken, but on the contrary is broadening and becoming stronger.'[25] Brutents points to the wave of nationalizations in the Third World, to the fact that industrial production there has increased over the last twenty years by a factor of 3.5, and to the historical fact that its number of employees amounted at the beginning of the eighties to 180 million, more than half of the proletariat in the whole capitalist world. According to Brutents the labour movement in the Third World has made much progress: 'Anti-imperialism now has a greater potential than ever before, even if it has not yet been realized.'[26] Last, but not least, we may quote Gorbachev: 'For all their might it is not the transnationals that will determine the Third World's development; it is more likely that they will be forced to adjust to the independent choice that has been or will be made by the peoples.'[27]

The re-evaluation of capitalism and the capitalist world market has led to a re-evaluation of Soviet policy towards the institutions of the world economy. The Soviet Union has applied for membership of GATT and shown interest in membership of the IMF.

Soviet–American Rivalry in the Third World: the 1970s and the 1980s

A combination of circumstances has brought about the qualitative shift in Soviet analyses of world politics and the Third World. With the advent of Gorbachev a new generation of leaders has come to the fore who did not play an active role in the Second World War and are less connected with the Stalinist past. They perceived a developing 'pre-crisis situation', and saw that to overcome this a radical new approach was needed. Internationally, also, the Soviet Union found itself in an impasse: worsening relations with the West, an American–Chinese alliance, unrest in Eastern Europe, a war in Afghanistan and the growing economic burden of sustaining the Soviet sphere of influence. A combination of military, technological and economic retardation particularly alarmed Soviet politicians.

Changing Soviet policy towards the Third World, however, can be fully understood only if the changing context of Soviet–American rivalry there is also taken into consideration. The United States and the USSR have always defined their respective Third World strategies largely as a function of East–West relations.

In the mid 1970s, the United States was internationally on the defensive. The trauma of defeat in Vietnam hindered an interventionist policy in the Third World, and this facilitated the emergence of a group of radical countries which sought actively to nurture links with the USSR. Moreover, a model of state-orientated development – as implemented, for instance, in Egypt, Syria and Algeria – was spreading all over the Third World. The aim was to shield national economies against the disturbances of the world market. Further commodity-based cartels of strategic resource-rich Third World countries raised price levels of fuels and raw materials. Hence Third World states asserted their interests more forcefully during the seventies, often in defiance of developed capitalist countries. This offered opportunities for the Soviet Union to enlarge its presence in the Third World.

At the beginning of the 1970s the Soviet Union attained what was regarded as strategic parity with the United States. It began to project its military power globally and to assist a growing number of progressive and anti-Western regimes in the Third World. During the same period US policy became more cautious as a consequence of the 'Vietnam syndrome'. The United States, of course, still pursued an active policy in the Third World. Within the Camp David process the USA tried to manoeuvre the Soviet Union out of the Middle East, and the Carter administration mounted a 'forthright human-rights campaign internationally'.[28]

The contrast with the eighties is nevertheless striking. The growing debt crisis undermined state-orientated economic strategies, protectionism and social policy in the Third World. The trend towards 'more plan' was transformed, with the help of the IMF, into a trend of 'more market'. The power of Third World raw material and fuel-exporting cartels was reduced and terms of trade improved for the developed capitalist countries. Most Third World countries, the Newly Industrializing Countries excluded, moved further towards the margins of the world economy, and socialism was on the defensive. The same can be said for the socialist countries, most of which encountered great economic difficulties during the eighties. These difficulties were primarily rooted in the malfunctioning of the traditional planning system, which could not adjust adequately to higher levels of economic development and new external circumstances.

These domestic developments were paralleled by changes in US and Soviet policies towards the Third World. The Reagan administration adopted a more activist US foreign policy, aimed at reasserting US economic and strategic power on a global scale after the perceived decline of the 1970s. On the southern flank of the Soviet Union, US military pressure was enhanced by the introduction of the Rapid Deployment Force (later Central Command) and the consolidation of Israeli–US strategic ties. Both the Soviet Union and the United States contributed to a substantial military build-up in the Northern Pacific. Moreover, US policy towards social upheavals and anti-imperialist states in the Third World changed. Reagan introduced a roll-back strategy with the invasion of Grenada and with support (often with sophisticated arms) for UNITA forces in Angola, the Contras in Nicaragua, and the Afghan resistance.

At first the Soviet leadership did not realize the impact of the change in American foreign policy. Brezhnev thought that the negative consequences of the invasion of Afghanistan would be of short duration and that economic sanctions against the Soviet Union would soon be lifted.[29] Later, Soviet leaders admitted that earlier analyses had overestimated the economic and political decline of American power.

The 1980s were also characterized by a technological revolution in microelectronics, computers and communications. The Soviet Union could not compete with the Newly Industrializing Countries for shares of Western markets for industrial products and found itself with even fewer economic assets than before to offer the Third World. The capitalist system proved more buoyant than earlier Soviet analyses had thought.

The Quest for Influence in a New Perspective

The Soviet Union is primarily a military, not an economic superpower. Its capacity to match its political aspirations with economic means has been increasingly constrained. The gross national products of the United States, the EEC and Japan are each greater than the estimated Soviet GNP. The average Third World country (socialist developing countries excluded) had in 1985 a mere 3.6 per cent of its total exports with the European CMEA states; for imports the percentage was even less: 2.5 per cent. In 1970 these percentages were respectively 6.3 per cent (exports) and 9.6 per cent (imports).[30] The trade patterns of developing countries are predominantly directed towards the developed capitalist world.

Moreover, Soviet trade with the Third World is concentrated on a few trading partners: the ten more important absorbed, in 1983, 74.6 per cent of Soviet exports to the Third World. Trade in services and transfers of capital and labour are insignificant in the relations between the Soviet Union and the developing world. Investments of all CMEA member states in the Third World, taken together, amounted in 1978 to no more than 270 million dollars.[31] Socialist economies tend to be autarkic, and this lessens their economic leverage in foreign policy. It may even be said that as a consequence of the specific socioeconomic structure in the Soviet Union there is no economic mechanism which provides an impetus towards geographical expansion.

The product pattern of trade flows between the Soviet Union and the developing world shows an unfavourable structure and negative trends. Increasingly, Soviet trade with the Third World is dominated by raw materials (especially food products and oil) and weapons.

The socialist Third World is not an economic asset for the Soviet Union but increasingly a burden. In a recent study sponsored by the RAND Corporation, the total costs of the Soviet empire were calculated. This empire was conceived of as the inner empire (neighbouring allied socialist countries) and client states in the Third World such as Cuba, Vietnam, Ethiopia, Nicaragua, Angola and South Yemen. The cost factors considered were trade subsidies, balance-of-payments surpluses, trade credits, open military operations (such as in

Afghanistan) and covert operations. Not counted were costs connected
with the deployment of Soviet troops in Eastern Europe. According to
this calculation, yearly total costs during the early 1970s were between
4.9 and 7.9 billion dollars. By 1981 they had grown sevenfold, representing 7.2 per cent of GNP, or 44.2 billion dollars. They subsequently
decreased, due to decreasing trade subsidies and decreasing military
support.[32]

Soviet leaders themselves draw attention to the huge expenses their
country has incurred through its commitments to the radical and poor
states. Addressing officials of his ministry in June 1987, E.
Shevardnadze said: 'To be completely honest, we not infrequently
promoted, and sometimes provoked, enormous material investments in
hopeless external political projects . . . which to this day are costing our
people dearly.'[33]

This increasing burden of the client states limits the possibilities for
the Soviet Union to provide aid to other countries. Cuba joined CMEA
in 1972; Vietnam in 1978. During the 1970s a series of association
treaties between CMEA and Third World countries was signed, but
Mozambique's request to become a full member of CMEA was refused
in 1981. The same happened to Ethiopia, Laos and South Yemen in the
1970s.[34] Meanwhile, Mozambique joined the Lome Convention (EEC
association treaty) and became a member of the IMF.

It is not only the erosion of the domestic material base of Soviet
power that limits the world role of the Soviet Union but also the economic slowdown in most allied planned economies, especially those in
the Third World.[35]

In the 1960s a series of friendly regimes which had received a considerable amount of Soviet aid were overthrown. As a consequence the
Soviet Union became more cautious about giving support, and realized
that economic aid could not provide sustained political leverage if the
countries concerned could turn to the West as an alternative source of
aid. During the 1970s arms sales became more important by comparison
with economic aid. Whereas during the 1950s and the most of the 1960s
the value of Soviet arms sales to the Third World was about equal to
that of Soviet economic aid, the value of arms transfers was twice as much
as that of economic aid between 1968 and 1972, and five times
greater from 1969 to 1982.[36] The Soviet Union relied increasingly on
arms transfers to acquire influence. From 1965 to 1973 Egypt received
more Soviet arms than any other Third World country, but these efforts
to exercise influence in Egypt failed and, indeed, appear to have been
counterproductive in view of what happened during and after the 1973
Arab–Israeli War.[37] The Soviet Union had similar experiences in other
Third World states.

It is also noticeable that the Soviet Union has rarely been able to acquire anything which could, in the proper sense of the word, be labelled a base in the Third World. No bases were acquired in Iraq, Syria, Libya, Ethiopia, Mozambique or Angola.

The Soviet Union hoped that the creation of vanguard parties on a Marxist–Leninist basis in second-generation socialist-orientated countries such as Angola, Ethiopia, Mozambique and South Yemen could furnish a solid base or durable Soviet influence. But these countries are extremely poor, strategically not very important, and did not succeed in creating broad domestic support due to economic crisis and/or war. Mostly the Soviet Union acquired influence in the Third World as a consequence of opportunities brought about by internal developments in the respective countries, not as a result of a deliberate policy or grand design. Moreover, the ease with which Third World countries could break their ties with the Soviet Union contrasts sharply with the difficulties those countries had in breaking their ties with developed capitalist countries.

Gorbachev's Policy towards the Third World

The weaknesses of the Soviet Union described above have not prevented a worldwide diplomatic offensive. The targets of this offensive in the Third World have tended to be large and strategically important Newly Industrializing Countries. In Asia, India has received much Soviet attention. Both in Gorbachev's report to the 27th Party Congress in 1986 and in his book *Perestroika*, it has been specifically mentioned. Gorbachev visited the country in November 1986 and held up relations between the USSR and India as an example of his 'New Thinking':

> To me personally, it is quite obvious that much of what we call new political thinking manifested itself internationally for the first time in relations between the Soviet Union and India. And that differences in sociopolitical system and ideology and our national, cultural and other distinctions have not hampered our dialogue is extremely important as a guiding example for others.[38]

The Soviet Union has extended economic and military assistance to India in spite of the decline in Indian demand for Soviet imports in the mid 1980s.[39] India has received $1.4bn in Soviet credits, entering into a four-year trade agreement in November 1985 and 1986. An agreement with the USSR to manufacture MIG-29 aircraft has also been signed.[40]

In Latin America, Mexico, Brazil, Argentina and Uruguay have been the foci of Soviet diplomatic activity. Shevardnadze has visited these

countries and Gorbachev intends to follow soon, trying to expand existing economic relations.

In the Middle East, the USSR established diplomatic relations with
Oman and the United Arab Emirates in September and November 1985
respectively. The prospect of Saudi–Soviet diplomatic relations is now
possible. The USSR has rescheduled Egypt's debt and is edging towards
diplomatic relations with Israel.

In the Persian Gulf the USSR responded to Kuwait's request to
protect its tankers threatened by Iran in May 1987 by permitting Kuwait
to hire three Soviet-flagged tankers to transport its oil, but tried not to
provoke Iran. In the Gulf War, it backed Iraq with military supplies and
also supported a peaceful resolution of the conflict by voting in favour
of UN Security Council Resolution 598. The USSR opposed sanctions
against Iran, and has entered into an economic agreement to build an oil
pipeline and a railway link with that country.

In South-East Asia and the Pacific, the USSR has been engaged in
bilateral visits to Malaysia, Indonesia and Thailand. The attempt to woo
the members of the Association of South-East Asian Nations (ASEAN)
has to do, in part, with an attempt to capitalize on their fears of China
and their conflicts with the USA.

The USSR has made a number of overtures to China. The Soviets
have begun to address those issues which the Chinese had previously
identified as posing obstacles to the normalization of relations between
the two states: Soviet troops in Afghanistan, Vietnamese troops in
Cambodia, and the stationing of Soviet troops and missiles on the
northern Chinese border. Sino–Soviet relations have improved considerably as a result of these recent Soviet initiatives.

The Soviet leaders also seem anxious to find ways of settling regional
conflicts in co-operation with the United States. In his political report to
the 27th Congress Gorbachev expressed his wish for a 'collective search
for ways to solve conflict situations in the Near and Middle East, in
Central America, Southern Africa and in all the seething points of the
planet'.[41] The advice is for reconciliation, urging belligerents to solve
their conflicts peacefully.

On the Middle East, Gorbachev has said that under the present
circumstances

> it is difficult to reconcile the interests of the conflicting sides. . . . However,
> we do not at all want the process of working towards a settlement, or the very
> goals of this process, in some way to impinge upon the interests of the United
> States or the West.[42]

He has also said: 'The Soviet Union does not bear any hostility towards

Israel in principle.' Diplomatic attempts to resume normal state-to-state relations between the USSR and Israel have reached an advanced stage.

The regional conflicts in the Middle East are incredibly tangled. Side by side with the major Arab–Israeli regional conflict go the interstate conflicts between Iraq and Iran, North and South Yemen, Iraq and Syria, Syria and Jordan, Syria and Egypt, Egypt and Libya, Algeria and Morocco and different fractions of the PLO amongst one other and other states in the Arab world. Adjacent to the Middle East lies the Horn of Africa, where the area's troubles spill over and influence the cycles of conflict between Ethiopia and Somalia, and Ethiopia and the Sudan.

Hitherto, Soviet support in the form of arms to the Arab side against Israel has helped to maintain the 'no war, no peace' situation in the Middle East. It still does, in spite of the USSR's setback in Egypt. The Soviet Union seems to be wary that radical Arab states might be the cause of involvement in mindless or needless confrontation with the United States. When the USA did its Rambo-style spectacular inter-continental raid against Libya, the Soviet Union condemned the attack but took no action.

The Soviet Union does not seem to take an optimistic view of the prospects of changing the internal policies of the feuding and inter-locking Arab states. It hopes to lessen regional tension within an overall agreement involving the USA, the USSR and the United Nations. Whatever the threshold of tension in the area, the new Soviet leadership has sent clear signals to friend and foe alike that it will not permit the situation to develop to an extent where the Soviet Union and the United States may engage in a head-on military collision.

The Soviet Union has begun the withdrawal of its troops from Afghanistan, although the prospects for peace there do not seem very good.

In Southern Africa, Angola and Cuba have agreed to withdraw Cuban troops as part of a settlement there. In Central America, the Soviet Union supports the peace process initiated by the Central American states. It cautiously supports Nicaragua. In South-East Asia, Vietnam has agreed to withdraw its troops from Cambodia by 1990. The Soviet Union itself is pulling out troops from the Chinese border and trying to lessen the tension there.

Hence, while the USSR is mounting a global diplomatic offensive, it is withdrawing from the excesses of the Brezhnev years. The Gorbachev group appears willing to control regional conflicts and prefers normal political, trade, economic and political relations. It does not seem to place much value on achieving political objectives by military means, in contrast to Brezhnev.

The balance sheet shows that the USSR wishes to defuse explosive regional conflicts on the basis of collectively worked out security guarantees provided by itself, the USA, Western Europe and the United Nations. It prefers moderate Third World regional powers to the socialist-orientated regimes. The picture that emerges is thus not a general retreat but a selective one, which involves reducing both the Soviet involvement in conflictual situations and the burdensome subsidies to Third World socialist-orientated regimes.

What are the Consequences of a New Detente for the Third World?

The new detente may be described as the outcome of a process of uneven decline for both superpowers. So far we have emphasized growing Soviet weaknesses in exerting influence in the Third World. But in the long run US power is also in decline, despite the fact that the Reagan administration tried to reverse this trend by boosting US military strength and notwithstanding the fact that the revolution in microelectronics, computers and telecommunications gives the USA new opportunities to reassert its role as a leading technological power. Rostow recently noted that 'the paradoxical fact is unmistakenly there that both superpowers are now in the grip of major productivity crises.'[43]

The growth of US labour productivity has continued to lag behind that of other developed capitalist countries. The mounting US trade deficit, the enormous national debt and Wall Street crash of October 1987 have drawn attention to long-standing weaknesses of the United States. The theme of US decline is now popular among American politicians and journalists. The quest for disengagement and for a readjustment of international commitments to capabilities is mounting in a way which may lead to a redefinition of the United States as a leader of the capitalist world.

Some US policy-makers have begun to revise fundamental assumptions which hitherto have governed policy towards the Soviet Union. It is now widely acknowledged that the decline of Soviet power since the end of the 1970s had not been taken into account by the Reagan administration, and that the ongoing process of perestroika and the redefining of Soviet foreign policy may bring about preconditions for a new detente which may provide the USA with more advantages than the detente of the 1970s.

William Hyland, chief editor of *Foreign Affairs*, recently wrote that Gorbachev is introducing innovative elements which are beginning to outweigh the elements of continuity. He thinks that the overall combination of circumstances suggest that it is a time of unusual opportunity for American policy. . . . The USA must continue to support and lead a powerful coalition of forces to contain the Soviet Union, but it will have to do so in an era vastly different from the period of the coalition's creation. We have won the ideological war; we are close to winning the geopolitical contest in the Third World, except for the Middle East.[44]

Another development which may affect the Third World is the process of multipolarization in the capitalist world. The ongoing multi-polarization of world politics was more or less concealed during the Reagan administration by the president's unilateralist approach to inter-national problems and worsening East–West relations. Although there is in the capitalist world nowadays no alternative to the USA as a hegemonic power, the opportunity for other centres in the developed capitalist world to exercise leverage may be enhanced, and this could enlarge the developing states' room for manoeuvre.

The Soviet 'New Thinking' on foreign policy seems to encourage the trend towards multipolarization, *rapprochement* in Europe, and the emergence of new centres of power in the Pacific. To a considerable extent, the question of whether the tendency towards multipolarization will be arrested by a reassertion of bipolarity depends on the success of perestroika in the USSR, and on political developments in the USA and Europe. Multipolarization opens up a political space for Third World countries. In this sense, the success of perestroika is in the interests of the Third World.

It remains to be seen how the United States will use the opportunities which might be offered by the relative Soviet retreat in the Third World. We may be entering a period of post-war history in which social struggle and revolutions in the Third World are less drawn into the orbit of Soviet–US relations, and in which both superpowers may find fewer arguments in favour of intervention.

Any comments on the reaction of the Third World to Soviet 'New Thinking' must be speculative at this stage. It seems to us that the following responses are likely to be voiced sooner or later.

– At the 27th Congress Gorbachev said that the European direction in Soviet foreign policy has become the top priority. Agreement with the United States is also a crucial priority. The position of the Third World as a whole seems to have been downgraded in spite of the upgrading of the newly industrializing capitalist countries within it. Hitherto the Soviet Union has often (even if sometimes only verbally) helped to enhance the international standing of the developing world, mainly in the shape of the non-aligned move-ment, and supported demands for a New International Economic Order. 'New Thinking' appears to be directed towards securing

agreements with the United States and the West, and neutralizing
China's enmity to the Soviet Union as a Pacific power. The articulate and conscious part of Third World opinion is likely to find this
orientation 'Eurocentric' at best.

–   In general, the Third World would see Gorbachev's disarmament
    initiatives and his seemingly sincere effort to reduce world tension as
    a welcome development. Third World countries would welcome
    superpower disarmament even further if funds released from stop-
    ping the rearmament process were to be used for their development.

–   The moderate and predictable system-maintaining role of the Soviet
    Union would be a welcome development to many of the capitalist-
    orientated states (for example in the Middle East). These Third
    World regimes often suspect the 'hand of Moscow' whenever they
    are embroiled in some domestic trouble of their own. The logical
    outcome of Moscow's 'New Thinking' is to abandon support for
    revolutionary groups in Third World countries.

–   New social movements in the Third World with revolutionary
    aspirations seem unlikely to find a ready and sympathetic friend in
    the Soviet Union.

–   The regimes that are likely to suffer most from the 'New Thinking'
    are the Marxist–Leninist ones. Their subsidies may be cut and, if
    they are in danger of being overthrown, Moscow's friendship
    treaties may not help. Disbarred from CMEA, advised to remain
    within the capitalist world economy but unable to obtain develop-
    ment aid, they may face worsening economic conditions. These
    regimes have begun to assert their independence from Moscow:
    some, like Ethiopia, Cuba and North Korea, stated their intention of
    boycotting the 1988 Olympic Games in Seoul. Fidel Castro has
    already criticized Gorbachev's international programme, and
    explicitly stated that Cuba would not follow the USSR's perestroika.

–   The other group which may find the implications of 'New Thinking'
    unhelpful are the peoples struggling for freedom in Palestine,
    Azania, Namibia and so on. On balance, the Soviet Union's record
    on decolonization has been good, even when Stalin formulated a
    rigid two-camp theory and lost the possibility of a Soviet role in the
    decolonization process. Doubts as to whether the Soviet Union will
    come to their support may be enough to make these peoples regard
    the Soviet Union as no different from the Western powers.

The reaction of the Third World as a whole to 'New Thinking' is
therefore likely to be broadly positive, but its radical component may be

uneasy about the possibly negative role the Soviet Union may come to
play in changing the world.

Notes

1. J. Ziegler and Y. Popov, *Ändere die Welt: sie braucht es – eine Dialog zwischen Ost und West*, 1986.
2. M.S. Gorbachev, 2 November 1987, *Moscow News*, no. 39, 1987, supplement.
3. Ibid. See also S. Shenfield, *The Nuclear Predicament*, London 1987, ch. 8.
4. The speech devoted just 2.5 pages out of 105 to the Third World.
5. Gorbachev, *Perestroika – New Thinking for our Country and the World*, London, 1987, p. 221.
6. Ibid.
7. Ibid.
8. Gorbachev, *Perestroika* (Dutch edition), p. 171.
9. Joint Soviet–Yugoslav declaration, *Moscow News*, no. 13, 1988, supplement.
10. E. Primakov, *Pravda*, 10 July 1987.
11. G. Shakhnazarov, 'Governability of the World', *International Affairs*, no. 3, 1988, p. 17.
12. Primakov, 'USSR Policy on Regional Conflicts', *International Affairs*, no. 6, 1988, p. 5.
13. R. Avakov, 'Novoe myshlenie i problema izucheniya razvivayushchikhsya stran', *MEMO*, no. 11, 1987.
14. G. Mirskii, 'K voprosu o vybore puti i orientatsii razvivayushchikhsya stran', *MEMO*, no. 5, 1987, p. 76.
15. Interview with Mirskii and Li, 'Sotsialisticheskaya orientatsiya v svete novogo politicheskogo myshleniya', *Aziya i Afrika Segodnya*, no. 8, 1987, p. 29.
16. W. Sheinis, 'Besonderheiten und Probleme des Kapitalismus in den Entwicklungsländern', *Gesellschaftswissenschaftliche Beitrage*, 1987, p. 409.
17. Avakov, p. 53.
18. A. Butenko, 'Nekotorye teoreticheskie problemy perekhoda k sotsializmu stran s nerazvitoi ekonomikoi', *Narody Azii i Afriki*, no. 5, 1982, p. 7.
19. Ibid., p..78.
20. Sheinis, 'Besonderheiten und Probleme . . .', p. 409.
21. Sheinis, *Rabochii klass i sovremennyi mir*, July/August 1987.
22. Avakov, p. 58.
23. A. Bovin, *Izvestiya*, 11 July 1987.
24. Avakov, p. 59.
25. K. Brutents, *Pravda*, 10 January 1986.
26. Ibid.
27. Gorbachev, *Moscow News*, 8 November 1987.
28. US House Foreign Affairs Committee, 1977, quoted in J.G. Whelan, and M.J. Dixon, 'The Soviet Union in the Third World, 1980–85; an Imperial Burden or Political Asset?', report prepared for the Committee on Foreign Affairs, US House of Representatives, Washington 1985, p. 363.
29. B. Parrott; in B. Parrott, ed., *Trade, Technology and Soviet–American Relations*, Bloomington, IN 1985, p. 47.
30. I. Dobozi, *Soviet and Eastern European Foreign Trade*, vol. 21, no. 1–2–3, 1985, p. 271 and *UN Monthly Bulletin of Statistics*, various years.
31. M. Lavigne, *l'Economie internationale des pays socialistes*, Paris 1986, p. 96.
32. See C. Wolfe, Jr, *et al.*, *The Costs and the Benefits of the Soviet Empire, 1981–1983*, Santa Monica, CA 1986 and *The Costs of the Soviet Empire*, 1973.
33. *Far Eastern Economic Review*, 3 March 1988, p. 16.

34. W. Kühne, 'Sowjetische Afrikapolitik unter Gorbatschow', *Europa Archiv*, 25 November 1986, p. 660.

35. See W. Andreff, 'Le Modèle d'Industrialisation soviétique: quelles leçons pour le Tiers Monde?', *Revue Tiers Monde*, no. 110, April/June 1987.

36. O. Cooper and C. Fogarty, 'Soviet Economic Aid to Less Developed Countries, 1954–1978', in US Congress, Joint Economic Committee, *Soviet Economy in a Time of Change*, vol. 2, 96th Congress, 1st Session, October 1979, p. 654.

37. R. Menon, 'Soviet Arms Transfers to the Third World; Characteristics and Consequences', *Journal of International Affairs*, vol. 40, no. 1, Summer 1986.

38. FBIS-SOV, 28 November, 1985, p. D/6.

39. *Problems of Communism*, September/October 1987, p. 7.

40. Ibid.

41. Gorbachev, Report to the 27th Congress of the CPSU.

42. Ibid., p. 175.

43. W.W. Rostow, 'On Ending the Cold War', *Foreign Affairs*, Spring 1987, p. 846.

44. W.G. Hyland, 'Reagan–Gorbachev III', *Foreign Affairs*, Autumn 1987, p. 41.

9

The Prospects for Conventional Stabilization in Europe

Karsten D. Voigt

Introduction

The alliance against Hitler disintegrated after World War II as political antagonisms developed between East and West. These resulted in the division of Europe, Germany and Berlin. NATO and the Warsaw Treaty Organization were political and military expressions of the tension between East and West which came to a head in the Cold War.

The NATO and Warsaw Treaty alliance systems assumed a new function at the beginning of the first phase of detente: the function of co-operation. In order to establish sufficient defence capabilities, the alliances had to balance the interests of individual member states (and, as in the CSCE process, between all European nations) and at the same time to contribute to co-operation and the reduction of tension. The shift of alliance functions with detente resulted in diverse and complex relationships between the alliances, amongst individual alliance members, and even amongst societal groups within individual nations. At the same time detente improved the long-term potential for security, peace and social emancipation, as well as the democratic process. The continuation and deepening of detente serves the interests of peace as well as sociopolitical interests.

Detente is a reform process. Reform policy is an attempt to achieve particular goals step by step. Individual steps cannot immediately resolve all problems, but this does not mean that achievable steps are unimportant or wrong. In the sphere of disarmament and politics, East and West have been able to come to an understanding with the INF Treaty. This acomplishment will be validated in the coming years if it leads to a continuation of the disarmament process: first, through cuts in shorter-range nuclear weapons; second, through steps towards conventional stability in Europe; and third, through changes in military strategies which bring about a structural inability to attack on both sides.

In a new phase of detente, we shall want to improve the conditions for achieving freedom. Progress in disarmament and the reduction of the threat of war remain, however, of independent value during this second phase. For this reason, the goal of freedom cannot be played off against the goal of peace. Rather, we should endeavour to tie the political challenges of freedom and peace to one another conceptually without making one a condition of the other, which would block progress.

This chapter focuses on the prospects for conventional stabilization which could be of great significance as preparation for a step-by-step demilitarization of the East–West conflict. Although Europeans may have a great deal of influence on the reformulation of nuclear deterrence, it does not lie within their power to overcome the nuclear-deterrence system entirely.

Conventional stability is here defined as a situation in which neither of the two sides in Europe possesses the ability to attack the other – that is to say, a situation in which the strategies of both sides are based upon purely defensive military intentions. Conventional stability must also rest upon the assumption that detente can remove the crises and the causes of war, enemy images and potential animosity in Europe. Arms control can succeed only if assessments of potential threats change and if the political disutility of aggressive military postures is understood. The Gorbachev leadership, for example, would have to be convinced that the USSR's conventional superiority in Europe is detrimental to substantial advances in the realm of conventional arms control. Should the Soviet Union come to an agreement on conventional stability, this would be proof of a new Soviet approach towards Western Europe.

The Asymmetrical Conventional Arms Race

The arms dynamic in conventional weapons in Europe is characterized by a number of asymmetries which are the chief sources of instability and the major reason why conventional arms control in Europe is faced with obstacles which can be surmounted only with great difficulty. The so-far unsuccessful MBFR negotiations are a primary example. First, there is the geographical asymmetry of the alliance systems. The Warsaw Pact has a cohesive alliance area with adequate territorial depth. It can deploy its troops in deep formation. To move units from the western USSR to the East–West border requires a land journey of less than

1,000 kilometres. On the other hand, Soviet access routes to waterways are extremely unfavourable. In addition, most of them are usable only with great difficulty or not at all during the winter months. In this respect NATO has an advantage and can control access to East European waterways with relative ease. NATO's major handicap, however, lies in its lack of alliance territorial depth. Furthermore, the Atlantic Ocean separates the Western European allies from the USA. American and Canadian reinforcement units must be transported more than 6,000 kilometres by air and sea in order to reach Europe.

In addition to this geographical asymmetry, there are differentiated military doctrines and strategies. In the event of a crisis, the Warsaw Pact hopes to defend itself on its opponent's territory. Its military strategy is therefore geared towards a territorial counteroffensive capacity: forward defence. The development of Soviet strategy has been aimed at a comprehensive conventionalized counteroffensive capacity. NATO fears an offensive following a brief period of preparation, and in fact fears this more than the possibility of the famous Blitzkrieg option. Even if no intention to conduct an aggressive strike can be attributed to the Soviet Union, its military strategy, from a Western point of view, still constitutes the greatest source of instability in Europe.

By comparison, the NATO flexible-response strategy is more defensively structured, inasmuch as NATO is in no position to mount a territorial offensive with ground forces. That having been said, NATO does not renounce the options of bomber and rocket tactical offensives deep into enemy territory. Attacks on military targets in Eastern Europe have always been one of the tasks of NATO air-strike units. In the future, this tactical offensive capability is to be reinforced under the planning directive Follow-On Forces Attack (FOFA) and above all to be conventionalized. The objective is to counter the second Soviet echelon in its approach areas. In addition, NATO reserves the nuclear first-use option in its doctrine. This so-called premeditated escalation option is incorporated into weapons systems and operational planning.

Sociopolitical asymmetry also influences the military situation in Europe. While the world-power status of the Soviet Union has hitherto been based on military might (the Gorbachev reform programme suggests medium- and long-term changes here), the West has far greater economic potential and a much more attractive social system. In connection with this, it should be borne in mind that the Soviet forces serve the function of guaranteeing Soviet influence in East European security and social policy. These military forces compensate for a lack of legitimacy in the political system. The systemic differences are also reflected in the differing degrees of openness and availability of military information to the public on both sides. In the conventional sphere, these asymmetries undoubtedly influence dynamic trends in armaments. The Soviet Union and other Warsaw Pact nations are gradually stepping up and conventionalizing their potential, which is suited for a territorial offensive. Conversely, there are also tendencies in the West which could be referred to as a 'Sovietization' of NATO military doctrine. This is to be found in the conventionalization and shift in capacity towards an emphasis on tactical offensives (for example FOFA and AirLand Battle). On both sides, trends in arms technology match these plans for the further consolidation of offensive options.

The long-range potential of conventional munitions is increasingly being extended. Both sides are striving to acquire ever greater capacities for the rapid deployment of military resources to enemy territory (for example conventional stand-off weapons, cruise missiles and, to some extent, ballistic missiles). There are certainly technical and financial problems which arise as a result of these new technologies, and they should not be underestimated. However, because of tendencies on both sides in both arms technology and military strategy, it should be understood that the dynamics of conventional arms in Europe will in the future exacerbate existing political and social instabilities, unless limitations can be agreed upon.

Within a conventional stabilization framework, both sides need to place more emphasis on the creation of a non-aggressive structural capacity. For the Warsaw Pact, this would mean permitting its military territory-taking counteroffensive strategy to be called into question and ultimately abandoning this provocative concept. NATO's response would be to reverse its trends towards the conventional consolidation of the airborne capacity to strike Soviet forces. Put simply, if the Warsaw Pact were to abandon its strategy providing for a territorial counter-offensive, NATO's threat to exercise nuclear first use would lose any military justification.

Structural inability to attack is unquestionably a more demanding goal than mere parity. If the military balance is complemented by arms-control policy following traditional ideas of balance, a contribution to the goal of conventional stabilization will already have been made. On the other hand, structural inability to attack requires both sides not only to disarm but above all to make adjustments within their force structures so that they embody a credible and clearly recognizable renunciation of offensive options. In this sense, both sides would shift from 'parity' towards defensive capacities.

Options for Conventional Arms Control in Europe

The history of conventional arms control in Europe until now presents a contradictory picture. The first attempt at conventional stabilization has so far been unable to produce a result; should the MBFR negotiations one day prove successful, the military situation in Europe would scarcely be altered. Such a treaty would, above all, be a significant means of setting out a declaration of principles, and illustrating that such collective agreements can be reached. The positive and negative experience gained during MBFR negotiations can be utilized in preparation for a broader European disarmament conference. It is my view that the MBFR negotiations should not be abandoned until the chances of substantive agreements at a European conference are seen to be greater than those of the MBFR negotiations. An extension of MBFR to include Denmark and Hungary would, from the perspective of arms control, create a sensible Central European subregion within a European disarmament conference.

The balance sheet to date in the area of confidence-building measures (CSBMs) is much more positive. The Stockholm agreement of the Conference on Confidence and Security-Building Measures and Conventional Disarmament in Europe constitutes, from a perspective of security policy, the first step towards improving the warning signals of preparations for a military attack. Although the agreement contains gaps – for example, it permits emergency alert exercises without prior warning – it does somewhat reduce the risk of surprise attack. The creation of a permanent pan-European institution, which could assess already agreed confidence-building measures and propose further ones, would assist this process.

Priority must now be given to the new conventional arms-control negotiations. It was General Secretary Gorbachev who proposed fresh talks on conventional reductions *from the Atlantic to the Urals* in East Berlin on 18 May 1986. In so doing he accepted in principle the old Western claim that stabilization of the European military situation requires that western military districts of the USSR be included.

The Warsaw Pact *Budapest Appeal* of 11 June 1986 elaborated upon and further defined the Soviet proposal. It called for negotiations on all components of land and tactical air forces, as well as battlefield nuclear weapons, from the Atlantic to the Urals. The reduced forces would be disengaged as complete and equal major units, both intermediate troop formations and units and their weapons. To reduce the danger of surprise attack, the concentration of troops along alliance borders would be reduced. The new conventional arms-control discussions were to be held within the CDE. In relation to verification, the Warsaw Pact stated that it would accept on-site inspections. Lastly, the *Budapest Appeal* contained one very attractive indication in connection with conventional stabilization discussions; both sides should base their military doctrines on 'defensive principles'.

Apart from this hint in the *Budapest Appeal*, there were further indications in the following year that the Warsaw Pact was prepared to question its military doctrine:

The SPD–SED agreement of 21 October 1986 concerning a nuclear-free corridor called for a reduction in the nuclear and conventional strike capacity of both alliance forces. The corridor agreement provides, *inter alia*, for the withdrawal of all artillery systems capable of carrying nuclear weapons, and thus of all heavy conventional artillery.

In his Prague speech of 12 March 1987, Mikhail Gorbachev announced his readiness to remove elements of asymmetry, should they exist. Reductions would have to be initiated by the party which enjoyed an advantage. As previously, the USSR now maintains that all in all, there is a roughly balanced power relationship in Europe. By adopting the Western concept of asymmetry, however, Gorbachev intimated a cautious turn which Soviet writers have long avoided.

Attention should be drawn to the latest Polish disarmament plan. Alongside some familiar elements, the Jaruzelski initative of May 1987 stressed that NATO and the Warsaw Pact should alter their military doctrines in such a way that their respective strategies can be recognized as 'strictly defensive'. Also significant in the Polish plan is the zone in Central Europe designated for nuclear and conventional reductions, which in contrast to MBFR includes Denmark and Hungary as well as the Federal Republic of Germany, the Benelux countries, the German Democratic Republic, Czechoslovakia and Poland.

Thus the Warsaw Pact nations have, in principle, accepted structural inability to attack as the goal of European conventional arms control. Moreover, the Soviet Union has indicated that it is prepared to take European security interests with respect to medium-range nuclear weapons more seriously than in the past – exactly how seriously remains to be seen in the ultimate conventional stabilization process. Over and above statements of principle, the signs of Eastern re-evaluations in the realm of conventional weapons must also be seen to lead to concrete actions.

Above all, it is important that the West should now find its way to a consistent arms-control strategy. It should be noted, however, that NATO reactions to recent Warsaw Pact proposals indicate that the alliance has difficulty formulating a common position. This may in part reflect feelings of being the conventionally inferior party, but it is none the less inexcusable.

NATO's High-Level Task Force in Halifax is proceeding with its work with great difficulty in response to the *Budapest Appeal*. The Brussels Statement of 12 December 1986 was very defensively worded and clearly demonstrated the reserved attitude of NATO members towards Warsaw Pact proposals. The current circumstances in Europe are regarded as disadvantageous to the West. The Brussels Statement intimated that reductions are primarily expected from the East and that the West hardly sees itself in a position to alter its own military strategy.

For a long time the High-Level Task Force could not even agree on the framework within which the arms-control discussions should take place. While France favoured the CDE, the US pushed for separate bloc-to-bloc negotiations between NATO and the Warsaw Pact. The compromise reached at the NATO meeting in Reykjavik in June 1987 produced a common Western position on the definition of the nego-tiating framework. The Western goals in these negotiations still remain unclear.

So far, NATO has been unable to draw up a negotiating concept. Over the years, insufficient attention has been paid to conventional arms control both in Brussels and within the individual NATO states. Within the alliance there is no apparent concept of demands that should be placed upon the Warsaw Pact, nor of what structural changes the Soviet military strategy must initiate – let alone of what concessions, if any, the West may offer the Warsaw Pact. Without such a negotiating concept, the West leaves itself open to suspicion that it is not sincerely interested in the stabilization of asymmetrical structures, capabilities and doctrines in Europe, but solely interested in obtaining improvements for itself in the sphere of confidence-building. Important though they may be, confidence-building measures are insufficient if conventional stabi-lization is genuinely desired; cuts and changes in capabilities cannot be avoided.

Options for Conventional Arms Limitation

Arms-control negotiations must, as mentioned above, be aimed towards the goal of mutual structural inability to attack, in the sense of the cri-teria also mentioned above. The MBFR forum is inadequate to serve this purpose since it focuses on troop levels and because the scope for reductions is, for well-known reasons, too narrow. Conventional arms control must be aimed at mutual reductions in attack potential after a

brief preparation period and at the elimination of periods of potential
offensive threat. In an initial phase, the European conventional arms-
control negotiations should concentrate on land-based weapons and
forces. As a matter of negotiating technique, naval forces should be
excluded from the negotiations. The air force should be included only in
the first phase in so far as a trade-off between renunciation of Warsaw
Pact offensive land-based options and NATO offensive air-based
options (for example FOFA) seems sensible and necessary.

Although the room for reductions at MBFR is too narrow, it continues to appear sensible to designate at least one subregion within the
pan-European negotiating zone from the Atlantic to the Urals (the
Central European zone) in which the main concern is reductions and
restrictions – as distinct from the rest of the territory from the Atlantic
to the Urals, where troop movements and activities would be restricted.
An agreement regarding reductions in the Central European zone
should be formulated by all the NATO and Warsaw Pact nations it
would affect. Participation of all CSCE nations in the verification
process could link this agreement with a further one dealing with the
pan-European negotiation zone. As the latest Polish proposal envisages,
the central reduction area should cover Denmark and Hungary in
addition to the MBFR zone. While there can be dispute about detailed
assessments of the balance between NATO and the Warsaw Pact, in
juggling figures such as 1:3, 1:2, or 1:1.2 the current debate misses the
real problems of such arguments about balance. The root of the problem
is that the Warsaw Pact will have to agree to substantial asymmetrical
reductions which are to its disadvantage. The primary source of military
instability in Europe is, after all, the Soviet territory-taking counteroffensive strategy. However, in the realm of medium-range nuclear
weapons the Soviet Union has demonstrated that it is prepared to accept
asymmetrical reductions if the West is willing to alter its own strategy. In
the conventional sphere, a deal might be struck which involved NATO
renunciation of nuclear first use and of new conventional options such
as FOFA. Here again, it is a matter of taking Gorbachev at his word.

In the final analysis, offensive options can be dismantled only if
capacities are genuinely reduced. Simple force cuts and restrictions on
movement, however important they may be, should not be the first
priority when mutual structural inability is at stake. In order to limit
strike options after a brief preparatory period, the reductions should be
concentrated on combat-ready active ground force units with more than
50 per cent of personnel (corresponding to Soviet Category I and II
units). From the outset, these unit reductions must include weaponry. In
addition, material reductions should be concentrated on mobile
weapons with high-firepower capabilities which serve strike options

(tanks, heavy artillery, combat helicopters and, in particular, tank guns).

To combat asymmetries, reductions of combat-ready units and their weaponry could be shared out according to the contributions of individual members of the respective alliances. The Soviet Union would then have to bear the lion's share of Warsaw Pact reduction, whereas NATO reductions would be more uniformly distributed. Senator Sam Nunn has proposed that the USA and the USSR withdraw half of their troops stationed in Western and Eastern Europe. For the USA that would be two and a half divisions, but for the USSR thirteen and a half. If these divisions are not dissolved but merely withdrawn from Europe, problems of geographical asymmetry arise. In the event of a crisis, the USSR could transport its troops to Eastern Europe more rapidly than the USA's units could reach Western Europe. One way of overcoming this problem might be to allow the Americans to store pre-positioned materials (POMCUS stores), as long as this did not conflict with the agreed limitations on equipment with an offensive capacity.

In addition, there should be limitations which serve as confidence-building measures and also reduce the risk of attack after a brief military preparation period:

- mutual transformation of combat-ready troop units into reduced-strength units (agreed strength reduction);

- selective reduction of armoured units;

- depletion zones in which the storage of materials suitable for attack – such as tanks, combat helicopters, heavy artillery, munition and fuel depots, and bridge-building equipment – is forbidden; however, defensive equipment such as barrier mines and tank barriers would be permitted;

- more rigorous CSCE provisions, particularly an obligatory advanced warning in case of emergency exercises of a certain size.

These proposals indicate the direction in which discussions should proceed in order to advance the conventional stabilization of Europe. The mutual creation of military means which correspond to the structural inability to attack is an ambitious long-term goal which can be achieved only at a gradual place. It is therefore all the more necessary for both sides to initiate the learning process which is needed for a comprehensive security and disarmament dialogue between East and West and to allow non-aligned and neutral states to participate. For this dialogue to achieve substantial results in formal governmental negotiations, it must be scientifically prepared and supported. Politicians, parties and parliaments can contribute to the development of a pan-

European security and disarmament culture in their discussions which,
given superpower participation, could assist in dismantling hostile
images and enmity in the East–West conflict. This process can improve
the chances of the intergovernmental negotiations achieving success.

Alternative Defence Models

Were the discussion concerning structural inability to attack independent of the increased efficiency of defence, one could leave this
debate to those militarists who count tanks, to strategy experts, and to
peace researchers. More important than the details of military planning,
however, is a change in the East–West political relationship so that the
military element is no longer a dominating factor; its influence must be
limited. The demilitarization of relations in Europe and the repolar-
ization of the East–West conflict are, for this reason, two sides of the
same coin. Arms control is a civilized political peace process in which
both sides gradually adapt to a non-violent method of conflict management. Such a learning process is also required in the discussion of
'structural inability to attack'. The debate has in itself had a civilizing
influence in affecting the outlook of those involved in the discussion. Its
main problems can be identified as follows:

-   the development of common criteria for the planning of armed
    forces;

-   communication and changes in the images of threat;

-   the orientation of military needs towards the principle of sufficiency
    instead of worst-case analysis;

-   changes in the definition of what is meant by standards of suf-
    ficiency when both sides adopt this principle.

The following comparison between different concepts and models which
fall under the category of 'structural inability to attack' accords with this
understanding of organization and stabilization as a learning process
between East and West. Here, a variety of models are outlined and
compared in the light of a number of criteria for conventional stabilization. These different concepts can most easily be distinguished
according to the structure and composition of their proposed component.

As distinct from the present NATO strategy, the alternative concepts
share one common characteristic: none of the models takes the use of
land-based nuclear weapons into consideration. The nuclear component
would be reduced to sea-based minimum deterrence. The overall role of

nuclear weapons would be drastically reduced and restricted to an assured capacity to compensate for an opponent's nuclear deployment. At the same time, with respect to battlefield deployment, the nuclear threat would be renounced. Horst Afheldt does not completely exclude nuclear deployment as a last resort.

(a) Covered Area Defence (Jochen Löser)

The basic principle of Jochen Löser's model consists of a combination of stationary barrier infantry forces with high-firepower (shield forces) and heavily equipped tank forces. The ratio of infantry to tank forces is 1:1. Along the border there would be a 40–60 kilometre strip in which 'fire brigades' would be stationed at protected points, in order to incapacitate the opponent and prevent him concentrating his forces. Mechanized conventional forces would conduct a counterattack within the covered zone in order to win back lost territory. Conventional security forces would secure the rear flank of this area in combination with extensive civil security capabilities. Löser envisages counterattacks conducted on enemy territory involving both weapons functions (up to 100 kilometres) and ground fighting forces (up to 40 kilometres).

(b) Integrated Forward Defence (Albrecht C. von Müller)

This concept also calls for a combination of light infantry and heavy tank forces; with respect to the latter, it is drastically reduced by comparison with Löser's. Along the border would be a five kilometre-wide 'fire belt' with a sensor net, mines, and intelligent (accurate) passive munitions. In the rear, light infantry uses anti-tank and anti-aircraft weapons in a so-called 25 kilometre 'net zone'. Finally, the tank forces, stationed in a 65 kilometre deep strip, serve the purpose of fighting the attacking units which have broken through and protecting the major centre from attack. If the enemy's attack should come to a standstill in the 'net zone', von Müller does not exclude the option of a counterattack on WTO territory. In addition, it should be mentioned that the 'fire-belt' weapons can strike up to 40–60 kilometres inside enemy territory.

(c) Structure of the Bundeswehr in the 1990s (Andreas von Bülow)

A further concept has been put forward by Andreas von Bülow. The ratio of tanks to infantry is greatly reduced by comparison with Löser's proposal. Von Bülow's model also consists of a forward defence zone of 40–60 kilometres in which underground light infantry forces fight with anti-tank and anti-aircraft weapons. This would be expanded by conventional mobile tank forces which would be stationed partly to the fore, but mainly in the rear of the forward defence zone. They would have the same function as in Löser's concept. Von Bülow also does not exclude the option of counterattacks conducted on WTO territory. Airforce and infantry weapon functions on the other side of national borders are foreseen as operating at a depth of 50–100 kilometres. Von Bülow portrays this model as one of transition. The mobile forces are vulnerable in view of certain changes in WTO force structure.

(d) Alternative Security Policy Study Group (SAS)

The SAS model is a mixed concept which renounces most of the mobile and, especially, heavy tank forces (mobile:reactive forces, 1:3.9 in respect of personnel). The greatest weight of defence relies on the light infantry forces ('capture net'), which robs the enemy of the initiative and delays its forward march by using barricades and prepared positions. Each of the 60-square-kilometre modules at the front of the 80-kilometre-wide 'capture net' would be occupied by twenty-eight soldiers. In the rear they would be assigned to cover a space of eight square kilometres. The 'capture net' would be equipped partly by light and partly by heavy tank and mobile forces ('fire forces'). The light tank units would fight in built-up areas; the heavy tank units in open areas while at the same time recovering lost territory. The mobile units are logistically and informationally notified by positioned modules, so that they are barely able to engage in combat operations outside the 'capture nets'. Light infantry and mobile fighting units would, under the SAS model, have the object of securing the rear defence zones.

The SAS model renounces all weapons functions designed to attack enemy territory. Air defence systems are to serve restricted purposes; they are to utilize land-based anti-aircraft and light fighter planes in combating infiltrating aircraft and weaponry.

(e) Defence Wall (Norbert Hannig)

This concept totally renounces mobile elements of defence. It involves a model of purely reactive, stationed conventional 'fire brigades' armed with both passive and active munitions. Mobility would be replaced with firepower. The border areas would be enclosed within a four-kilometre zone stocked with passive munitions (for example mines). In this zone, supplementary guided weapons would be fired from infantry combat vehicles dug in throughout the area. The artillery rockets possess a range of 20.5–200 kilometres; the guided weapons of the infantry range from

50–60 kilometres. The rocket launchers are removed from the border in relation to their ranges. These would do more than cover the border zone, as they would also cover rear areas (this is based on the principle of overlapping circles). In the event of mobilized action, the infantry combat vehicles would dig themselves into positions in such a way that the layered system created field barricades and bunkers. Hannig states that the civilian population should at the same time be evacuated from battlefield areas.

(f) Technocommandos (Horst Afheldt)

This is a proposal for reactive stationed area defence, which calls for three overlapping light infantry (fighting commando) nets equipped with short- and long-range rocket artillery as well as an information/ communication and control system. It is the most frequently quoted concept in public debates in the FRG. The technocommandos would be evenly distributed throughout the entire Federal Republic of Germany; however, Afheldt renounces either mobile or heavy equipment (for example tanks) for his forces. The net of fighting commandos would have anti-tank weapons and conventional artillery to explode mines, mortars, and similar weapons at their disposal. The fighting forces (twenty-five men per unit) operate within an area of 10–15 square kilometres along the border. They would wear out the attacking forces. The rocket artillery net possesses short-range weapons with which to explode mines, and other munitions such as accurate artillery rockets of middle-range capacity. This net begins 20 kilometres behind the border and is intended to fight enemy strike forces.

Horst Afheldt renounces the use of air strike forces in his concept; their functions would be taken over by the artillery rocket net and the control and communication net. He has also developed a transition model for this concept, which resembles that of the SAS.

Comparison between the Alternative Defence Models

(a) Strategic Stability

The most difficult problem for strategic stability lies in the question of what constitutes a defensive concept. Defensiveness and offensiveness are not unique features of individual weapons systems, but emerge from the overall structure of a defence concept – the combination of tactical-operative principles and the military options of the available capacities. Furthermore, it is hard to imagine pure defensiveness: even light infan-

try forces could advance from Bonn to Moscow if the opponent did not
defend himself sufficiently. For this reason, in terms of defence
concepts, it is better to speak of 'more defensive' and 'more offensive'.

This alone, however, does not resolve all the problems. Structural
inability to attack may be becoming a household phrase, but its meaning
is hardly clear. If considered too narrowly it implies that this inability
should be independent of the enemy's capacity and options, and none of
the models presented here promotes a structure incapable of engagement. Hannig's infantry combat vehicles alone could, circumstances
permitting, push forward (though logistical problems would surely then
arise). If considered in a broad sense, the concept could be taken to
mean an inability to occupy enemy territory for a long period of time;
given present circumstances, neither side would then be in a situation to
count on a rapid military victory.

A force structure which can conduct a rapid offensive into enemy
territory is something very different from one in which the weapons and
soldiers are immobile and incapable of reaching it. A serious debate
about structural inability to initiate an offensive must also clarify a range
of problems, including: does pure defensiveness mean the complete
renunciation of mobile forces? Renunciation of heavily armoured
forces? Renunciation of weapons which function deep within enemy
territory? These questions should not be answered in the abstract.
Whether or not a defence concept can be defined as defensive and non-
threatening depends on the presumed enemy's perception of it. That
which is defined as structural inability to attack cannot be determined
unilaterally, but only in agreement with the WTO.

The next question to be addressed is: What conditions can guarantee
Europe's strategic stability? The strategic situation would be especially
unstable if both sides were to have offensively orientated strategies as
well as corresponding options and capacity at their disposal. The defensive intentions behind their offensive options would not be considered
credible. In a crisis both sides would suffer an overwhelming pre-
emptive impulse. The result would be an eternal arms race in which each
side would attempt to take away the other's offensive options while
concurrently maintaining its own ability to attack.

Fortunately, this situation does not exist in present-day Europe. Only
the Warsaw Treaty Organization has such a strategy – that is, offensive
and orientated on to the opponent's territory. NATO, however, is
currently expanding its counteroffensive abilities in the shape of FOFA
and other plans which provide conventional military options designed to
fight deep within enemy territory. This trend of 'Sovietization' in
Western military strategy does not correspond to the requirements of
strategic stability.

Europe's strategic stability would be best guaranteed if both sides possessed a truly reactive defence structure. If both sides were independently to have access to so-called defence forces and no longer possessed tanks, a change in their offensive capacities would have occurred. But we should remember that political problems cannot be resolved by military means.

If NATO were to abolish unilaterally its mobile and armoured forces and rearm along the lines of a strictly reactive military structure, would the entire strategic stability of Europe improve, even if the East were to maintain its forward strategy? This question is more than difficult to answer. On the one hand, such a step would improve political stability because the non-threatening character of NATO would be more clearly expressed. One could further plausibly argue that strategic stability, in the sense of structural inability to attack, could be reached more easily if mobile and armoured forces focused specifically on enemy territory were renounced. This is where Afheldt's and Hannig's proposals differ.

On the other hand, the overall European strategic situation would stabilize if the 'defence-efficiency hypothesis' could be met in full. This states that reactive stationary units have an advantage over mobile forces. It must also be demonstrated that, in terms of military effectiveness, reactive concepts such as those of Afheldt and Hannig are convincing to the present NATO structure on the conventional level. Even supporters of the alternative models express doubts about this. That in itself demonstrates that the majority of the proposals addressed here involve mixed forms of stationary and mobile elements.

These mixed concepts, however, entail problems of their own in the realm of strategic stability. It is questionable whether mixed concepts which make use of mobile and armoured forces can contribute much to the building of confidence. Jochen Löser's proposal can hardly claim to have a particularly defensive character. His reform concept is not particularly guided by the goal of strategic stability. However, von Bülow's and von Müller's concepts cannot escape doubts as to their non-threatening character, especially when they fulfil their efficiency postulates. Given particular circumstances, a potential enemy may find them especially threatening. For example, light infantry with heavy firepower can bring a WTO offensive to a standstill; the rear flank could then come forward and launch a counterattack, pushing the aggressor out of NATO territory. On the grounds of deterrence, von Bülow and von Müller have stated this as an express intention. They argue, however, that only following a WTO offensive need the WTO fear such a counterattack. Under such conditions, a NATO offensive would not be feasible.

In that respect, the defence-based defence structure's inability to attack a fully armed opponent would be reduced. Is this not equally valid today for both the WTO and NATO? And how does the non-threatening character of such mixed concepts look in the event of an attack which is not intended to serve the purpose of victory, but is the result of a politically calculated escalation process? It must be kept in mind that the defensive characteristic of mixed concepts based on stationary and also conventional forces (von Bülow's model sustains fifty-six mechanized brigades, even if the number of personnel would be reduced) can become unclear from the potential enemy's perspective. Whether or not the concepts can satisfy the criterion of strategic stability therefore appears questionable. The SAS model, which brings out more clearly the firepower capability of armoured forces, appears to meet the criterion better.

A combination of offensive and defensive elements can awaken doubts about the non-threatening character of the defence structure. This problem also exists for the purely reactive models like that of Horst Afheldt, especially during the phase of transition from the existing structure to the alternative defence option. If one were to begin unilateral rearmament, there would be a problematic transition period. On the grounds of stability one would be required to sacrifice one's restraint capacity, for the dismantling of one's mobile and armoured forces would take place before the reactive infantry and rocket artillery forces were functional. Were one to supplement the present tank brigades with the reactive capacities, one would increase one's offensive capacity instead of destroying it. Strategic stability would collapse. The sectoral introduction of more defensively structured forces in individual elements could only partially solve this dilemma. A minimal prerequisite of strategic stability would be a challenge to the placing of heavy armoured forces in the rear during the transition period. Even then, doubts remain about the non-threatening character of the defence structure as portrayed in von Müller's and von Bülow's proposals.

Any attempt to stabilize the entire strategic situation unilaterally therefore shows itself to have limitations. The criteria themselves must become mutually and reciprocally operational, but even then only Afheldt's, Hannig's, and the SAS's model could increase strategic stability. Their non-threatening character can be clearly recognized. But these concepts cannot be realized overnight. All the alternative strategies involve offensive–defensive mixed concepts during the transition phase, which could be considered as especially threatening when there are no doubts concerning the concept's military efficiency. In order to improve strategic stability a co-operative solution is necessary; both sides should, right from the beginning, rearm in a defensive direction.

(b) Crisis Stability

One of the most important starting points for many of the alternative proposals is a criticism of flexible response's unstable character in a crisis. The present defence structure requires rapid mobile action in order to be capable of countering (disarming) an attack following a short warning period. NATO, therefore, offers its opponent attractive targets that must be attacked quickly in order to achieve military advantages. Many NATO weapons systems must be rapidly and potentially pre-emptively deployed, to avoid the risk of capture or destruction at an early stage of the fighting. By virtue of renouncing land-based nuclear weapons, all the proposals discussed above entail a large number of heavy armoured forces and of centralized command and control centres which still offer the opponent attractive goals but nevertheless reduce the risk of pre-emptive action in the event of a crisis. In reality they would probably fulfil the criterion of crisis stability better than today's 'flexible response'. Horst Afheldt's model comes closest to an optimal structure of crisis stability, while in the concepts as set out by von Bülow and von Müller (to say nothing of Löser) attractive targets are available after as well as before, in that strong armoured forces and a well-equipped air force would be maintained. Norbert Hannig's 'defence wall', however, would increase crisis stability if one could be sure that the buried vehicles, artillery and rocket stations and the information and control systems could not be easily detected by the enemy (for example by their radar signals).

(c) Disarmament-Compatibility

In addition to dealing with the improvement of crisis stability, the alternative concepts speak of making it possible to step out of the European conventional armaments race, for the most part unilaterally. By contrast, flexible response is supposedly tied to an endless arms race because one's own defence is directed against the enemy's capacity, thus necessitating constant further reactions. Here there are doubts concerning the compatibility of arms control with the present NATO strategy, while the room for manoeuvre for Western reductions is restricted in view of WTO conventional superiority.

If one defines disarmament-compatibility in the realm of conventional weapons such that rearmament would foster a defensive structure, then all the concepts analysed above are by definition more arms-control orientated than the present NATO strategy. For that matter, most advocate unilateral stabilization in the conventional field without placing demands on the WTO. In every case, however,

discussions with the East are vital for the purpose of clarifying misunderstandings.

Acceptance of unilateral initiatives for stepping out of the conventional arms dynamic in Europe is likely only when the cost–effect
hypothesis of defence is valid, which once again is closely connected to
the efficiency hypothesis. It is argued that it must be cheaper for one
side to establish a reactive defence structure than for the other side to
establishing corresponding forces with an offensive orientation. It is
easier for the defender to make counteradjustments, so the attempt to
overcome the reactive concept leads to a dead end.

No strong argument in support of this hypothesis has yet been put
forward, and the case has usually rested on certain beliefs. The supporters of these alternatives tend to underestimate the costs of ensuring
immunity against any reaction by the offensively armed side, and to
overestimate the military efficiency of static defence. This is especially
evident in Hannig's model, which provides for unilateral mounting of
rocket and artillery firepower. When the cost–effect analysis alone is
valid, a complete unilateral stepping out of the conventional arms
dynamic is politically impossible in the face of alliance and domestic
concerns, and irresponsible in terms of security policy. Should the WTO
stand by its offensive strategy even after the restructuring of NATO, it
would try to arm against the new Western defence structure. NATO
would then have to make further costly adjustments.

The Western reactive defence structure rearmament could serve to
make NATO's non-threatening character clear, and could in the long
term put pressure on the WTO to renounce its offensive strategy. One
would have to maximize the non-threatening character of the structure –
that is, rearm in the direction of Afheldt's proposal.

The question remains whether changes on the NATO side can have
any effect on the East's forward strategy. One need not presume an
aggressive intention on the East's part to come to the conclusion that its
offensive strategy has as much to do with historical experience – with
alliance policy considerations as well as traditional military beliefs – as
with the details of Western armament. If so, a gradual strategy of unilateral initiatives might have very little effect on Eastern armament.

In conclusion, this means that the alternative concepts which are
more compatible with arms control may have clearly defensive effects on
the East. Whether or not their unilateral realization could end the
conventional arms race depends on questions of the reactive character
of firepower as against the mobility of traditional conventionally
armoured forces, especially on relative efficiency and costs. The validity
of this hypothesis cannot be determined due to a lack of actual and
comparative examination. Even less certain – and, at least in the past,

irrelevant – has been the hypothesis that the WTO would react to a unilaterally defensive restructuring of NATO. One therefore remains dependent on co-operative measures if one wants to control the conventional arms race in Europe.

(d) Ability to Exercise Restraint

The controversies between opponents and supporters of flexible response and, for that matter, alternative concepts have been over-concentrated on the question of how militarily efficient the individual structures would be against aggression. Many advocates of the defensive models often label their recommendations independently as contributions to a functional NATO defence, so that the benefits of political stability are reduced. This analysis is something of a war of beliefs in which enthusiasm for the alternatives makes up for a lack of knowledge regarding the concepts' performance capability. Of course, it is hard to see how one would make a practical comparison between the alternative models and flexible response, from the point of view of military efficiency. Those in official positions in NATO and defence ministries have, up to this point, barely taken the trouble to analyse the defensive concepts seriously. The following thoughts are therefore preliminary and provisional.

One key question concerns the extent of flexible response's deterrent effect. Even if one has doubts about the credibility of the deployment of nuclear arms, the deterrent effect against an enemy counting on victory can be considerable. There is also, however, the risk of rapid conventional and nuclear escalation, and the factor of the damage which conventional and nuclear weapons threaten against targets deep in WTO territory.

It is clear that the risk of nuclear escalation is reduced by the concepts described above. Most of these alternative concepts are based on a scenario involving large forces conducting an offensive after only brief military preparation, in an attempt to break rapidly through the defender's positions. The alternative concepts would probably increase NATO's ability to ward off an attack in such a scenario. Today, the West's only option, once the forward defence line has been broken through, is nuclear escalation. Because of this, Afheldt and Hannig envisage a longer conventional war of attrition in which the attacker becomes entangled in the defence net. After John Mearsheimer, the prospect of a long-lasting war of attrition has been considered an especially effective deterrent against a conventional attack. Afheldt's concept of a space-covering defence net, by which a rapid breakthrough appears impossible, could also restrain attacks effectively.

But how do other scenarios look, for example, in the event of an attack with limited goals, when a war does not involve the goal of victory? The more a structure is based upon static defence, the less flexible it is to engage itself in changed circumstances. But in the case of a large-scale attack, the restraint capability of the alternative models does not meet the criteria of the efficiency hypothesis. The defender's advantage in familiar and prepared areas should be stronger when reactive-orientated forces with optimal firepower are engaged. Mobile units can then be equipped for any type of battle which the aggressor might choose. As mentioned earlier, it is impossible to make a final judgement on this point at this time. First, it is to be doubted whether a reactive structure such as Afheldt's is of the same value as flexible response in early forward defence, in view of present WTO strategy. Afheldt and Hannig do not renounce mobile elements indiscriminately; all the other proponents of alternatives suggest mixed concepts in the light of this.

'Fire versus Mobility' controversies are closely linked with the efficiency question. The supporters of a static defence structure argue that modern technological development (for example, sensors, optics, information technology, munitions technology) have led to an enormous increase in firepower. Because of this, improvements in armour are not sustainable. Those who do not suffer from a technological fetish (for example Hannig and Löser) argue that fire can replace mobility to the extent that static rocket and artillery positions can also concentrate their fire on targets over wide distances. (In other words, they can change the location of fire coverage.)

It is certainly true that the element of firepower has taken on considerable significance. It is, however, by no means clear that improved firepower alone can give a defensively orientated side a decisive advantage. An offensive operational strategy can also make use of technological advances. This point is particularly valid for Hannig's defence wall, but also has some bearing on the other concepts.

A further argument against the static models states that the renunciation of mobility and armoured forces would lead to the complete loss of any territory taken by the enemy. An aggressor would have to pay a high entry price and face a higher rate of attrition, but would face no risk of counteroffensives. This is the debate which prompted the SAS, von Bülow, von Müller and Löser to accept armoured forces, at least in terms of 'firepower', in their concepts. The consensus between followers of alternative models agrees that mobility and armoured forces cannot be completely abandoned in a unilateral restructuring.

The defence concepts also renounce the capacity to inflict damage deep in enemy territory. The ability to restrain is reduced when the enemy's territory becomes a sanctuary. The aggressor then risks becoming trapped in the defence net – that is, not achieving his goals – but need not fear retaliation; destruction would be suffered only on the defender's territory. In addition, the attacker's reinforcement forces could march unchallenged on to the defender's territory and concentrate on exerting power there.

This criticism does not concern Löser's, von Müller's or von Bülow's proposals, which maintain a limited 'deep-strike' option within WTO territory. Such capacities are thinkable under Hannig's model, but without heavy rocket launchers would have to be stationed less than 200 kilometres from the border. Afheldt and the SAS both renounce the threat of massive damage to Eastern territory on the grounds of defensiveness. There is obviously a conflict of purpose here between stability and restraint capacity. The concept of sea-based nuclear weapons which strike back should be taken into consideration. An aggressor could then not exclude the possibility that NATO would deploy these against its territory in the event of a threatening situation.

It remains clear that a final judgement on the alternative concepts is impossible. This cautious evaluation has indicated that all the alternative models would mean a loss of deterrence in comparison with flexible response. When they are unilaterally initiated, with some mobile and armoured forces still in existence, the threat of limited damage on enemy territory persists, in order to hinder the concentration of enemy forces. To satisfy the criteria of restraint capacity, von Bülow's and von Müller's concepts are preferable to those of Afheldt and the SAS, although neither satisfies the stability criterion. Hannig's concept appears to suffice, because of its unilateral optimization of rockets, in respect of the stability and deterrence criteria. For none of the concepts can the criteria of stability and deterrence be fulfilled simultaneously and sufficiently by a unilateral restructuring.

(e) Alliance Compatibility

Many supporters of alternative concepts argue that they could be unilaterally established by the West without challenging all the alliance partners to co-operate. This method of argument overlooks the fact that structural inability to attack cannot reveal its non-threatening character when it is a tactical-operational concept unique to the German Bundeswehr. It must become the military strategy of the entire alliance. Take, for example, a situation in which the Bundeswehr rearms its forces defensively while the USA – the second largest contingent of conventional forces on the European continent – not only maintains its offensive capabilities but also develops them further in respect of

AirLand Battle. The result could be a WTO presumption of improvements in NATO's attack capacity in that the defence capacity is optimal while offensive forces are being built up simultaneously. The same problem remains: there would be disputes in connection with the mixed concepts and the transition phase.

If one wants to achieve stability in Europe, the rearmament must be planned and established by the entire alliance. At the very least, the NATO partners who field the largest conventional forces in Central Europe must be involved from beginning to end. That includes the USA. Without the agreement of the most important alliance power, the alternative concepts are barely feasible. It is also a large problem for the practical establishment of the alternative concepts.

In principle, all the models presented are compatible with the alliance in so far as the tactical-operational level of all alliance fighting forces is dealt with. The political and practical problem also exists in the operational concept of current US army developments. Although AirLand Battle in its entirety is not feasible due to its technical and financial implications, this trend, which stresses high mobility and a strong offensive capability, is a trend in a very undesirable direction.

One could attempt to assimilate the operational concepts of the Bundeswehr and of the armies of smaller countries such as Belgium, the Netherlands and Denmark in the direction of greater defensiveness, but this is no substitute for a German–American agreement. Arguments which state that the establishment of the alternative models could in the long run involve a renunciation of the presence of American troops in Western Europe are counterproductive. For the political purposes of peace and security, Western Europe remains supportive of the US presence as long as the USSR maintains its troops in Eastern Europe. More so than the nuclear weapons stationed in Europe, the 300,000 or so US forces there ensure that every European military issue between East and West poses an imminent danger of a war between the superpowers, encompassing the risk of escalation. There are therefore serious problems with any recommendations which call for a division of responsibilities within the alliance, for example with the Bundeswehr assigned land defence and the Netherlands and Denmark required to concentrate on naval duties. Although this is feasible to some extent, it should not be permitted to endanger the multinational structure which maintains forces committed to forward defence.

Enormous practical problems are posed for NATO in establishing the alternative concepts. First, the USA must be convinced that rearming the defence structure on a reactive basis would not pose unacceptable disadvantageous risks. Overall, models such as von Bülow's are better designed in terms of the alliance compatibility criterion than concepts which distance themselves more sharply from flexible response.

(f) Damage Limitation

The present NATO strategy of deterrence sacrifices the possibility of limiting damage in the event of war. Should deterrence fail, what is to be defended would more than likely be destroyed. This flexible-response risk was the starting point from which alternative concepts developed. In respect of limiting damage in war, it could be argued that the alternative concepts are better designed than flexible response. A defensive defence structure in theory offers less attractive conventional and nuclear targets. Herein lie problems for several concepts. In this sense, von Bülow's, von Müller's and Löser's models do not satisfactorily fulfil the criterion of offering less attractive targets: the number of stationary heavy armoured forces in the rear area is too high. Hannig's proposal lacks the possibility of minimizing damage, for as soon as the first shot is fired it is too late, and concentrated counterfiring is inevitable.

A purely reactive defence structure like Afheldt's is faced with the problem that its ability to bring war to an end quickly is nonexistent. It would probably lead to a long-lasting conventional war of attrition. In view of this, the ability to exercise restraint is required. Whether or not this should limit damage remains doubtful. A conflict of goals follows in the conventional realm: restraint capacity or damage limitation. Those who want to strengthen conventional deterrence must prevent the success of Blitzkrieg operations and rapid enemy breakthroughs. If deterrence fails, a war of attrition, which inevitably affects the cost of damage limitation, becomes likely.

These considerations make it obvious that the best method of minimizing the damage caused by war is to prevent it. Political strategies such as detente and confidence-building and the connected structural incapacity to attack, which together create a structure of common security in Europe, are much more meaningful to the prevention of war than a unilateral restructuring of forces.

(g) Societal Compatibility

It has become a truism that the level of financial and human resources required today by flexible response cannot be maintained in the future. The Bundeswehr of the 1990s would be more or less bankrupt. All the alternative concepts appear to be cheaper, since they could be staffed by fewer personnel than the present Bundeswehr structure. It is often pointed out that expensive large weapons systems could be abolished. The cost comparisons of the individual models are unavailable to their respective authors and, for that matter, costings are very difficult in any case. It seems, however, that the costs of more modern rocket and information technology have been somewhat overestimated. This affects models which are especially dependent on high technology (for example, Hannig's). Should the optimistic prognosis which supporters give the defensive concepts be provable, these models would indeed be much more acceptable to society than 'flexible response'.

A frequent accusation made against the defensive models states that they would lead to a militarization of society by virtue of their militia-like structure and high number of reserve forces. Supporters argue, against this, that such models do not imply the militarization of society; rather, a civilization of the military. The question should not be dealt with at this level of polemic. Even the empirical examples of countries with militia-like structures do not offer any further help. Switzerland surely has a militarized society in comparison with that of the FRG, but Austria would be a counterexample.

It is understood that concepts based on militia-like structures would largely penetrate the civilian and military sectors, as is the case today. Theoretically, the direction in which this develops cannot be predetermined: it depends on the political framework. If the restructuring is embedded in detente and the creation of a supra-bloc security structure, the danger of militarization can be considered low.

It must be taken into account, however, that the majority of infantry structures envisage concepts which, during peacetime, station individual units in areas which are to be defended. In this manner, familiarity with the area can be increased so that the advantage of the defence can be utilized to the utmost. This would allow for an even distribution of military burdens throughout the FRG. Until now, the burdens have been most heavily felt in border areas. On the other hand, overall burdens might increase.

Concluding Analysis

The above comparison of the various alternative concepts shows that the problems of 'structural inability to attack' have not yet been sufficiently addressed. A purely defensive force structure, capable of anticipating geostrategic asymmetries as well as the enemy's potential and capacity, is nonexistent. If the WTO were to disarm unilaterally, the West would be in a situation to initiate an offensive into opposing territory – this would occur even with Afheldt's concept. If the WTO maintains its present concept, one can say that NATO, under the conditions of flexible response, is at present unable to attempt an offensive.

The comparison makes it clear that conventional stability in Europe could be improved by a restructuring of armaments. *Ceteris paribus*, highly mobile heavy armoured forces are more offensive than the fighter commandos and rocket artillery troops found in Afheldt's and the SAS models. One should consider that, on the one hand, a purely non-threatening military strategy is impossible. On the other, stability means more than concentrating on factors of mobility.

In terms of stability and policy, *Horst Afheldt's* proposal is better designed than the others. His concept sets out to optimize strategic and crisis stability. Whether or not it could remain stable when confronted with an arms race remains an open question. Because Afheldt's model is so rigid, there must be great doubts about its restraint capacity. The technocommandos serve purposes other than those of retrieving lost territories, so that this concept renounces the threat to damage enemy territory. The enemy is to anticipate a war of attrition in which there is great ability to exercise restraint. Whether this concept can meet the standards of the damage-limitation criterion is doubtful. This does not alter the fact that Afheldt's proposals come close to providing the ideal model, in the event of both East and West creating stability-orientated structures.

Norbert Hannig's buried artillery bases could not serve political stability, despite their restraint capacity. His model is based on a unilateral form of reactive war, one that can easily be assessed by the enemy. Since the rocket bases are readily provided with information, this concept would be stable in the event of a crisis.

Further options to be evaluated are those of *Jochen Löser's* model, which attempts to integrate concepts completely contradictory to those of FOFA and Space Defence. It remains to be seen how far it correlates to 'structural inability to attack'.

Two proposals to be taken more seriously are those of *Andreas von Bülow* and *Albrecht von Müller*. Measured against the conventional criteria of restraint capacity, their military efficiency is unquestionable. In this respect they are probably better designed than those of the status quo. Both concepts are more strongly orientated towards damage limitation than is flexible response. On the other hand, there are doubts concerning the capacity of von Bülow's and von Müller's concepts to meet the demands of political stability. The question here concerns the combination of conventional armoured forces and light infantry with high firepower. The potential enemy could perceive such structures, under certain circumstances, as capable of initiating aggression. This would be especially true once the restraint-capacity criteria are satisfied. The WTO could see these models as attempts to check the enemy's attack while heavy armoured units simultaneously prepare a counter-attack. In terms of promoting political stability, these concepts are not significantly different from the status quo.

The *Alternative Security Policy Study Group (SAS)* proposal can be
considered between Afheldt's and von Bülow's (or von Müller's). The
SAS model could fulfil the requirements of political stability, since it
comprises low mobility and few heavy armoured forces ('fire forces'),
which are tied to the logistics of the relatively stationary module net.
This concept's restraint capacity could be better than that of Afheldt's
model. It is trifling by comparison with von Bülow's and von Müller's in
terms of damage threatened upon the enemy's territory. In renouncing
this option, the possibility of hindering enemy-force concentration is
sacrificed. An 'SAS-Plus' model could avoid this problem by altering
the limited fire effects deep in enemy territory. Cuts in the model's non-
threatening character would have to be made.

One confronts a never-ending conflict of goals in discussing the
premisses of defensive rearmament. Either one optimizes the defence
concept in terms of conventional stability (in which case the losses
incurred due to restraint capacity are almost inevitable), or one concerns
oneself with the maintenance of efficient military functioning in the first
place. The criteria of political stability are hard to attain. For that
matter, under some circumstances the situation could deteriorate.

The gravity of the implied conflict of goals is not to be underestimated; it depends on the one hand on the assessment of European
force comparisons, and on the other, which causes of war are considered
most imminent. Even those who appreciate the conflict of goals between
stability and military functions must consider the problem posed by the
transition phase during which both reactive and offensive capacities are
possessed simultaneously. The military situation would probably become
even more unstable upon supplementary establishment of static defence
elements.

This conflict of objectives cannot be avoided. Anyone truly
concerned with the improvement of conventional stability in Europe,
and with not lessening NATO's ability to respond properly to an attack,
must see the need for the co-operative planning of defensive rearmament. Arms-control negotiations in this field will not emerge as a
result of political tactics, nor from domestic or alliance political
pressures. They are stimulated by political problems in the realm of military and stability concerns, which will arise in the course of the application of alternative defence concepts. Without the enemy's
co-operation, without the integration of changes in military structures
within a mutual concept of detente, conventional stability cannot be
achieved in Europe. This is shown by the inability of the WTO to
determine what constitutes a non-threatening and confidence-building
European security structure.

The disagreements between arms-control supporters and followers of unilateral defensive rearmament can be overcome when both images are tied together in one proposal for conventional stability in Europe. Exclusively defensive rearmament should not become dependent upon the results of arms-control negotiations, nor should one submit to the illusion that a long-lasting functional stability structure in Europe could be created in the absence of a co-operative initiative to rearm defensively.

Through this defensive rearmament, arms-control negotiations and unilateral stabilization could both complement and challenge each other. It would be the responsibility of negotiators to bring about WTO reductions. Negotiations concerning the cutting of conventional armaments in Europe to minimum levels should begin with the goal of mutually dismantling mobile and heavy armed forces. From that point the talks can determine acceptable criteria for stabilization and discuss threat assessments. They must in any case establish and mutually set forth a definition of sufficient defence capacity. It then becomes a two-sided process of learning how to organize conventional stability.

As long as a sufficient defence capacity is not placed at risk, stabilization can begin to develop independently of the results of arms control. Some limits must be defined, lest restraint capacity no longer be guaranteed. In view of the enormous potential stationed along its borders, the Soviet Union has more room than NATO to take unilateral steps in Europe. A truly decisive step would be for the WTO to renounce its forward strategy and establish one of forward defence. This presumes changes in both the doctrine and the structure of WTO forces, which would in turn provide NATO with more room to take unilateral steps.

There is now considerable potential for such an integrated reform-orientated strategy to succeed in improving the military situation in Europe. Gorbachev's 'New Thinking' does seem to have stimulated new thought processes throughout the WTO. Their possibility of further development must be tested by corresponding initiatives from the West.

10

Soviet 'New Thinking' in Security Policy

Gerard Holden

One of the most important factors which has contributed in the late 1980s to a new climate of detente has been the USSR's 'New Thinking' on security policy. This aspect of Soviet policy can be related both to foreign policy in the broadest sense and to the specifics of military strategy, and contributed greatly to the conclusion of the INF Treaty in December 1987. In this chapter, I focus in particular on changes in Soviet conventional military strategy which seemed to be projected during the first three to four years of Gorbachev's general secretaryship. I shall seek to show how important these changes may be to the future of detente; describe them in some detail; and discuss their effect on East–West relations and on intrabloc relations within the Warsaw Treaty Organization (WTO).[1]

Political and Military Detente

There is a fairly popular conception of detente, represented in some of the contributions to this book, which sees it as a kind of progression from the political to the military sphere. According to this conception, the detente of the 1970s came to a halt in large measure because political relaxation and 'normalization' could not be extended into regional security agreements or arms-control treaties which were radical enough to halt the technological/strategic arms race or reduce threat perceptions on either side. The essentials of this argument can be found along a geographical continuum from American liberals, through Western European social democrats and Eastern European foreign-policy specialists, into the Soviet community of civilian writers on security policy.[2]

Other contributions to this book have raised a challenge to this conception both analytically and historically, focusing instead on the political and social tensions generated within the blocs and within individual societies by the historical process of detente. They have argued that the politics of a new detente depend more on these processes than on the technical aspects of military confrontation, particularly within Eastern Europe.

My purpose in this chapter on Soviet policy is not to adjudicate between the two conceptions of detente or to attempt a synthesis, but in a way to avoid a straight choice by showing how both can serve to illuminate Soviet policy in Europe and within the WTO, which has been from its inception an alliance with both internal and externally directed functions. I shall develop the argument by illustrating the relationship of 'New Thinking' in the 1980s to both these functions.

The formation of the WTO in 1955, although it took place six years after the creation of NATO, amounted in many respects to the superimposition of a multilateral organization for the Eastern bloc on to a European security system whose shape had been visible for a number of years. Prior to the creation of the WTO, the USSR had sought to ensure its security interests in Eastern Europe through a combination of bilateral treaties and troop-stationing agreements, and the widespread appointment of Soviet personnel within Eastern European military and internal security establishments. The decision to form the WTO can be related to a variety of external and internal considerations: the reintegration of the Federal Republic of Germany into the Western bloc and NATO; the need for a diplomatic bargaining chip with the West as the tentative beginnings of East–West detente got under way; the need to reestablish Soviet–East European relations on a less directly coercive basis as de-Stalinization proceeded within the bloc; and the need to lay the foundations for a military organization which could function effectively once the most direct Stalinist controls were somewhat eased.

This interplay of internal and external factors can be traced throughout the subsequent history of the WTO. One important aspect of the bloc system as a whole has been the need to ensure the cohesion of one's own bloc even at times when relations with the opposing bloc are improving. The cycle of Cold War and detente periods since 1945 has also shown an underlying evolution of both external and internal relations. Even during the period identified as the 'Second Cold War' in the early 1980s, there did not seem to be much serious likelihood of political conflict turning into military conflict. The likelihood of direct military intervention within blocs also seemed to have diminished. However, considerations of alliance cohesion remained of considerable importance from the 1950s right through to the 1980s, and the military strategies which evolved on both sides throughout the period did not necessarily develop in more accommodating directions to accompany the political relaxation. By the late 1980s, however, military strategies did seem likely to become less offensive, at least on the Eastern side.

As far as the internal dimensions of Soviet policy are concerned, the history of military interventions in Eastern Europe in 1956, 1968 and 1981 is too familiar to need repetition here. It is unarguable that one of the WTO's central internal functions has been to ensure an ultimate Soviet veto over political developments in Eastern Europe, to be exercised either through direct Soviet military action, as in Hungary and Czechoslovakia, or via an allied regional elite, as happened in Poland. One or two caveats, however, should be raised about the geopolitical signifiance of this function. First, the declining effectiveness of military intervention in terms of solving the region's political crises has become apparent to observers both within and without the bloc; secondly, it is inaccurate to see the WTO as an institution dedicated solely to the preservation of a certain state of Soviet–East European relations and a certain kind of regime in Eastern Europe, without reference to external relations.

This second point relates to the influential analysis of the WTO put forward by Christopher Jones, who sees the alliance as in essence a device for ensuring a continued Soviet interventionary capacity against potentially dissident regimes in the region.[3]

The inadequacy of this analysis as an overall characterization of the WTO lies partly in its failure to see Eastern European territory as of any importance in an externally directed military strategy, whether this strategy is considered to be offensive, defensive, or some combination of the two.

In fact, a brief historical survey of trends in Soviet strategy serves to bring out the region's military significance from before the creation of the WTO into the late 1980s. In the early post-war years the region made an important contribution to Soviet air defence capabilities, and during the late 1950s and early 1960s the 'nuclearization' of Soviet strategy resulted in the introduction of nuclear-capable weapons systems with both Soviet and Eastern European units, though it is unlikely that the Eastern Europeans received nuclear warheads. The WTO itself also became a more active military organization in the early sixties, when a multilateral exercise programme with apparently joint internal and external functions got under way. From the mid to late 1960s onwards, both NATO and the WTO were shifting away from 'nuclear-only' assumptions in their military planning, and assuming that a conflict in Europe might start at the conventional level and continue for a period

before nuclear weapons were used. A variety of influences have been
suggested to account for these developments on the Soviet side: a fairly
straightforward response to NATO's flexible-response strategy (formally adopted in 1967); a strategic gamble that a conventional offensive
into Western Europe could defeat NATO and prevent the nuclear
devastation of the USSR (see below) – perhaps even an act of institutional self-preservation on the part of the Soviet Ground Forces,
which had earlier seen their role diminishing as the emphasis on nuclear
weapons increased.

Whatever the reasons may have been, these developments continued
into the early 1980s, by which time the West was beginning to turn to
Soviet strategy for inspiration in the field of conventional war-fighting,
and new Soviet concepts identified by Western analysts as 'Operational
Manoeuvre Groups' were being interpreted as a qualitative increase in a
supposed Soviet threat to Western Europe. It could be argued that
developments such as these restored greater significance to Central and
Eastern European territory in classical military terms.

After 1945, the USA's initial monopoly of nuclear weapons and
subsequent prolonged superiority seemed to nullify the protection
apparently afforded the USSR by its newly acquired territorial control
over Eastern Europe. Once strategies began to shift back towards
conventional options, however, the strategic role of Soviet forces
stationed in the region revived in importance. In any event, by the early
to mid 1980s authoritative Soviet writings on military strategy were
showing a pronounced shift towards conventional operations, by
comparison with work published twenty years earlier.[4]

Much of the mainstream Western literature on Soviet strategy has
taken too crude a view of Soviet foreign policy as a whole to assume
anything other than an offensive policy towards Western Europe, and
offensive Soviet military concepts have been regarded as evidence for
this. Nevertheless some Western scholars, notably Michael MccGwire of
the Brookings Institution, have made serious attempts to reconstruct the
military planning process in terms not of an offensive push westwards,
but of a strategy aimed at preventing nuclear attack on the USSR in the
event that a war with the West seemed inevitable. In MccGwire's
account, from 1966 onwards Soviet strategists no longer believed that a
conflict with the West would inevitably escalate to nuclear war. It
followed, therefore, that there was a chance of deterring a US attack on
the USSR by seizing Western European territory; hence an enhanced
requirement for a conventional offensive capability.[5]

There are still some weaknesses in MccGwire's overall argument, as
he assumes a rational decision-making process and also commits the
reverse error to that of Jones by neglecting intrabloc influences on

security policy. However, one strong point in favour of his analysis is that it assists us in making sense of Soviet negotiating policy over arms control in Europe during the 1970s detente.

In surveying the history of detente in the 1970s, it is useful to remember that the Eastern bloc was the originator of the call for a European security conference, which eventually materialized as the Helsinki process. The primary motivation here was a desire for confirmation of the territorial (and thus, it was assumed, political) status quo in Europe. Although the West managed to put the Soviet bloc on the defensive in the human-rights 'basket' of Helsinki, the original *quid pro quo* between the two sides was the MBFR talks, which started in 1973.

The MBFR talks never succeeded in reducing conventional forces or weapons in Central Europe, but this is hardly surprising. The West sought either to gain compensation for US forces which had been slipping away from Europe or to freeze their levels, and to open the Eastern bloc up to inspection; the East resisted inspection and sought to protect its conventional capacity in Europe from reductions. The virtue of MccGwire's analysis is that it provides a plausible explanation of why the USSR followed such an unpromising negotiating strategy in MBFR. Although the Soviet desire for European stabilization, as represented by the European detente treaties, was genuine, *military* strategy in the region required the maximum possible numbers, capacity and freedom from inspection, and for these reasons could not accede to some central Western demands. This contributed a good deal to the MBFR deadlock. The absence of doctrinal or strategic considerations from the negotiating mandate may also have served to obscure some of the problems.

This brief historical survey has outlined some political and strategic factors in Soviet security policy in Europe. I shall now turn to the developments of the mid 1980s which may have improved the prospects for a revived detente in the next decade.

Changes in Soviet Policy

The developments which have taken place in Soviet security policy under Gorbachev need to be set against a broader background of foreign policy. A number of strands can be observed in areas where 'New Thinking' has had an impact: the ideology of war and peace which underpins foreign policy; manifest foreign policy in arms-control negotiations with the USA; statements on military doctrine and strategy which are of particular importance in Europe; and aspects of policy advice, discussion, and formation.

Programmatic statements of 'New Thinking' have been made by leading figures such as Gorbachev and Foreign Minister Shevardnadze, and a number of other journalists and academics like Aleksandr Bovin and Evgenii Primakov. The principal themes of these statements have included the idea of security as a political rather than a military concept in the nuclear age; a concept of global interdependence and security which covers the political, economic, ecological and humanitarian spheres; and the need for flexibility and compromise in negotiations. Few of these ideas have seemed entirely new to anyone familiar with global discussions of 'common security', but they do provide a striking contrast with more traditional Soviet formulations of the need for 'parity and equal security', with their emphasis on numerical equivalence in weapons.

Stephen Shenfield has provided the most convincing account of the ideological basis of these reformulations. Drawing on Soviet debates which go back well before the Gorbachev era, he has traced the challenge which the danger of nuclear war posed to official optimism about the communist future of humanity. In the ideological debate which arose out of this challenge, peace and interdependence were placed above the growing strength of socialism as factors working in favour of detente, and even though an intersystemic competition was still held to be in progress, military factors began to be downgraded within the 'correlation of forces'.[6]

As far as nuclear arms control and disarmament were concerned, Gorbachev's statement of January 1986 on a programme for global denuclearization by the year 2000 fitted in well enough with the aspirations of 'New Thinking', even though it was not supported initially by much detailed work on how such deep cuts in nuclear forces could be effected. However, the revision of earlier requirements for 'parity' was reflected in the conclusion of the INF Treaty in late 1987, involving deeper cuts for the USSR than for the West. This step seemed to confirm the analyses of other Western observers who had noted the increasing role being played by civilian writers on security. These civilian writers interpreted the arms race as an interactive process rather than as a simple response by the USSR to Western armament, and by implication some of them endorsed unilateral cuts as a way of starting a disarmament process.[7]

An accompanying aspect of 'New Thinking' in the security sphere was the introduction by Gorbachev of the new criterion of 'reasonable sufficiency' in armaments. For nuclear forces this seemed to approximate to a minimum-deterrence posture as a desirable goal, though perhaps the most interesting facet of the new criterion was that it was evidently introduced before the Soviet political leadership, Gorbachev included, had spent much time thinking about its content. Foreign-policy scholars in the Soviet civilian think-tanks seem to have been asked, both privately and publicly, to elaborate the concept. In a development of major potential importance for both Western and Eastern Europe, publications and statements from Gorbachev and others began to expound the concept of 'reasonable sufficiency' as including a criterion of non-offensiveness for conventional armed forces. This suggested (and sometimes explicitly stated) acquaintance with Western research and writings on alternative defence.

A non-offensive conventional interpretation of 'reasonable sufficiency' was not universal, for some military writers preferred to see it as a more restrictive and purely quantitative concept. The goal of non-offensive military doctrines and strategies was also endorsed by the WTO in a statement of May 1987, although again it was possible to deduce differences over content and implementation from the continued emphasis in military writings on the importance of the counteroffensive.[8] The evolution of this debate was also important for its indications about the role of civilian analysts in providing advice and expertise relatively independently of the Soviet military establishment. Gorbachev and Shevardnadze clearly encouraged this development, and although the school of civilian commentators may not have had access to classified military data, they began to publish more adventurously, particularly on issues of conventional strategy, and this affected the general climate of the Soviet security debate.

I have outlined some of the aspects of Soviet 'New Thinking' which have been most visible in terms of public statements as well as possible implications for arms control and disarmament. It is also important to step back a little, and try to account for these phenomena within a broader picture of East–West relations and of Soviet reform policies. One might set out Gorbachev's view of the connection between domestic reform and foreign policy as a combination of two complementary considerations. On the one hand, the need for domestic economic and political reform necessitates a stable external environment and, if possible, the redirection of resources into the civilian economy. On the other, the USSR's ability to compete with the West in an economic and technological capacity has declined significantly, making the task of domestic reform all the more urgent.

Setting the problems out in this exclusively 'hard-headed' way does something of an injustice to Soviet foreign policy. It fails to account adequately for what are evidently sincerely held beliefs about the urgency of the need for denuclearization and relaxation, or for the emerging degree of consensus between Western liberal and Soviet thought about issues like common security and non-offensive defence. However, Gorbachev and other commentators have repeatedly used an argument about the socialist system's lag behind capitalist development as a way of mobilizing and motivating the Soviet population in support of reform, so one needs to pick one's way with some care through these arguments: was 'New Thinking' brought about by the pressure of inter-systemic competition from capitalism, or can progressive internal rethinking on the Soviet side provide an adequate explanation on its own?

It would certainly be unfair to deny the Soviet system any capacity for self-reappraisal and domestic renewal which did not stem from external pressures. Many of the reform advocates close to Gorbachev and of his own generation had seen their expectations of political and cultural revival collapse after the fall of Khrushchev, and they were joined in the late 1970s and early 1980s by a younger generation of party intellectuals who had grown up under Brezhnev and knew that the system was not working fairly or efficiently. Having said that, it would also be unrealistic to deny that the more candid reappraisals of the Soviet position in the world which came to the surface in the early 1980s were based on an increasingly pessimistic view of the future of the socialist system in a world economy still dominated by capitalism, and a fear that the USA's scientific–technological advantage might be turned into an identifiable military superiority.[9]

Some formulations of 'New Thinking' did make these considerations fairly explicit, and so left themselves vulnerable to a conservative charge that the new policies amounted to an admission of Soviet weakness *vis-à-vis* the West. The contentiousness of this point was reflected both in Soviet debates and in Western assessments of the Cold War state of play. During 1987 and 1988, commentaries from mainstream US analysts veered between triumphant assessments of Soviet decline and US Cold War victory, and expressions of alarm at the decline of US hegemony within the capitalist system (which often focused on Paul Kennedy's book *The Rise and Fall of the Great Powers*).

These two accounts could be reconciled if it is accepted that both superpowers have become overextended and are in periods of relative decline. However, the Soviet decline has been both steeper and of more immediate military–technological relevance. One would also have to conclude that the Soviet polity made a more coherent attempt to come to terms with the new situation via its explorations of 'New Thinking', but that the USA could afford to be rather more complacent: whatever the USA's own national problems, its system was certainly not losing the competition with socialism.

Soviet debates over foreign policy became more public during 1988, and one particularly sharp clash between Shevardnadze and Yegor Ligachev occured just after the 19th Party Conference in June–July of that year. Shevardnadze made a speech to diplomats in which he called for a more pluralistic discussion of foreign policy, and Ligachev responded sharply with a statement that international relations remained based on class principles. Others expounded the contemporary meaning of peaceful coexistence as a 'deideologization' of international relations. Criticisms of previous foreign policy-making even included an account of Brezhnev as a Reaganesque figure who was incapable of reading through the advisory texts prepared for him on foreign policy.[10]

Since my main concern here is with military policies, I shall try to reframe the question about external and internal influences on 'New Thinking' to see how one can best account for more specific reforms in security policy. Where nuclear forces are concerned, one can see Gorbachev's disarmament diplomacy as fully consistent with the trends within military thinking sketched above, whereby nuclear weapons and war-fighting doctrines were seen as of declining relevance to the maintenance of Soviet security. Up to a point, therefore, military professionals might be prepared to accept a substantial denuclearization of security policy; there might be some resistance if and when the interests of the armed services came under imminent threat (for example those of the Strategic Rocket Forces).

For this reason, it may be more useful to focus attention on the implications of 'reasonable sufficiency' for conventional military planning, where the possibility of a change towards a non-offensive conventional posture would be both a radical departure for Soviet policy, and a possible source of greater dissonance between the military professionals and the political leadership. Once again, it is worth comparing the relative importance of internal rethinking and external pressures. I have already mentioned the influence of Western alternative defence writing on Soviet civilian analysts. These analysts clearly had encouragement from the political leadership, and were able to take advantage of an environment in which their inputs into policy discussion would be heard. Nevertheless, it is difficult to argue that their influence alone was responsible for Soviet rethinking of conventional strategies, if only because such a high degree of Western influence seems unlikely.

One should therefore seek an explanation at a rather more basic and traditional level of security policy-making. Something of a shift towards a more defensive strategic emphasis has in fact been detected from about 1984–85 onwards. Michael MccGwire, in updating his earlier analysis, seeks to account for this in terms of a further important reassessment which took place in the early years of the decade.[11] He argues that Soviet planners were at that time becoming increasingly pessimistic about the state of East–West relations and saw a serious danger of conflict with the USA, not in Europe but in the Persian Gulf

region. It was considered that such a conflict would not necessarily
escalate to world war, so that the previous requirement for an offensive
into Western Europe would serve no purpose and could be relaxed or
abandoned. Hence a new strategy could be developed which allowed for
the reduction of forces in Europe, and perhaps by extension a more
flexible relationship between offence and defence elsewhere on the
Soviet periphery.

It would follow from MccGwire's analysis that behind Gorbachev's
declarative statements about non-offensive postures, a decision-in-
principle had already been taken, one in which military planners had
been involved from the start. The civilian specialists would then appear
to have been asked to contribute ideas on ways of implementing the
decision, and there could be room for disagreements over the pace and
military–technical details of change, and perhaps over the degree of
reciprocity to be demanded or sought from the West. The full process of
transition was in any event envisaged as a long one, so some of the
immediate Western responses, to the effect that no changes in Soviet
postures were yet visible, could be considered to have missed the point.

The study of Soviet security decision-making is also a long-term
enterprise, and even if MccGwire's account is not entirely correct it
gives us a challenging thesis to test against future developments. One
respect in which it appears deficient is its apparent lack of attention to
specific *Western* strategic developments to which Soviet strategy may
have been in part reacting – notably more offensive land and sea
concepts such as AirLand Battle, Follow-on Forces Attack, and the US
Maritime Strategy. In addition, anyone who found MccGwire's rational
actor model unconvincing in his earlier work is likely to feel that his
explanation of the defensive shift is also rather too clear-cut. Jack
Snyder has offered an alternative explanation in terms of a deliberate
decision on Gorbachev's part to challenge conservative institutions
which retain a zero-sum approach to foreign and military policy, and (by
extension) to use Western ideas in doing so.[12] Snyder's account also
entails a greater likelihood of civil–military disputes.

Without trying to adjudicate between these different versions, I would
reiterate the point that the 1985–88 period saw some significant
developments which are likely to affect Soviet military policy in Europe,
even if they have not yet been translated into practical policy. In trying
to assess their possible impact over a longer new detente period one
needs to look at their relationship to Western and Eastern Europe in
turn, and to the new negotiations on conventional forces which
promised to follow in the wake of the INF Treaty.

Alternative Defence and Alternative Security

In certain respects, Gorbachev's new security thinking amounts to a fundamental challenge to European Cold War structures. Nevertheless, it leaves some central problems unresolved, notably in connection with Eastern Europe.

As far as Western Europe is concerned, Gorbachev has evidently set out to confront and undermine received wisdom about a Soviet military threat to the region. In making such a public issue of the need for change in military doctrines, Soviet commentators have effectively acknowledged that some Soviet actions and postures have contributed to the misrepresentation of Soviet intentions in the West. They are arguing that these doctrines need to be changed, though the West must also abandon the offensive elements in its own posture.

This position comes very close to the central argument of many Western European alternative defence writers, some of whose concepts have been outlined in Karsten Voigt's chapter in this book. There is also a more diffuse but equally significant sense in which Soviet reform policies of the late 1980s have served to reorientate the country more clearly towards the West. At the same time, however, Russia's historical ambivalence towards the West has re-emerged as more conservative, Russian nationalist traditions have also benefited from political relaxation. Gorbachev has spoken repeatedly of a 'common European home' identified by its cultural heritage. The concept may be historically debatable, but I would suggest that it can be understood in two related ways: first, as the expression of an aspiration that the USSR (or perhaps Russia) should not be considered a backwater of European/world culture, and secondly in a more geopolitical sense with a military subtext – the USSR is now an unambiguously status quo power; the West has nothing to fear except a more relaxed social and political competition.

One might argue that these developments can be traced back to self-interested economic causes: the Soviet system needs greater integration into the capitalist world economy in order to remain effective and viable. But this would be an unduly deterministic argument. In the cultural sphere, other developments may have contributed as much to a Western assessment of the USSR as any number of statements of military doctrine. The publication of Pasternak's *Doctor Zhivago*, and the appearance of such powerful anti-Stalinist historical fiction as Grossman's *Life and Fate* and Rybakov's *Children of the Arbat*, serve as evidence of a society engaged in a long-delayed reappraisal of its own past and present. The publication of Roy Medvedev's *Let History Judge* also seems possible.

Eastern Europeans reading my previous three paragraphs are likely to respond with a variety of wry smiles. And indeed, if we return to geopolitics, the question of Eastern Europe cannot be fudged. The status quo does assign Eastern Europe to a sphere of Soviet military-political hegemony or domination, even if the limits of Soviet toleration in the region appear to have widened considerably over the past twenty years. How far, then, does 'New Thinking' apply to Eastern Europe?

One can approach this question by looking again at the internal functioning of the WTO, and also at differences of approach within the Western debate on alternative defence. Although some Western analysts of the WTO have argued that there has been an organic connection between offensive military strategy and a Soviet capacity for intrabloc intervention, I would argue that things are not quite so simple. To put it another way: it would seem possible for Soviet strategists to devise a posture which appeared less threatening to Western Europe, but did not render impossible internal intervention either by Soviet forces or by domestic military establishments, as in Poland. The point here is that although the Soviet tank divisions which so alarm the West were used in Hungary in 1956 and Czechoslovakia in 1968, they played no direct role in Poland in 1981, even if their existence provided a backdrop to the imposition of martial law.

A related point has been made by Western critics of overtechnical approaches to alternative defence, who see a danger that even clearly defensive postures and technologies could merely freeze the confrontation in Europe and leave the sociopolitical problems of Soviet–East European relations (and, for that matter, of US–European relations) unresolved. One of the weaknesses of the alternative project in the West has certainly been its vulnerability to misappropriation: Ronald Reagan abducted its language for his Star Wars speech; the British Labour Party found it expedient to combine the advocacy of defensive defence with a commitment to use resources saved on nuclear weapons for conventional forces.

One could not, however, argue that Soviet–East European relations in the late 1980s had not evolved since the invasion of Czechoslovakia twenty years earlier. Although the fact may be of little comfort to the population of Poland, the emergence of Solidarity ten years before 1980 would probably have led to a much bloodier Soviet intervention, rather than domestically imposed martial law. By the end of the 1980s it was also clear that martial law had been no more successful in resolving Polish political and economic problems than a Soviet intervention would have been, and this must have been clear to the Polish and Soviet leaderships alike.

It is also reasonable to assume that the Soviet leadership is fully aware that any future military intervention in Eastern European politics, even a domestic one, would have grave repercussions both on Soviet domestic reforms and on the Soviet foreign-policy reform project. These existing disincentives to intervention were strengthened by the signature in September 1986 of the Stockholm Agreement on confidence-building measures, which included a clause obliging its signatories to refrain from the threat or use of force against any state, regardless of its social system. The advance notification of military exercises also constitutes a psychological barrier. During a trip to Yugoslavia in early 1988 Gorbachev signed a declaration whose wording seemed to strengthen the disincentives still further, by disavowing claims to a monopoly of truth over social developments, asserting that each Communist Party is responsible only to its own working class and people, and even applying the term 'peaceful coexistence' to relations between *all* states, not just between those with different social systems.[13]

Of course, such verbal statements do not necessarily dictate crisis behaviour, and similar ones have been made in the past. One cannot rule out the possibility of a future crisis in which the question of using military force arises. These developments do, however, suggest that Gorbachev knows how high a price the USSR has paid for its past interventions, and that any future attempt to impose a solution by force would amount to an admission of defeat. The Eastern European contributions to this book suggest that the most crucial problem for a new detente in the region is not so much the issue of Soviet intervention in itself, but the question of how the existing leaderships will deal with rising domestic expectations of political reform, which have been fuelled in part by the emergence of Gorbachev in the USSR. The situation is not without its historical precedents: Khrushchev's leadership failed to appreciate fully the extent to which Eastern European societies would become more volatile than the more stable USSR in conditions of reform. Gorbachev is shrewder than Khrushchev, but his reforms are bolder, and no prudent Westerner would assume that he has foreseen all eventualities in Eastern Europe.

The public Soviet debate on alternative defence and security had steered clear of the Eastern European question until late 1988, even though internal military discussions may still have been incorporating intervention options into their planning models. Nevertheless, there did seem to be a possibility that the complementary issues of foreign-policy reassessment and alternative military modelling might eventually converge in an explicit discussion of intervention as an element in Soviet/WTO strategy. Throughout 1988 there was an increasing boldness in the journalistic treatment of foreign policy in general and Eastern Europe in particular, with some indications of reassessment of the Czechoslovakian intervention appearing around the time of the twentieth anniversary in August. In addition, some civilian analysts who had been in the forefront of the debate on non-offensive alternatives were by mid 1988 shifting from general conceptual writing to the more concrete exposition of alternative postures.[14]

It became clear from around mid 1986, when an INF agreement began once again to appear possible, that after such a treaty had been signed the focus of arms control in Europe would shift towards negotiations on conventional forces. With the MBFR talks still in progress, after a fashion, it was not immediately clear what form the post-MBFR forum would take, nor was it yet clear by the time this chapter was written (September 1988). Presumably that will no longer be the case by the time this is published, but one can still be fairly confident that the resulting negotiations will be complex and long-drawn-out. Among the most contentious points at issue during consultations over the mandate were the inclusion or non-inclusion of nuclear-capable weapons, and whether doctrines could be incorporated into the agenda, as favoured by the WTO.

Perhaps the most ominous portent for the success of the new talks was the example of MBFR itself. Even if the data stumbling block which has so dogged MBFR could be removed, it was hard to see the West formulating a negotiating position which was both acceptable throughout NATO and able to offer attractive trade-offs to the East. The Eastern negotiating strategy might well offer substantial trade-offs, perhaps on the lines of troop withdrawals from Eastern Europe in exchange for cuts in Western nuclear-capable forces, but it is by no means clear that there is any preparedness on the Western side to give up anything of substance.

Nor does the Eastern approach appear entirely unproblematic, in part because of the very state of flux in strategic discussions which I have tried to document in this chapter, and especially if the Soviet debate on strategic requirements in Central Europe remains unresolved. It could also be hard to incorporate comparisons of doctrine and strategy into a cumbersome multinational or bloc-to-bloc forum, even if a clear Eastern position were finalized. Even so, the assumptions on which the USSR and WTO approached the new talks might differ in one highly important respect. If MccGwire's analysis of the assumptions behind Soviet MBFR negotiating strategy in the 1970s is approximately correct, very little leeway was available for serious constraints on military capabilities. By 1988/89 more defensive assumptions would leave much more room for flexibility, given that a defensive posture does not require a surprise-attack capability, and so can be more relaxed about issues like the notification of exercises and on-site inspection (which was of course provided for in the 1986 Stockholm Agreement and the 1987 INF

Treaty). If that position is reflected in the post-MBFR conventional talks, the onus for making a success of those talks will rest more squarely on the West.

The question of Soviet conventional forces in Eastern Europe and the Western USSR remains one of the issues most central to Cold War politics in popular perceptions and Western elite calculations, however inaccurately it may have been portrayed and interpreted. It is therefore not very encouraging to contemplate the prospect of a negotiating forum which either proceeds through the 1990s at an extremely slow pace, or becomes completely bogged down at an early stage. One can hope that this does not happen, but if it does it is likely to be presented to Western European public opinion as proof that Gorbachev's 'New Thinking' was never to be trusted anyway. My argument in this chapter leads to a different conclusion. If these negotiations do indeed become stalemated, then this is because the chosen forum is inadequate and inappropriate as a way of translating into negotiated agreements the more profound developments in Soviet–East European relations, US–West European relations, and Soviet civil–military relations, which this chapter and others have examined. Whether more appropriate fora or processes can be devised is another matter.

In conclusion, it is worth trying to relate the largely strategic concerns of this chapter to some of the broader geopolitical analysis which has been offered by Richard Falk, Mammo Muchie, and Hans van Zon. Europe has not been a unique focus of Gorbachev's diplomacy. Other regional powers on the Soviet periphery and beyond have also seen an increase in Soviet diplomatic activity since 1985 (Japan, China, Indonesia, India). The overall pattern of this diplomacy supports the analysis offered here of the USSR as a status quo power which, according to Muchie and van Zon, is now much more pessimistic about socialism's ability to compete with capitalism in the Third World. In some respects, as with the withdrawal from Afghanistan and apparently greater Soviet reluctance to take on additional commitments in support of Third World allies, not even the status quo is assured, whether for good or ill.

Richard Falk captures these processes challengingly and disturbingly in his characterization of a 'new geopolitical bargain' being offered by Gorbachev to the USA: in exchange for nuclear disarmament, relaxation and perhaps even the ending of the Cold War in Europe, the USSR will not challenge the West elsewhere in the world. The analysis I have offered suggests that one region where the outcome of that bargain would still be problematic in terms of East–West politics is Eastern Europe. If this is somewhere near the truth, there is all the more reason, in seeking to create and extend a new detente in the 1990s, not to

neglect the interconnection between these apparently disparate aspects
of geopolitics and demilitarization.

Notes

1. A much-expanded version of the argument of this chapter can be found in Gerard
Holden, *The WTO and Soviet Security Policy*, Oxford 1989.
2. For a range of contributions, see: Raymond L. Garthoff, *Detente and Confrontation: American Soviet Relations from Nixon to Reagan*, Washington, DC 1985;
Horst Ehmke, 'A Second Phase of Detente', *World Policy Journal*, vol. 4 no. 3, Summer
1987, pp. 363–82; Péter Déak, 'Postwar Trends in Military Policy: Hungary's Role in the
Warsaw Treaty Defence System', in *Hungary and the World: Külpolitka 1987*, Budapest
1987, pp. 62–75; D. Proektor, *The Foundations of Peace in Europe: Political and Military
Aspects*, Moscow 1984.
3. Christopher D. Jones, *Soviet Influence in Eastern Europe: Political Autonomy and
the Warsaw Pact*, New York 1981.
4. The most frequently cited works from the later period have been: N.V. Ogarkov
Istoriya uchit bditel'nosti, Moscow 1985, and M.A. Gareev, *MV Frunze: Voennyi
Teoretik*, Moscow 1985.
5. Michael MccGwire, *Military Objectives in Soviet Foreign Policy*, Washington, DC
1987.
6. Stephen Shenfield, *The Nuclear Predicament: Explorations in Soviet Ideology*,
London 1987.
7. See Pat Litherland, *Gorbachev and Arms Control: Civilian Experts and Soviet
Policy*, University of Bradford School of Peace Studies, Peace Research Report No. 12,
November 1986.
8. For example in a book by General Yazov, who was appointed Defence Minister in
mid 1987. see D.T. Yazov, *Na strazhe sotsializma i mira*. Moscow 1987.
9. See Stephen Shenfield, 'The Changing Soviet View of the Future', *Futures*, vol. 20,
no. 4, August 1988, pp. 367–84.
10. 'Round table – Perestroika, the 19th Party Conference and Foreign Policy', *International Affairs* [Moscow], no. 7, 1988, pp. 3–18, 40.
11. At the time of writing, MccGwire's most recent exposition of his updated account
was: 'A mutual security regime for Europe?', *International Affairs* [London] vol. 64,
no. 3, Summer 1988, pp. 361–79).
12. Jack Snyder, 'The Gorbachev Revolution: A Waning of Soviet Expansionism?',
International Security, vol. 12, no. 3, Winter 1987/8, pp. 93–131.
13. *Pravda*, 19 March 1988; *Soviet News*, 23 March 1988.
14. For example: A. Kokoshin and V. Larionov, 'Protivostoyanie sil obshchego
naznacheniya v kontekste obespecheniya strategicheskoi stabil'nosti', *MEMO*, no. 6, 1988,
pp. 23–31.

PART III

European Co-operation and Domestic Change

11

Problems and Prospects of East–West Economic Co-operation: An East European View[1]

Andras Köves

Fifteen to twenty years ago the mutual dependence of East–West detente and co-operation was widely accepted.[2] There was almost complete consensus that the improvement of political conditions would naturally lead to intensified economic relations, and also that if strong permanent economic ties were established between East and West, this could constitute the 'material' foundation of a lasting detente.

By the mid 1970s, however, even before the meeting of heads of state and government in Helsinki, East–West detente and trade had already passed their zenith. The emerging detente between the superpowers was followed by renewed tensions in the second half of the decade and in the early 1980s, in the same period the rapid growth of economic relations began to stumble, and was soon replaced by stagnation and even decline.

1 Detente and Co-operation

Post hoc, ergo propter hoc? Rising tensions in Soviet–American relations – which also had an adverse effect on European East–West relations – did not necessarily lead to stagnation or decline in economic relations. 1975 was not followed by anything like the Cold War of the 1940s and 1950s, when the decline of economic relations was the *exclusive* consequence of political motives.

In the absence of international tensions, economic co-operation would certainly have developed more favourably in the 1970s. It is rather easy to demonstrate this proposition; one can find dozens of examples of the way in which trade, credits, and the growth of new and

253

widely preferred forms of co-operation have been and are still hindered
by the absence of political detente. Nevertheless, it is equally obvious
that all this still fails to explain adequately why economic relations have
evolved as they have, why their relatively fast development was halted so
abruptly, and what is preventing a renewed development.

It was the Soviet Union's relations with the West rather than the rest
of Eastern Europe that were mainly characterized by political tensions.
Yet during the last fifteen years, Soviet trade with the West has been
growing faster than the trade with the West of any of the East European
countries. Moreover, Soviet–Western trade was growing rapidly even
when, in the early 1980s, that of the East European countries was on the
decline. The explanation is well known and simple: the Soviet Union is
an oil exporter and the resulting improvement in its terms of trade had a
much stronger *favourable* effect on the development of its trade
relations with the West than the *unfavourable* effects exerted by tension
in the international political situation.

Later in the course of this analysis, it will be made clear that the fast
increasing trade turnover enabled by the oil-price explosions was in
more than one respect just a sham result which melted away when oil
prices on the world market fell from the $30 per barrel level. This had
nothing to do with the changing international political conditions – at
least, not directly – but it was certainly related to the traditionally closed
character of the Soviet economy, which has not lessened despite the
rapid growth of trade.

Political tensions between the Soviet Union and the West did have
repercussions on the economic relations between *Eastern Europe and
the West*: they led to economic policy restrictions, credit difficulties, and
a worsening general atmosphere. Disappointed in detente, the Western
countries, led by the United States, increased their efforts to prohibit or
restrict the sales of strategically important high-technology equipment to
Eastern countries. Irrespective of the declared aims of the embargo
policy, these measures affected the small East European countries most
severely. These countries were attempting to modernize their economies
and this entailed greater reliance on technological relations with the
West. They therefore made efforts to further their relationships with the
Western countries despite the tensions between the superpowers.[3]

East European economies were fraught with yet other difficulties.
The more strained are international relations, the stronger is the argument for prudence in developing economic relations with the West, on
the grounds that it is in the vital interest of the CMEA countries to avoid
'exaggerated and one-sided' dependence on countries which are
potential adversaries. This approach, which still survives, is an important
element of the whole attitude of the CMEA countries towards the outer

(non-socialist) world; it has ideological–historical–political roots going far beyond the scope of this chapter. In the period of detente this attitude could be suppressed; but it always comes into prominence at times of rising tensions.

Confronted with accumulating foreign economic difficulties, East European countries could choose, broadly speaking, between two strategies: one was *opening towards the outside world,* export-orientated economic development, and finding a niche in the international division of labour; the other was *turning inwards*: attempting to cope with economic difficulties by developing co-operation within the CMEA, *instead* of and to the detriment of relations with the West. Because of the international situation, East European countries tended to prefer the latter method, even though it had never been efficient and was now increasingly difficult to achieve.[4]

In Eastern Europe, the nature of the exogenous constraints on rational economic action is frequently debated. Of course, it is mainly policy-makers who refer to hard constraints, whereas analysts point out that on the one hand, action based exclusively on economic considerations has a wider scope than what is seen by the economic policy of a particular country, while on the other hand, it can be made wider exactly through economic policy action. It is only through effective deeds that acts, methods of procedure, and courses of action earlier considered quite impossible can now be accepted either tacitly or explicitly. As a matter of course, such debates – like similar ones in other parts of the world, now or in the past – are not to be declined *in general.* During the last decade, however, numerous instances have shown in Eastern Europe that economic necessity forced out the transgression of constraints. For example, when it was impossible to postpone the decision any longer, because of the country's financial situation, Hungary (later followed by Poland) decided to join the International Monetary Fund and the World Bank – a decision it had refused to make during the previous fifteen years, in a period of detente.

Taking into account these as well as other considerations, this chapter starts from the proposition that the causes of the ups and downs of East–West economic relations are to be sought, first of all, in economic processes themselves. Likewise, the future prospects for recovery and strengthening of economic co-operation are to be found in the economy, although of course economic processes should be treated as functions of social and political processes.

In this context, it is important to mention the evolving reform process in the Soviet Union and how that might improve the chances of a new detente and of a wider East–West economic co-operation based on it. The results of reforms in socialist countries depend, above all, on

internal circumstances, but favourable or unfavourable external conditions might play a role, too. In my judgement, a Western policy based
on sound self-interest would include a positive attitude to reforms in the
socialist countries and contribute to establishing favourable overall
conditions for social, political and economic reforms.

In the following pages, after a brief summary of how East–West economic relations have declined due to growing external indebtness of
CMEA countries (Part 2), some reasons for Eastern European debt will
be analysed. These include the global process (Part 3), the systemic
reasons (Part 4) and the reasons inherent in economic policies (Parts 5
and 6). Recent dilemmas of Soviet–Western economic relations will be
discussed separately (Part 7). A greater openness of the CMEA
economies (that is, establishing direct links between the domestic and
international economy) as well as their more intensive participation in
the institutional system of global division of labour, are regarded as key
issues in the future development of East–West trade (Parts 8 and 9). We
shall conclude (Part 10) that in spite of the unfavourable short-term
outlook, domestic reforms and a more profound detente may lead to an
upswing in economic relations in the long run.

2   What Went Wrong?

East–West economic co-operation has consisted up to now mainly of
trade and credit relations. The CMEA countries have been using credits
to cover their trade deficits, which have increased rapidly since the early
1970s. By the turn of the decade, the accumulated debt of most East
European countries, except the Soviet Union, forced these countries to
take serious restrictive measures.

By 1981, of the six East European countries the gross external
convertible currency debt amounted to $67 billion; the net debt (gross
debt minus assets and international reserves) being $61 billion. The
latter amount was more than double the total export receipts in convertible currencies in the same year. These countries had to spend more
than two-thirds of total export receipts on servicing the debt.[5] It became
quite impossible to raise any further credits, at least by the usual
channels. The only way for these countries to meet their liabilities was to
realize a surplus on their trade balance, or significantly increase it, without delay. Two countries (Poland and Romania) who were unable to
achieve a surplus, became insolvent and had to ask their creditors to
reschedule their debts; other countries also faced serious financial
troubles.

In the wake of inevitable restrictions, the relatively fast economic growth of East European countries suddenly fell (in a few countries, stagnation or even recession followed), the rate of investment had to be reduced, technological lags and structural problems were aggravated, the rising standard of living slowed down or stopped, there was no further improvement of commodity supply to the population, and acute shortages again became a characteristic feature of some of these economies.

Trade with the West declined; even today, the total trade of the six East European countries has not reached the peak value of 1980. During recent years imports have once again increased somewhat; nevertheless, imports from the West in 1986 were still no more than two-thirds of their 1980 value. Indebtness, which had fallen for some years, is growing again. Other statistical data covering the mid 1980s indicate some improvements, but there are still very serious economic problems. This is, in the final analysis, what constrains economic relations with the West.

3   Eastern Europe and World Debt

As to its causes, nature and consequences, the problem of East European debt has much in common with the processes of running into debt in other parts of the world which began in the mid 1970s. The large-scale indebtedness of different countries which has led to a world debt crisis is rooted in the world economic and international financial processes which followed the first sudden rise in oil prices. Banks had to reinvest the huge amounts of oil money flowing mainly into the Euromarket. With stagnant investment activities in the industrial countries, it seemed natural to invest much of this money in other parts of the world. In these areas – in the developing and socialist countries – the demand for external resources to be used for economic development was very high. Relatively fast economic development, also promoted through credit, increased the demand for imports, especially products from industrial countries. The growing export markets offered by the debtor countries constituted, in turn, an important factor in offsetting the economic situation of the industrial countries. Therefore these countries did not restrict new credits, as long as the borrowers could meet their debt-service obligations relatively smoothly.

Financial difficulties arose for several reasons of which some, but not all, were predictable. For example, it was possible to foresee and to calculate that alongside the growth of the debt, instalments of interest and capital would also increase, and that the slow growth of demand on the world market would stem the growth of export receipts. It could also be predicted that the ratio of export receipts and import costs would be influenced by the changing terms of trade. However, the majority of the countries which found themselves in financial trouble later on wrongly estimated the future trends of their terms of trade; they expected that prices not only of primary sources of energy, but also of other raw materials exported by them would continue to rise so that the terms of trade would continue to improve, thus facilitating the management of the debt service. Those debtors who were also oil importers had to abandon this assumption finally during the second oil-price explosion. The oil exporters had to do the same from 1982. *Nor was it predictable* that the second oil-price shock would be followed by a severe recession in the OECD countries and that interest rates in the United States would suddenly rise in the early 1980s as a consequence of the tight monetary restrictions applied by the Reagan administration.

As for Eurocredits, it was a *given condition* that interest rates could fluctuate according to changes in the market conditions; thus it could be *presumed* that the real rate of interest – the difference between the nominal rate of interest and the rate of inflation – would not always be negative, as had occurred when debts increased most rapidly.

For this reason it could not have been predicted, either, that the strongly credit-orientated development policy of the developing and socialist countries would so suddenly switch over to restriction: that the large net capital inflow would be replaced by large net capital outflow, as actually happened in the early 1980s. This constitutes one of the most serious obstacles to world economic development in the present period.[6]

4   Indebtedness and a Few Particularities of the East European Economies

For Eastern Europe, the rapid accumulation of debt was possible only because there were liquid monetary means available in the world. Had there not been potential creditors, debts could not have accumulated either. The fact, however, that the *possibility* of incurring debts had been created – in this sense – by external circumstances does not mean that the *explanation* of indebtness should be sought exclusively in those external circumstances.

We shall come closer to an explanation if we compare certain immanent features of the East European economic systems with world economic conditions and look at the aggregate effect of the accumulation of debt. East European planned economies are characterized by the constant reproduction of macroeconomic shortages: there is high unsatisfied demand for investment goods, production input material, parts, consumer articles, and so on.[7]

In a market economy, an increase in exports may help to ease tensions arising from insufficient domestic demand; in a centrally planned economy the increase of imports is held to be the most obvious method of relieving shortages. Part of the imports of individual East European countries come from within the CMEA, and these imports grew rapidly until the second half of the 1970s. However, the bulk of intra-CMEA trade is carried out within the framework of bilateral clearing accounts, so that there is a limit to the amount that one particular country can increase its imports. This is not only because the partner countries also face shortages (and often in the same kinds of goods) but also because the partners are willing to increase their supply only if they, too, can acquire the additional quantity of goods they need, in order to maintain an even bilateral trade balance.

This is why there is a persistent demand for imports from outside the CMEA region which are not subject to the same constraints. It is quite easy to see that the intensity of this demand may fluctuate according to the seriousness of the shortages within the region at a given time and depending on the extent to which the CMEA economies are capable of satisfying their mutual demands. We shall revert to this question later. However, it is important to mention that the pressure to increase imports from outside the CMEA is not typically concomitant with growing capacities to increase exports outside the CMEA region. In a sense, this is another aspect of the same problem. In a market characterized by macroeconomic shortages, the basic difficulty is the purchase of goods (acquiring inputs), not the sale of outputs. If the goods produced sell easily on the domestic market (or in other CMEA countries) it is difficult to stimulate enterprises to compete in the world market. Many producer enterprises feel it is a burden, or even a punishment imposed on them by superior authorities, that they have to export their goods to non-CMEA countries.

Viewed from another angle, the problem is that in these countries, *production for the world market beyond the CMEA has not been among economic policy priorities for several decades. These economies are artificially separated from the outer world* so that external impulses (changes in prices, demand and supply conditions, and so on) are received in a roundabout way, with much delay, as a result of economic policy decisions. For all these reasons, the structure (above all *micro*structure, the structure of firms) of the economy is generally different from what would be needed to produce for the world market – that is to say, the economic actors (the state and the enterprises) do not have the necessary abilities and capacities to increase exports so as to keep pace with imports.

Thus, because of unsatisfactory export abilities, the planning and economic management and control organs are compelled, despite constant pressure, to restrict imports, portioning them out as a special privilege. Constraints are relieved only in so far as it is possible to finance the current trade deficit through credit. The relaxation of credit for Eastern Europe in the 1970s which allowed this constraint to be relieved is what accounts for the rapid accumulation of debt.

That the constraints were relieved 'by far too much' is ascribed by a few analysts to the decline of the order and discipline demanded in traditional planned economies. In the traditional planned economy, 'policy-makers act to balance imports and exports by virtue of their wide-ranging control over resource allocation', and 'imports, thus, are *effectively* restricted' (emphasis added) 'by the country's ability to export' (Brainard, 1982). It is possible that the increasing role of the industrial (branch) ministries and of the large industrial conglomerates in decisions on imports at the expense of the Planning Office did indeed contribute to Polish indebtedness. The planners therefore did not sustain 'order': that is, they did not ensure that imports and exports were balanced. Weakness of the central management and control organs in relation to pressure from branch authorities and enterprises may have been characteristic of other countries as well. But in general, the order and discipline of the traditional planned economy are quite different in practice from what is assumed in planning decisions.

If the commodities planned for export cannot be produced, or if they are produced but cannot be sold (or not at the price planned), the plan will be upset, as it will also be if imports cost more than anticipated, either because unplanned domestic shortages have to be covered from imports, or because of unfavourable price developments. Earlier, the traditional planned economies did, on the whole, avoid running up large debts – not because the central allocation of resources was more effective, but because their economic policies were less import-intensive. In the seventies, however, the rapid growth of import requirements meant that even the most centralized and traditional planned economy could not avoid the growth of indebtedness – as can be seen from the example of Romania.

5 Economic Policy Mistakes and Maladjustment

In retrospect, it is not difficult for the majority of analysts in both East and West to identify the grave economic policy errors and failures which led to the accumulation of debt in Eastern Europe. The Polish debt – the most serious of all – is unanimously attributed to the greed with which Polish leaders of that time made use of the seemingly favourable prospects for raising loans. They did this, in the spirit of the priorities they had developed themselves, with a view to double-quick modernization and the building up of a 'second Poland' within just a few years. The situation was made worse by the fact that in one or two years the economic control organs lost control, not only over imports but most of all over investment and thus over economic processes in general. This was precisely because they were in so much of a hurry. The rapidly increasing imports could not lead to the expected growth of exports because they lacked an export-orientated economic policy and a corresponding economic mechanism for carrying out such a policy.

In order to understand the economic policy errors that were committed, we must take a further step. I have already mentioned the general tendency to increase imports which characterizes East European economies – the internal pressure on policy-makers and planners, although it is not always of the same intensity. The pressure to import has been a more important factor in influencing the balance of payments than the inadequacy of the capacity to export. Beginning in the late 1970s, however, *increasing import demands have been* characteristically *concomitant with decreasing export abilities.*

The problem is often explained by exogenous factors which also affect other regions in debt: worsening terms of trade because of changes in the relative world market prices, loss of value of traditional export items on the world market, the geographical restructuring of the world market away from the Atlantic region, and growing trade restrictions. Of course, those problems did contribute to the widening gap between import needs and export capacities. The important question is the failure or delay of the East European countries in adjusting to these phenomena.

In my view, the fundamental error of the economic policy-makers, perhaps the primary factor accounting for the large-scale indebtedness, still exists and still prevents appropriate adjustment processes. This is *the failure to realize that the demand for Western imports would increase inevitably in the long run, independent* (or even in spite) *of policy intentions and decisions, whereas the parallel increase in exporting capacities requires a fundamental revision of the objectives and instruments of economic policy* – that is to say, the development of an alternative economic policy.

6   Changing Conditions – Unchanged Priorities: CMEA Co-operation

1.   A substantial quantity of the goods required for modernization – that is, the structural transformation of the East European economies – has always had to be procured from the West, as with all the other regions of the world wishing to 'catch up'. Beginning as early as the 1960s, the growth of the labour force was slowing down, domestic resources needed to sustain an increase of investment of the same vintage became increasingly scarce, cheap sources of energy and raw materials began to dry up. In CMEA usage, the resources of extensive economic development have been exhausted, so that it has become necessary to switch over to intensive development based on improved economic efficiency. Parallel with this process, the demand in these economies for Western imports has been growing. It was not so much that the modernization efforts of East European economies led to the rapid growth of machinery imports from the West (although this did happen in a few countries for a few years). Rather it was that even if imports of machinery were selective and restricted, such imports led to a chain of rapidly increasing supplementary demands for imported production materials, parts, and subassemblies.

This phenomenon can be explained in terms of the level of develop-ment, size and, above all, *way of functioning* of the East European economies: because of excess demand, weak and – from the buyer's point of view – unreliable horizontal relationships exist among enter-prises. That is why even when, theoretically, an enterprise could buy equally efficient domestic products, the buyers may prefer imported inputs. In any case, however, it is the inevitable and general *consequence of modernization* based on imported technology (as is demonstrated by the world trade turnover figures for this type of product). Despite the indignation of the economic policy-makers and the noisy campaigns for substituting domestic products (or one of the CMEA member countries' products) for these imports, such inputs constitute the major share of imports from the West in all the East European countries.

2.   The major share of the foreign trade of the Eastern European coun-tries is with the other CMEA countries. For a long period, trade with the West had developed in parallel with the rapid growth of intra-CMEA trade. In the late 1970s, however, there was a slowdown in the growth of the East European countries' intra-CMEA imports. This is partly the consequence of the general East European economic slowdown, especially the weakened supply capacity of the Soviet Union, which is the biggest trade partner of all these countries.[8]

One has only to study the harsh criticism that the current Soviet leaders have levelled against the economic policy of the Brezhnev era, and what they say about the country's economy having come to stagnation by the turn of the last decade, and about the difficulties of achieving the goals of restructuring and acceleration, to understand the causes of the slow-down. The development of the traditional branches of Soviet exports to Eastern Europe (energy and raw materials) had halted (even reversed in a few fields). Moreover, domestic consumption in the Soviet Union has continued to increase, and the same goods which were previously exported to Eastern Europe have been increasingly needed in order to offset imports from the West. This has led first to reduced growth, then to stagnation, and finally, in the case of certain important products (e.g. oil) to a reduction in exports.

While the volume of Soviet deliveries to Eastern Europe has stag-nated, East European exports to the Soviet Union have grown rapidly since the turn of the decade. The rapid expansion of exports has been forced upon the East European countries by the continuous rapid deterioration of their terms of trade with the Soviet Union under the conditions of bilateral clearing trade.

Because the volume of exports to the Soviet Union has grown much faster than imports over a long period, resources have been absorbed which might otherwise have been used to increase exports to the West. Moreover, the fast increase in exports (of manufactured goods) to the Soviet Union was possible only because imports of Western production materials, subassemblies and parts, which were built into the finished products, were growing as well. At the same time, the stagnation in imports from the Soviet Union limited the availability of commodity stocks for export to the world market, and indeed led to the purchase of such goods from the West instead of the Soviet Union. All this has gradually increased the pressure on the balance of trade between East European countries and the West.[9]

The initial reaction of the East European countries to these changes was slow. Throughout the entire period after 1973–74, these countries systematically overestimated the prospects for growth in intra-CMEA relations. Despite the more or less significant economic policy changes that have taken place everywhere, the traditional economic development strategy and approach continued to predominate and left their mark on the efforts made within the CMEA as well as on the development priorities of the individual economies.

The fundamental issue is the difficulty of modifying the deeply rooted strategy of the last forty years, in which a decisive role was assigned to adjustment to CMEA needs (and the production capacities of CMEA partners) in shaping the direction of economic development, the mechanisms of economic management, and the overall structure of the economy and of enterprises. In the context of East European indebtedness this presents a serious problem, not only because so many resources are tied up in intra-CMEA trade, which inevitably dominates the economy in the long run, but also because if development and production are adjusted to a market whose patterns of demand, methods of operations, types of inputs, and so on, are radically different from those of the world market, it will inevitably reduce the ability to conform to world market standards.

Owing to the nature of CMEA co-operation, which I have analysed in detail elsewhere (Köves, 1987), the industries which produce energy, raw material and primary products still carry a disproportionately large weight in East European countries' economic development. In most cases these industries are characterized by extremely low efficiency and are mainly used for import substitution. Hence traditional development policy conserves the backwardness of East European economies and reduces the prospects for 'catching up'; infrastructure continues to be neglected, the environment is further polluted, and not enough money is available for development in those fields of the manufacturing industry which offer a potential basis for an export-orientated development policy.

In the 1980s this situation has worsened; despite the scarcity of investment resources, huge amounts have been spent on national or international energy projects, which – while further aggravating the problems of economic efficiency and exports – even fail to alleviate the difficulties of energy and raw-material supply. This is the main reason why the necessary changes in export structure have not taken place so far, and why the balance-of-payments difficulties have not eased.

7 The Soviet Union and Trade with the West

Recently, Soviet trade with the West has also suffered considerable decline. Oil dominates Soviet exports and therefore the sudden fall of world market prices, combined with stagnating oil production, has led to a decline of several billion dollars in export receipts. Exports of manufactured goods to the West have never been significant. After 1973, when oil prices were high, the increase in receipts from oil exports seemed to be sufficient to cover the import demand growing even more rapidly in the Soviet Union than in the East European countries. The situation totally changed in 1985–86. Not even import restrictions could avoid the need to raise huge credits. The net foreign debt stock of the country grew in 1986 – in a single year – by more than $9 billion, reaching $24 billion.[10]

The general view is that in the short run this does not constitute an obstacle to further credit, but all credits can do is prevent an intolerable reduction of imports. It is not possible to finance any substantial *increase* in imports through credit, and in the long run constraints on raising credit will increase.

Official statements make it clear that there is no intention today to increase imports from the West. Given the problems of the balance of payments, this is no surprise. Yet in Gorbachev's programme of acceleration and restructuring, fast technological progress, structural transformation, and catching up with world standards at a forced pace are priority objectives. Other countries' experiences, as well as the Soviet Union's own economic history, prove that considerable quantities of imports constitute an indispensable condition for speeding up the modernization process (Köves, 1985). This does not seem to be understood, however, since several of the more recent Soviet declarations blame earlier leaders for flooding the country with a 'plague of imports', which led 'to the stagnation of certain branches of science and technology' and dependence on foreign countries (Alexandrov, 1986).

Even the most sketchy knowledge of world economic trends and world trade figures shows that Soviet imports, by any measure except for Soviet export capacities, are not too large but too little, even though the most up-to-date branches of the Soviet civilian industry which determine today's technological standards have been based on Western technological imports. In fact, modernization, innovation and technical development are mainly hindered by the domestic socioeconomic mechanism: its rigidity, the conflicting interests of producers, bureaucracy, and so forth. As for dependence, that is of course a real problem between partners of unequal economic power who are not dependent on each other's deliveries to the same extent. However, this problem is not solved through not importing. Indeed, unwillingness to import may lead to lower technical–economic capacities than otherwise, so that the country could become not less but, on the contrary, *more* vulnerable than if those imports were realized.

8   Towards a More Open Economy?

Quite apart from the way the volume of imports is likely to develop as a result of economic policy and the foreign-exchange situation, from the viewpoint of the future development of the Soviet economy (or the viewpoint of Soviet–Western economic relations) it is of key importance that the economy should grow more open: its institutional isolation from the outside world must diminish; such institutions and mechanisms should be established as are able to maintain direct connections between the home and foreign economy. This has to be an integral element of glasnost (openness) and perestroika (restructuring). A policy aimed at socioeconomic development and catching up with the world economy requires changes that are incompatible with the prevailing degree of seclusion from the outside world.

The declared aim of 'catching up' with world development standards remains a vague concept which can be elaborated only if more information is made available about global economic processes; if permanent direct channels of professional or other contacts are established in all those fields which play a role in the 'acceleration' process; if the majority of Soviet products can be measured by world market standards (which is at present impossible because of the artificial isolation of the domestic economy from the world); and if Western imports are considered as permanent channels of supply selected on the basis of efficiency instead of being regarded as a necessary evil, an unpleasant source of material and food supply, the use of which is not advisable, except for a few exceptional and individual cases, as at present.

Mutatis mutandis, these statements also hold for the East European countries. Because their economies are so much smaller and their involvement in the international division of labour so much deeper, the establishment of a more open institutional system for these countries is practically the same as market-orientated economic reform. It would involve the development of domestic markets for commodities, capital and labour, the breaking of monopolistic positions, differentiation of producers according to criteria of efficiency. The monetization of economies is possible only through the organic linking of domestic and external markets.

9 Participation in the International Division of Labour, and Joint Ventures

So far, I have suggested that the explanation for the rising tension between import needs and export capacities of CMEA member countries is to be found in the nature of their economic systems. However, East–West political factors are also important. Some of these have already been mentioned. The Cocom system and the restrictive American trade policy which gained strength again under Ronald Reagan's presidency have undoubtedly constrained Soviet and East European modernization efforts.

Greater importance should, however, be attributed to another factor. Partly because of Western policies and partly as a consequence of their own political and ideological biases – and, indeed, the mere logic of a politically divided world – the CMEA countries have excluded themselves or are, on the whole, excluded from the institutional system and mechanisms of the global economy.

The European CMEA countries have collectively refused, over a long period, to take part in international financial organizations (IMF, World Bank; even today, only three are members: Hungary, Poland, Romania). They joined GATT relatively late (and still not all[11]), and did not recognize the EEC for fifteen years (while the latter concluded important trade agreements with almost all the significant and less significant countries and groups of countries of the world).

On the one hand this has entailed trade and financial disadvantages which can be demonstrated with data. On the other – and this is the main problem – this outsider's status – being 'different' – discouraged quite a few potential economic partners, thwarting the prospects of developing economic relationships with the CMEA countries.

Until recently, the CMEA countries have been left out of the international division of labour. Only a few allowed the import of working capital and the founding of joint ventures on their territory, and even in those cases there were considerable limitations. Yet during this period, many developing and industrializing countries improved their chances of catching up by attracting foreign investment. The CMEA countries were hardly affected by global redeployment and were very vulnerable to the export offensive of the Newly Industrializing Countries.

It is fashionable to argue that the introduction of new forms could shift the current deadlock in East–West economic relations. It would, in any case, be good to renew the traditional forms of these relations. But, more importantly, new content can make new forms meaningful.

The establishment of joint ventures between CMEA and Western partners is now permitted and, indeed, promoted in many CMEA countries. This is undoubtedly an important instrument in achieving the triple goal of foreign capital imports, technological development, and an increase in exports. It is especially timely now that other methods for importing capital (new loans) are growing more difficult and have been shown to be inefficient, when investment resources and imports are scarce because of restrictions, and when reserves available for increasing exports have declined during the decade of pushing exports. Despite all this, very little progress has been made in the establishment of joint enterprises. There are very few *realistic* plans for joint ventures which are capable of satisfying the interests of all parties equally. In comparison with the multitude of investment possibilities offered in other regions of the world, the advantages which CMEA countries can offer to foreign investors are rather modest. The new form of joint venture could gain actual macroeconomic importance only with a higher degree of openness on the part of the CMEA economies.

What does this involve? For example, plans for joint ventures often fail because the CMEA countries stipulate that the enterprise should sell its products abroad, *against convertible currencies*, or at least that the export–import transactions of the enterprise should not be negative. Given the foreign-currency situation of these countries, this standpoint is quite understandable. However, the main interest of the foreign investors is to find a market for their products in the CMEA countries – to sell the products of the joint venture on the domestic market (or in another CMEA country).

This, of course, limits the scope of joint ventures. It should be stressed, however, that the problem stems from the closed character of these economies and the absence of an export-orientated economic policy. It is the organic linking of foreign and domestic market and the ending of the disadvantageous position of exports to the West (as against domestic sales and exports to the CMEA markets) that could initiate a process which would assure the supply of the domestic market with up-to-date products of higher technological standards and quality. This process, in which joint enterprises would also have a part, would *at the same time* contribute to increasing the exporting capacities of the country and, *indirectly*, to creating the possibility of producing larger export commodity stocks which conform better to market demands.

10   In Lieu of a Forecast

The foregoing has been intended to make it clear that it is first of all the inward-looking economic policy and the isolation of the CMEA eco-nomies from the world economy that bar the way to progress in East–West economic relations. It is not in the spirit of this chapter to suggest that the revision of economic policy and the economic reform aimed at increased openness are simple to put into effect, that they can produce quick results, or that a new, at last 'genuine' boom in East–West eco-nomic relations is at hand.

Difficulties lie in the political–social–economic costs of the changes and the very high risks involved. The accumulation of mistaken decisions and missed opportunities makes it harder to break with the past and to make radical changes. In the Hungarian experience, the real difficulty is not that economic policy-makers, planners, or economists-researchers do not agree on the *necessity* of discontinuity. It is, rather, about its *possibility* that opinions diverge: 'We know that we should do something else and in a different manner, but we can't.' One cannot even say that such arguments are groundless; one can say only that *nevertheless* changes must be made now, since further postponements of decisions and further advances in the wrong direction would further worsen the economic situation and make radical action even more risky.

Because of these difficulties, it might be worth making a distinction between two time horizons concerning the prospects for East–West economic co-operation:

In the short run, today's difficulties are unlikely to diminish and may even grow worse for some East European countries. The balance of payments will continue to constitute a severe constraint. In a few countries a moderate growth rate is possible; in others the governments will have to struggle further, perhaps for years to come, to find some kind of tolerable balance between import restriction and export enforcement by which the tensions of the domestic economy can be kept under control. The prospects for raising credit are not expected to improve. The notion that credit could be raised through the import of foreign working capital does not hold out the promise of quick results.

In the long run, the conditions of East–West economic co-operation may change; thus trade trends are not predetermined. Several factors may be important:

1.   *World Economic Conditions.* It is *not* reasonable to assume that world market demand will grow at a much higher rate than today, that the pattern of demand will become more favourable for the CMEA countries' existing pattern of exports, that competition between exporters will ease, or that changes in relative prices will favourably affect the CMEA countries *on the whole*. It is, however, possible that certain changes will take place in the management of international debts, so as to make it easier for debtor countries to fulfil their debt services alongside economic growth and structural transformation. Although the Baker Plan conceived in this spirit is still just a plan, a few debt-facilitating procedures and methods are already spreading. Today, one of the gravest worries of OECD countries is that they cannot – or can hardly – increase their exports, and they are therefore genuinely interested in finding some solution to the debt problem (Lever-Huhne, 1985; Bogdanowicz-Bindert, 1985; Solomon, 1985; Entwicklung . . . 1987).

2.   *World Political Conditions.* East–West political relations seem likely, as of now to improve further. It is too early to make any predictions about how far this process will go. However, as long as it continues, it may help economic relations during the critical stages. It could

improve the institutional framework of trade, and help to abolish continuing administrative restrictions. The indirect effects are even more important: an improvement in political relations could result in an atmosphere favourable to long-term transactions which could establish *mutual dependence.* This would result in a higher degree of openness in the East European countries, as well as wider participation in the international division of labour, and create a situation in which economic rationality comes less into conflict with real or imaginary political interests.

The Soviet Reform. During the last twenty-odd years, the idea of reforming the socialist socioeconomic system has been alive only in one or two East European countries. Thus the kind of internal changes which constitute the indispensable conditions for deepening East–West economic co-operation were possible only within very narrow limits. This situation has fundamentally changed with the announcement of the Soviet programme of restructuring and radical economic reform. As Mikhail Gorbachev himself put it, it is an enormous task and only the initial steps have been taken: 'favourable changes are slow, the transformation has proved more difficult, and the causes of the problems accumulated in society deeper-lying than it has been assumed' (Gorbachev, 1987).

It is impossible to deal here with the range of issues involved in the Soviet reform, but it is important to note that Soviet leaders trace today's economic troubles back to the political practice of the Stalin era and the ideology developed in support of it. Current Soviet economic thought has gone so far as to formulate explicitly the argument that the system of central planning that has prevailed for more than fifty years in the Soviet Union, and is identified with socialism, is in fact just one of the possible forms of planning, and it is feasible – indeed, necessary in the Soviet Union at present – to substitute another form of planning; such a new form would not specify enterprise action in every detail – what and how much should be produced, from whom the inputs should be procured, and to whom the outputs should be delivered. Rather, it would be concerned with macroeconomic development only, determining the overall direction of the economy, laying down the general conditions of enterprise management, and so on. Internal questions of enterprise management would be decided by the workers' collectives, so that the independence of enterprises can grow.

The emerging reform process will, of course, affect trade with the West only indirectly and in the long run. Nevertheless, a genuinely critical evaluation of past and present, and the translation of plans for restructuring into practice in the Soviet Union and other CMEA countries, could result in an unbiased consideration of the influence of alternative foreign economic policies on economic development. Thus the prospects of a greater degree of openness towards the world economy are likely to brighten and, should this process elicit favourable reaction in the West, the future of East–West economic relations would look hopeful.

Notes

1. The author acknowledges helpful comments by Gábor Oblath, Eva Palócz and László Szamuely on an earlier draft of this chapter.
2. For the purposes of this chapter, *East* includes the European member countries of the Council for Mutual Economic Assistance (CMEA), and *Eastern Europe* the CMEA countries outside the Soviet Union (Bulgaria, Czechoslovakia, the GDR, Hungary, Poland and Romania).
3. On the US export controls and the underlying debates, see Bertsch (1980, 1981), Gershman (1979), Gustafson (1981), Hewett (1982), Huntington (1978) Jacobsen (1980, 1982) and Stern (1982).
4. For a detailed discussion of the economic policy alternatives, see Köves, 1985, pp. 136–58).
5. Source of data: Developments . . . (1987).
6. On international debt crisis, see, among others, Cline (1985, 1985a), Lever-Huhne (1985), Entwicklung . . . (1987), Nunnenkamp (1985), etc. For a comparison between the accumulation of debts in Eastern Europe and Latin America, see Köves (1986).
7. Of the numerous approaches to this question in English-language/Hungarian literature, we call attention to the works of Bauer (1978) and Kornai (1980, 1986). Franklyn Holzman investigates the question from the balance-of-payments perspective (1979, 1979a).
8. In the mid 1980s the Soviet share in the global trade of the East European countries was typically 35–40 per cent, and above 60 per cent within their intra-CMEA trade.
9. For a more detailed analysis of those problems, see Köves 1983, 1985 (pp. 81–112), 1987.
10. Developments . . . (1987), p. 26.
11. The Soviet Union has recently applied for observer status – to which, however, the United States is implacably opposed.

References

Alexandrov, A.P. (1986) 'Contribution to the 27th Congress of the Soviet Communist Party', *Pravda*, 27 February 1988.
Bauer, T. (1978) 'Investment Cycles in Planned Economies', *Acta Oeconomica*, vol. 21, no. 3, pp. 243–60.
Bertsch, G. (1980). 'US–Soviet Trade: The Question of Leverage', *Survey*, 26/2. pp. 66–80.
Bertsch, G. (1981) 'US Export Controls: The 1970s and Beyond', *Journal of World Trade Law*, vol. 15, no. 1, pp. 67–82.
Bogdanowicz-Bindert, C.A. (1986) 'World Debt: The United States Reconsiders', *Foreign Affairs*, vol. 64, no. 2, pp. 259–73.
Brainard, L. (1982) 'Poland's Foreign Debt Crisis. Background and Perspectives'. Submitted as Testimony to the European Subcommittee of the Senate Foreign Relations Committee, 27 January.

272 THE NEW DETENTE

Cline, W.R. (1985) 'Changing Stresses on the World Economy', *World Economy*, June, pp. 135–52.

Cline, W.R. (1985a) 'International Debt: From Crisis to Recovery?', *American Economic Review*, May, pp. 185–90.

Developments . . . (1987) 'Developments in East–West Financial Relations in 1986 and Medium-Term Prospects', *Financial Market Trends*, no. 36, OECD, Paris, February.

Entwicklung . . . (1987) 'Entwicklung und Stand der internationalen Verschuldung', *Monatsberichte der Deutschen Bundesbank*, January, pp. 38–49.

Gershman, C. (1979) 'Selling Them the Rope', *Commentary*, April, pp. 35–45.

Gorbachev, M.S. (1987) Address at the January Session of the Central Committee of the Soviet Communist Party. *Pravda*, 28 January.

Gustafson, O. (1981) 'Selling the Russians the Rope? Soviet Technology Policy and US Export Controls'. Prepared for the Defence Advanced Research Projects Agency. Rand Corporation.

Hewett, E.A. (1982): 'The Pipeline Connection: Issues for the Alliance', *Brookings Review*, vol. 1, no. 1, pp. 15–20.

Holzman, F. (1979) 'Some Systematic Factors Contributing to the Convertible Currency Shortages of Centrally Planned Economies', *American Economic Review*, May, pp. 76–80.

Holzman, F. (1979a) 'Some Theories of the Hard Currency Shortages of Centrally Planned Economies', in *Soviet Economy in a Time of Change*, a compendium of papers submitted to the Joint Economic Committee, Congress of the United States, vol. 2, Washington, DC, pp. 297–316.

Huntington, S.P. (1978) 'Trade, Technology and Leverage: Economic Diplomacy', *Foreign Policy*, no. 32.

Jacobsen, H.D. (1980) *Die Ostwirtschaftspolitik der USA, Möglichkeiten und Grenzen einer "linkage" – Politik*, Stiftung Wissenschaft und Politik. Forschungsinstitut für internationale Politik und Sicherheit. Ebenhausen.

Jacobsen, H.D. (1982) *Die Ostwirtschaftspolitik der Reagan-Administration*, Stiftung Wissenschaft und Politik. Forschungsinstitut für internationale Politik und Sicherheit. Ebenhausen.

Kornai, J. (1980) *Economics of Shortage*, Amsterdam, North-Holland.

Kornai, J. (1986) 'The Hungarian Reform Process. Vision, Hopes, and Reality', *Journal of Economic Literature*, vol. XXIV, December 1986.

Köves, A. (1983) ' "Implicit Subsidies" and Some Issues of Economic Relations within the CMEA', *Acta Oeconomica*, vol. 31, nos. 1–2, pp. 125–136.

Köves, A. (1985) 'The CMEA countries in the World Economy: Turning Inwards or Turning Outwards', Akadémiai Kiadó, Budapest, 248p.

Köves, A. (1986) 'Foreign Economic Equilibrium, Economic Development and Economic Policy in the CMEA Countries', *Acta Oeconomica*, vol. 36 nos. 1–2, pp. 35–53.

Köves, A. (1986a) 'Is opening still topical?', *Acta Oeconomica*, vol. 37, nos 3–4 (forthcoming).

Köves, A. (1987) 'Some Questions of Energy Policy of the East European Countries', in R. Dietz, K. Mack, eds, *Energie, Umwelt und Zusammenarbeit in Europa*, Springer Verlag, Wien-New York, pp. 57–68.

Lever, H. Huhne, C. (1985) *Debt and Danger: The World Financial Crisis*, Penguin Books, p. 160.

Nunnenkamp, P. (1985) 'Die Entstehung und Bewältigung von Verschuldungskrisen in Entwicklungsländern,' *Die Weltwirtschaft*, no. 2., pp. 183–198.

Solomon, A.M. (1985) 'LDC Dept: Where Do We Go from Here?', *The Banker*, August 1985, pp. 14–18.

12

The State and Society: Reflections from a Western Experience

Hilary Wainwright

Critical socialists in the West and in the East now start their thinking from a common premiss. State intervention in society, even where that state is formally under the control of 'the representatives of the working class', is part of the problem as much as part of the solution.

It is obsolete state forms, as well as Realpolitik, which underlie the problem of the military blocs. The ideology of the Cold War presents the political choice as one between the totalitarian state, monolithic in its internal structure and monopolistic in its relation to society, and, on the other hand, the parliamentary state, with its limited levers for democratic control. A condition for 'dealignment' is the development of realistic visions East and West, of alternative, genuinely democratic political forms.

This is not a matter of converging trends towards a single model, as some commentators have, rather arrogantly, argued – frequently implying Eastern adaptation to a Western ideal. Rather, it is a matter of different experiments in popular power, growing out of diverse circumstances and therefore combining a variety of institutions and values. What such experiments might share and what could bring them together in joint action is a refusal to acquiesce in the rule of those whose power derives from the Cold War. Only dialogue between the associations and movements participating in these experiments can establish what values and political visions we share. One problem in such a dialogue is language: not so much the problem of different languages, but the fact that in the East the concepts of socialism and democracy have become empty, even mocking of the meanings they have had in the past. They cannot easily, without new phrases and qualifications, be used to communicate anything positive or precise. In the West, too, their use has muddied their meaning. But still in the West they contain a critical political point if they are used without rhetoric. For this reason I find myself automatically using these terms when referring to the goal of a society whose members are emancipated from inequalities of wealth and power.

Amongst some people, East and West, disaffection with existing state–society relations has led to a somewhat uncritical discovery of the joys of the private market. Amongst others, however, it has led to a search for new forms of democracy, both in social and economic life and in the state, and in the relationship between the two. In the West at least, where there is some scope for autonomous political initiative, this has involved practical experimentation, particularly through local government.

Local government in Britain, especially the government of major cities, provided several favourable conditions for innovations in political structures – until, that is, Mrs Thatcher decimated their power. Most important, given the powerful conservative influence of the military in ossifying established state structures, is the relative autonomy of local councils from the defence imperatives of the nation-state.

Also, new ideas about democracy gain much of their vitality from local initiatives – in different social communities and workplaces, as well as the local institutions of political parties – so local authorities provide an ideal opportunity for innovation to gain political expression. The political administration of the Greater London Council (GLC) between 1981 and 1986, when the government abolished it, provided one such moment of innovation.

The GLC was responsible for running London-wide services such as transport, waste disposal, certain forms of housing, and also for carrying out the strategic planning of the use of London's valuable land. The left's attempt to run this vast city government in a new way was incomplete, as any social experiment inevitably is, especially when it faces the determined hostility faced by the GLC. In some ways it was a failure; in others, a success. But a sharper sense of the issues facing socialist democracy, and even an idea of some of the solutions, can be gained by reflecting on the experience.

The Labour left gained control of the GLC in May 1981, thirteen years after the events of May 1968. Those thirteen years had been years of disillusionment with the limited democracy of conventional British politics – disillusionment stirred in part by the glimpse in '68 of real possibilities for change. The years since then were also years of debate, conflict and experimentation about alternatives. At the risk of being schematic, there were two main directions to these debates. For a brief moment, the GLC brought them together – though not always in harmony.

THE STATE AND SOCIETY

First, there was a sustained rebellion against the limits of a democracy restricted to political representation. It was a rebellion by the first generation which had benefited from the results of a fully democratic franchise: the reforms achieved by a majority Labour government. For the students of '68, the shop stewards' movement of the same period – and, amongst others, the feminists who asserted themselves soon after – the bureaucratic benevolence of public-sector provision was not enough. They aspired to choice. Not so much consumer choice – they had that, and were not satisfied – but democratic control over the social and economic decisions which shaped their daily lives; the discipline of the college and the courses available, the pace of the assembly line and the organization of work, the provision of childcare and the division of domestic labour.

Initially, these rebels were taking the rhetoric of liberal democracy at its word and contrasting its political claims with the inequities of economic and social power. The kinds of democratic control they wanted varied (perhaps not enough: there was a tendency for certain practical procedures appropriate in particular circumstances – for example, collective decision-making – to be abstracted into moral principles). And since they were concerned with institutions of daily life rather than political institutions at several removes, they explored new – new to them – forms of democracy: forms with a strong direct, rather than representative, component.

In the creation of their own organizations and wherever they had any social and economic space of their own – in their own courses, producer co-ops, their own collective childcare arrangements – they tried to prefigure these forms. In general, then, the concern of these movements was civil society: social relations separate from the state – though given the extensive role of the state, the two spheres of state and civil society cannot easily be separated. Where these initiatives came into conflict with the power structures (as distinct from social resources) of the existing state, they found themselves against them. But their creative practice – rarely theorized – concerned society outside the realm of government and political parties.

The second impetus of debate and initiative about democracy came from within the Labour Party and was focused, at times too narrowly, on the institutions of political democracy. The experience of Labour in government backtracking on party commitments – in 1966–70 and again in 1974–79 – produced a build-up of frustration with the party's lack of influence on the government. Labour prime ministers, with their cabinets, seemed to be in the grip of the Treasury, the City and the IMF rather than Parliament, let alone the party. The power of these institutions, the influence of unaccountable sectional interests on the main

Whitehall departments combined with official secrecy and prime ministerial patronage, had drained the idea of parliamentary account-ability of all meaning. Labour Members of Parliament had become stooges of their government. Faced with this, Labour activists tried to build some kind of counterpower through the only instrument at hand: their party.

The result was a struggle to hold MPs to party policy by making them subject to mandatory reselection by their constituency parties and making elections for the leadership a matter for the party as a whole rather than purely the parliamentary party. Although in effect it was a movement about democratizing the state, it was carried out so exclu-sively through the party that the wider issues of political democracy, or lack of it – the political role of the civil service, the powers the prime minister holds in the name of the crown, the position of central govern-ment in relation to the regions and localities – rarely got an airing, except through the speeches of Tony Benn. No new model of demo-cratic political representation emerged – only the need for one and some of the problems it would have to address.

One such problem – the fundamental one, in fact – is the relation between the state and the rest of society: civil society, as these economic and social relations have historically been called. At the time of the struggles within the Labour Party, this did not appear to be an especially important problem: the activists were concerned with how to make the executive arm of the state accountable to the legislature and how to make members of the legislature responsive to the party in whose name they became legislators – all intrastate, or at least intrapolitical, relationships.

The importance of wider relationships did, however, begin to emerge: for example, over the issue of how to exert social control over invest-ment, given that the nationalized industries did not provide a democratic and socially responsive industrial model. Workers like those in Lucas Aerospace, instead of seeing the state as the sole source of the solution, tried to test out how political power could extend worker's industrial power to transform industry in a socially responsible and democratic direction. But unfortunately, these were just occasional concerns. Now, however, the issue of the state and society is being posed in stark nega-tive relief as Mrs Thatcher pulverizes all civil society beyond the private entrepreneur. In a paradoxical way this advocacy of market economics is politicizing society, or at least parts of it, in a way which is reminiscent of Eastern Europe. The Thatcher government has politicized – that is, sought to control – every previously autonomous body except – and this is the difference with the 'planned' economies – private economic interests, financial and industrial.

Against this background a twin focus on democracy in civil society and in the state has become as urgent in the West as in the East, albeit in a very different way. This means giving credence to recent attempts to democratize economic and social life. This latter point needs to be reasserted because the special importance of those movements referred to earlier, which had this concern, was lost. One reason for this is that the success of Thatcher has rather dazed parts of the left and knocked it on to the defensive, producing a stream of *mea culpas* wiping out the past. Another reason is that we detracted from the innovative details of our ideas by accepting the all-encompassing description 'extra-parliamentary'. It has its uses, but the indiscriminate way it was flung around (by me as much as anyone else) lumped two different phenomena together. It muddled into one blurred image 'extra-parliamentary' in the sense of mobilizations outside parliament but around political decisions, with 'extra-parliamentary' in the sense of outside the realm of conventional political power. In so doing it damaged the understanding, including self-understanding, of these movements. It overpoliticized, in too narrow a fashion, those attempts to democratize economic and everyday life.

Of course such attempts at change *are* political in the sense of trying to change society. But they are specifically not political – in fact, almost anti-political – in that by changing social relations independently of conventional politics, they are challenging the limits which the existing state places on democracy. Before the left gained control in certain local councils, the social movements were mainly agnostic about the state. They made specific demands – to scrap nuclear weapons, to provide childcare for all, to take action to preserve jobs – but they rarely had any positive view on how their sphere of activity and that of parliamentary politics and the state, which in theory Parliament controls, should connect, if at all.

It was not until politicians sympathetic to these movements gained office in local councils – subordinate, dependent parts of the state – that the question arose of how activity in spheres independent of the state should relate to representation within the state. This was a question which ran through many of the experiences of the left's control over the GLC. It is a question which has two sides, depending on whether your approach was formed primarily by the experience of social movements and independence from party politics or whether it was formed by the internal battle for power within the Labour Party. From the former standpoint the question, in its extreme form, was how to gain support from the local council of a sort which strengthened your organization's ability to achieve the social changes for which it aimed, without losing the organization's self-determination. From the inner party standpoint the problem was how to support social movements – and in turn win their support for the Labour council – without losing control of the direction of social and political change.

These two contrasting sides tugged at the relationship from opposite directions. There was no model they could turn to, from an industrial society, of a party using state power to contribute to revolutionary change, but without the pretensions that such change could be achieved through the state alone.

Almost by force of circumstance, the solutions worked out by trial and error in the experience of the GLC – from inside and outside – established some principles for the future. Two circumstances were crucial. On the one hand, the statutory powers available to the GLC fell far short of what would be needed were the GLC by itself even to try to carry out all its objectives. This was particularly so given that its limited power would be undermined rather than complemented by national government. In other words, if the GLC were to carry through its manifesto rather than go the way of radical-sounding Labour administrations before it, it *had* to turn to sources of power and initiative other than its own – though few politicians consciously thought of it this way. On the other hand, movements and organizations in society – in the black community, amongst women, in localities facing particular problems and in all manner of workplaces – were at a low ebb compared to the strength and confidence of many of them in the 1970s. They were down enough to be on the lookout, though warily, for support; but not so down that they had lost their capacity to demand it, press for it, and insist on their own terms.

A point to bear in mind, in the following discussion of the principles which in practice were developed in this situation, is that these were circumstances of conflict with institutions outside the control of the GLC and popular movements. Consequently, the principles I am discussing do not provide a blueprint for a democratic socialist society. They are principles concerning the state and civil society in the struggles for transition towards such a society, although I hope, too, that they begin to prefigure the kind of society we want.

A first principle towards which we edged was that whenever the GLC intervened in a community or workplace, it would do so only on the basis of a respectful relationship with allies on the inside. At first the GLC did not do this. Like any other government – socialist or liberal-technocratic – it administered from on high, as if so long as it was in charge, the detailed character of the social relations into which it intervened was irrelevant. It took over a furniture factory, for instance, with the aim of saving jobs and transforming the production process. It – the GLC, that is – had great expertise about the furniture industry, and much money.

Nevertheless, in the end, the factory collapsed. More money, more power – a stronger state body – could well have postponed the collapse. But what could have made a lasting difference was a close relationship between the GLC managers and accountants and the foremen and shop stewards in the factory who welcomed what the GLC was trying to do and had watched the previous manager/owner make a mess of production. They knew, on the basis of their own skills and experience, how production could be improved. For this knowledge to be released, however, and turned to practical effect, there would need to be a change in the division of labour and authority within the factory, as well as its ownership and source of finance.

The GLC's intervention could have been midwife for such a change, though it could not have carried it through. However, at the time when the GLC – via its Enterprise Board, GLEB – first came into contact with the furniture factory, it was operating with the traditional notion of state intervention: as the knight on a white charger. This was a notion of the state which tended to see itself intervening as if it, and it alone, could bring about the changes required. The opposite of this is to leave things alone: leave it to the self-regulating market; as if the market were based on equality and freedom and would arrive at the optimum solution for all. Then there is the mixed approach: the market needs nudging this way and that; some functions even need to be taken out of it. We arrived at an approach quite outside these options.

Our approach stemmed from a belief, based on the experiences of recent social movements, that political parties do not have a monopoly of the power for social change. For instance, for the purposes of saving jobs and changing production there are forms of knowledge, skill and power outside the capacities of the state, including the national state, however socialist its intent: forms which lie only with the workers in particular and related companies – workers at all levels. We and they shared certain common interests in saving and transforming production – interests which the owner and/or shareholder, in an enterprise whose immediate profit prospects were low, usually did not share: for capital is mobile in a way labour is not. The task, then, was to negotiate an alliance which released the skills and capacities for self-organization amongst the workers within a wider framework set by the policies on the basis of which the GLC was elected.

The character of such alliances illustrated further general principles that can be drawn from the GLC experiences. The aim of 'releasing skills and capacities for popular self-organization' involves the state in two very different kinds of relationship. On the one hand, it requires strong negative or restrictive action against sources of economic and social inequality and exploitation. On the other, it requires supportive, enabling action to create the conditions for popular self-determination.

The GLC's approach to land use and development provides a good illustration of the two-sided relationship. In the decade before the left's control over the GLC, citizens in inner London had put up determined resistance to rapacious property developers. For the property market, these inner-city areas – by the river, round the docks, near the City of London – were 'prime sites': sites for major office developments. Throughout these years community groups lobbied the GLC, without much success, to use its planning powers to protect existing residential, recreational and service uses of the land. Then, amongst the new councillors who made up the left majority in 1981, were several people who had played a leading part in the community movement; in fact in several cases these individuals had made the effort to become councillors specifically in order to use the GLC's powers to block the property market. Their allegiance was to the community groups whose aspirations for the areas they supported and whose capacity for self-organization they respected.

The best action the GLC could take, they decided, was to buy the threatened land from the property developer, with a compulsory purchase order if necessary, and put development under the democratic management of the community groups, with GLC finance where necessary. Many community groups had already worked on alternative plans to those of the office developers, as a positive focus to their campaigns. Such plans became the basis of the development. The GLC, with the groups, would agree guidelines, consistent with the standards and principles on which the Council was elected. On this basis the groups would manage and direct the development, identifying the needs and drawing on the ideas of their members. They would send a representative to a GLC committee every month or so to report unforeseen problems or needs or share ideas from which groups in other areas could benefit. GLC staff, architects, accountants sometimes gave practical support, but the drive and imagination behind the development came from the groups based in the community.

These two functions, then, are very different, involving distinct forms of state action. The first function is controlling and instrumental, with a determinate outcome: the GLC buys land in, for instance, Waterloo in order to stop office development. The second is supportive and enabling: it involves a relationship based on mutual respect. For if the autonomy of the popular organization is undermined in its relationship with the state, if it becomes a mere arm of the state, it loses its capacities for change and creation. Thus the political order which is based on popular alliance must be a political order to which uncertainty is not a threat.

In a sense a problem with socialism, historically, is that it has concentrated on the former, controlling function and let the latter, supportive function fall away. The result is that where 'socialism' has held sway, autonomous popular organizations have shrivelled, as in the Soviet Union and many parts of Eastern Europe. And where it aspires to hold sway, they appear as a threat, as is illustrated by the attitude of Labour and Social Democrat parties to progressive movements outside their sphere of influence. The Cold War solidified this exclusion of popular movements from any distinct role – beyond crowd scenes – in traditional scenarios of socialism. Its atmosphere was 'if you are not with us you are against us'; an atmosphere which denied space for the tensions which come from plural spheres of struggle and change. One of the practical and ideological repercussions of the rejection of Cold War politics in '68 was, as I have already implied, a renewed confidence in struggling for social change beyond the conventional boundaries of the political.

The most powerful and lasting expression of this was modern feminism. Its slogan 'the personal is political' summed up its belief that the liberation of women required changes in social relations far deeper than those that conventional politics, liberal or socialist, could reach. Post-war social democracy had raised the education and expectations of women as citizens but let them down as women. The barriers of gender threatened to restrict our fulfilment as equal citizens. The clash of expectations and personal experience led women themselves to search out the roots of their subordination: subordination in every sphere of life from work, both waged and domestic, to sex. For fifteen years before the GLC's Women's Committee appeared on the scene, women – collectively, informally, individually – had been resisting these divisions, transforming these relationships. Their concerns rarely surfaced as politics.

By the early 1980s and the first major electoral breakthrough of the left in local government, feminists in many different circumstances were increasingly clear about what they wanted from the state, including the local state. They were not demanding that the state solve their problems; they were demanding resources, and also an influence on how public services were provided. So by the time the GLC opened its maze of corridors to feminists, the scene had been set for a new relationship between the local state and the daily lives of women. Instead of the politicians and civil servants deciding and implementing what they thought was best for women, women demanded state support for activities they were already doing or knew could be done if the resources were available. They also presented well-worked-out proposals that would make every service and power of the GLC more responsive to the needs and desires of women. By trial and error, conflict and argument,

mechanisms evolved under the authority of the Women's Committee by
which the GLC provided resources, with certain agreed conditions, for
the dense network of women's activities whose direction remained self-
determining. In the same way mechanisms were constructed by which
the GLC, sometimes only half-heartedly, opened up its mainstream
policies to the influence of feminists whose expertise had been gained
outside the local state apparatus and who continued, by choice, to
remain outside.

Here I have used the ways in which the GLC worked with
autonomous organizations in industry and the community to illustrate
the emergence – still in practice rather than in theory – of a view of
socialist transformation which is not monopolized by the state. Underlying these practices were two understandings, sometimes painfully
learned, that point both to the necessity of state intervention in civil
society in achieving socialism, and to its limit. First, there was an awareness of the exploitation and the inequalities of power and status on
which civil society in the West is based – inequalities which are continually reproduced. Secondly, there was a recognition that resistance had
grown independently of the state, and to a large extent of political
parties, and that this resistance – resistance by the people who had previously, as victims, been daily reproducing inequality and exploitation –
is an unsubstitutable condition for emancipation.

A final question flows from this reflection on the relations between
socialist political representation and different classes and groups in the
economy and society: what kind of state, under the control of what sort
of party(ies), can be both strong against sources of economic and social
inequality and supportive towards autonomous popular movements or
associations? I cannot answer this in detail here, but I draw certain
conclusions from the experiences described above. First, for the state to
be strong it needs to be independent of those who have a vested interest
in the inequalities of civil society, whether they be the property
developers against whom the GLC took action, or the City institutions
against which the left needs to move at a national level. This clearly
implies a radical rehaul of the civil service and its present external
relations.

Secondly, the restrictive actions of a socialist administration will face
intransigence and reaction. To overcome this, the administration will
need its actions to be backed by expressions of popular support and
reassertions of its democratic mandate. The state itself cannot actually
mobilize such support: to be genuine, and therefore sustained, it would
require the energies and commitment of the political party(ies) on whose
policies the administration was acting. But for political parties to be willing and able to build an independent and popular defence of their

administration's actions, there need to be direct connections between the government, its parliamentary supporters and the base organizations of the party. In Britain, the Labour Party, from its foundation onwards, acquiesced in a political system in which these connections were mediated – in effect blocked – by the power that the executive inherited, in the name of the crown, from Britain's half-hearted democratic revolution. Labour prime ministers and senior cabinet ministers have slunk away from their election commitments behind the elaborate protection barriers of official secrecy, patronage and the royal prerogative.

One of the advantages of the GLC for developing, in a modest way, new forms of democracy was that as a relatively recent local authority it lacked this dead weight of history. (This is not to imply that conservative institutions need centuries to mature – the GLC's permanent hierarchies exerted plenty of pressure towards inertia.) The new breed of left politicians coming into the GLC, fresh from struggles within the national party for the accountability of the parliamentary party, were determined to give a strong political drive to the GLC machine and to be open to the party and the public about the difficulties they faced. When manifesto commitments came up against problems, the politicians went public, explained their plans and gave all the information they could about the opposition. Sometimes, as the administration clashed with national government – over cheap fares, over taking over London Transport, over abolition itself – people took action, but rarely through the Labour Party.

This leads to a problem for both the controlling and the enabling functions of a socialist administration. Political parties are crucial potential links between action by the state and autonomous groups in society. The Labour Party, however, has been shaped according to the needs of state socialism – in practice, state pragmatism. All the muscles of the party are trained for is to get their candidates elected; then it is up to the parliamentary party or the Labour group in council, until election time comes round once more. Even now that mandatory reselection is built into the party's constitution, Constituency Labour Parties rarely take further action either to support their MPs or to pressure them, unless the MP him- or herself gives a lead. In London then, when the GLC needed the energetic support of the people who believed in their policies, the party's reflexes were inert. *Ad hoc* campaigns grew up and sometimes stimulated local parties into action. All too often, however, the GLC itself filled the vacuum, employing full-time officials to do the campaigning which really only a voluntary political organization can do with any lasting credibility.

The enabling function of the state shows up yet further limitations of the Labour Party – and, indeed, most West European traditional parties of labour. But before exploring these, let us ask what kind of state this function requires. In a sense, modern capitalist countries have long had enabling states: states supporting institutions in civil society at the same time as respecting their autonomy. They have been enabling the institutions of private capital. For this purpose and as a result of this process, state institutions at every level are enmeshed in reciprocal relations with private corporations and financial institutions. An administration which instead gave support to the associations of those without property would therefore need to dismantle many established relationships and ways of doing things. As a small-scale illustration: the GLC did literally dismantle the offices and dispersed the staff of the 'London Industrial Centre', which gave unconditional aid to business – and promoted the low wages of the London workforce to entice investment. The GLC replaced this Business Centre with the 'Popular Planning Unit', which worked with trade-union and community groups on their plans, bargaining positions and campaigning demands, and with the 'Greater London Enterprise Board (GLEB), which invested in companies conditional on an agreement with the trade unions.

The state's relations with private capital are opaque. They are not immediately obvious in the institutions of parliamentary democracy. There is no formal representation of capital, no delegates from the Chamber of Commerce on local councils, no representatives of the Confederation of British Industry (CBI) in the House of Lords. The workings of the market determine which are the most powerful companies, and informal agreements determine who deals with whom in government. A democratic alliance with those who are not players in the market requires formal, transparent procedures to determine access to political resources and influence over political decisions: procedures which respect the necessary autonomy of popular organizations. At the GLC this need led to the growth of forms of direct and delegate democracy complementing parliamentary-type institutions. The latter retained ultimate power over the framework of policy. But parliamentary-type, broadly· representative democracy was not sufficiently flexible to respond to the very specific needs and initiatives of different groups.

Parliamentary democracy has always dealt with the public as individual constituents with problems to be seen to, sorted out by the MP and civil servants. An administration committed to enabling popular organizations, however, is one where the constituents have plans and powers of their own with which they work from their independent base with politicians towards shared, or at least consistent, aims. This requires intermediate levels of participation: more intense than voting, yet not as totally political as being a councillor or an MP – citizens' actions, one might call them. It also, I would argue, requires political representatives who are responsive and empathetic to the processes of non-political popular associations. This implies a political system and values with a bias against career politicians and in favour of movement between politics and organizations in civil society.

The GLC's attempts to extend democracy beyond council, or representative, democracy left the Labour Party far behind. We have discussed the limitations of its electoralism; but deeper than this is the limitation of its exclusive focus on state power – or rather, state office. The GLC – implicitly rather than consciously – was acknowledging other sources of power for social and economic change: in black organizations, the movements in London for lesbians and gays, workplace trade-union committees, women's centres and tenants' federations. From these, however, the Labour Party was absent. As a result, when the GLC was abolished by the Conservative government these autonomous groups had no political focus, no political platform or amplifier for their insights and demands. That requires new kinds of parties which take seriously the importance of social movements and their autonomy. Many socialists in Europe, active in social movements but wanting also a political representation, are experimenting with what national and international forms such parties might take.

Unlike many contributors to this book, I have focused on the West. All I have said in reflecting on one Western experience implies that the relationship of social movements in civil society with the state and socialist parties is quite different in the West, at least in their starting points for change, from that relationship in the East. In the West, on the basis of the analysis above, the movements have sufficient autonomous strength in spheres outside politics to benefit from some kind of partnership with elected political representatives. Indeed, such a partnership is necessary to overthrow the inequalities and exploitation they face. In the East, by contrast, civil society is not riven with inequality because it lacks autonomy entirely. There is equality in powerlessness. Inequalities stem from the state's concentrated power. The democratic resistance in the East immediately faces the state; its objective, frequently, is simply to establish a social life autonomous from the state. Only when such autonomy has grown is it possible to consider a new kind of state, a state which supports and respects democratic associations with a life of their own under conditions of economic and social equality. So social movements, both East and West, are working from opposite directions but perhaps with similar hopes. A dialogue which constantly throws these contrasts and mirror-images into the discussion may well be fraught with misunderstandings, but it will help to clarify and make specific the pluralist socialism we both want.

13

Ecology and the New Detente

Martin Ryle and Kate Soper

This chapter is concerned with what we might term the 'green alternative' and with its implications for East–West understanding at both official and unofficial levels. It is a strategically important notion, not only in the attention it directs to ecological issues but in its suggestion that the transitional period we are now entering may develop along widely divergent lines. In so far as they reduce tension, minimize risks of accidental nuclear war and build a degree of mutual confidence, we must welcome such recent political developments as the Gorbachev reforms, the INF agreement, and the general *rapprochement* between the superpowers. At the same time, we need to develop political thinking and political alliances 'across the blocs', capable not only of contesting a Cold War which may at last be thawing, but of influencing the kind of 'post-Cold War' settlement which is eventually reached.

It is quite possible that such a settlement might embrace welcome measures of detente and disarmament, while remaining inimical to the building of the permanent order of peaceful coexistence which is the ultimate aim of the peace and ecology movements. A lessening of East–West tension in Europe is beginning to make itself felt and may eventually begin to take us 'beyond the blocs', but this is happening within an overall political and economic orientation still tied to exterminist tendencies of our First World industrial culture: to its exploitation of poorer countries, and to its pursuit of economic expansion regardless of ecological consequences. Within this overall orientation, military force and the threat of force are likely to remain central to nation-state identities and to the identity of the (nuclear-armed?) 'Western European front' which may develop in response to any US withdrawal from Europe.

Hence the importance of the green alternative, which must continue to oppose Cold War conservatism and to give a cautious welcome to official detente, but which also calls in question the truly progressive nature of any 'technocratic detente', based as the latter is on the common wisdom of politicians, administrators and many citizens/voters in East and West alike – a common wisdom which asserts that human well-being is identical with economic expansion, vaunts the leading role of technology, and regards pollution and resource depletion as an inevitable price for all this civilization.

Such themes were officially orchestrated in the aftermath of Chernobyl: a dreadful calamity, it was agreed, but valuable none the less for what it taught us about nuclear accidents and the need for East–West co-operation in dealing with such hitches in the future.[1] Recently, the USA and the USSR have publicly floated the idea that they might surmount their verification problems by detonating some nuclear warheads in each other's test sites. What will come next? Soviet astronauts launched from Cape Kennedy? Mutual assistance in retrieving obstreperous (understandably obstreperous) monkeys from outer space? Across-the-blocs shopping sprees in the hypermarkets of Freedom and of Socialism? Barter arrangements to enable easy tourist access to the blocs' respective military parades? Some of these things are happening already. Which are to be judged as progressive, and by what criteria are we to judge?

In the West, the new social movements and Green parties have for some time been arguing that there is a link between policies of uncritical 'economic growth' and the phenomena of militarism, nuclear exterminism, and ecological degradation. Green ideas have begun to penetrate mainstream political thinking, though with little concrete effect to date.

In Eastern Europe, too, the environment is increasingly the focus of public and scientific concern and of political campaigning. Disastrous levels of chemical and dust pollution, particularly in Poland and Czechoslovakia, have been the most immediate cause of anxiety; but the Chernobyl accident was of historic significance in alerting the public to the particular dangers of the nuclear industry – and has generated more sympathy on the part of the various independent peace and human-rights groups in Eastern Europe for the centrality accorded the nuclear issue by disarmament activists in the West.[2]

There remain important differences of emphasis in the disposition of ecological groups in East and West Europe: differences attributable partly to the discrepant political and institutional contexts in which they must work, partly to differences in experience and history, and partly to diverse ideological perspectives. Greens in the West have moved on from a concern with pollution and the environment to a direct contestation of the economics of growth, whereas environmental degradation remains the essential concern of ecological protest in the East, where affluence is understandably thought to present a less compelling problem and where, as we have indicated, the ills of immediate pollution are that much more severe. These differences of emphasis and asymmetries of experience are reflected in the chapters in this book (especially in those by Andras Köves and Istvan Rev), and we discuss them in the remainder of this chapter. By stressing the interrelationship of our respective concerns, and by extending the dialogue around them, we believe we can build on the existing recognition that the ecological crisis transcends national and bloc boundaries, and can search for a common political language to express and give effect to our common disquiet.

From Ecology to Green Politics

The West European 'ecology movement' began as a diffuse protest movement: a series of often unrelated campaigns on environmental and other issues. The broader green movement still includes such 'single-issue' bodies as (in the UK) the Council for the Protection of Rural England or the *ad hoc* local campaigns which resisted proposals to bury radioactive waste in shallow land sites.

However, the two largest environmental pressure groups in the UK (both of which have extensive international affiliations), Greenpeace and Friends of the Earth, link together a variety of initiatives, sometimes placing them in a broader social and economic context. Greenpeace may still be best known for its efforts to prevent the killing of whales and baby seals, but among its first actions was an attempt to stop French nuclear testing in the Pacific: here, environmental issues were indissolubly fused with questions of militarism and colonialism. In its campaigns on the felling of tropical rainforests and on public transport in London, FoE has highlighted social and economic dimensions of environmental issues. And in marking the first anniversary of Chernobyl, FoE joined forces with CND, the most politically prominent and controversial of protest movements, in a demonstration calling for unilateral steps by Britain to dismantle both nuclear power plants and nuclear warheads.

The development of eco-protest into green politics has also been influenced by the 'alternative lifestyles' movement (or ideology) which is a legacy of the later 1960s. As well as formal political initiatives like the Future in Our Hands movement associated with Erik Damman, there have been community-based practical alternatives of the kind recently advocated by Rudolf Bahro.[3] Numerically insignificant and politically marginal, such groups are none the less important because they express a conviction, which we believe is well founded, that both global justice and ecological sustainability require the adoption of simpler lifestyles by the inhabitants of rich countries.

The crucial moment in the development of the green alternative, however, has been the institution of Green parties and electoral alliances. By autumn 1985, nineteen such groupings were active in a dozen European countries. Since then, the green electoral presence has continued to grow. In Italy, the establishment of a co-ordinated 'Green List' has been followed by the formation of a Green Party, and in West Germany (where *Die Grünen* enjoy a parliamentary representation and a political influence which are the envy of greens elsewhere) the 1987 Bundestag elections demonstrated a clear increase in support for their radical position, despite some disagreement and even incoherence inside the party.[4]

These developments are important for the internal politics of Western European countries. It should be borne in mind that as well as having representatives at every level from local councils up to the European Parliament, the Greens are impelling the major parties to rethink their policies from an ecological standpoint, and thus have an impact larger than their share of votes might suggest. Here, however, we are concerned less with this than with the consequences, for green/ ecological thinking itself, of the move into electoral politics. For once it has been decided to enter the electoral arena, a grouping whose focus was once primarily environmental finds itself led to develop policies on a range of issues – in principle, on every issue with which voters are concerned. 'Ecology' must be placed in the framework of a broader social and economic programme.

How will those citizens of Eastern European countries who share the greens' initial environmental concerns react to these wider programmes? One general point needs stressing. The very move from eco-protest to green politics involves a certain 'loss of innocence'.

Environmental protest, with its resistance 'from below' to economic–bureaucratic imperatives, has until now been in many ways an embodiment of the 'anti-political politics' favoured by such writers as Vaclav Havel and George Konrád (and this, together with the pronounced anarchist–decentralist orientation of many greens, seems to support the idea that the green movement might be enlisted as part of some 'league of opposition' to both communist and capitalist states.[5] 'Anti-politics' naturally commends itself to people whose experience of comprehensive social and economic programmes, imposed from above in the name of all-embracing ideology, has been so bitter. Autonomous and unofficial groups in Eastern Europe are constrained, for reasons of self-preservation and political realism, to eschew grand political proclamations, and the weakness or nonexistence of a pluralist civil society and political culture has made it in any event impossible to organize support for such proclamations; but the avoidance of overall 'alternative programmes' has also, perhaps, been a matter of principle. Thus Havel welcomes the 'proclaimed non-ideological stance' which he finds in the Western Green parties.[6] In a considerably earlier essay, 'The Power of the Powerless', written in 1978 and anticipating several themes that have since come to the fore in green politics, Havel explained:

> 'dissident movements' . . . understand systemic change as something superficial, something secondary, something that in itself can guarantee nothing. Thus [they adopt] an attitude that turns away from abstract political visions of the future towards concrete human beings and ways of defending them effectively in the here and now . . .[7]

The concern with 'concrete human beings' is naturally what most people, regardless of political affiliation, would claim to feel. But the distrust of 'abstract political visions', while it may be salutary, cannot relieve parties that operate in a pluralist political culture of the duty to state just what 'vision' they in fact entertain, how it differs from the status quo, and what kinds of 'systemic change' they believe necessary to its realization. Nor is this a duty faced solely by the Green parties, which could be avoided if environmental pressure groups continued to operate 'from below', from outside formal political structures: for within major political parties and institutions, 'concern for the environment' must be translated, if it is to mean anything, into particular and perhaps contentious proposals for action (or inaction), and set in the framework of other policies which concerned citizens, both East and West, may or may not find convincing and attractive.

In sum: while they just 'stand up for the environment', green and ecological groups draw on a good deal of straightforward sympathy – from most quarters of the Western party-political compass, and from those in the East who share their ecological concerns. However, once they take up specific positions on difficult and controversial issues, some of that sympathy may no longer be forthcoming. Which of these controversial issues are likely to be of especial weight in discussions between Western greens and autonomous Eastern European thinkers, and thus in the construction of an ecologically informed project of detente from below?

Economics is obviously crucial; moreover, it involves questions of capitalism/socialism which are particularly delicate in the context of a

joint East–West critique. The next section of this chapter briefly surveys
this area. Questions of gender and feminism have also been central to
green politics, as they have to the rethinking of Western socialism, and
any citizens' dialogue between East and West is likely to include them
among its themes.

More immediately, perhaps, one thinks of what is already the best-
worn item on the East–West agendas, both official and unofficial: peace
and disarmament. Here, while the Greens have in certain respects been
quick to respond to Eastern European perspectives (on the militarization of society, on the need to preserve and enlarge the space for
an autonomous Eastern European discourse, on the necessity of non-
aligned 'beyond-the-blocs' projects), they have at the same time continued to uphold an uncompromising unilateralism which some Eastern
European groups find naive.

Die Grünen have signalled their support for independent peace initiatives both in the GDR and in the USSR.[8] In the UK, the Green Party's
non-aligned perspective is clearly reflected in the manifesto which they
produced for the 1987 election. These Green parties – and the 'Beyond
the Blocs' booklet produced by the European Greens collectively in
1986 demonstrates similar concerns among some other Western European Green parties – have recognized that disarmament cannot be a
matter of nuclear weapons only but must take account of militarism in
general, and of the role of superpower armed forces in enforcing the
political status quo. They have espoused the long-term objective of
creating a new political order across the continent, and they recognize
the importance of civic and democratic rights in this process.

Meanwhile, they have in general – and certainly in the UK and the
FRG, the two key NATO allies in Europe – advocated unilateral-
disarmament measures of a more 'extreme' kind than most political
groups. In Germany, their influence has pushed the social democratic
opposition towards a more uncompromising anti-nuclear position; and
were the British Labour Party to modify its current unilateralist policies,
the Greens would certainly retain theirs. Moreover, they are not just
unilateralist but anti-NATO (though this is less clearly so in some countries, such as Belgium; and the issue does not arise in this form for
Green parties in neutral countries like Austria, Sweden and the Irish
Republic). They would see this not just as a question of morality and of
the need to refuse unconditionally to participate in preparations for the
ultimate crime of a nuclear attack on civilian populations, but as consistent with their ecological commitment: nuclear war would be the final
environmental catastrophe, and nations which possess, or allow the
deployment on their territory, of nuclear arms, or who continue to
remain part of an alliance based on those arms, are potential accom-

plices in an act of ecocide. And the Greens' opposition to nuclear energy, where once again they take positions more 'extreme' than those favoured by the Social Democrat opposition (whose leading representatives tend to equivocate about the future of the nuclear industry), commits them to a refusal of nuclear weapons.

This latter aspect of their policies is likely to inspire reservations among those in Eastern Europe who regard unilateralism as an ingenuous or self-indulgent response to Soviet military power. Discussion of the differing perspectives involved here has been at the heart of the continuing citizens' dialogue promoted by END and other peace movements:[9] in that sense the green position, whatever reactions it may elicit, comes as nothing new.

Capitalism, Socialism and Ecological Economics

It is possible to attribute many of the environmental ills of Eastern European countries to features specific to Soviet-style communist economic management. In this perspective, the responsibility may seem to lie with overcentralized and unaccountable hierarchies and institutions, unhampered by an organized expression for the interests of civil society; with a technology often backward and inefficient compared with what is available in the West; with geostrategic objectives that have tied the Comecon countries into energy dependency on the USSR (one motive for Soviet expansion of nuclear electricity); with a headlong industrialization that has subordinated to its demands not only the ecological viability of whole regions but the very lives of millions of labourers and peasant farmers; and with a continuing attempt to keep up with the West, despite technical inferiority, which still forces the cutting of ecological corners in the name of faster 'progress'.

But to conclude from this that there is something inherently more beneficial for the environment in a capitalist organization of the economy would be wilfully simplistic. It would be to overlook the fact that in accounting for the particular ecological troubles of the countries of Eastern Europe, much stress must fall on their emulation of capitalist methods and productive goals; and to overlook also the terrible and more secular ecological damage that has been the result of this quest for productivity within the capitalist nations themselves. The phase of rapid heavy industrialization can take traumatic forms in more than one type of socioeconomic system – as witness the heavy human and environmental toll of the early years of the Industrial Revolution (one of whose most eloquent chroniclers was Friedrich Engels[10]). Today, phenomena such as the recent massive poisoning of the Rhine, the chemical disaster of Seveso, or the excessive nitrate levels found in East Anglian drinking water remind us that even in the privileged heartland of Western Europe, capitalist industry and agriculture cause frequent and serious damage.

But very relevant also to any assessment of the ecological record of the capitalist order is its 'success' in exporting to poorer parts of the world the more negative consequences of its own prosperity. While citizens in the metropolitan countries are able to reap the benefits of this prosperity in relatively healthy conditions, chaotic urbanization, unbridled pollution and oppressive and unsafe labour conditions continue to destroy human lives and natural environment in Mexico City, in the Amazon rainforest, at Bhopal, or in the uranium mines of Namibia. The international capitalist institutions which have managed this 'export' are unaccountable enough, in all conscience, even if their allegiance is to profit and 'market freedom' rather than to 'progress' and scientific socialism.[11]

What is the conclusion of this polemical matching of ill for ill? Do we subscribe to the view, widely held within the green movement,[12] that contemporary capitalism and 'actually existing socialism' are just two variants of a more general historical phase that we can call 'industrialism'?

Well, not altogether. Without suggesting that actually existing socialist societies offer a model for the future (ecologically or in many other respects), we would insist that a critical understanding of capitalism as an economic system is an essential prerequisite for the formulation of an 'eco-alternative' in the economic field. In particular, we would ask those who are inclined a priori to favour 'free markets'[13] to bear in mind two features of the market economy which are of key ecological importance: its inherently expansive tendency; and its separation of 'economics' from 'politics'.

The inherent expansiveness of capitalism is generally presented as a plus, 'stagnation' being regarded as the most morbid condition that can afflict any economy. And it is in this light that we are being asked to appreciate the merits of the attempted economic perestroika in the USSR. Western commentators have tended to assume that once Gorbachev has established himself, his next step must be to 'modernize' the economy by introducing greater and greater market-style incentives,[14] that this will be the ultimate test of how far he can 'revolutionize' things, and that the unambiguously positive outcome, in the economic sphere, will be a Russian industrial–commercial–consumer system capable at last of competing with the West on equal terms in the great game of 'economic growth'. But it is, of course, also the express intention of the Gorbachevian reform to render the Soviet economy more efficient, competitive and productive, and in this sense the thinking behind it follows the logic of these capitalistic assumptions despite its professed commitment to continue along the socialist path.

The development of economies better able to meet basic needs – to provide a varied and healthy diet, good housing and health care, and so on – is incontestably progressive. It may be that the adoption of market-like mechanisms will enable socialist societies to meet some such needs better (though it is clear from the example of full-blown market societies such as the UK or the USA that quite basic material wants can be very poorly and inequitably satisfied within a 'growing' economy). It may be, too, that a modernization of technology will bring direct environmental and ecological benefits through the replacing of inefficient and polluting factories, energy installations and transmission lines, and so forth. However, in so far as perestroika envisages an essentially indiscriminate increase in production, and an adoption of market accounting as the principle index of economic efficiency, its overall ecological impact is likely to prove ambiguous at best – especially if ecological questions as such are simply ignored in the pursuit of what Andras Köves (who himself ignores them) calls 'socioeconomic development and catching up with the world economy'. For the kinds of 'growth' permitted – and, indeed, enforced – by market capitalism lead inexorably to ecological problems and crises: 'the ecology crisis' is in fact, in the broadest terms, a crisis of our consuming too much, too heedlessly of the future and the basic needs of poor countries: the dynamic of 'growth' is also a dynamic of depletion.

We must, then, be wary of any 'detente', whether from above or below, which is built around a simple faith in the powers of the 'free market' to correct the current ecologically destructive tendencies of the socialist economies or improve on their overall level of material well-being. This form of detente – which was well imaged in the recent Hungarian Grand Prix (the first of its kind to be held in a communist state) – may be welcome politically, even in a limited sense 'culturally', but its ecological implications are hardly very cheering.[15]

Even more vexed questions arise if we ask whether the 'freedom' of the capitalist market is the sole or final alternative to the unfreedoms of bureaucratic state socialism. From a purely ecological point of view, Rudolf Bahro (who now holds a grass-roots 'commune' perspective) once argued for the advantages, *ceteris paribus,* of centralized economies when it came to formulating and implementing ecologically sound policies:

My positive evaluation of the non-capitalist base of the Eastern bloc rests on two fundamental points. First, the relations of command are much easier to establish than in the capitalist system. Secondly, and perhaps even more important, the problems facing our civilization require centralized social planning if they are to be solved, and this aspect must not be abandoned in the necessary changes in Eastern Europe. It is always possible to discuss whether the market has a role to play in satisfying the needs of the population, but the general proportions of the reproduction process must be planned.[16]

Politically, however, the advantages of planning are at present largely nullified – leaving aside all questions of technological backwardness – by the lack, in Eastern Europe, of popular accountability and information. This point is wittily made in Istvan Rev's chapter, which stresses the *political* emancipation latent in the introduction, within societies governed by a supposedly omniscient central plan, of the uncertainties and the distinct interests represented by the market: 'the legalization of the market has a significance which is not limited to the marketplace'.

On the other hand, Rev himself also writes that 'the market has no inherent guarantee for the protection of the environment'. We would go further, and reiterate that its inherently expansive dynamic is a grave long-term *threat* to the environment. The question then is: can we invent political-economic forms which go beyond the antithesis plan/market? Can 'the plan' be conceived, and instituted, not as centralized omniscience but as flexible democratic instrument, reflecting local as well as national interests, ecological as well as economic needs? What balance should we strike – in environmental as in other matters – between bureaucratic/legislative intervention, public education and individual responsibility, and 'economic rationality'?

To ask these questions is to confront some important discrepancies between Eastern and Western societies in the potential power of their citizens to influence the course of economic life. In the capitalist nations, such is the divorce of economic and political spheres that popular intervention in the hierarchically organized domain of the economy is well-nigh impossible, despite the liberal and democratic institutions enjoyed at the political level. In Eastern Europe, by contrast, as George Konrád has pointed out, 'the demand for democracy makes itself felt in every social organization, in economic and cultural as well as political institutions.'[17] It is for this reason, he suggests, that self-management, 'the question of questions', has hitherto become a demand precisely in those places where capitalist rule has ceased to be legitimate. But as he also points out, it is a demand with no easy answers:

If economic decisions are not to be legitimated by capitalist ownership of property, then either the government must legitimize them or else the associated producers collectively. If it is the latter, then there arise the key questions for self-management: who decides in the name of the associated producers?

An elected body or a person? Or is it possible to create a flexible legal and financial system, with social property at the disposal of individuals, which could serve as an economic formula for self-management?[18]

These are admittedly not new questions, nor does Konrád have specifically ecological issues in mind when he poses them. Indeed, the problems they raise have been a perennial preoccupation within the democratic socialist tradition, and it must be recognized that they allow of no 'purely ecological' response. Conversely, however, in that the democratic socialist project must now itself encompass an ecological dimension, they admit of no 'purely economic' or 'purely political' solutions either. The greens have injected into them the additional and constant question of nature and its needs – which are also our needs. In so doing they have in a sense 'updated' the agenda to which all those, East and West, who are seeking emancipation must now address themselves.

'Politics from Below' and the Role of Minority Movements

How can we build on the potentiality offered by the 'greening' of minority protest, East and West, and render it more concretely effective both nationally and internationally?

Let us begin by noting two very positive features about the emerging concern with ecology among the minority groups in Eastern Europe. The first relates to the relatively 'unpolitical' – and therefore 'safe' – campaigning status accorded ecology in the Eastern bloc. Many people – including a number of quite prominent cultural figures, academicians, scientists and members of the administrative bureaucracy, who would not want to associate themselves with anything smacking of dissidence – have felt able to express themselves quite openly on issues of pollution and environmental damage, and to participate in the various officially recognized ecological groups and clubs.[19] What this reflects, in part, is the USSR's official line that ecology is an 'international' issue not bearing directly on its own internal domestic policy or relations with other Eastern European countries. Issues of 'peace' and 'human rights', on the other hand, are perceived very differently, being regarded either as part of Soviet propaganda or else as part of the agenda of the political opposition.

Given the current fluidity of the situation in Eastern Europe, one can do no more than speculate on the possible effects of this expansion of the political platform of dissident groups to include ecological issues. On the one hand, it may serve to politicize ecology in a way that renders it a more controversial area for campaigning than hitherto – though this is unlikely to happen except at the cost of a desirable enhancing of public awareness of some of the key connections between environmental degradation, militarism and the commitment to industrial growth. But equally, it may well have some impact on the credibility of the dissident groupings themselves among more 'respectable' citizens, thus allowing their programmes to be reviewed more sympathetically now that they are seen to be embracing issues of such immediate day-to-day concern; and this in turn may have its effects on the degree of tolerance and space accorded such groups.

The second positive feature of the developing ecological orientation of dissident groups has to do with the more constructive dimension of protest which it represents. To campaign on such issues as conscription, human rights, censorship and freedom to travel is essentially to campaign *against* something – and, moreover, to campaign against a 'something' whose various repressions and privations obtain by and large only in Eastern Europe, by comparison with which the West is viewed as a haven of liberty. To campaign on ecology is also certainly to campaign against something, but the something (pollution, waste, environmental disease, the destruction of nature . . .) is less easily located in any specific legal forms or institutions, nor is it exclusive to this or that social system. And it is by virtue of this more diffuse, transnational and transinstitutional quality of the negative forces opposed by ecological protest that this protest ceases to be primarily reactive and becomes a movement *for* something.[20]

The 'something' may as yet be ill-defined and overly abstract, but its core idea is that of a fundamentally altered pattern of human production and consumption based around quite different values to those prevailing in either capitalist or socialist societies at the present time. It is a pattern, then, without exemplars either East or West, but one whose beacon of hope is being recognized and relayed back at many points around and across the blocs. What is beginning to emerge, in short, is an 'eco-politics' which not only unites minority groups within and across the blocs, but takes them beyond their own previous analyses and perceptions of both their own and other societies.

This point may be re-expressed in terms of the key role played by ecological concern in breaking through some of the more difficult and sensitive barriers to understanding and co-operation between movements of the left in the West and dissident groups in the East. For one might say that it has offered itself as a kind of 'neutral' terrain of consensus wherein the market-fixated conceptions of freedom and progress which prevail in many East European dissident circles can be more persuasively challenged by their Western counterparts; and wherein

Eastern groups in turn have been able to win a more sympathetic ear for their resistance to the unaccountable and bureaucratic authoritarianism of their own societies.

Hitherto, for example, independents in Eastern Europe have found themselves impatient with the relative indifference of much of the European left to what for them is the key issue: the democratization and self-determination of their own societies, which, as they rightly argue, are indispensable to demilitarization and to the exercise of any real citizen control over the economy. But equally, many in the West, including those appreciative of these Eastern priorities, have also found themselves frustrated by the failure of East European dissidence to develop a more critical approach either to capitalist society or to the subordination (different in kind to that of Eastern Europe to the USSR, but a subordination for all that) of the Western nations to the economic and military hegemony of the United States. Nor has it been easy to convey to East European independents (who tend to see any endorsement of their own system as an apology for totalitarianism) a 'Western' sense that there are certain features of Soviet society and some values sustained by its system which are welcome antidotes to the consumerism, aggression and cultural banality which flourish under the banner of 'freedom and democracy'.

Through appeal to ecological values, however, we have been able to engage in a more dispassionate appraisal of our respective societies, to look upon their supposedly negative or positive qualities in a somewhat altered light, and to derive from this assessment a shared conception of a possible alternative transcending the 'communism versus capitalism' and 'totalitarianism' versus 'freedom and democracy' oppositions. And in speaking of a 'new detente', we are surely speaking of precisely this kind of transcendence: of a process of East–West reconciliation which evolves through transformation of the existing political systems and alliances of both blocs and has the construction of an ecologically responsible political order in Europe at the centre of its concerns. Since so much of this new thinking converges around the question of human needs, this must become a key area of discussion if any such process of reconciliation is to be fostered.

The priority now accorded by many greens in the West to the issue of lifestyles and consumption is indeed a progressive move, and rightly regarded by them as a necessary sharpening of ecological protest. But it is important that in focusing their polemic on the (causal) economic growth rather than the (symptomatic) pollution, they do not alienate potential eco-friends in the East, for whom the supposedly 'softer' issue of the environment remains the main concern. After all, those who have never enjoyed the luxury of the private motorcar or disposable nappy are unlikely to summon up quite the same level of alarm as their

counterparts in the West about the oil and paper they consume. This
does not mean that greens in the West should hold back on their analysis
of the connections between ecological attrition, pollution and private
consumption, or be any less forceful in their resistance to the growth
economy. But it does mean that they must recognize the complexities of
the situation: the most ecologically devastated areas of Europe (Poland,
Czechoslovakia) are inhabited by people whose lifestyle is by no means
luxurious – indeed, often quite primitive in Western terms. By the same
token, when an official in Eastern Europe speaks of environmental
pollution as 'the price that has to be paid for industrial development of
civilization',[21] it may not strike citizens in Eastern Europe lacking basic
plumbing and heating facilities as quite the cliché it has become for
green activists in the West, with their relatively generous property, in
jeans and sticker-bedecked cars.

Moreover, shocking as it may seem to us here that ecological awareness was first raised through the campaign to have the scheme for a
highly polluting hydroelectric dam at Nagymaros replaced by a 'clean'
nuclear power plant, we must also take account of the actual levels of
chemical and dust pollution affecting Eastern Europe. In Czechoslovakia, 30 per cent of fish, reptiles, birds and mammals and 60 per
cent of amphibians are now threatened; 45–60 per cent of woods and
forests in Bohemia and Moravia will be irreparably damaged or
destroyed by the end of the century. In Poland, less than 1 per cent of
water is classified as 'first-class' (inhabitable by salmon) and current
rates of cancer and infectious disease are reputedly among the highest in
the world. (Officials in Poland now classify twenty-six regions as ecologically dangerous: two of them – Gdansk and Cracow – as cata-
strophically so.) In the Northern Bohemian coal region, infant mortality
is higher than in any area in Britain; only 38 per cent of teenagers are
free from respiratory, digestive, skin or bone disease. With statistics like
these, the obsession with the environment is perfectly understandable
and hardly to be viewed as reflecting a politically naive approach.
Indeed, the antithesis between 'environmentalism' and 'lifestyle'
campaigning begins to break down in situations where standards of
living are falling precisely because of environmental conditions. Of
course, the pollution which detracts from the quality of life today is the
effect of the quest for 'improved' material lifestyles tomorrow, and it is
important to keep this contradiction in mind. But we must also understand the reasons why short-term local environmental campaigning has
been given such priority in Eastern Europe. There is, in short, a practical
urgency about the situation there of which we need to take account in
the West, integrating its level of immediate regional environmental
imperatives into our wider green demands.

Turning now more directly to the question of strategies, it must be admitted that here too the problems are knotty and complex. Differences in the political systems of East and West Europe not only have their practical effects on the modes of campaigning available to minority groups, but have made for significant divergences of perception of the political process itself and the ways it may be influenced. And to this must be added the new complexity introduced by the relative liberalization in the USSR.

In the West, the multiparty, democratic system of government has meant that a great deal of ecological and peace protest has gone into influencing the political establishment itself, through pressure upon its mainstream parties. It means, too, that it has been possible for green politics to find representation within the official political spectrum itself as a result of the constitution of the Green parties. By contrast, in Eastern Europe, where no such moves are possible, groups such as Freedom and Peace (WiP) in Poland or Charter 77 in Czechoslovakia have tended to view their activities as primarily 'anti-political' or 'countercultural' – as making sense, that is, in terms of the construction and diffusion of an alternative political culture alongside that of the state and party apparatus. For them, any accommodation with the official process carries the risk of co-option and can proceed only at the cost of a blunting of their political demands, and this has contributed to the widespread sense that the only viable and principled action must go into cementing a genuinely autonomous opposition to the state.

This is not to imply that eco–peace politics in the West does not have a similar 'countercultural' inspiration and mode of functioning alongside its more conventional political campaigning. Moreover, the recent right-wing victories in the West have added to a general sense of frustration at the failure of ecological politics to make any significant impact on the electoral process, and led to a growing scepticism in some circles as to the value of channelling so much energy into party politics. It is in this spirit that there has been some talk of late of the need to consolidate the 'detente from below' strategy which has always been a central axis of eco–peace campaigning by uniting its various common-minded groups and individuals into some trans-bloc 'league of opposition'. This, it is said, would not exclude continued 'outside debate with officials and parties, but it would represent a seizure of initiative on the part of autonomous groups, allowing them to set the conditions on dialogue rather than continuously being pulled into the one-sidedness which has afflicted eco–peace movement relations with the Eastern bloc.

The widespread exasperation at the obstacles which the conventional political institutions in the West place in the way of furtherance of any genuine ecological alternative, combined with the pervasive disappoint-

ment that, glasnost and perestroika notwithstanding, we have yet to see
any really substantial break with old attitudes towards independent
activity in the East, makes these arguments timely and compelling. But
there are none the less a number of factors that should be allowed to
weigh in any discussion around this strategic option.

In the first place, despite the obvious attractions of an international
network confined to the fellow-minded, it risks becoming a cosy forum
for the converted to discourse among themselves while the rest of the
world is left to continue in its former, predictable and unconstructive
ways. It could, in effect, represent a retreat from the process of education and persuasion of unsympathetic elements – a process which,
admitted, has proved very uphill and registered few concrete achievements to date, but which for all that has had a very definite impact on
the way in which the Cold War is now perceived by both public and
politicians, and has placed the issue of ecology on the agenda of official
politics, from which it was all but absent as recently as five years ago.

Secondly and relatedly, a deliberate cold-shouldering of the social
democratic parties in the West and of officialdom in the East could have
the effect of alienating the more well-disposed elements within those
circles and hardening attitudes which might otherwise have proved more
flexible over time. What we may see as an inevitable response to their
intransigence they are likely to regard as an elitist move confirming their
sense of the 'marginal' or 'subversive' quality of ecological arguments –
which they can hence cheerfully continue to ignore or condemn.

It is also important to remember that despite its oppositional and
relatively clandestine mode of operating, dissident campaigning on
peace and ecology in Eastern Europe is not motivated simply by a spirit
of stoical rebellion or of opposition for opposition's sake. Many of the
groups in question have entered into serious consideration of their
relations with the official process and have argued the need for maintaining some dialogue with it, even if this has proved possible at times
only through the 'mediating' role of their allies in the West. Consistently,
too, they have addressed their appeals openly to their own governments
– in some cases with notable success.

Charter 77 has presented numerous demands for action on the environment to the government, including a letter of protest following the
Chernobyl disaster; in Poland, WiP has demanded the abandonment of
the country's first nuclear power plant at Zrkowiece and demonstrated to
that effect in Wroclaw; in Hungary, the Blues have petitioned over the
Nagymaros project and even distributed door-to-door leaflets, while the
Danube circle numbers prominent scientists among the signatories of its
letters of protest and has published two books on the plans for the dam;
in Yugoslavia, where campaigns have gathered momentum after

Chernobyl, a demonstration attended by some 2,000 took place in Ljubljana and the petition circulated by the Slovenian delegation to the Yugoslav Youth Congress in June 1986 linked together the themes of peace and ecology and called for a moratorium on the construction of nuclear power stations in Yugoslavia; finally, in the GDR, where peace and ecological protest has the protection of the Protestant Church – and hence occupies a semi-official space and enjoys a mode of official tolerance rather different from that obtaining elsewhere in Eastern Europe – events around the themes of peace and ecology have been fairly openly and regularly staged since the early eighties, and the Church itself has been in the forefront of the protest following the Chernobyl accident.

Unwelcome and technically illegal, then, as a good deal of autonomous ecological activity remains in Eastern Europe, it also enjoys a measure of state tolerance – a tolerance in part reflective of the degree to which this activity has remained engaged, non-aligned and openly contestatory in its methods (resisting, as far as possible, manipulation by reactionary elements in the West and the cloak-and-dagger politics of outright 'subversion').

This tolerance has already been extended as a result of the Gorbachevian reform and there are good reasons to suppose, granted the continued dynamic of the perestroika process, that the space for more independent activity will continue to enlarge. This is likely to result in new forms of political growth and more open representation of the existing but hitherto under-expressed (and in the West too little recognized) plurality of critical opinion in the USSR and Eastern Europe. Just as we risk marginalizing ecological protest in the West by insisting that it must speak only in certain places and with a single voice and philosophy, so we should not assume that there is only one authentic form in which it can surface in Eastern Europe, or that it has only openly confrontational modes of action at its disposal. There are some signs now, in fact, that perestroika is generating a new and critical appraisal within oppositional groups of their own analyses and strategies within the new situation, and that something more complex and sophisticated than can be contained in the notion of 'dissidence' or 'subversion' is now afoot in Eastern Europe.

There is no reason, moreover, why only progressive elements should seize the opportunity of perestroika to pursue their autonomous activity, and neo-Fascist and neo-Stalinist elements are already to be heard voicing their particular brand of reaction to the official policies of the state.[22]

In this situation, it is important that ecological protest be associated with a more discriminatory politics than that of a simplistic 'anti-statism'. (The same might be said of the inadequacy of purely anarchist responses in the West to the libertarian politics of right-wing government.)

Finally, there is an assumption of East–West symmetry in the 'league of opposition' approach which may need to be questioned, at least as regards ecology: namely, the assumption that this is as 'oppositional' and as much a minority concern in the East as it has shown itself to be in the West. To date, the very lack of political pluralism in the East has made it difficult to judge how far the idea of an ecological alternative to technocratist conceptions of progress commands public interest and respect. But some register of popular feeling on this issue is to be found in the mass audience for works of poetry, fiction and film treating of ecological themes in a fairly serious kind of way[23] a cultural interest to which there is nothing corresponding in the West. To this we may add the pervasive expressions of concern over the environment within mainstream official politics in Eastern Europe – to which, again, there is rather little that corresponds in the standard pronouncements of Western establishment figures. Certainly, Gorbachev's dismay over 'the excessive loads on the natural systems as a consequence of the scientific and technological revolution and the increasing extent of man's activity'[24] is hardly consistent with his paeans to Soviet technical achievement, but it remains a fact that we have yet to hear anything very much of the need for a more rational use of the world's resources as an asset belonging to all humanity from the lips of Mr Reagan or Mrs Thatcher.[25]

No doubt to attach too much weight to these indices would be a mistake, but they suggest a groundswell of public sympathy for ecological argument of a type and scope which has been lacking in the West. The sentiment in question may be religious or romantic in its leanings (more of a celebration of Mother Nature or lament over a lost pre-industrial past than a serious engagement with the construction of a viable eco-politics) but it may none the less represent a basis in popular feeling for that project rather different from anything obtaining at the present time in the West. This is not to deny that there is extensive public unease about the environment in the West too, and some evidence of mass concern at the destructive tendencies of our affluent culture in the support given to such projects as Band Aid and Live Aid. But this has not been registered to any significant degree in people's voting patterns: when put to the democratic test, ecology has not hitherto proved itself a very popular option. Conversely, of course, we must question how far ecological issues would be given priority over the furtherance of Western-style consumption were the opportunity given to people in the East to give electoral expression to their wishes.

What conclusions might one draw from these considerations? Perhaps their most depressing – though also their most challenging – implication is that the market-dominated, liberal-pluralist society

contains elements inherently inimical to the emergence of the spiritual
values and (dare we say it?) measure of asceticism in personal consumption that are requisite to serious engagement with our ecological
crisis. For not only does it encourage consumerist definitions of progress
and individual well-being, it also squeezes out the space for expression
of people's desires for more communal and less tangible forms of grati-
fication. It is not that the market eradicates all such desires, but that its
'privatizing' dynamic has a repressive influence on the ways in which
these are experienced: too often they persist only in the form of a vague
malaise whose underlying challenge to the values and logic of capitalist
existence goes unrecognized for want of any positive channels of
expression.

But the totalitarian regimes have in their own way proved no less
contradictory in the desires they have promoted and repressed: for while
they have condemned the 'consumerist ethic' as a Western degeneracy,
they have committed themselves to an indefinite industrial expansion in
the name of ever higher material standards of living. Also, in tending to
conflate all forms of freedom enjoyed in the West with a 'decadent'
market freedom, they have encouraged a sense that democracy itself is
incompatible with the realization of communal and social values – when
in truth these can genuinely flourish only where they are not authori-
tarianly imposed.

The questions which arise when we attempt to account for East–West
differences of public attitude are among the most awkward we have to
confront. They require us to acknowledge that there are divergences in
the patterns of response to ecology (and in the conflicts of feeling these
may embody) which derive from differences in forms of social organization and cannot be accounted for in direct anthropological terms.
This in turn suggests that we cannot rest the case for an ecological
politics simply on the appeal to a 'common humanity'. Certainly there is
a distinct vein of public sympathy for its values discernible in both
systems, but if we are to build on this it has to be channelled into a
common politics.

Notes

1. See the article by the present authors in the *END Journal*, Summer 1986.
2. On acid precipitation and its effects in Eastern Europe, see Steve Elsworth, *Acid Rain*, London 1984, especially pp. 100–02. On environmental issues generally in Eastern Europe, and on the response to Chernobyl, see the paper by Michael Waller cited in note 19 below.
3. See Erik Damman, *Revolution in the Affluent Society*, London 1984. Bahro's 'commune perspective' is outlined in several essays in his *Building the Green Movement*, London 1986: see, for example, pp. 92 ff., 174–5.

306 THE NEW DETENTE

4. On the situation in autumn 1985, see Martin Ryle's 1986 paper for the UN University, *Green Politics and Socialism in Britain*, pp. 1–18. On internal alignments in *Die Grünen*, see the articles by Werner Hülsberg in *New Left Review*, nos. 152 and 162. The formation and electoral fortunes of the Italian Greens are referred to in the UK Green Party Newsletter, *Econews*, no. 35, p. 9.

5. Anarchist/decentralist/direct-action perspectives are found in many of the articles in the Oxford-based magazine *Green Line*. On the 'league of opposition', see the article by Lynne Jones in *END Journal*, Summer 1987.

6. See *END Journal*, Spring 1987, p. 14.

7. Jan Vladislav, ed., *Vaclav Havel: Living in Truth* (essays by and about Havel), London 1987, pp. 92 f.

8. Most notably in the Alexanderplatz demonstration, when a number of Green deputies showed their support for the 'Swords into Ploughshares' group in the GDR. See the account in F. Capra and C. Spretnak, *Green Politics*, London 1984, p. 73 – where it is made clear that some left-wing members of *Die Grünen* were not happy about the action.

9. The *END Journal* has published many contributions to this dialogue; see also END's pamphlets on autonomous peace groups in the GDR, Hungary, Czechoslovakia and the USSR.

10. In his *The Condition of the Working Class in England*, 1845 (now available in the Marx/Engels *Collected Works*, published by Lawrence & Wishart).

11. Transnational companies implicated in these environmental disasters include VW (Amazon deforestation), Union Carbide (Bhopal) and RTZ (Namibia).

12. See, for instance, Jonathon Porritt, *Seeing Green*, Oxford 1984, pp. 216–17.

13. Who, of course, include many Western socialists: see, for instance, Alec Nove, *The Economics of Feasible Socialism*, London 1983.

14. Following Gorbachev's speech on the seventieth anniversary of the Bolshevik Revolution, a discussion on BBC Radio 4's 'World Tonight' (3 November 1987) – Alec Nove was one participant – congratulated the Soviet leader in just such terms as these.

15. But we should also note here that Charter 77 has been campaigning over the damage that will result from the building of a new motor-racing circuit in the green belt near Brno (see END Briefing Sheet on 'Ecology in Eastern Europe').

16. Rudolf Bahro, *From Red to Green*, London 1984, pp. 101–2.

17. George Konrád, *Antipolitics*, London 1984, p. 140.

18. Ibid., pp. 143–4.

19. For example, see the discussion of environmental protest in the GDR, Hungary and Poland in the END Briefing Sheet on 'Ecology in Eastern Europe' and in Michael Waller's paper on 'Autonomous Movements for Peace and Ecology in Eastern Europe' (delivered to the annual conference of the National Association for Soviet and East European Studies, Fitzwilliam College, Cambridge, 28–30 March 1987 – available through END, 11 Goodwin Street, London N4). On ecological campaigning by leading cultural figures in the USSR recently, see Simon Cosgrave, 'Thoughts on the 8th Writers' Congress', *Detente*, Autumn 1986, p. 18.

20. A point well made in Michael Waller's paper (See note 19): 'Until recently, East European dissidence has been above all a reaction *against* the perceived evils of a political system. It is in the process now of becoming a movement, very heterogeneous, very fluid, *for* something.'

21. *Zycie Warszawy* (an official Warsaw newspaper), November 1982.

22. For an account of such developments and a most interesting insight into contemporary cultural trends in the USSR, see Boris Kagarlitsky, 'The Intelligentsia and the Changes', *New Left Review*, no. 164, July/August 1987, pp. 5–26; cf. also Simon Cosgrave (see note 19) and 'The Russian Complex – the Eidelmann–Astafiev Correspondence', *Detente*, no. 8, Winter 1987.

23. We have in mind here, for example, the popularity of the novels of Rasputin, of Voznesensky's poetry and the cinema of Elim Klimov.

24. Mikhail Gorbachev, 'A World in Crisis' (Speech to the 27th Party Congress), included in *Socialism, Peace and Democracy*, London 1987, p. 14.

25. Ibid. [This was written before the 'greening' of Mrs Thatcher – Ed.]

14

The Anti-ecological Nature of Centralization

Istvan Rev

In Central Europe and in Hungary, those who actively worry about the deterioration of the environment fear not only environmental but economic pollution as well. The expansion of the market, they argue, could further limit the possibilities of protecting the environment; short-run market calculations could make human existence impossible in this region of the world. (In the end the whole region will cease to exist and the man, too, who would miss the sight of the nonexistent countryside.) Many of those who worry argue that only decisive central intervention could save the dangerously declining environment for the future: central intervention which is able to overcome short-sighted economic speculation. In opposition to the worm's-eye view of local short-sightedness, only the bird's-eye view – capable of understanding global interconnectedness – may offer some hope. But for those who fly over it the countryside is but a map, and they cannot see the small cormorant (*Phalacrocorax pygemus*).

I

Most environmentalists fear the economists. For specific historical and political reasons, reform has merely changed the façade of economic policy. Economic reformers have existed in Hungary since 1953 and although it has been advisable for them to remain silent for long periods, they have managed to reappear on the surface of the water. They managed to survive the hard times, succeeded in getting a foothold in research institutes and in consultative bodies. They multiplied, became more refined, more radical, more professional. And naturally, like any reformers – especially those who have to be reformers for others, as well – they tend to squint. When nobody else has the opportunity to put forward reform ideas, then the economists have to be not only reformers of the economy proper, but of something else as well.

The reformer is not simply a critical intellectual; he or she is the person who knows how to cure the disease, who has prescriptions – prescriptions which can be used only inside a given political and economic framework. Prescriptions are written for use: the reformer has to market the ideas; he or she has to persuade somebody. In a political system where power is monopolized the only available audience is those who are in power, who monopolize the political institutions. The reformers have to make those who are in power believe that it is in their best interest to adopt these reforms, which would limit their power.

Theoretically, it ought to be possible to start a dialogue with somebody else, with different groups within society. But in a system where political expression is the exclusive right of those who monopolize the political institutions there is not much choice for those who consciously try to stay inside the given framework – this is why they are reformers. Those who are in power will adopt the reforms only if it can be proved that the suggested reforms will not limit the political power of the authorities. In this way, the economic reformers have to prove that their ideas are neutral from a political point of view. Of course, the majority of these reformers have known perfectly well, ever since 1956, that the desired economic reforms cannot be introduced without major political changes, that the stability of existing political institutions makes the reforms completely uncertain and reversible. But what can one do when it is impossible to speak about political issues? One hopes that the economic changes will induce political changes which will have some effect upon the political institutions too. If the legalization of the market legalized different economic interests, if it were admitted that the interest of the buyers and that of the producers do not coincide and that the interest of the state-owned firms is not a *raison d'état*, then one might hope that these differing interests might be articulated not only in the marketplace. The economic reformers hoped that the economic rationality would convince the authorities that one interest is not necessarily superior to another, and that the interest of the individual would not be dismissed on the grounds that the interest of the state is always, and by definition, superior.

The economic reformer is hoping, but naturally he cannot talk about his hopes: he must behave as if he had no secret ideas, as if political questions did not enter his mind. He wants to convince the party, he talks to the officials, he is present at the important consultative bodies, and at the same time he knows perfectly well that the strongest obstacle in the way of economic reforms is the political monopoly of that party which he tries to convince. His thoughts differ from his words, his words from his hopes. He hopes nobody will be able to detect his real hopes. After a while he himself does not know what his real hopes are, what is the connection between his words and his thoughts. Who is he in reality? He does not know what to think.

Until very recently the most important obstacle to open speech was not so much censorship as this tendency to squint. Until the end of the 1970s only economists were allowed to become reformers; sociologists were under strict surveillance. It was not only the lack of official permission which prevented the sociologists from becoming reformers, but the lack of tradition as well. Sociology was reborn only at the beginning of the seventies, political science was discovered at the end of the seventies, ecology was almost unknown until the beginning of the 1980s. All these disciplines were considered completely superfluous compared to dialectical materialism and scientific socialism, the two basic disciplines entitled to answer all the basic questions of mankind. In such a situation it was no wonder nobody was in the position to counterbalance the understandably one-sided economic orientation of the reform ideas. Not only the dogmatists and conservative Stalinists but even the anti-Stalinist sociologists and ecologists were afraid of these ideas.

According to reliable sources, Budapest became one of the capitals of Europe most polluted by lead, at a time when the market played a completely insignificant role in the economy. The erosion of the soil, the denuding of the forests, were not the consequence of market competition. And it would be difficult to blame the market for the yearly loss of one hundred thousand tons of iron ore which occurred at the beginning of the 1950s because of the chimneys of the largest steel mills in Hungary. The steel mills of north-eastern Hungary were the pride of the socialist industrialization policy, but because they lacked ore condensers – which were not considered productive investments – one hundred thousand tons of imported iron ore entered the air in the form of dust, increasing the rate of cancerous diseases – the region has a cancer rate three times higher than the rest of the country – and decreasing the value of the productive forces.

According to the experts, including those who are concerned about life expectancy, the ecological situation of the country is disastrous. Judging from the leaked information and dust, it is constantly worsening. The most the authorities do is to spare no pains to spare the population from worrying too much. We get more dust than information.

The social reformers, those sensitive sociologists who are fighting for an alternative social policy, feel that the economic reformers are hostile towards real social reforms. They accuse the reformers of becoming neoliberal conservatives who would let the most needy fight armless on the market. At the same time, the economists accuse the sociologists of being politically blind, as their ideas would require central redistribution and would increase the role of the central apparatus once more. One can empirically prove that there is more to worry about than the self-limitation of centralization. Nevertheless the centralized system does not offer any more guarantees for the survival of the human species and its environment than societies where the economy is governed by the market. Naturally this does not mean that human and environmental values are defended in the marketplace.

The market was not invented in order to save the human environment. The market has no inherent guarantee for the protection of the environment, just as it does not guarantee the undisturbed working of democratic institutions. The market guarantees only the working of some (never perfect) rules of the game. (The most polluted capital of Europe is the centre of an ancient market economy.) Milton Friedman, the prophet of the self-regulating market, got the opportunity to put his theories into practice in a totalitarian – even, according to Latin American standards, extremely anti-democratic – regime. Neither trees nor the man living under the trees will be better off because of the undisturbed working of the market.

But there is a crucial difference between the working of the market and the gesture which legalizes the market. It is one thing to live in a situation where the market regulates itself, and quite another to live at the moment when the political authorities feel compelled to legalize the market because they have to admit that they do not know everything in advance and do not know better than those who bargain with each other in the marketplace. This is the moment when the authorities have to acknowledge that their power is not omnipotent and that there are forces stronger than their central will. The market creates (never perfect, always limited) openness only on the marketplace, but in a system where not only the economic sphere is centralized, the legalization of the market has a significance which is not limited to the marketplace.

II

From the beginning of the first three-year plan (1947) both ideology and political practice were based on the conviction that life is inherently difficult, that society tends to pass through different stages of thesis and anti-thesis (as is well known from the laws of dialectical reasoning). Behind the symptoms are hidden, complicated relationships which one cannot notice with lay eyes. The world of appearance which the layman imagines has nothing to do with objective reality. These firm convictions of the Hungarian leadership are characteristic of the early European modernists. The modernists believed that the essence of things is always concealed and only the privileged few are able to understand what is really significant.

But the Hungarian leadership was not only the heir to the European modernists but to the Enlightenment as well. And as enlightened modernists they were convinced that the difficult reality could be conquered, contradictions could be solved, constraints could be overcome. All that was needed to accomplish this was a strong, centralized system led from the top. The world of contradictions needed a leadership without illusions, able to comprehend the objective reality. The supposed and propagated discrepancy between illusions and reality served to legitimize the centralizing regime.

Not only was the leading role in political actions the privilege of the central authorities – they even had the right to identify the problems. All those things which from below seemed to be contradictions, barriers, limitations, or possible sources of conflict from above were called illusions, feelings of inferiority, sabotage by the class enemy. Actual and possible issues became non-issues as a consequence of the work of the central authorities. Only the business of the centre could acquire the status of a real issue. Most of the problems were sublimated before they could be articulated. Certain spheres of life simply did not exist, or were lost in the darkness of the nameless world.

Naturally, in the smoggy world of total centralization, ecology or even loud, open concern for the environment were absolutely unknown. All references to the ecological consequences of industrialization were called naturalism. In a system which had supernatural ambitions, naturalism was equated with feelings of inferiority, capitulation, treason. Those experts who warned the government that the goals were too ambitious, impossible to reach, were labelled as retrograde bourgeoisie unable to grasp the strength of the revolutionary masses – and the workers unable to increase their efforts were stigmatized as petty-bourgeois, uneducated, ideologically backward.

It is not easy to see that Stalin or his best pupil, the Hungarian leader of the 1950s Rakosi, had anything in common with the turn-of-the-century avant-garde, but these brutal utopians were real futurists. They wanted to crush nature in order to build on its ruins a second, man-made nature, the result of the conscious actions of the men of the new world. Political power stood not only above the governed but above nature as well. Nothing but superhuman – and supernatural – goals could legitimize these extraordinary political techniques. There was no democracy, but then there could be no democracy. Only the leaders were able to understand the world around them; only they were able to visualize the bright future. The majority of the people would have elected faint-hearted democrats who would have wasted all the time by hesitating to fulfil the tasks of history.

III

Although their effects are global, ecological dangers are produced locally. It is rational and economical to deal with them locally. When the need for regional, national or worldwide intervention arises, the tasks are much more difficult. Local efforts aimed at preventing catastrophe cannot be compared to the organizational, economic and political dimensions of any national or international actions aimed at repairing the damage resulting from an ecological catastrophe. In order to eliminate the source of the problem, to maintain the ecological balance, local measures are necessary.

A regime which aims at complete centralization cannot tolerate autonomous localities. For the centralized system to exist, a unified fictitious community is necessary – a macro-community without any communal network, without any communication, without any spontaneity, without any autonomy. For the centralized system to exist undisturbed, the complete atomization of society is an absolute precondition. The atomized individual has to look into the distant future, without thinking too much about the problems of the present. He has to fix his eyes on the end of the road, but only the selected (not elected) few, the leaders, know how to get there without hesitation.

There is neither room nor need for any discussion. The leaders know everything perfectly well. In a centralized system there is no uncertainty, there is no need for any discussion. In a non-centralized, democratic system there is always uncertainty, there are always debates. The results of the elections are uncertain, developments on the marketplace are unpredictable, the people just do not know the future for sure. A certain naiveté prevails in these societies: the society respects the decision of the majority, and knows that the professional politicians behave as if they respected the choice of the majority. Both parties take the rules of the game seriously. This is why the would-be result is always uncertain.

Because of the fortunate genetic, educational, cultural differences of the human species, that macro-community, in the name of which the regime liquidated all real, existing small communities, was necessarily fictional. The only real result was the dangerous erosion of local self-sustaining capacities. There were no longer any local organizations or communities which might have been able to protect the environment and the nation from deterioration. It was risky to organize, it was risky to act together, it was risky to act at all. Not even the local authorities had any power to act; no power was delegated to the local level. Everything was decided in the centre, which acted according to the interest of the state and of the party, and based its decisions on distorted distant information.

It was almost unimaginable to report local catastrophes; even natural disasters were treated by the centre as the conscious sabotage of the class enemy. It was better to hide the problems, and wait for central measures or for miracles. But miracles have seldom happened, and the local officials, who in most cases were newcomers to the region, had no local knowledge, no local experience to do anything effective. The local apparatus, just like the central authorities, needed immediate, measurable results. Progress had to be measured every day. The regime had to find visible, measurable forms of legitimacy that could be propagated – new factories, new chimneys, more and more tons of steel, more harvesters, increasing numbers of co-operative members. The protection of the environment is not an immediate result. Cancer is a relatively slow disease; its negative effects cannot be felt immediately. (Today Hungary has the shortest male life expectancy in Europe.) It would be misleading to say that the mind of the atomized population was preoccupied with the problems of the distant future. No, they were worried about the present or about the next day; all their energies were needed for the struggle for survival.

IV

Even day-to-day survival is based on local knowledge. From the experiences of generations, the peasant knows exactly when it is possible to seed, when it is necessary to fertilize, when to start the harvest. But in the illusory world of total centralization it was not possible to let local knowledge and local practices loose. If local knowledge is better, then why do we need centralization? To acknowledge or ever refer to local knowledge would make it possible to advocate local interest, thus questioning the essence of the system. Local colour is deviance in the grey world of homogenized uniformity.

So the timetable of agricultural work was decided centrally. There were regions where – according to the central timetable – the peasants had to seed in January and harvest when the grain was still green. It was more important to follow central directives than to work rationally, to feed the city, the industrial proletarians. And not only the peasants' but the artisans' local skills became superfluous. In the strict hierarchical system, where one has to obey directives without question, any special knowledge becomes dysfunctional. The hierarchical system in the sphere of production goes beyond itself; it institutionalizes the inferior status of any local knowledge.

V

The more centralized a system, the more self-confident it seems to be. This is the system of inherent distrust. Because of the pervasive suspicion of the authorities everybody tries to escape from being called into account, and this need to escape forces everybody to keep the inputs, the possibilities, the problems secret. Life is covered by the dust of thick secrecy. The centre does not know the secret, it has information only about its existence, so it cannot give credit to the difficulties, to the scarcely audible local voice. The centre knows that everybody tries to cheat the authorities immediately above them but it is not in a position to acknowledge that it knows what is going on, since this would under- mine the legitimacy of the system. There is no real communication between the centre and the people; there is silence on the surface. But people talk to each other; the weaker the vertical voice, the more inten- sive the horizontal voice becomes. In this way people know perfectly well that the authorities know the secret but do not dare to speak about it. This is another reason why people do not respect the evaluations of the centre. This mutual distrust is fatal for the environment. Central- ization is inherently anti-ecological. The society gains less from that never-realizable advantage of a centralized system – that theoretically, it would be able to concentrate effort and capital on solving the ecological problems – than it suffers from the liquidation of local knowledge and local organizations.

VI

In the world of centralization the only real shortage is time. One has to hurry. According to the promises, today's sacrifices will be reimbursed in the shortest possible time. Time will bring its fruits (it is another question whether those fruits will be edible). Planning does not start with counting the given resources but with the desired output. The inputs are then attached to the planned output. The plan is the forcing of the central will on nature. The planner tries to manipulate society and nature in such a way as to make the desired goal seem attainable.

At the time of the first plans the priority was to turn the environment upside down, to change the political, social, cultural, natural, even historical environment. At school the children learned about the great Acts of Remaking of Nature, about the GOELRO plan of electrification in Soviet Russia, about Mitchurin's ingenious biological experiments, about all the bright achievements of Stalinist science. To imitate the Soviet example a huge dam was built on the River Tisza, the second most important river in Hungary, which is crucial for agricultural production on the Great Plain. The dam ruined the agricultural production of the whole region. The interest of agriculture was not taken into account at that time. The future belonged to industry: the less agriculture produces, the less its share in the gross national product, and in turn the shares of industry will increase, according to the statistics. The easiest way of industrializing the country is to liquidate agriculture.

Now it is the Danube's turn. A hydroelectric power plant is under construction at the beautiful Danube Curve, endangering not only some of the loveliest countryside in Europe but the rich agricultural region of Western Hungary as well. The plant is being built with the help of the Austrians, for whom ecological concern stops at the national border. They, who with widespread popular support stopped the construction of the Hainburg hydroelectric plant, made good use of the impossibility of a national referendum in Hungary. Instead of supporting the popular protest in Hungary, they supported that government which once more tries to prove its strength *vis-à-vis* nature and society. It seems that nothing has changed; time stands still. Life and the government are just like their predecessors in the 1950s. But this is only the surface.

VII

Although no dramatic, spectacular events took place in Hungary at the end of the 1970s, some fundamental changes started around 1979. Naturally the way things happen here is that changes are not introduced by earthquake-like events. Although many things were evident to spectators, those who made the decisions neither talked nor even knew about them. What happened was that the leadership gave up insisting on running the country according to strict ideological premises and adopted a more practical standpoint. Until the very end of the 1970s the only indicator of economic, political and cultural success was an ideological standard: things went well if they went according to certain ideological considerations. Reality was forced into the Procrustean bed of theoretical vision; things had to happen according to something. The centralized system wanted to force its vision on reality instead of acting according to an understanding of the environment. Not taking the (natural) constraints into consideration was the proof of man's ability to make history. Not accepting the blind fate of the world was thought to be the real revolutionary behaviour.

After the introduction of the New Economic Mechanism in 1968, when the classical, direct planning mechanism was abolished, the ministries and the party apparatus no longer had any direct means of compelling firms, managers and producers to act according to the will of the centre. The classical planning mechanism whereby the firms, the individual workers, were given obligatory tasks from the centre was abolished; the reform was supposed to replace this mechanism by monetary and fiscal techniques, and by the automatism of the market. But in the absence of any institutional reforms, the ministries and the party remained the crucial decision-makers. The market became but a simulation of automatism. A bargaining mechanism developed. The managers, the firms, all the factors of the economy started to bargain with the ministries and the party apparatus for preferential terms, for subsidies and for privileges. He who had the better connections had better chances, more tax exemptions, more subsidies, greater opportunity to increase prices. But this bargaining mechanism could not be institutionalized. This was already the post-reform period. The ministry had no direct control; it was not allowed to intervene directly. This is why bargaining had to take place below the surface. The economy was managed in the underworld. Centralization became uncertain and in some cases unconstitutional; verbally, everybody had to support the reform, the revitalization of the market. The centralizers, the planners, the managers became more and more schizophrenic; they could not say what they really wanted and they could not do what they said.

Sometimes the managers and the centralizers acted according to their words, according to some of the expressed values; sometimes according to their hidden thoughts and practices. Sometimes they behaved according to the explicit rules of the new game; sometimes according to implicit rules of the real game. This is how economic life has become more and more polyphonic. The same phenomena can be observed in other spheres as well. If differing and even contradictory interests could be tolerated in the sphere of the economy, then why not in other spheres too? Although the politicians acted as if they still possessed the only real knowledge about the real interests of society, it was admitted that some different, inferior, particular interest might exist in society which could even be articulated by scientists, artists, and sometimes even by lay human beings. Nobody knew exactly where the boundaries of tolerance were; what was permissible and what was not. The centralizers did not know what to take seriously, for the borderlines of tolerance were openly nonexistent; the border belonged to the world of non-issues.

There was nobody who was able to give guidelines to the authorities; they had to act according to the implicit rules. It was admitted that life cannot be governed solely by central directives, but this finding has never become explicit. Those in the apparatus who had such thoughts did not have the courage to think them. How is it possible to act without speaking, to speak without thinking, to think without thinking? That was the secret of the so-called 'social contract'.

It was understood that one of the most important elements of this 'social contract' was the constant increase in the standard of living after 1956 in Hungary. This policy could work as long as there was always something more to redistribute. But what can one do when one has to redistribute the decrease of the gross national product? How does one redistribute the decline, the economic problems? How can one maintain the illusion of a national consensus when one is not in the position to give anything? In such a situation, what one can give is the closing of one's eyes: tolerate the illegal second economy, the underworld of economic life, without admitting that one's eyes are closed. One cannot close one's eyes openly, it is against the existing laws. It was a new secret pact; what one gets is what one is able to get secretly. The authorities tolerated this secrecy; this was the most they could give in that situation. As long as people did not ask questions, the centralizers decided to behave; and not ask questions either. But gradually, the people came to understand that the authorities know the secret but are unable to do anything about it. And the authorities have learned that the people know their inability to do anything about it. This is how the crisis of the Central European version of post-modernity began.

VIII

Until the end of the 1970s, the modernists and modernizing regime acted as if they were able to eliminate all kinds of conflicts in the foreseeable future, as if everything was just a matter of time. This was one of the most important legitimating factors. The regime propagated and truly believed that it would solve all the basic conflicts of mankind, since the basis of all these conflicts is material. Development, the modernizing potential of the system, would make possible an advanced material world where conflicts no longer exist. By the end of the 1970s – when not even self-exploitation in the second economy could compensate any longer for the growing economic difficulties – this utopian idea became clearly obsolete, even though this was not stated explicitly.

By that time, all this was becoming clear in other parts of the world. A worldwide crisis of modernity and modernization was already evident in the more industrial parts of the globe where other indicators of social well-being started to gain significance. At the end of the 1970s the discovery of these new indicators in Central Europe was not too difficult. In the 1970s the borders were already relatively open – not only people but even ideologies and acid rain travelled through the slightly open doors.

In the West, this was a time of disappointment. Nobody trusted the Grand Theories, the Great Promises, the Bright Utopias any more. This was the time of the revival of localism, the victory of the Greater London Council, the municipal movement in Madrid, the socialist reforms in the French public administration. This was the time of the strengthening of green movements throughout the Western hemisphere, the time when Western governments and oppositional parties started to experiment with the co-optation of some of the ecologists.

By this time, the state of public health in Central Europe had become alarming. Silesia became perhaps the most unhealthy region of the continent, the Czech forests were dying, in Hungary the infant mortality rate was on the increase, average life expectancy was decreasing, and the nitrate content of drinking water was in most of the country above the hazard level. The economic crisis, the political problems, the growing consciousness of the population, the increasing uncertainty of the central apparatuses all had their role in making the atomized people more active, in making activities more open, and making openness one of the most important political demands. The Central European governments understood that in a situation of stagnation and decreasing standards of living, less easily measurable indicators have some real significance. To prove that the government has some interest in the health of the population costs less than over-ambitious industrial projects. To be concerned with the well-being of the population might be some compensation for growing economic difficulties. And by showing some concern for the problems of the environment, the government hoped to take the wind out of the sails of probable citizens' initiatives. As a combined result of the economic and political situation, and the interpretation of the Western developments by the government and by society, naturalism changed into ecology in the official vocabulary. The policy of the party and the government became more eclectic. Society became more polyphonic (but not more pluralistic, since the articulation of the different interests had no institutional framework and no political guarantee).

IX

The existence of the market does not provide better circumstances for reclaiming the locality, for regaining nationalized public space, or for winning back the right to organize. We, here in the middle of Europe, know the market perfectly well. It is not unknown to us. We have constantly been living with it, although it has not had a name. Even before 1968 or before the end of the 1970s we had to pay when we came into this world. Although we have a free medical service, we had to pay the doctors. We had to pay when we died; we had to give money to the gravediggers. And whenever we wanted to live, to survive, we had to pay as well (sometimes too dearly). They only real difference is that now the market has a name; we know what to call it. What formerly belonged to the underworld has come up to the surface. Now we are able to talk about it. Since it has a name, we might be able to speak about our dissatisfaction; we can say what we do not like. The existence of an open market means uncertainty. This is a real novelty in the world of deadly certainties. Uncertainty means the possibility of open discussions, open social debates in a society where even in the sphere of the economy the centre knew everything better and in advance, where there was no room for economic debates. The gesture which legitimizes the market differs from the place which we call the market. There is nothing inherently good in the market, but uncertainty is certainly better than certainty for ever.

X

This was the atmosphere in which a group of people, breaking with the long tradition of atomized individual actions, started to organize a blue (the colour of clear water and that of peace) movement. We wanted to act legally, inside the given legal framework, and in this spirit we asked for permission to form an ecological association. But to tolerate something and to legalize it, to close one's eyes or to face up to the situation, are different things. We did not get permission, and some of us decided to continue our ecological activities as a non-registered social movement. We organized public debates, circulated material about the ecological effects of the planned hydroelectric power plant, collected thousands of signatures for our petitions, initiated a national referendum, and tried to use, in our circumstances, the repertoire of similar movements in other parts of the world. We tried to make contacts with other Hungarian and foreign groups. We tried to persuade the Austrians that their eight billion schillings which they had lent for the project would not make the Central European energy, ecological and political situation better, and we tried to persuade our fellow-activists that it was better to act autonomously than to be co-opted by some existing institution. We won the Alternative Nobel Prize but we failed to stop the construction of the plant. We have learned a lot, helped others to learn something as well, and although our movement is in deep crisis now, we are not alone any more.

It is extremely unfortunate that at a time when more and more people try to move away from our special historical tradition of surviving with the help of informal techniques, there is no money to help citizens' initiatives. The state, the local authorities, are not in the position to give anything; the citizens do not have enough to help their own movements. But this is all natural. Had the state or the local authorities been rich enough, there would be no need for them to be tolerant. For long decades the state legitimized itself by claiming that it would take the responsibility for all the social needs of the country. Citizens' initiatives were not permitted to exist on the grounds that there was no need for such grass-roots organizations; the state would be able to solve all problems alone. Today when, because of grave economic problems, the central authorities are not in a position to promise so much any more, they try to evade these responsibilities. This is why the churches are allowed to take a more active part in social work, and why citizens have the right to do something – at least locally. This is why the state called the market in to help. The market will not help to solve the most pressing social problems. It will not help to get rid of social inequalities. It cannot help to solve the growing problems of ecology. But as I have tried to show, at least in this situation the market means something more than itself.

XI

Within certain limits, poverty is ecological. By the middle of the 1970s, when in Hungary it became clear that there was no money for extensive urbanization, the state stopped the bulldozers. Instead of demolishing the old city centres, a new rehabilitation programme was started. Instead of the huge, inhuman housing estates, less ambitious, human-scale projects have been planned. There was no money for local council housing, so a programme has been initiated instead to make old dilapidated housing stock comfortable. For more than thirty years the state-owned houses (more than 80 per cent of all the houses in the cities) have not been repaired; all the money was concentrated on the more spectacular task of erecting huge housing estates. The first result of this new programme was to repair the houses along the Grand Boulevard, without making the apartments inside more comfortable. This is the façade, and for those who are in power the façade is still the most important thing. But one can admit that for those who walk in the Grand Boulevard, even the colours of the façades mean something.

Traditional building materials and techniques, which for decades had been considered anachronistic, have been rediscovered. Concrete is *passé*, partly because of lack of capital. Labour exchange, that centuries-old tradition, is alive again, and labour exchange is not only a construction technique, it is a technique of rebuilding local communities. It is not the technique of the atomized individual but that of the living community. (More than 90 per cent of the houses in Hungarian villages are being built by labour exchange.) We are alive once again.

A closer scrutiny of most of the important and long-lasting economic, social and ecological reforms in all the Central European countries indicates that they are nothing more than the legalization of already existing illegal or semi-legal practices. What seems to be the work of professional reformers is in fact the consequence of continuous social resistance. The reformers act as intermediaries: they have the opportunity and the skills to articulate the pragmatic consciousness of atomized citizens, individual producers, and a growing number of associations – real communities.

Between the citizens and the professional reformers there is a 'division of linguistic labour'. Reformers assign a different value to the acts of ongoing resistance; their interpretation differs from the citizens' and from that of the apparatuses. The citizens are not weak. The emergence of the reformers was already a sign of the regime's accommodation to the citizens' resistance, but the actual reform, the legalization of illegal practices, is nevertheless different from the real meaning of resistance. The reform results from the way the reformers interpret citizens' actions and the way, in turn, the party interprets the reformers' ideas. What the people have to do is to force the real meaning of their actions upon those who interpret them. The environment is in danger; we can no longer allow the luxury of misinterpretation.

15

Perestroika: The Dialectic of Change

Boris Kagarlitsky

To Western observers, Soviet society at the end of the 1970s seemed hopelessly conservative, and arguments over the 'unreformability of communism' became commonplace among dissidents and the liberal intellectuals who sympathized with them. Pessimism reigned even among official experts, many of whom, on their own admission, 'had fallen into the depths of despair'.[1] There seemed no prospects for the future of the country other than an expectation of slow decay. However, with the coming to power of Mikhail Gorbachev, the general mood rapidly changed. People who, until recently, had had no faith in even the possibility of reform began to speak confidently of its irreversibility. The experts were gripped by reformist euphoria and the Western press, of both left and right, began to write of the success of the changes in the USSR with unprecedented enthusiasm. Although nobody denied the difficulties being encountered by perestroika – particularly the opposition of the bureaucratic apparatus and the complex economic situation of the country – nothing was capable of shifting the general mood of triumph. Hopeless pessimism was transformed into so much unbridled optimism although the actual dynamic of social development was much more complicated and contradictory than was generally recognized.

Soviet society has never been as monolithic as it was presented by Stalinist ideology or the oversimplified Western conceptions of totalitarianism. Numerous interest groups, forming both within and outside the apparatus of power, have always exerted influence on decision-making and engendered a variety of conflicts. In Stalin's time these conflicts were one of the reasons for the mass 'purges' within the party when the executions of prominent party and state figures signalled changes in the relationship of forces between different groups within the apparatus. Under Khrushchev the terror was brought to a halt, but a continuation of the open struggle between factions led first to the downfall of the all-powerful Minister of State Security, Lavrenty Beria, and later to the removal of Stalin's 'veterans' Molotov, Malenkov and Kaganovich. In the last analysis, Khrushchev himself was a victim of this struggle.

It was not simply a matter of clashes between people sharing power, or of a conflict of opinions. Each of the participants in these events leant for support upon definite structures in the apparatus and championed their interests. It was precisely the lack of faith of the broad bureaucratic 'mass' in Khrushchev's programme of reforms, and the absence of a social base for it outside the apparatus, which led to the fall of Khrushchev in 1964.

Brezhnev and the Eclipse of Reformism

At the moment of Brezhnev's accession the reformist faction in the ruling circles had practically no serious backing. The rehabilitation of victims of the terror in 1954–56, the debunking of Stalin's 'cult of the personality', the loosening of state control over cultural life and the vital extension of individual rights in that period were a very great historical achievement, but it should be remembered that all these radical measures also played a major role in the struggle between apparatus interests by weakening the position of one faction and structure and promoting the role of others. Khrushchev's early success was connected with the unanimous desire of the ruling circles to put an end to the omnipotence and irresponsibility of the repressive organs at that time, and to place the reorganized state security service under party control. At the next stage the impulse for continuing the political (but not the economic) reforms was the striving of the younger generation of *apparatchiks* to strengthen their own position and to edge out and discredit Stalin's 'old guard'. From the moment these goals appeared to have been achieved, the reformist potential of Khrushchev's thaw was exhausted and those people who had risen to their positions thanks to de-Stalinization were interested not in continuing the changes but in preserving stability. Since Khrushchev, carried away with his own reforms, did not wish to take this into consideration, he was removed from his post and replaced with a more suitable leader – Leonid Brezhnev.

The most important peculiarity of the Brezhnev period consisted in the ability of the leadership at that time to maintain a stable compromise between factions in the apparatus while simultaneously raising people's standard of living. It was necessary to guarantee significant and consistent economic growth so that each social group could increase its share of the cake without affecting the interests of others, and to a certain degree this objective was achieved. In the late 1970s and early 1980s workers' incomes grew rapidly and their way of life changed. There was a sharp increase in the number of privately owned cars, nearly every home acquired a television and refrigerator and millions of people continued to be rehoused from the 'communal quarters', where several families shared a kitchen, into normal, modern accommodation. The quality of building and the general provision of living space also improved. It is characteristic of the period of Brezhnevism that there were virtually no major strikes or disturbances comparable to the events at Novocherkassk in 1962 when the Khrushchev leadership was forced to send in troops to crush workers' protests against a rise in prices.

All of these social successes were achieved with a simultaneous growth of the armed forces and a rapid expansion of the government apparatus (which, from the point of view of the bureaucrats, served as the most important indicator of progress). Military–strategic parity was gained with the USA and the influence of the USSR in the world, particularly with developing countries, increased rapidly. Contrary to the popular view which formed towards the end of the Brezhnev era, the 1970s were undoubtedly one of the most prosperous and successful periods in Soviet history. What means were employed, and at what price these successes were achieved, are another question . . .

If Khrushchev attempted to blend political reforms with the maintenance of the traditional principles of economic management then Brezhnev, at first, chose to do directly the opposite. Political stability had to be combined with economic reform, the intention of which was to broaden the rights of the intermediate link of the economic apparatus and to form a layer of 'Soviet managers'. This reform, begun in 1965, could have accelerated the growth of the country and, at the same time, have satisfied the technocrats whose specific weight within the ruling circles was steadily increasing in proportion to the modernization of society. However, it very soon became clear that in practice the reform was only exacerbating contradictions between the economic and party apparatuses within the economic apparatus itself. It is not surprising, therefore, that the Brezhnev leadership, which valued stability so highly, rapidly curtailed the changes. By 1970 the reform had in fact ground to a halt.

The reform was accompanied by hopes for improving the efficiency of the economy. In so far as these proved to be without foundation, however, Brezhnev and his supporters were forced to make maximum use of other, extensive factors of growth. Enterprises had no real incentive to renew equipment (it was quite enough to fulfil the plan with the old machinery, and reconstruction placed the fulfilment of the plan under threat). As a result massive centralized investments in new enterprises became necessary. All the material, labour and financial resources that existed in the country had to be used to the utmost in the realization of this programme. Not surprisingly, the economy began to 'overheat' fairly quickly. The rapidly rising volume of money in circulation was not guaranteed by the supply of goods and the means devoted to the construction of new enterprises did not bring the planned return: building works dragged on because of the inefficient organization of labour, construction costs were rising all the time and the incipient shortage of money was concealed with the aid of the printing press. In order to receive additional resources, ministries were compelled to undertake new construction before completing the old. In the first half of the 1970s official propagandists loved to say that the whole Soviet Union had been turned into 'a gigantic building site'. By the end of the Brezhnev period they preferred not to recall this image. Many projects remained uncompleted over the course of several five-year plans, the cost of labour had increased fantastically, and there was a shortage of building materials, labourers and energy resources.

The maintenance of fixed prices for food, despite an extremely low productivity of agricultural labour and an uninterrupted expansion in effective demand, led to the state being forced to pay millions in subsidies while the population had to stand in queues complaining about the shortage of produce.

For a time all such problems were offset by increasing links with the West. Detente was a vital necessity for the Brezhnev leadership, and during the 1970s the Soviet economy became significantly more 'open'. However, the position occupied by the Soviet Union in the international division of labour clearly did not correspond to the status of our country as a strong industrial power. 'The basis of our exports', wrote the economist A. Byko in *Literaturnaya Gazeta*,

> was, and still is, raw material resources, primarily oil and gas, which account for approximately 80 per cent of our hard-currency exports. The sharp upward trend in world prices in the 1970s led to an almost twelve-fold increase in the price of oil and it seemed that such a situation would be maintained, at a minimum, until the end of the century. So why change the structure of exports and seek new reserves?

In its turn the imported equipment, acquired with 'petrodollars', could not be utilized with sufficient effectiveness 'because of bad management, chronically unfinished projects and slowness in familiarization'.[2] Despite the income from oil, the external debt of the USSR and the deficit on the balance of trade with capitalist countries grew appreciably. After the Polish events of 1980–81, Brezhnev's supporters came to the conclusion that it was essential to correct the situation in some way. The rates of growth of imports declined and debts were promptly paid off. Nevertheless the position of the USSR on the world market remained extremely precarious, as was revealed by the sharp fall in oil prices in the mid 1980s.

The Crisis of Brezhnevism

The years 1979 to 1980 proved fateful for the Brezhnev model. Contradictions and errors which had been concealed over many years began to drift to the surface. Tempos of economic growth began to fall appreciably, relations with the West steadily worsened and in Eastern Europe, 'pacified' for a full twelve years after the suppression of the 'Prague Spring', the situation suddenly destabilized. In Poland, the crisis quickly assumed a political character and led to a direct confrontation between the government and the workers' movement Solidarity, but other countries of the Eastern bloc were also encountering serious difficulties. When, in December 1979, Brezhnev decided to send Soviet forces into Afghanistan to save the 'fraternal regime' from the brink of collapse, nobody expected this to be the start of a prolonged conflict; it was perfectly clear, however, that the old political methods were no longer appropriate to the new reality.

The crisis of detente, the beginning of the war in Afghanistan and the events in Poland were, of course, not only the result of Brezhnev's policies. The West had entered a phase of structural changes, and a 'neo-conservative wave' had emerged in the majority of capitalist countries. Brezhnev and his supporters bore direct responsibility for the political failures of their allies in Poland and Afghanistan, but events in the rest of the world exposed the complete inconsistency of the political thinking which predominated within that leadership. With its orientation to stability, it expected, in an utterly irrational way, that the outside world would maintain an unaltered appearance and that qualitative changes were improbable. If oil became more expensive this was 'until the end of the century', if liberals dominated American politics this was an 'irreversible shift', and so on. The Brezhnev elite seemed psychologically quite unprepared for the explosions of the 1980s. Attempts to maintain the status quo through force, as happened in Afghanistan, only complicated the situation.

By the beginning of the 1980s the opinion had formed among the

most varied strata of Soviet society that Brezhnevism had exhausted
itself. The new generation, which had grown up during the years of
'stability', was more educated and demanding. An inconsistent modernization of the way of life had generated new demands and, in the end, a
new dissatisfaction. People felt themselves more independent and
demanded respect for their civil and human dignity. The years of 'stability' had passed to the benefit of society: social bonds had been
strengthened and people had a better conception of their collective
interests. In their turn the contradictions between bureaucratic departments were exacerbated to the point where it became clear that 'the
epoch of fine pies' was at an end. The shortage of resources provoked
interdepartmental clashes and made planning and decision-making at all
levels much more complex. The emerging lag in the field of modern
technology produced a feeling of horror among the military, especially
when the United States proclaimed its idea of 'space-based defence'.
Thus not only the lower classes were seized with discontent but also a
significant section of those at the top.

A paradoxical situation had arisen. On the one hand, society was
fully ripe for change, but on the other, there was no serious movement
of any kind for reform. Dissidents had never, even in their better years,
proposed a programme of social transformation. Throughout the whole
period of its existence, the dissident movement had advanced the
slogans of human rights and defence of the freedom and dignity of the
individual, but its incapacity to formulate a constructive programme
meant that the slogans became ever more abstract and divorced from the
real problems of the lives of the masses. As a result the dissidents pinned
their hopes more and more on diplomatic pressure from without. It was
proposed that the 'free world' should force the Brezhnev leadership into
concessions in the sphere of human rights. Such a strategy, for all its
questionable aspects, was at least understandable in the epoch of
detente. But it became perfectly suicidal in the conditions of heightened
international tension in 1979–82.

Compared with the 1960s, when the human-rights movement was
born, a significant evolution had taken place by the end of the Brezhnev
period. After the defeat of the 'Prague Spring', a general move to the
right could be discerned in this milieu. Academician Andrei Sakharov,
who initially favoured 'socialism with a human face', had, little by little,
adopted a liberal standpoint and many of his statements (for example on
Vietnam and detente) were utilized by American hawks in their efforts
to strengthen their position morally. An even more serious shift to the
right took place among the 'new emigration', whose numbers had begun
to grow rapidly from the mid 1970s. The most surprising thing is that
the dissident movement, though in desperate need of detente, practically

never recognized this fact.[3] Many in the dissident milieu welcomed the coming to power in the West of such figures as Margaret Thatcher and Ronald Reagan as a sign that 'at long last a decisive stand had triumphed in the free world'. In practice the immediate consequence of the crisis of detente proved to be a new round of repression against 'anti-socialist elements' and a worsening of the situation with regard to human rights.

By the end of the 1970s the dissident movement was in serious crisis. A significant section of activists had left the country, many had been arrested, some had dropped out of public activity. The most important cause of the crisis, however, was not repression but the absence of a political perspective. While the influx of people into the movement had declined, this in no way signified that there were fewer dissatisfied people in the country. Rather, in the new conditions, protest had assumed other forms.

A New Opposition and the Rebirth of Reform

The characteristic features of the 1979–82 period were, on the one hand, a strengthening of reformist tendencies within the establishment and, on the other, the emergence of a new socialist opposition. Unofficial left groups existed among the youth back in the 1950s, but under 'mature Brezhnevism' their number was insignificant. People who had suffered for such activity during the 1950s and 1960s had either given up the political struggle or joined the dissidents, losing their socialist ideology in the process. The situation swiftly changed in connection with the crisis of the dissident movement. New samizdat journals began to appear whose authors declared their Marxist orientation, discussion circles sprang up and there was a sharp growth of interest in socialist theory. The intensification of cultural links between the USSR and the outside world in the epoch of detente had had an influence on the ideology of these groups. As opposed to their predecessors in the 1950s, the 'young socialists' had a fairly thorough understanding of the ideas of the Western Left, from Gramsci and Rosa Luxemburg to the Frankfurt School, and they could utilize the experience of the reformist and 'revisionist' movements in the 'fraternal countries' of Eastern Europe.

In many respects the ideas of the left intersected the projects of official reformist experts, both attempting to formulate a realistic programme of changes on the basis of a socialist perspective. Both recognized the need to combine planning and market principles in the economy and the inevitability and necessity of democratization from above. However, in contrast to the reformist academic establishment, the left placed an emphasis on self-management of production. If the official experts, with rare exceptions such as B.P. Kurashvili, have advocated a unique Soviet 'managerial revolution', the left has declared workers' democracy as its aim. Moreover, in the opinion of the majority of young socialists, the supporters of official reformism have evidently re-evaluated the potential role of 'Soviet managers'. Workers in the government apparatus were genuinely interested in definite changes but, at the same time, were afraid of them. The industrial management apparatus in the localities was dissatisfied with the departmental bureaucracy at the centre but, at the same time, was tied to it by indissoluble bonds. Relations between the 'captains of industry' and the local party apparatus were shaped in a similar manner. In the opinion of the left this limited the reformist potential of the technocracy, even in the implementation of a moderate technocratic project. Successful changes could be begun only on initiative from above, but could be completed only by a mass movement from below.[4] Relying on the intermediate strata not only does not guarantee profound changes in society; it does not even allow the consistent implementation of a programme of limited reforms along the lines of Hungary in the 1970s. (It is no secret that it is precisely this 'model' which has inspired the majority of liberal experts.)

By the beginning of the 1980s such ideas were being developed in the pages of three samizdat journals – *Varianty* ('Alternatives'), *Poiski* ('Searches') and *Levyi Povorot* ('Left Turn'). Radical groups had formed primarily in Moscow and Leningrad, but the demand for such publications also grew rapidly in other cities, particularly among the youth. Nevertheless, the left was still very weak and had no political or organizational experience. In April 1982 most of the more active representatives of the new Left were arrested. *Levyi Povorot* and *Varianty* discontinued publication, as *Poiski* had done even earlier.

Because of the crisis in the dissident movement and the weakness of the left, official reformism remained the only real alternative to Brezhnevism. This current had also experienced certain difficulties. The reformist experts were mainly clustered around research institutes in Moscow, Novosibirsk and Leningrad. Their mouthpiece became the Novosibirsk journal *EKO* which, under the editorship of Abel Aganbegyan and Tatiana Zaslavskaya, attempted to combine scientific profundity with popularity of exposition. What could not be said in the text because of censorship was often 'spoken' by the wicked cartoons illustrating almost every article. The popularity of *EKO* grew rapidly in the late 1970s and early 1980s, although the readership remained fairly mixed. The editors conducted a special investigation to determine 'Who are you, our readers?' In fact *EKO*, like the reformist current itself, had numerous supporters in the most varied strata of society 'from the worker to the minister', but could not count on the support of any broad social group. The apparatus of economic management proved to be divided almost equally between supporters and opponents of reform; in the party apparatus, groups which were orientated towards change were compelled to coexist with conservatives, whereas the intelligentsia supported the reformist project 'for want of something better'.

The reformist programme's social lack of direction had its positive aspects. Reformist experts appealed more to an understanding of 'objective necessity' than to specific interests, and this created the feeling of an unbiased approach and an interest in the highest objectives of the state. Moreover, the indispensability of change was indeed acknowledged among the most varied social groups. Even conservatively minded figures saw that the USSR's growing lag in the field of 'high technology' could lead to an undermining of military might and that economic weakness could prove debilitating for a world power.[5]

Paradoxically, what the left saw as the greatest failing of the liberal experts' project – namely, its vagueness and lack of direction – assisted the formation of a broad and diverse coalition of supporters of change. Credit should be given to Yuri Andropov who, during his tenure as head of the KGB, began the very difficult job of uniting various factions and groups in the apparatus into a bloc of 'healthy forces'. Naturally, different individuals and groups expected different things from the changes. Some merely hoped to force out the Brezhnev 'mafia' from leading positions and to occupy the empty seats, while others wished to reinforce the military and political might of the country; a third group dreamed of a redistribution of power and rights among departments; a fourth was sincerely concerned to make Soviet society more free, just and dynamic. In any event, all were united by the understanding that it was 'impossible to go on living in the old way'.

Both those at the top and those at the bottom of society felt they were coming to the end of an epoch. Everyone desired renewal. The problem was that its meaning was not uniformly understood.

It was generally felt that Brezhnev's death came about two years too late. From 1980 the country was already living in expectation of this event.[6] When it finally happened even functionaries could not, at times, conceal their satisfaction.

The selection of Andropov as General Secretary was testimony to the political crisis of Brezhnevism but not yet to its final demise. In his very first declarations the new leader gave notice of his intention to carry through transformations not only in the economic but also in the political sphere. Experts began to elaborate draft reforms, overloading the leading bodies with them. The word 'reform', which had almost disappeared from the pages of official documents, began to appear more and more often in the press. A resolute struggle was launched against corruption, which had become virtually a way of life for Brezhnev's elite. Some activists of left groups who had been arrested in 1982 were released and their places in Lefortovo Prison taken by embezzlers and bribe-takers. Meanwhile Brezhnev's supporters, recovering from the initial shock of their leader's death, became aware of the impending danger and began to mount energetic resistance. Not a single one of the reformist projects considered at the highest level became an official document. Reform of the schools, proclaimed in the summer of 1983, was reduced to a list of good intentions and then, in practice, killed off.

The Impact of Chernobyl

Andropov's death and Chernenko's coming to power complicated the situation still further. In the person of Chernenko, the country had gained a leader who openly aspired to make his principle 'Brezhnevism without Brezhnev'. However, the lack of perspective in such a policy was apparent from the very first months. The economic situation continued to worsen and the struggle between departments and groups over the drawing-up of any directive document was exacerbated to the highest degree. The country lived in expectation of a succession of solemn funerals.

The death of Chernenko and the selection of Mikhail Gorbachev as General Secretary in spring 1985 brought an end to the protracted interregnum. The reformist current again found itself at the helm, but of the tasks set at the beginning of the eighties not one had been achieved. Almost another year was required to secure a working majority in the Politburo, Central Committee and Council of Ministers for supporters of the new leader. From day to day the newspapers reported on the permutations within the highest echelons of power. The 'veterans' of the Brezhnev mafia, Romanov, Tikhonov and Grishin, gave up their posts, but it proved much more difficult to undermine traditional bureaucratic 'claims' in the national republics. Here Brezhnevites maintained their positions for a long time, even within the highest party organs. The protracted struggle of the Moscow reformist leadership against the Kazakh Party leader, Kunaev, ended in December 1986 with his removal as First Secretary of the republic's Communist Party, but this provoked serious disorders in Alma-Ata. Many national-Brezhnevites can look on these events with satisfaction. After Alma-Ata, Moscow became much more careful in similar situations – which helped the traditional leaderships in the Ukraine and a series of other republics to retain their positions.

Nevertheless, the Gorbachev faction was undoubtedly triumphant. The 27th Congress consolidated its success by electing a new Central Committee and the idea of economic transformation and democratization was reinforced, at least in general formulations, in the new edition of the party programme. The word perestroika was heard from the highest platforms. However, in reality, society felt the changes only after the Chernobyl catastrophe in summer 1986.

The atomic reactor accident at Chernobyl revealed at once the numerous weaknesses of the traditional management system and its incompatibility with modern technology. Long before the disaster many specialists had pointed to the economic and ecological miscalculations attendant on the seventies strategy of developing atomic energy. The reactors were built too close to densely populated industrial centres and construction was carried out with infringements of the design. Nevertheless, the Brezhnev leadership insisted on the most rapid fulfilment of the 'atoms for peace' programme, which it saw as the magical means of resolving the aggravated energy problem. When the catastrophe happened it became clear that the power station was being run by incompetent people, that the firefighters, sent to the site of the incident, were unprepared for duty in conditions of radioactive fallout (although the existence of such a danger was mentioned more than once in the specialist literature), and that the local bosses concealed information on the real state of affairs from the highest echelons of power, as a result of which the situation deteriorated even further.

No one believed the first newspaper reports, which patently understated the scale of the catastrophe and often contradicted one another. The confidence of readers was re-established only after the press was allowed to examine the events in detail and without the existing censorship restrictions. The policy of openness (glasnost) and 'uncompromising criticism' of outmoded arrangements had been proclaimed back at the 27th Congress, but it was only in the tragic days of the Chernobyl disaster that glasnost began to change from an official slogan into an everyday practice. The truth about Chernobyl which eventually hit the newspapers opened the way to a more truthful examination of other social problems. More and more articles were written about drug-abuse, crime, corruption and the mistakes of leaders of various ranks. A wave of 'bad news' swept over the readers in 1986–87, shaking the consciousness of society. Many were horrified to find out about the numerous calamities of which they had previously had no idea. It often seemed to people that there were many more outrages in the epoch of perestroika than before although, in fact, they had simply not been informed about them previously. After the information on the crimes and errors of the contemporary period, new material about Stalin's evil deeds began to break through. Writers, journalists and cinematographers, aware of the new opportunities, rushed to make use of them.[7]

If the first period of perestroika, which lasted from spring 1985 to spring 1986, can be called a time of struggle in the apparatus, events clearly entered a new phase in summer 1986. The 'golden age' of perestroika had begun.

Glasnost and democratization became the watchwords of the day. Reformist, left-wing and anti-Stalinist ideas were obviously predominant in the mass media. The old mechanism of economic management functioned as before, but the political situation had changed. A majority of representatives of the Brezhnev group had already been ousted from their positions in the Politburo and the 'intermediate link' in the apparatus had gone over to passive resistance, defence of their privileges and blocking the implementation of reforms. Draft changes passed many times through innumerable commissions, one version of the text being replaced by another and endless amendments and elaborations being introduced. The bureaucracy had selected the tactic of filibustering, drawing out the decision-making process to the maximum extent. Many resolutions, adopted at the centre, were not implemented in the regions and every possible 'instruction' and 'position' was devised to limit the reforming effect of the new legislation.

The official programme of changes, based on the ideas of Aganbegyan, Zaslavskaya and their 'Novosibirsk group' was initially quite moderate. It proposed an expansion of enterprise autonomy while maintaining the system of centralized planning, the admission of a small private sector, mixed international enterprises in some branches of the economy and the regulation of the administrative and legal systems. The restraint of this programme was its chief political virtue in that representatives of the most varied currents within the party elite and the country as a whole could put their names to such minimal demands. For the left the idea of mixed corporations was rather uncomfortable from an ideological point of view, but this was not a central point and the left anyway still played no significant role in events.

The Logic of Democratization

However, even such a moderate programme proved difficult to carry out in the face of resistance from the bureaucracy, and some sort of untraditional means of pressure on the government apparatus was required. Essentially, even the realization of the most lukewarm programme of economic restructuring demanded radical political shifts. Democratization was to become an *instrument of reform.*

The state of affairs in the economy remained extremely unstable. After Gorbachev came to power the slogan of acceleration [*uskorente*] of socioeconomic development was advanced and enterprises were required to increase their output at any price. In reality, enterprise directors called into circulation hidden reserves of raw materials and components put by 'for a rainy day'. Many managers were working sixteen hours a day. All this could not fail to yield results. The economic indicators for 1985 were appreciably better than for the preceding year. On the one hand, department heads had demonstrated that there was no need to hurry with the reforms because it was possible to achieve reasonable results with the old management mechanism and that it was necessary only to increase the pressure on directors. On the other hand, directors now had to maintain the achieved level at any price so as to avoid serious trouble. In practice, it was impossible to fulfil the plan according to the traditional indicators while simultaneously redesigning the system of management. Something had to be sacrificed. The opinion spread even among official experts and reform-minded planners, that the real restructuring would have to be postponed until the 1990s and that the current five-year plan (1986–90) would have to be extended somehow on the basis of the old mechanism. Meanwhile economic growth in 1985, despite the selfless efforts of workers, engineers and many production leaders, remained highly unstable. Chernobyl showed how unreliable was the old system of management. The catastrophe strengthened the arguments of those in favour of quickening the pace of reform. Moreover, the capitalist world, having overcome the most recent phase of its structural crisis, was experiencing a period of rapid growth. The neo-conservative wave was reaching its apogee and the Reagan administration did not conceal its intention of utilizing the increased economic superiority of the USA over the USSR to alter the military–strategic balance in its favour. The war in Afghanistan continued without any serious military or political successes and the situation in the countries of Eastern Europe remained confused and unsettled. As before, the West treated Soviet declarations about restructuring with mistrust.

Political democratization created the only possibility of unblocking the situation and quickening the pace of change. The press, which had gained quite a lot of freedom, had to ensure independent monitoring of the implementation of decisions and to assist the 'pressure from below' on the bureaucracy. The return to Moscow of Academician Andrei Sakharov and the freeing of political prisoners enhanced the authority of the Soviet government in the international arena and provided evidence to the whole world of the effectiveness of perestroika. Many representatives of the sixties intelligentsia, who under Brezhnev had stayed on the political periphery or bided their time, returned to prominence. The left also became much more active.

The January 1987 Plenum of the Central Committee had to reinforce the shifts which had been taking place throughout the previous year. By Gorbachev's own estimation, the plenum 'advanced democratization as the major driving force of perestroika'.[8] A whole series of proposals put forward at the 27th Congress were made more concrete. Gorbachev directly declared the necessity of changing the electoral system in such a way that there would be more officially nominated candidates than seats in the Soviets. The plenum also discussed the election of enterprise directors and section heads and the creation of self-management organs in production. A special Party Conference on problems of perestroika was called for June 1989, although its powers and tasks were not precisely defined.

Although the reforms proposed by Gorbachev were quite moderate, the intermediate link of the bureaucratic apparatus continued to resist. Implementing even a part of what had been discussed at the plenum proved extremely difficult. 'Experimental' elections of factory directors were conducted in a series of enterprises which, for some reason, were without a boss. No existing directors, however, wished to subject themselves to this experience, and section heads and administrative personnel were appointed, as before, by the director. Although the new law on state enterprise, which envisaged the democratization of industrial life, came into force on 1 January 1988, almost nowhere did the administration permit workers to intervene in the process of decision-making. In addition, many points of the law had been formulated very vaguely. Councils of Labour Collectives were established in the factories, but in most cases the administration itself laid down their powers and tasks and the method by which they were to be set up. Very often the directors headed the new 'organs of self-management' and turned them into an appendage of the administrative apparatus.

Elections to the local soviets in summer 1987 took place on the basis of the old electoral system. In several districts an 'experimental' list contained one candidate more than there were deputies' credentials, but even here candidates who finished in last place were given the status of 'reserve deputy' if they had managed to gain more than 50 per cent of the vote.

Nevertheless, in almost every 'experimental multi-mandate district' the electors were able to take advantage of their new rights. In a majority of cases it was precisely the local bosses, who had traditionally sat in the soviets, who were finding themselves 'overboard'. As *Izvestiya* acknowledged, the list of 'reserve deputies' included a 'whole string of leaders'. Among those who had failed at the elections were regional committee secretaries, chairmen of the executive committees of soviets and their deputies, and so on. 'Several "leading" candidates made it into the soviet with difficulty, their fate being decided by a majority of one or two votes.'[9] Even in districts where the old system had been maintained the electorate often acted in an unusual manner. Students at Moscow University voted against a functionary of the university administration responsible for the student canteen. According to a report in *Literaturnaya Gazeta*, official candidates failed to be elected in 1,076 districts of the country.[10] It should be noted, incidentally, that the press covered these events in detail and even spoke of attempts to 'correct' the voting records which had taken place in certain instances.

The elections testified to the change in the psychological climate in the country. The life of society was reviving. Politics was no longer perceived as a pursuit of the privileged, nor criticism of authority as dissidence. In the conditions of liberalization all political and ideological currents existing in society came to the surface. Right-wing liberal dissidents grouped around the samizdat bulletin *Glasnost* and the Moscow seminar 'Democracy and Humanism'. Russian nationalist and Fascist groups united under the banner of the *Pamyat* ('Memory') society. National minorities also voiced their own demands. In the Baltic states there were demonstrations marking the anniversary of the Stalin–Hitler pact in 1939 by which these territories came within the Soviet sphere of influence. In Vilnius several hundred people came on to the streets and in Riga the demonstrations were much bigger. The Crimean Tatars held a meeting in Moscow to demand rehabilitation and a reversal of Stalin's order expelling them from their native land. The left groups also underwent rapid growth.

The Club Movement and Yeltsin's Dismissal

The political situation which arose after the January Plenum was extraordinarily propitious for the left. On the one hand, its demands coincided completely with the slogans of the day and, on the other, the left was able to attract to its ranks a growing number of people who were disturbed by the slow tempo of real change. The swift growth of 'informal associations' began back at the end of 1986. The Club for Social Initiatives (KSI) and the Perestroika club in Moscow quickly became centres of attraction for the socialist and left-liberal intelligentsia. Ecological and 'cultural-democratic' groups were formed or gained in strength. The movement in Leningrad developed particularly rapidly. On 16 March, following the call of the 'cultural-ecological'

group *Spasenie* ('Salvation'), hundreds of young people gathered at the
Hotel Angleterre, which had been earmarked for demolition. They were
joined by representatives of other ecological and left groups, pupils from
technical colleges and schools, workers and students. Stewards from the
Forpost ('Outpost') group ensured that order was maintained. Journalists who were present acknowledged that everything was superbly organized: 'there were no excesses of any kind'.[11] Participants in the demonstration were unable to prevent the demolition of the building, but they made
the larger point that citizens have the right to influence decisions taken by
the authorities. The leader of *Spasenie*, Aleksei Kovalev, immediately
became a well-known figure both in Leningrad and beyond. Independent left groups advanced his candidature for the city soviet, but the
electoral commission refused to register him. In its turn the Moscow
press came out in criticism of the Leningrad authorities and in support
of Kovalev and *Spasenie*.

By the summer of 1987 it was already possible to speak of a mass
movement in which thousands of people were taking part in various
regions of the country. The platforms of the different groups varied in
important ways from one other, as did the forms of their activity. The
desire for unity was combined in many clubs with distrust towards other
groups, sectarianism and mutual rivalry. Nevertheless, participants in the
movement increasingly felt the need to elaborate a common platform
and to set practical collaboration under way.

In August 1987 the KSI held a conference in Moscow of the fifty-two
leading progressive groups at which the founding of the Federation of
Socialist Social Clubs (FSOK) was announced. While preserving their
various differences, the groups within the federation jointly declared
themselves in favour of socialist pluralism, self-management of production and the democratization of planning. FSOK's Declaration
advanced specific political demands: the abolition of censorship and the
right of clubs to put up their own candidates in elections. The economic
section remained the least worked out and it was decided to prepare
special documents at a later date which would concretize FSOK's
positions on the questions of self-management and planning. The clubs
unanimously declared that the reform must be carried out without a
drop in workers' living standards and must maintain social provision for
cheap accommodation, free medical care, full employment, and so forth.
The extension of the role of market factors in managing the economy
was seen as natural and inevitable, but stress was also laid on the
dangers of triumphant technocracy and of a substitution of market
fetishism for plan fetishism.

FSOK was joined by clubs not only in Moscow and Leningrad but
also in Kuibyshev, Krasnoyarsk, Novorossiisk, Ivanovo, Saratov and

elsewhere. Throughout autumn 1987 the federation experienced continual growth. Publication commenced of its samizdat bulletin *Svidetel* ('Witness') – later, in recognition of tradition, it was renamed *Levyi Povorot*. FSOK representatives had an opportunity to speak before foreign journalists at the official Novosti Press Agency, and material about FSOK appeared in several newspapers. However, in November the situation suddenly changed.

On 31 October, Central Committee Secretary A. Lukyanov, speaking at a Novosti press conference in front of foreign and Soviet journalists, reported that at the regular plenum which had just taken place disagreements had arisen over a speech by Boris Yeltsin, and he had been forced to resign as Moscow party leader. This report had the impact of an exploding bomb, but public opinion was shaken even more by the silence of the official newspapers. Lukyanov's words were reported in Western Europe, China, Hungary and Poland but Muscovites were obliged, as in the first days of the Chernobyl disaster, to hear the news about events in their own country from foreign radio. Yeltsin was well known as one of the most stalwart supporters of perestroika and his resignation seemed an ominous sign. The left clubs unanimously protested against the silence of the mass media, although within a majority of groups there were pointed discussions about what could be done in such a situation. FSOK activists began collecting signatures on the streets of Moscow to a letter demanding complete openness (glasnost) in the Yeltsin affair. Vladimir Kurbolikov from the *Obshchina* ('Commune') club, who had come down from Leningrad, Kovalev and several other members of FSOK were detained by the police while doing this. The crisis intensified even further when the central newspapers and local Moscow press published the record of the plenum of the Moscow Party Committee at which Yeltsin had been removed from his post and accused of a multitude of political sins. At Moscow University students held a spontaneous meeting and organized an initiative group which made contact with KSI and FSOK. Many Party organizations in Moscow refused to support the decision of the plenum.

Later, in January 1988, Gorbachev acknowledged that because of the 'Yeltsin affair', the party leadership had suffered serious criticism from the left and that the removal of the Moscow leader had been interpreted 'by a certain section of the intelligentsia, particularly the youth, as a blow against perestroika'.[12] In their turn, conservative-minded officials saw Yeltsin's dismissal as a signal for counterattack. Serious administrative pressure began to be exerted on the clubs and several activists were forced to abandon their jobs. It became extremely complicated to engage in any activity on an official basis. Clubs were not able to use premises and their reports did not pass through the press, although back in September there had been no problem with this. The Krasnoyarsk section of FSOK, the Committee for Assisting Perestroika, found itself in an extremely difficult position. After activists from the committee had accused a series of figures in the local leadership of corruption, the Party Regional Committee took a special decision against this group, and one of its members, V.B. Chetvertkov, was expelled from the party. Similar events occurred in other cities.

A majority of clubs continued to emphasize the legal character of their activity and their preparedness to collaborate with progressive groups in the party and state apparatus. This did not, however, prevent them from being accused of 'unconstructive positions' and 'attempts to undermine the foundations'. In winter a genuine Stalinist campaign commenced in the press against the left. *Komsomolskaya Pravda*, *Pravda*, *Vechernyaya Moskva* and *Moskovskii Komsomolets* all came out with attacks against FSOK and individual clubs. *Pravda* also attacked the noted playwright Mikhail Shatrov, who was in favour of a more consistent analysis of the Stalinist past and historical justice with regard to Stalin's opponents (including Trotsky). Judging by the tone of some articles, the conservative groups in the apparatus were seriously frightened by the growth of left activism after the events of August and November 1987. Liberal journalists preferred to keep quiet in the expectation that this 'conservative wave' would soon pass.

In liberal reformist circles reference was made to Gorbachev's winter vacation and the illness of one of the leaders of the progressive faction, Central Committee Secretary Aleksandr Yakovlev. The Stalinists' counterattack was not triggered, however, by a fortuitous set of circumstances. Perestroika had entered a new phase and the political delineation of society had been sharpened.

Technocracy and the Market

If, during the earlier stages of perestroika, the slogan of change had been capable of uniting the most varied currents within society and the apparatus, it was clearly no longer sufficient. Many representatives of the 'new generation' of *apparatchiks*, who had been able to acquire important responsibilities during the course of events in 1985–86, were inclined to consider the fundamental tasks of perestroika fulfilled and to regard with apprehension any 'experiments' which might threaten their hard-won prosperity. The comparative warmth in international politics and the Soviet–American treaty on intermediate-range missiles – which to a significant extent were a result of the changes in our country – also, in their own way, reinforced the conservative mood in the apparatus. If many bureaucrats viewed internal political liberalization as a kind of 'price' to be paid for the trust of the West and a resumption of detente, their interest in political change clearly diminished when this goal seemed to have been achieved to a significant degree. Indeed, there were further misgivings, after the November outbursts by young people over the 'Yeltsin affair', that the democratic process had already gone 'too far'.

Of course, perestroika was continuing. The rehabilitation was announced of Bukharin, Rykov and other old Bolsheviks falsely accused by Stalin of creating 'the bloc of Rights and Trotskyites' in 1937. The journal Oktyabr ('October') published V. Grossman's long-banned novel Life and Fate, and the first issue of Latinskaya Amerika ('Latin America') for 1988 carried a short note on Trotsky's life in Mexico. The withdrawal of Soviet forces from Afghanistan was being prepared and the press openly wrote of the failure of the 'Afghan campaign': 'the fundamental goals have just not been achieved'; 'the presence of Soviet forces in the country has lost all sense. Withdrawal is inevitable and logical.'[13]

Nevertheless, the dynamic of events was not as it had been in 1986, and among reformists there was a feeling of some dismay. Many radical slogans were repeated in a ritualistic way without any serious resolve to try and carry them out. Experiments with the election of directors were curtailed (although the law which formally made elections obligatory had come into force). The ideologists of economic reform, dissatisfied with the results which had been achieved, advanced all sorts of new proposals and, having lost their former unity, argued all the more furiously among themselves. In the words of the eminent Soviet jurist B.P. Kurashvili, the measures taken in the period 1985–87 were so superficial and half-hearted that perestroika risked 'not even reaching its hazily presented final goal'.[14] It was essential to formulate more precisely the tasks of economic and political reform, and to develop a specific project.

Whereas at first the technocratic and democratic concepts of change had more or less peacefully coexisted, it was now necessary to draw a clear distinction. The technocrats, more and more obviously defending the interests of the industrial management apparatus, saw the way out of this complicated situation in the partial elimination of social provision and the importing on to Soviet soil of the recipes of the neo-conservative theoreticians of the West. Nikolai Shmelev, one of the most fashionable authors of this trend, quite candidly defined his programme with the words: 'Everything that is effective is moral.'[15] Together with other theoreticians of the technocratic school (G. Lisichkin, G. Popov, et al.), he has viewed social provision as a brake on development and a 'survival of feudalism'. The technocrats no longer concealed the anti-democratic character of their proposals. In the pages of *Literaturnaya Gazeta* Lisichkin declared that the starting point of reform had to be the interests of the 'advanced' minority, hampered in its development by the slow backward majority. The task of perestroika was to overthrow the 'tyranny' of the majority and to assert the superiority of the elite.

The expansion of market relations is the main slogan of technocratic ideologues. In fact, however, the 'market' phraseology of this group should be treated with extreme caution. The structure of the Soviet economy, formed under Stalin, guarantees an absolute monopoly position to the leading enterprises and departments. For decades the major part of investment has been devoured by the factory giants producing means of production. Everything has been organized in such a way that the consumer is subordinate to the producer, and this is explained not only by the absence of a market but frequently by the absence of any real choice. The economy is orientated not to the satisfaction of human need but to self-reproduction. This 'self-devouring economy', to use the expression of the noted scholar V. Seliunin, cannot become more humane through the proposed reorientation from central directives to profit criteria. The means are changed, but not the goal.

In these circumstances the proposed 'playing of the market' can only turn into a rise in prices, inflation and increased exploitation of the consumer by monopolist organizations. It is typical that the technocrats, who continually emphasize that the market will solve a majority of problems, are highly disdainful of structural reform in the sphere of production and of a redistribution of investments, although it is perfectly obvious that without such measures 'normal' market competition would simply just not happen.

The concrete recommendations of this school are reduced to the removal of food subsidies and the raising of prices in the name of improving financial health. At the same time they propagandize the slogan of 'self-financing', which is understood in practice as the freedom for monopolists to increase prices. Since January 1987, when a series of departments transferred to the principles of self-financing, the newspapers have begun to report fast-rising prices on the most varied goods and services, from trips abroad and window-cleaning to . . . funeral services. Analysing the higher cemetery prices for 1987, the Moscow sociologist. A. Rubinov remarked, not without irony, that 'the economic prospects for this branch are "indeed marvellous".'[16]

The essence of the matter is that under the guise of 'reform', workers are being forced to pay for the economic miscalculations of the bureaucracy, bad management, structural imbalances and the pre-crisis situation of the economy. It is perfectly clear that such proposals cannot find mass support. In data obtained from surveys more than 70 per cent of the population are opposed to them.[17]

The concepts of the new technocratic school have not been accepted as an official perestroika strategy and on several occasions have even been criticized by Gorbachev. However, the influence of its supporters in the apparatus has been steadily growing and particular concepts can be detected more and more frequently in official documents. There is nothing surprising in this. Technocratic ideologists have suggested methods which, under a veneer of radicalism, are completely acceptable to the bureaucracy, and have also proposed the retention of traditional structures within both the economic and political systems of society. Despite its anti-Stalinist rhetoric, the technocratic current has converged more and more with the conservative-Stalinists. The brutal apparatus of political control has proved an essential element in a strategy based on frustrating the interests of society and lowering the standard of living of those at the bottom. It is also patently obvious that glasnost and self-management – the watchwords of the previous stage of perestroika – have no part in these concepts.

It is no accident that G. Kh. Popov, one of the major ideologists of the technocracy, appeared in the press with denunciations directed at Yeltsin while bluntly suggesting that in this complicated situation, the left might prove more dangerous than the conservatives. After Yeltsin's downfall the technocrats and Stalinists began to act more often as a united front, propagandizing for a rise in prices and for the elimination of those figures who, in their opinion, were too far to the left and on whom they had pinned the label 'vanguardism'. Naturally, both sides have viewed this compromise as purely tactical, but the objective dynamic of events has pushed them into each other's arms.

In many factories the workers have begun to demand changes in the organization of labour, glasnost at the workplace, dismissal of incompetent and corrupt leaders, a shortening of working time and an end to overtime. The press reported on strikes and spontaneous meetings in many enterprises towards the end of 1987. In December sharp conflicts arose between workers and the local authorities in Krivoi Rog and Volgograd when an absence of money at the bank and the much tighter financial discipline resulted in the non-payment of wages. The workers protested, proving that they, at any rate, had legally earned their money and could not be held responsible for non-fulfilment of the financial plan. Officials mourned the passing of the good old days when it was possible simply to use force. In accordance with the classical laws of the revolutionary process, a polarization of forces was taking place in the country.

The Party Conference and the Formation of the Popular Front

The 19th CPSU Conference, scheduled for summer 1988, was planned by Gorbachev and his allies to be an important stage of perestroika. If the 27th Party Congress had not satisfied the expectations of the proponents of change, and had not taken a single concrete decision on the reform programme, this conference was expected to get the transformation of the political system under way again. According to rumours which were circulating in Moscow from February onwards, transfers of cadre personnel were also expected, but it became clear fairly soon that even if Gorbachev and his group had wanted this, they were not strong enough to carry out a serious reshuffling of cadres in the highest party positions.

The defeat of the Brezhnevite faction in no way signified the political death of the party conservatives. On the contrary, the place of the senile and corrupt Brezhnevites was quickly taken by younger and more energetic people who were prepared to put into practice changes within the administrative system, but were categorically opposed to structural reforms and refused to share with society the tiniest part of their power. Western journalists and Soviet intellectuals usually identify Yegor Ligachev as the leader of this new conservative faction, and he rapidly became an object of hatred to the liberal public. Needless to say, the real point is not the individual personality but the serious shifts going on within the ruling elite. The 'neo-conservatives', as distinct from the Brezhnevites, seemed capable of speaking in the language of modernization and of responding, in their own way, to many of the demands of social development. They could find a common language with the technocrats on concrete problems. Criticism of Stalin, which had been made one of the main manifestations of perestroika in ideology, touched them less than it did the Brezhnevites, since none of the neo-conservative faction had been direct or indirect accomplices in Stalin's crimes. Nevertheless, the neo-conservatives were well aware that the anti-Stalinist campaign in the press was getting out of control, and launched energetic attempts at an ideological counteroffensive.

In March 1988, the newspaper *Sovetskaya Rossiya* published Nina Andreeva's letter 'I cannot waive my principles'. The author (or authors, for there was a suspicion that behind Andreeva stood a whole group of people) spoke out against 'left-wing intellectual socialism' and demanded that J.V. Stalin's achievements should be respected. Andreeva's letter at once became a kind of programme for the conservative forces, and the unknown Leningrad chemistry teacher became a celebrity throughout the country. In thirty regional party committees it was decided to disseminate the letter as propaganda material for the political training system, and a number of provincial newspapers reprinted the text.

In response, *Pravda* published on 5 April an official criticism of Andreeva's letter in the form of an editorial piece backed by a Politburo decision. Many of the *apparatchiks* who had been most zealous in propagating Andreeva's letter were forced to admit their mistake. All this testified to a sharpened struggle at the top, but the spring test of strength did not turn into an open split. Moreover, before the conference itself both factions were able to find a common language.

As always, democratization turned out to be the victim of this compromise. The Theses of CPSU Central Committee for the party conference largely consisted of declarations which suited both factions, and the selection of delegates was carried out under the strict control of the *apparat*. Plenums of the regional committees took the final decisions, and the mass of CPSU members, not to mention non-party people, had to make do with making suggestions which the *apparat* could either pay attention to or ignore, as it wished.

Such an understanding of 'democracy', however, by no means satisfied the workers. If in the early days the ideologues of perestroika had complained about the passivity of the people, the situation began to change quickly before the 19th Party Conference. In Kuibyshev, Yaroslavl, Omsk, Krasnoyarsk, Moscow and Astrakhan there were mass meetings. In Yuzhnosakhalinsk there were strikes. It was significant that this activity arose not as a result of appeals from above for support for perestroika but out of mass dissatisfaction with the way in which this perestroika was put into practice, and from the workers' unwillingness to become mere spectators of another political compromise worked out at the top.

The authorities' concern over these events was expressed in the form of a tightening of censorship. A whole series of publications which were ready for the press, and in which the preparation for the party conference came under criticism, were hurriedly removed from the production process. Naturally nothing was officially said about this, but a few days before the opening of the party conference the socialist samizdat journal *Levyi Povorot* published a photocopy of an article from the newspaper *Sovetskaya Kultura* which had already been typeset, but was pulled out on the orders of the party leadership (*Levyi Povorot*, no. 10, 1988).

For their own part, the left-wing groups felt the need to form a single broad organization which could have a real influence on the course of events. The socialist clubs played a most active part in the mass actions of May and June 1988. Most of the groups began to grow rapidly. But at the same time, the limitations of the movement's initial organizational forms became evident. The Federation of Socialist Clubs, where there were still strong elements of sectarianism and disunity between the groups, was not capable of forming the basis for a mass movement. There was a need for a joint platform and a real unity of action. The majority of groups with a left orientation in the whole country united into the Organizing Committees of the Popular Front. At the same time, the right-wing and liberal groups formed their own 'party', the Democratic Union (DU), and the Black Hundreds group *Pamiat* turned itself into the 'National-Patriotic Front'.

Subsequent events confirmed the necessity of consolidating the left-wing forces. The discussions at the party conference brought out the profound differences between the supporters of a radical course and the conservative part of the *apparat*. Academician L. Abalkin, well known for his sympathy towards Scandinavian social democracy, spoke of how economic growth rates were continuing to fall, and of the need for more serious structural reforms. B.N. Yeltsin demanded a sharp cut in the party *apparat* and the abolition of all privileges. Ligachev criticized Yeltsin harshly, and many delegates went out of their way to dissociate themselves from Abalkin. The liberal writer G. Baklanov, head of the journal *Znamya*, was simply not allowed to speak.

Nevertheless, the party forum did not give a decisive answer to any of the urgent questions. The most important resolutions of the party conference were not even formulated beforehand in the Theses, and were not anticipated either by the delegates or by society as a whole. On this occasion resolutions were not adopted unanimously, but the leadership's proposals were invariably passed. The conference decided to conduct early elections for a Congress of People's Deputies in spring 1989, and to ensure an increase in the role of the soviets by combining the leading positions in the soviets and the corresponding party committees.

The left-wing forces criticized the plan for a Congress of People's Deputies, in which about a third of the places would be reserved for representatives of party organs and official 'social organizations' (the Komsomol, trade unions, and so on), as 'a new element of class representation'. The experience of the preparations for the 19th Party Conference had shown that such a decision would guarantee places in the Congress to the *apparatchiks* even if the masses voted decisively for other candidates. The actual powers of the Congress, which in fact would involve only the election of a new Supreme Soviet, without legislative functions, seemed to the supporters of the Popular Front to be unacceptably limited. Nevertheless, the left-wing forces intended to participate actively in the pre-election struggle. This required the strengthening of the Popular Front's organization, a widening of its social base, and the creation of its own information channels (the circulations of the samizdat monthlies 'Left Turn' and 'Open Zone' were already clearly insufficient: hundreds of copies were in circulation, but the local left groups were demanding thousands).

The incredibly complex tasks which confronted the activities of the Popular Front had to be tackled in a very short time, by people with very little political or organizational experience. And all the time the movement was continuing to grow and to form its own structures and ideology.

On 31 July, after a whole series of unsanctioned demonstrations, the Popular Front succeeded in holding its first authorized meeting in Moscow – a meeting which attracted, according to *Izvestiya* (1 August 1988), 'about a thousand people'. *Moscow News*, the mouthpiece of the liberal circles, reacted to this initiative of the Popular Front with open disapproval – to the left of the familiar technocratic reformism the shape of a new, radical political force had begun to appear.

Conclusion

In January 1988 the well-known Soviet economist V. Seliunin wrote that two years of perestroika had revealed the bankruptcy of the fundamental concepts of official economic science. The reformist current had proved to be in no condition to elaborate and propose to society a radical project that could arouse the enthusiasm of the masses. The major achievement of perestroika remained glasnost, but it could not automatically resolve the country's social and economic problems. Now, wrote Seliunin, 'structural shifts are required in the economy – it is necessary to turn from work for its own sake to people and their needs.'[18] Such a perestroika would, in its turn, be possible only if it maintained the living standards of the masses and developed the industrial, political and local democracy which gives workers the opportunity for real participation in decision-making.

The aimless projects of the first years have proved unrealistic. The experience of Soviet society has once again demonstrated that the most moderate decision is not always the most sensible. In the place of abstract notions of the 'common good' has come a consciousness of the real conflict of interests in society. 'The struggle is not simply between bureaucrats and non-bureaucrats,' wrote one of the commentators of the popular journal *Novy Mir* ('New World'),

> but between social groups on which they both depend for support. The major question is: who is capable of leading the mass forces that have a real interest

in perestroika, in scientific, technical and cultural progress, and are its fundamental vehicle and thus the vehicle for the general interest – the workers with
the highest skills, embodying the most advanced productive forces, and the
scientific, technical and humanitarian intelligentsia.[19]

Thus the radical wing of official reformism has finally come to the
conclusion, as a result of two years of perestroika, that the changes
cannot be completed without the support of specific social interests.
However, the strategy proposed by this current – to mobilize the
modernizing intermediate strata – in no way solves the problem of finding a mass base for the transformations. Only if the real collaboration of
the intermediate and lower strata can be secured within the framework
of a radical, reformist project will it be possible to forge a powerful
social bloc capable of opposing the bureaucracy. What is needed for this
is not a boost to the social egoism of the 'advanced' (and essentially the
most prosperous) social groups but, on the contrary, a struggle to gain
their utmost solidarity with the wider masses. Such a broad platform is
entirely possible. Within it are included political democratization, the
development of industrial and local self-management, the maintenance
of social provision, a redistributive, anti-bureaucratic policy under
democratic control from below, defence of the interests of the consumer,
and a gradual reorientation of the economy, taking into account ecological
and humanitarian factors, towards the satisfaction of human need.

Socialist democracy must also provide the individual with social and
legal guarantees. It is important to change economic priorities in such a
way that people really become the major goal. Decision-making must be
decentralized and democratic procedures must be created which are
incompatible with both bureaucratic and technocratic approaches to
administration. Finally, the half-measures which are convenient for the
bureaucracy must be replaced with new, consistent, democratic legislation. It is not a question of choosing between plan and market (in any
modern society there are both). The genuine choice today is between a
developing civil society and bureaucracy. Upon which forces gain the
upper hand depends the future of socialism in our country and, perhaps,
the whole world.

Notes

This piece first appeared, in a shorter version, in *New Left Review* 169, May–June 1988.

1. See the very candid interview with Nikolai Shmelev in *Knizhnoe Obozrenie*, no. 1,
1988.
2. *Literaturnaya Gazeta*, 10 February 1988.
3. At this time the only exceptions were the brothers Roy and Zhores Medvedev, who

always emphasized the connection between detente and human rights. It should be said that, in general, the majority of dissidents did not consider that 'the Marxist Medvedevs' belonged to the movement. They continually attacked them, bringing all possible accusations against them right up to 'collaborating with state security'.

4. This programme was formulated in the samizdat journal *Sotsialism i Budushchee* ('Socialism and the Future') (*Levyi Povorot*) nos. 3–4, 1980.

5. Typically, the research of Academician Tatyana Zaslavskaya, which proved that the management of the Soviet economy was steadily deterioriating, aroused a considerable echo.

6. During this time the following anecdote was popular in Moscow: A person is reading a lengthy newspaper obituary and a neighbour on the Metro asks: 'Already?' The reader replies: 'Not yet'.

7. See my article 'The Intelligentsia and the Changes', *New Left Review* 164, 1987, pp. 5–26.

8. M.S. Gorbachev, *Perestroika i Novoe Myshlenie* ('Perestroika and the New Thinking'), Moscow 1987, p. 60.

9. *Izvestiya*, 7 July 1987.

10. *Literaturnaya Gazeta*, 1 July 1987.

11. *Izvestiya*, 26 March 1987.

12. *Literaturnaya Gazeta*, 13 January 1988.

13. *Literaturnaya Gazeta*, 17 February 1988.

14. *Izvestiya*, 15 February 1988.

15. *Knizhnoe Obozrenie*, no. 1, 1988, p. 2.

16. *Literaturnaya Gazeta*, 17 February 1988.

17. Data taken from the research conducted jointly by the Central Economic-Mathematical Institute and *Literaturnaya Gazeta*. Material from the research was published in part in the FSOK bulletin *Levyi Povorot*, no. 5, 1988.

18. *Sotsialisticheskaya Industriya*, 5 January 1988.

19. *Novy Mir*, no. 11, 1987, p. 188.

16

From Class Obsessions to Dialogue: Detente and the Changing Political Culture of Eastern Europe

Milan Šimečka

What to the West looks like the ebb and flow of a dark threatening tide or an alternating pattern of Cold War and detente actually feels to us in the East like an alternating pattern of brutal and less brutal forms of political culture, and the ebb and flow of the internal frustrations of the system we inhabit. That is about the extent of our selfish insight into European and global issues. It is why we are incapable of taking the current East–West talks really seriously or contemplating them with any real hope. What we do know is that the most important questions are not being discussed – such as, for instance, what can be done to give us, the smaller nations of Eastern Europe, the freedom to decide our own future for ourselves, one for which we can bear personal responsibility. For this reason we are unable to identify with the problems of Europe's free nations, such as the crisis of the EEC, inflation, unemployment, agricultural surpluses and the importance of whether Conservative or Socialist governments will be elected. They all look such calm, unruffled waters to our eyes.

Here in the East, politics have traditionally been quite a lethal occupation. The sort of crises to which we have been accustomed here were capable of casting an entire nation into a state of economic despair (for example, Poland), creating such social and political apathy that the very meaning of the nation's existence was jeopardized (for example, Czechoslovakia) or giving rise to grotesque manifestations of nepotism (for example, Romania). It is all the more striking if one turns one's gaze to the Soviet Union. Soviet historians are still unable to account for the 25 million people in 1923 or 46 million in 1946 who in 'normal' circumstances would have survived and whose offspring would be living there now. Our insight into European issues is tragically coloured in this way.

351

We feel, with no particular pride, that the West has nothing that competes with us in this respect.

The conviction has taken root in our consciousness that the only real crisis over the past forty years has been the crisis of Eastern Europe. It is this crisis which is responsible for the East–West confrontation which has occasionally worked itself up to the brink of war – as happened in Berlin in 1953 – or merely dragged on in the trenches of dreary propaganda warfare. This 'Eastern crisis' of ours was built into the system foisted on us, and from the outset was inherent in its ideology and political culture. This is why we believe that for the past decades the West has not been under threat from the violent export of revolution; the only threat came from the frustrations created by the system's endemic crises – frustrations which governed the ebb and flow of the Cold War. During the periods of hopeful changes detente was an inevitable component of foreign relations, whereas in times of inertia and ideological stagnation a cooling of East–West relations was always bound to occur.

This egocentric viewpoint (one which I also adopt when assessing the changes of detente) does not necessarily regard the West as only a passive deflector and neutralizer of Eastern frustrations. I am aware of the part played by the West in helping us to cope with the dangerous situations we have experienced over the past forty years. I quite simply feel a certain regret that I am incapable of viewing this issue with Western eyes, since I am one of the 'shaken' (as the Czech philosopher Jan Patocka once called us), which means that I have been marked willy-nilly by my experience here in the East and by what I once enthusiastically embraced as my nation's fate. No doubt my reflections on it occasionally display a kind of preposterous pride in the fact that our particular *theatrum mundi* was the setting for more authentic and tragic political dramas than elsewhere; that history here was in some way more challenging; that it is not so many years ago that we believed in certain ideals which were capable of turning even brothers into enemies for life. It is a degenerate sort of pride, of course, and the only reasonable excuse we have for it is that the historical experience of Eastern Europe might still serve as a lesson to the rest of the world.

Crude Beginnings

Two days before Christmas 1953, the former Politburo member and KGB chief, Lavrentiy Beria, was executed in Moscow. He was shot as an English spy. (How is it actually done? Does the condemned person stand with bound eyes before a firing squad? Or does it happen as described by Arthur Koestler in *Darkness at Noon*: the victim being led off by the executioner to some vault where all he hears is the creak of a leather holster behind him?) Stalin was dead, but the political culture of high treason and espionage lived on. Later still, Imre Nagy and other leaders of the Hungarian uprising were to be executed as spies and traitors. Even in Czechoslovakia people were being executed for 'espionage, high treason and oppositional intrigue'.

On 13 September 1964, the Politburo members informed Khrushchev that they were all ranged against him and that it would be better if he took voluntary retirement. Being intimately acquainted with the political culture of inner party struggles, Khrushchev did not resist. He was dismissed from his post and became a pensioner. According to Roy Medvedev, when he got home he said: 'Well, that's it. I'm retired now. Perhaps the most important thing I did was this – that they were able to get rid of me simply by voting, whereas Stalin would have had them all arrested' (*Khrushchev*, Oxford 1982, p. 245). Khrushchev was the first high-ranking Soviet leader in forty years to have been dismissed from his post on the basis of a majority vote in the highest organ of power without being at the same time pilloried and consigned to the scrapheap of history.

When Alexander Dubček was taken off to Moscow in 1968 after the invasion of Czechoslovakia, Brezhnev is supposed to have asked him what he expected his fate would be. Dubček apparently replied that he was expecting to be shot. At this Brezhnev took umbrage and rebuked Dubček for treating him as a barbarian. There's progress for you! It took fifty years for the lumbering political culture of the proletarian revolution to realize that people who in Soviet eyes objectively threatened the party's monopoly of power did not necessarily have to be shot out of hand.

The Soviet Union's barbarous political culture was undoubtedly a psychological barrier against which all the old attempts at East–West dialogue shattered. What sort of confidence could the East inspire with its offers of 'peaceful coexistence' when those who voiced them could not even guarantee to stay alive back home, let alone stay in office? What sort of assurances could Soviet leaders offer about eventual agreements if, from the moment they entered high office, they could not be sure of their own survival? None the less, my view is that since the end of the crude period of Soviet political culture – since the mid fifties, in other words – the West's suspicion of Soviet offers was not always entirely justified. Irrespective of the personalities involved, by then there were certain factors in Soviet foreign policy which could be relied on. Above all there was the desire to preserve the status quo in Europe and maintain good relations with certain of their neighbours, such as Finland

and Iran. Other factors included respecting Austrian neutrality and keeping on good terms with India. Unhappily, the Soviet political culture of those days was totally in the grip of an ideologically loaded language which seriously impeded the achievement of the sort of dialogue which would do something other than shore up the military blocs.

Time and again I would find myself wondering whether, in the period of elation following Stalin's death, the West had had an opportunity to influence the evolution of the USSR's political culture in favour of greater willingness to co-operate in politically neutral fields, such as trade, the exchange of scientific and technical information, and so on. The point is whether a more vigorous policy on the part of the West could have fostered a sense of shared responsibility and strengthened to some extent the hopeful features of Soviet internal developments at the beginning of the sixties. One thing is certain: positive achievements in that respect were largely responsible for the more moderate domestic and foreign policies of the East. It would be difficult to assume however, that outside influence would have had the effect of ridding Soviet political culture of that particular sense of permanent threat from within and without, of continuing encirclement, its feeling that the sacred legacy of the Revolution was somehow in jeopardy. And even though Soviet propaganda invariably projected an image of steadfastness, indestructibility, might and strength, one could always sense behind the façade a feeling of inferiority and lack of self-assurance. I rather fancy that it was something left over in Russia from the Revolution, rather like the after-effects of a neglected bout of flu.

It is a well-known fact that the Bolshevik takeover of power was almost unbelievably trouble-free: the sheer theatricality of the storming of the Winter Palace is reminiscent of the attack on the Bastille. The gradual disintegration of society had previously so weakened the old authorities that they virtually fell apart of their own accord. What emerges from accounts of the discussions within the top party leadership of those days is that this development had taken the Bolsheviks as much by surprise as anyone else and sowed a certain degree of confusion in their ranks. The overwhelming majority of the revolutionaries were unprepared for a victorious revolution in Russia and had no wish at all for the country to remain isolated, faced with the task of preserving revolutionary power and starting to build socialism on its own. Lenin, Trotsky, Bukharin and others always counted on Russia being the third or fourth country in Europe to start on the road to socialism, following in the wake of Germany, France, England, and others. What happened subsequently consisted entirely of improvisation and stopgap measures which were not hailed as pioneering achievements until much later. It was precisely such stopgap measures that gave rise to the Soviet political culture which was to survive right up to the 1950s and 1960s. As a result of the relative isolation of the country, Jacobin terror was to take root as a permanent feature of the political culture. (I am not at all sure that Trotsky's obsessive assertion that the terror of the thirties was Thermidorian stands up to historical scrutiny.)

The Bolsheviks held on to power for want of any alternative. At the end of the Civil War, the only people to whom they could possibly have handed over power were their archenemies who, meanwhile, had even been joined by some of their former allies. This vital need to hold on to power at all costs formed the basis of Soviet political culture and shifted it in the direction of the sort of barbarism which could not be concealed behind such euphemisms as the 'dictatorship of the proletariat'. What had once been a diminutive party gradually swelled with the huge influx of members of the state bureaucracy and economic administration who were thereafter to regard the preservation of power as their supreme class interest. And this class interest, as we are all aware, shored itself up by means of a maniacal system that resulted in social stagnation. From then on, the only threat was external. I am convinced that subsequently what counted most in confrontations with the outside world were not the old illusions about world revolution but chiefly the effort not to show any sign of weakness that might open the way to outside subversion.

Self-perpetuating Power

Even though we were only a backwater compared to the Soviet Union, the example of Czechoslovakia provides quite a good illustration of how a political culture committed entirely to perpetuating the established power can come into being. The rule that communists take power once and for all, a rule derived from the Russian Revolution, coloured all the strategic considerations of the Communist Party of Czechoslovakia even before February 1948. Even though the party had taken part in the regular democratic parliamentary process during the pre-war years and had countenanced the formation of a whole series of coalition govern-ments, it never regarded itself as an ordinary political party dependent on the voters' favour. It openly spoke of itself as a 'party of a new type', but the civil parties never fully appreciated what this implied in the battle for power, depending instead on traditional parliamentary prac-tice. By now, however, it is all too obvious that even meticulous study of the *History of the CPSU(b)* would not have helped them very much.

Inspired by the glowing picture of Soviet experience purveyed by the distorting mirror of propaganda, the East European Communist parties took on board the utopian notion that merely by holding on to power and using the means of the state, everything was possible: a backward country could be transformed into an industrialized one, a poor land into a rich one, a class society into a classless one, a con man and thief into a conscientious citizen and a layabout into a workhorse. This misconception was to plague the political culture of Eastern Europe, wreaking havoc everywhere. It was no doubt partly due to its influence that even large numbers of intellectuals endorsed the utopian aim of radically restructuring the whole of society, even though they ought to have realized by then that things were not quite so simple. However, the majority made no objection to the new political culture which was getting rid of everything that was 'old-fashioned'.

At the age of twenty, I found nothing particularly dangerous in the idea that all the instruments of the state (including coercion) had to be used to further communism's noble goals; on the contrary, it seemed quite logical to me. The visionaries in power obviously knew better than ordinary people what was best for society as a whole. By assuming total power and by taking the correct decisions, the supreme organs of the revolutionary vanguard could transform a desert into a flowering garden. Many politicians continue to be ensnared by this illusion, even though it has been clearly demonstrated that 'correct' coercive measures in society always degenerate and result in nothing but confusion and barren violence. Even though this was obvious in Czechoslovakia after the very first years of totalitarian rule, the illusion took root in the political culture anyway. The new political culture clung like a limpet to the postulate that no disaster or failure was ever so irredeemable as to justify handing over power to anyone else.

Without a doubt, the political culture of self-perpetuating power was prepared, up to a point, to accept certain purely technical measures and sheer pragmatism in the exercise of power. The utopian element became so prominent because right at the outset it was dignified and given a cultivated gloss through art, literature and propaganda and projected in this form at the public at home and abroad. The less refined methods of coercion were kept hidden in the cellars of power. There the grimy labourers of repression toiled away, partly under the spell of the fanatical notion that someone had to carry out filthy and thankless tasks in pursuit of communism's noble goals. It took no more than five years to achieve the virtual subjugation of the entire Czechoslovak population and put everyone on the state's payroll. In purely technical terms it was no mean achievement, one that could be carried out only in a country like ours that had been ordered and structured since Austro–Hungarian days, and whose population was well administered, disciplined, cultured and literate. What took place here was a revolution of typewritten decrees, which was no less ruthless for all that.

There was virtually no resistance to these changes. For this reason I have always wondered, over these past thirty years, why it was that the violence used and the crudeness of the political culture far exceeded what was 'necessary'? (Though may I be forgiven for posing what is in essence an immoral question.) Why were the futures of millions of people shattered? Why were people sent to prison camps in their droves? Why did defenceless and often only imaginary enemies of the regime face possible death sentences in show trials, when it was patently obvious that most people were willing to assist the strange social experiment with their work and talent, or at least earn an honest living in some socially beneficial employment? I have not the least doubt that in every revolution and every violent takeover of power, violence merely continues as the most expedient way of governing. However, the main cause of such violence is the maniacal yearning for permanence, irreversibility and self-perpetuation which is built into the political culture.

And that is one reason why the communists – perhaps unwittingly, perhaps deliberately – created situations which ruled out all chances of reconciliation, or of consensus with the broad mass of the population. They seem to have been in some kind of trance in which they spread evil and drew as many people as possible into their demonic circle so as to prevent them ever having any means of retreat, to implicate them as much as possible and give them a sense of shared guilt. This was the mechanism used to assemble the 'new class' of which Djilas writes. What held them together was not just the sharing of power, privilege and material benefits, but above all an awareness of sharing the 'original sin', as well as the thought of their eventual fall from grace or of the revenge that others might eventually wreak. This was one of the reasons for the disastrous outcome of the Prague Spring. The 'normalizing' regime made ingenious use of the 'original-sin' technique, by involving more and more people in its immoral doings with a view to preventing them ever receiving absolution. Every change in the East European countries is hampered by this phenomenon, and it is bound to cause the Gorbachevites headaches too.

Changes

The political culture thus created in Eastern Europe was quite a reliable way of preserving the established order for several long decades, despite the shock waves that we registered here from time to time. From the beginning of the sixties, however, East European political culture lost its gruesome aspects. In other words, politics ceased to be such a lethal business. So long as establishment members steered clear of embezzle-ment or the crassest stupidities, they enjoyed the prospect of guaranteed careers well into old age. The dramatic unmasking of traitors was a thing of the past, or at any rate did not end in execution. When the political culture is moderated in this way, it enables the expression of alternatives among the middle-ranking officials or within the top party leadership. Fear no longer paralyses thinking to the same degree, and groups of reformists can start to emerge within the ruling party.

Frequently this seems like a process of people 'seeing the light' and rethinking their ideas. Sometimes it is, but most of the time it is an act of self-preservation: the reformers reacting in crisis periods to an imminent collapse of the entire system and destruction of the established order. These were the motives of the successive reform attempts in Hungary and Poland, and finally in Czechoslovakia in 1968. Of course, I am not trying to say that the reformists' motives in promoting change were never anything but selfish (as in the case of Gomulka, for instance). It always included somewhere the vision of a 'better' socialism, as well as a genuine appreciation of society's needs, a desire for reconciliation, national ambition, and so on. Dubček, for example, sincerely believed in the possibility of harmonizing the interests of the majority of the people with the interests of the party.

It was changes in the political culture which also enabled the rise of Gorbachev and paved the way for the USSR's present planned reforms. In a political culture of the earlier type, Gorbachev would not have stood the slightest chance. There would have been no scope for elaborating a reform programme, let alone manoeuvring with it to the heights of political power. It is extremely important that in the changed political climate, Gorbachev arrived at the summit of power in what was an incredibly civilized manner by East European standards. In this respect, Gorbachev has an enormous moral advantage over Kádár, Jaruzelski or Husák, who came to power in the wake of national dis-asters and in ways which would normally cause qualms of conscience (if politicians possessed such a thing).

The beneficial influence of the milder political climate which set in, paradoxically enough, during the Brezhnev era of stagnation and inertia also helped preparations for the explosion of liberalization – or glasnost, if you like – in Soviet culture, journalism and public life. By now it is clear that the suddenness of the phenomenon was actually an optical illusion, that explosive material had been accumulating for years in Soviet society and the changes in the leadership merely served as a detonator. The people who helped to assemble the explosives are nowa-days referred to in the Soviet Union as 'sixties-ites', this roughly denotes people whose ideas were formed in the 1960s during that celebrated initial 'thaw' which formed their present attitudes. They subsequently found themselves in isolation, particularly in the seventies, silenced by the primitive political culture of the Brezhnev leadership. However, although they were certainly marginalized, they were not annihilated as they would have been under Stalin. These people found ways to survive according to hallowed Soviet tradition. Some of them prospered, others went from one scandal to another. Some collaborated less, others rather more. Many emigrated in despair – yet another option previously unthinkable.

The 'sixties-ites' fall into two main groups: open dissidents and covert dissidents. So far, the present glasnost has accorded freedom of speech only to the latter, although names I knew from the dissent of the sixties and seventies are already beginning to crop up in the Soviet press. And although relations between the open dissidents at home and abroad and the glasnost-conscious 'perestroika intelligentsia' are still far from easy, it requires very little progress in the present political climate to turn these relations into a meaningful dialogue. Admittedly, in its 'bitter' and 'painful' search after the truth, Soviet culture would make it much easier on itself if just ten, say, of the best books of Soviet dissent were to be published in the home country, because the facts are there for all to read, and have been for a long time. The trouble is that there is now a tradition here in the East that many people fail to value truth until they have found it after bitter search: it is too easy to pop round to the library and find it in a book.

Gorbachev himself belongs to the same generation as those 'sixties-ites', but he operates in a far riskier field than Soviet intellectuals do. If he really is as intelligent and perceptive as his Western interlocutors suggest, then it is unlikely that his private ideas differ greatly from the mainstream of reformist thinking as developed in Hungary, Poland and Prague Spring Czechoslovakia. They are ideas I can readily imagine, since I once shared them. Unlike Gorbachev, though, the feeling I have as I write these lines, for instance, is one of enjoying the luxury to let my mind wander at will. Indeed, I find it hard to imagine the heartbreaking task Gorbachev had during his holidays when he was writing his celebratory speech to mark the seventieth anniversary of the Russian Revolution. 'Blast! what am I going to say about Stalin? How far can I go in my criticism of the Brezhnev period, seeing that there are still so many Brezhnevites around? How should I put it so as not to cause a revolt?' And to have to write it aware of the fact that throughout the land every single word will be turned over and over again like a new coin, and that thousands of Kremlinologists in the West are waiting to pounce on these coins, in order to weigh them and assess their worth, is by no means an enviable task!

Soviet political culture confronts its Western counterpart on unequal terms. In the dialogue between them, the Western side only ever takes into account those things that are stated explicitly. The trouble is that we in the East always have two replies to the same question – one public, one private. In such a situation discussions are not easy: there is no way of recording the concealed, private element in the minutes. Within the bizarre political culture of the East there is no lack of awareness of the true state of the world; nor is this awareness confined to the intellectuals. On the contrary, it is widespread – 'popular' in the true sense of the word – and is also shared by a large proportion of the ruling elite. Unfortunately, the 'law of conservation of power' decrees a game of blind man's buff: in spite of our blindfolds we are able to see how things are, but we pretend to see nothing. This state of split thinking, which is schizophrenic in many ways, affects everyone who is engaged in any sort of public activity, however minor. The sole exceptions are those blinkered individuals who deliberately close their minds lest they lapse into the sin of doubt.

This schizophrenic state of mind has always existed here, and it will take more than glasnost to eradicate it. The coexistence of lies and licensed truth in one and the same brain and one and the same language is a principal feature of our political culture. The West is unacquainted with such schizophrenia, so that when Western journalists talk with their Soviet colleagues or interview Soviet leaders it is sometimes as if they are talking to simpletons. I have often watched such interviews on television and always my heart goes out to the poor Soviet participant. Soviet history is one ghastly pitfall after another, so that when someone from the West draws the conversation round to such a trap the interviewee has the impression that they are being pushed into it out of sheer spitefulness. The Soviet leader thinks to himself: why are they trying to get me to talk about something so dangerous and risky when they know the answers already and have the opportunity to read them in a hundred books?

The invasion of Czechoslovakia in 1968 is just such a pitfall. When asked straight out why twenty years ago they suppressed in Czechoslovakia the very things they themselves are doing now, Soviet leaders will sidestep the question with a quip. During Gorbachev's visit to Prague, they asked a Soviet spokesman what was the difference between the Prague Spring and perestroika. 'Twenty years', was his glib reply. Gorbachev himself was teetering between truth and lies like a regular tightrope walker. The only thing that amuses me about this whole comedy by now is the theoretical question of the relation between an admission of the truth and the social reality. Is it really conceivable that a single admission of error could have the power to pull the ground from under the feet of the entire normalizing establishment and throw the country into confusion and anarchy, as everyone seems to think? We all know the truth of the matter anyway. Could it really be that by removing our mental block it would turn the whole country upside down? Surely it is nonsense to think of the entire nation as if it were a patient on a psychoanalyst's couch?

In the final analysis, there is a point at which all changes in the political culture find themselves up against a locked door in political thinking and reality. It is a barrier which the imperative of permanence – the system's trumpeted timelessness: its radiant tomorrows – is loth to traverse. None the less, we are all aware that the guarantee of radiant tomorrows is no more than a euphemistic extrapolation of the guaranteed survival of the established order. It is a guarantee that the power of individuals and entire *nomenklaturas* ends only with their biological demise, as we are able to witness. Popper puts it in a nutshell when he says that the only difference between democracy and dictatorship is the fact that in dictatorships there is no way of getting rid of bad governments in a normal manner. This is a very telling simplification because it shows precisely where the ceiling for developments in the political culture of Eastern Europe is fixed.

A political culture which once abandoned palace revolutions and unbridled power struggles is now a prisoner of its own yearnings for stability and permanence. And, as has been demonstrated time and again, this makes it impossible for the system to solve its crises as they arise, and it has to wait either for the crises to come to a head or for the old ruler to fall down dead. Eastern Europe desperately needs even just a touch of plurality in its political culture, but the question is how to reconcile fire and water, how to introduce pluralism without jeopardizing the established order? It looks as if this will be the cardinal issue facing the Gorbachev generation, far outweighing in importance all the economic reforms put together. Even if they were to go only halfway towards solving this problem, earlier periods of detente would become no more than matters of academic interest to historians.

The Present Changes and Detente

The argument continues over whether the Soviet Union's present readiness for detente and its unprecedented desire for co-operation – and its obvious concessions, particularly in the sphere of arms control – are the outcome of the USA's firm stand, or are chiefly the result of internal changes in the USSR. The truth of the matter is not easy to determine, because both phenomena happened to occur simultaneously. Faced with such a puzzle, the conclusions people draw depend on their own particular sympathies. In any case, those involved in the debate are concerned not so much with the truth of the matter as with national prestige. Understandably, the Americans ascribe their success to having negotiated from a position of strength, whereas the Soviets are by nature incapable of admitting that they might have succumbed to pressure. The insight I have gained from my historical experience of this area makes me a partisan of the view that internal changes within the Soviet Union constituted the chief reason for the dramatic changes in the international climate. I believe, quite simply, that if Brezhnev's health had held out for four more years there would be neither detente nor the prospect of the first nuclear disarmament ever.

Since we remember much more clearly than people in the West how things used to be, we are much more aware of the sort of ideological and psychological inhibitions that Soviet politicians had to overcome before Gorbachev could accept the USA's Zero Option. After all, commentators on this side had just been earning themselves fat salaries to malign it. In its relations with the West, the political culture has been transformed in a way never before known. The very idea of a NATO officer setting foot on Soviet territory for verification purposes, let alone in restricted zones, would have been unthinkable even five years ago. Quite simply, the present phase of detente, and particularly the Soviet approach to the process of relaxation, is incomparable to any we have ever seen in the past. It truly needed the 'quantum leap' in Soviet attitudes which currently goes under the name of 'New Thinking'.

This 'New Thinking' would have Marx turning in his grave, not to mention Stalin or Brezhnev. Gorbachev has abolished the class-based interpretation of the world more or less without any great theoretical rumpus, East or West. He has placed the interests of the human species above those of the working class, and justified this on the grounds that nuclear weapons do not discriminate between classes. (Not that ordinary bombs in the last war were any more discriminate.) What he has done is to jettison the dogma which, for decades, had hampered the Soviet Union in its dealings with the rest of the world. Although it had not been a motive for aggression as such, it had come in very handy for justifications *ex post facto*. This was still true in the case of Czechoslovakia in 1968, when we were treated to a spate of class-based arguments. By now Gorbachev has buried a great number of the old principles without troubling to raise any memorials. In this respect the new leader differs radically from Khrushchev, who considered it his duty to refute old dogmas theoretically before adopting new ones.

None of this was the product of outside pressure – it was largely due to the realization that society was riddled with symptoms of economic, political and moral crisis. Recognition of the even more glaring crises in the smaller states of Eastern Europe no doubt helped the process along. The golden rule that all difficulties in Eastern Europe are the work of enemy agents, and that working-class demonstrations are the work of provocateurs and hooligan elements, has been abandoned. At long last, policies based on rational analysis – in so far as this is conceivable in our system – have taken root in the political culture.

Detailed examination of the ebb and flow of detente has always shown that the phenomenon is dependent on internal conditions in the Soviet Union. Detente has only ever achieved tangible results in periods of attempted reform – that is, under Khrushchev and Gorbachev. I doubt very much that the seventies can be regarded as a period of detente at all. However, I freely admit that my attitude is strongly coloured by my experience of 1968. I remember how all those disarmament talks in the seventies – and even Helsinki itself – looked very dubious dealing to us, or like a party at the expense of the Eastern European countries, something we paid for in the currency of imprisonment, decline and stagnation.

This was not entirely true, of course, and as it turned out, what seemed no more than agreements on paper about human rights were, amazingly enough, to prove instrumental in achieving certain improvements. The third basket at Helsinki was originally intended as the price the Soviet Union had to pay for recognition of the status quo in Europe. The Soviet Union was only too happy to pay it, since our political culture contained thousands of artfully contrived methods for skirting human-rights obligations. Indeed, in Czechoslovakia the immediate post-Helsinki period was a time of the worst persecutions. A deaf ear was turned to any references to the Helsinki Final Act and, as I know from personal experience, any talk of Helsinki in those days would send police officers into fits of laughter.

That all assumes a different aspect, however, if looked at in longer perspective. Over these past years – which, alas, Czechoslovak culture will never regain – much has changed. Concepts have emerged which were previously unknown. These concepts undoubtedly penetrated the reform thinking then coming to fruition in the Soviet Union. If nothing else, by confirming the outcome of World War II Helsinki served to rid the Soviet Union of its old obsessions about external threats, and this subsequently had a positive effect on its attitude to detente.

The various agreements that were confirmed by treaty during the seventies mostly benefited the two superpowers. The countries of Central and Eastern Europe went on much the same as before, except that some of them were even worse off. Probably only the Hungarians managed to derive any benefit from the new climate – the Poles only ran up debts. But during that period, Soviet political culture remained virtually unchanged. As a result, this superficial detente quickly caved in after the invasion of Afghanistan and the Polish crisis. In those situations, the Soviet leadership acted according to old stereotypes and without any concern for detente and Western public opinion – not even for the opinion of the Western Communist parties. Such stereotyped thinking is illustrated perfectly in Brezhnev's talks with Waldeck-Rochet: the Soviets were always aware that there was more than one way of solving a crisis, but they invariably opted for the most brutal solution as the most effective, and relied on the fact that after a while the ripples would die down and talks with the West resume as the only alternative.

The conclusion to be drawn from all this is that the second period of detente did not truly begin until recently – not, however, because Gorbachev managed, in a short space of time, to strew the world with disarmament proposals and present it with his vision of a future without nuclear weapons. No, the new detente is emerging because there has been a major shift in the Soviet Union's attitude to the world and its own role within it. At the same time we are seeing the creation of a political culture capable of conducting a wider and more meaningful dialogue. In the new climate traditional European concepts are being reconciled semantically, so that eventually not even the concepts of freedom and democracy need mean something completely different in East and West. Because of our historical vantage point, we have a heightened awareness of this fundamental shift. Viewed from the West, the Soviet perestroika does not necessarily appear so revolutionary, since the totalitarian administration of society is still in place. In historical terms it is certainly intended as a revolution and to someone like myself, accustomed to our own tedious eventlessness, it even looks like one sometimes.

There has certainly been a revolutionary change in the thinking of Soviet society and its self-image. I remember how dreadful it was to be confronted by certain Soviet intellectual stereotypes. The feeling of amazement and despair which they aroused was like coming up against a high stone wall. As one looked on helplessly at the public display of lies whose transparency was evident to the smallest child, one gradually lost all faith in reason. It would be almost impossible to believe without experiencing it at first hand. It would be hard to credit the destructive effect it can have on people's minds and its baleful influence on our entire nation. On the whole, therefore, I can understand the revolutionary Soviet film-maker Elem Klimov when he said in an interview with *Der Spiegel* that it all seemed to him like a dream.

Naturally, I often discuss with friends the possibility of this revolution taking a nose dive. My arguments against scepticism derive from the fact that this is the first authentic liberalization of 'existing socialism' that cannot be suppressed from outside, as happened everywhere else. So far, no attempt at liberalization has ever lost a domestic contest. I know how things were here: had it not been for outside interference, a return to the old order would have been unthinkable. I do not entertain any illusions, however, about those inner forces which are working against perestroika. Above all, I have in mind the inertia of an enormous nation. That is something we can feel even from this distance.

I must admit that I am rather irritated by the sort of scepticism voiced by those whose obsession with the system causes them to repeat *ad nauseam* that the system remains intact and perestroika could even reinforce it in the long run. I would ask all those who think along these lines how *they* conceive of a change of system in the Soviet Union. Lacking our 'lived experience', they lose sight of historical reality. It is not that I am incapable of taking into account what the Soviet Union owes to Europe and its different nations, not to mention its debt to Czechoslovakia. However, it is a well-known fact that debts of history are never paid off in one go. There is just no other way of getting down to the job but what is happening now. It is first of all necessary to get rid of the absurd, artificial ways of thinking which have so far held the Soviet Union in their iron grip. Furthermore, it is important for that country to free itself gradually from its historical burden and start to come to terms with its past: the famine, the utopian experiments, the Gulag, and the fanaticism which devalued human life. And the rest of the world should have some understanding for this perestroika. One can hardly expect the Soviets, at this stage in their history, to start translating the American Constitution as the basis for a fresh start. However, if thinking continues to develop and mature along present lines, it cannot be long before the realization hits them that they are not in fact the last innocent nation in Europe, one which has only ever acted in self-defence.

With half of their minds, people here resist the thought that the habits created by the existing system are not really ingrained and are inclined to think that it is merely an unnatural skin which will fall away at the first contact with living reality. With the other half, however, they are aware that forty years of history constitute a burden which crushes everything beneath it, including human nature. For ages now I myself have been trying desperately to find someone among my fellow-citizens who does not consider it daft to think and express oneself freely. A hundred years ago, ordinary Czechs in the Habsburg monarchy probably had difficulty imagining the idea of electing their local council by voting for one single candidate. Nowadays, I overhear people asking what is the point of the proposed reform of the voting system, seeing how hard it is to find anyone ready to accept a post of responsibility. The regime that suppressed virtually every freedom liberated the people in one respect, however: it freed them from responsibility. At first it was the declared ambition to educate every servant-girl to be able to hold government office; nowadays, however, servant-girls have not the faintest desire to do so.

Doubts continue to be expressed about the sincerity of present Soviet efforts in favour of detente and about the trustworthiness of Soviet proposals. Sincerity in politics is something that is very hard to assess – always supposing it has a place there at all. When I recall how sincerely Brezhnev hugged and kissed Dubček in Bratislava just two months before the invasion. . . . As for the trustworthiness of Soviet initiatives, this should be measured against the degree to which they are anchored in society. When one looks at them in this way, one has to conclude that they are. I even fancy that the policy of peaceful coexistence as formulated by the post-Stalin leadership was intended seriously and was based on the country's internal need for peace and for time to reform. What emerged clearly from the Cuban crisis was that the Soviets had no intention of staking everything they had, above all their existence, on some possible superpower advantage.

Moreover, I have the feeling that from about 1956 onwards, talk of a Soviet threat had no real basis. In the immediate post-war years, the façade of peace slogans concealed a covert acceptance of the possibility of East–West military conflict. At that time, to speculate on conflict was still consistent with the Soviet image of the world as being somehow pregnant with the final worldwide victory of socialism. Admittedly, such an attitude was by then extremely unrealistic, but by inflating the significance of such phenomena as the decolonization of the Third World they had something, at least, to support their ideological vision. However, with the death of Stalin misgivings began to take root in the Soviet leadership concerning a global solution to the class struggle between the capitalist world and the world of socialism, as it was then called. It was obvious from the practical measures of the Soviet leadership that it was concentrating entirely on strengthening 'existing socialism' while deep down it no longer believed in worldwide implantation of socialist 'achievements'. Western Europe and other developed industrialized countries maintained their security far more effectively by means of their achievements in the economic, scientific, technical and social spheres than by building up their armed forces and creating military blocs. This trend was already obvious by the sixties, and everything that happened subsequently in the arms field was no more than an infantile balancing act. If humanity ever manages to survive these war games unscathed, that period will be looked back on with shame for the next hundred years.

In view of the Soviet Union's subsequent acknowledgement of its severe difficulties in coping with all contemporary challenges and its adoption of policies geared to catching up on the West's lead in terms of civilization, all ideas of action to achieve the salvation of the world proletariat, let alone predatory aggression, were ruled out. One does not slaughter a milch cow. The important thing is that this awareness evolved within the Soviet Union and was not imposed from outside – that it gradually matured, albeit belatedly and with difficulty. It went on to influence the political culture in its relations with the West. Of course East–West relations are still fraught with misunderstandings – after all, it is an encounter between two planes of different heights – but I still think that a higher position provides a better view of things, and from such a vantage point the West can try to grasp some of the more baffling phenomena.

There is obviously a strong temptation to force the Soviet side into admitting explicitly that the Revolution and everything that happened afterwards was a historic error, but I do not see what useful purpose this would serve. It is an extremely risky approach. One can hardly impose, on several generations who strove desperately to do something sensible with the legacy of the Revolution, the destructive idea that everything they did was in vain. In the event of a profound identity crisis, all the suffering which the nations of the Soviet Union had accumulated over the years could be turned against the West, and this option is always present in the Soviet mind. In all events, that enormous country is bound to have problems over its identity. After all, everything so far has been based on an artificial history, and no one can predict how Soviet society will react when confronted with a true picture of its past.

I do not regard the specific talks on disarmament and other issues to be so very important in the present detente. What *is* important is that detente should influence the process of developments within Eastern Europe in favour of greater openness, that it should give Soviet society time enough to define its place in the contemporary world, free from ideological preconceptions. It will benefit Europe as a whole when the Soviet Union finally rids itself of its domestic frustrations and openly demonstrates how glasnost and democratic choice among freely articulated alternatives is benefiting its society.

Soviet political culture has changed more in the last few years than we are sometimes prepared to admit when our single-minded concern with the system blinkers our gaze. If the evolution within Soviet society continues along the lines of the main slogans of perestroika, it will change even more significantly. The various processes which have got under way in this closing period of the century have all served to revive time-honoured European values, loosen schizophrenic ideological inhibitions, and start to budge all those structures that seemed petrified for all time. This represents an opportunity for Europe as a whole. I can well imagine, though, all the things that need to be done if our wing of 'the European home' – a concept which has finally been given a seal of approval here in the East – is to become properly habitable. The list of alterations is so enormous that it scarcely bears thinking about. Is there an alternative? Yes – we could leave everything the way it is. But who finds that prospect appealing?

17

From Anti-nuclearism to a New Detente in the 1980s

Elisabeth Gerle

The Western European peace movements have often been described as primarily anti-nuclear movements. For some of them this has been true, especially for those emerging during the late seventies and early eighties, as well as for the earlier movements against the neutron bomb in the seventies. When 100,000 people demonstrated in Hamburg (June 1981), in connection with the Evangelical Church's Congress; when 500,000 marched against the nuclear threat in Rome, 350,000 in Bonn and 300,000 in London in October; 500,000 in Amsterdam in November and 100,000 in Paris the same year, the focus was definitely on resistance to nuclear weapons, especially the deployment of cruise missiles and Pershing II in the UK, the Netherlands, Belgium and the Federal Republic of Germany. This was also true for the peace marches initiated by the Scandinavian women. Thousands of Scandinavians walked from Copenhagen to Paris in July 1981 for a nuclear-free Europe. The next year they went to Moscow and Minsk with the message 'No to nuclear weapons East and West' artistically expressed with beautifully designed and embroidered banners and dresses in pink and all the colours of the rainbow. The next year they went to Washington.

The INF Treaty, signed by President Reagan and General Secretary Gorbachev at the Summit in Washington, DC on 8 December 1987, is an agreement to remove these nuclear weapons from Europe. Does this imply a decline or disappearance of the Western European peace movement? Political commentaries have for some years been talking about the growing silence from the Western European peace movements and the lack of huge street demonstrations against nuclear weapons. The only voices quoted from Western Europe after the Iceland Summit in the American mass media were those of Helmut Kohl and Margaret Thatcher, expressing deep anxieties about being left without the nuclear umbrella. The peace movements were said to be quiet.

The INF Treaty is in many respects a victory for the anti-nuclear movements in Europe, and celebrated as such. It is, however, too limited to be seen as anything more than a first step on a long road to nuclear disarmament. The question of what the peace movements will do after INF is in a sense already answered. Long before the INF Treaty was signed the anti-nuclear movements had broadened their agenda to encompass far more than anti-nuclearism. They had also gained an awareness of the fact that the nuclear threat is related to a deeper understanding of democracy and the cultural roots of militarism, human rights, the relationship between rich and poor countries in the world, and overall questions about the environment. Earlier established peace movements have had this broader approach to the issue of peace all along, trying to get rid of images necessary for the Cold War and seeking to raise consciousness about the roots of the military build-up in post-war Europe.

The evolving character of the Western European anti-nuclear movements is a result of the social learning process many of them went through after their emergence in the late seventies and early eighties. The fear of nuclear war in Europe was the starting point, a fear that became widespread after public expressions from Washington of support for limited nuclear wars, Europe as a nuclear theatre and the American president's description of the Soviet Union as an evil empire. This fear was crystallized by the proposal to deploy cruise missiles and Pershing II in Belgium, Italy, the Netherlands, the UK and the FRG. Ordinary citizens without earlier contact with established peace organizations, now facing the prospect of becoming close neighbours to a military base with nuclear weapons, decided that traditional descriptions of security connected with nuclear deterrence and alliance politics constituted a myth that had to be challenged. Instead of increased security, people living near NATO military bases felt that they were being increasingly drawn into a risk zone and becoming prime targets in the event of an outbreak of war. An awareness of computer mistakes committed over the years, combined with the awareness that a Pershing missile could reach Moscow within three to nine minutes, fuelled this fear.

The Soviet response was to describe their new strategy as 'Launch on warning'; in effect, they would respond with nuclear forces immediately if their computers signalled a nuclear attack from the West. The deployment of nuclear missiles in the German Democratic Republic and in Czechoslovakia made many people feel that they were living in an invisible concentration camp. Their lives and their future were in the hands of two distant superpowers, who had assumed the right to decide about life and death in an apocalyptic scenario. During these years President Reagan was more influenced by right-wing fundamentalists who were expecting our time to be the last one, and almost seemed to be looking forward to Armageddon as the last struggle against evil.

Democracy in the Nuclear Age

The political strategy of the peace movement in Western Europe during these years was to create mass public opposition to nuclearism through the provision of information. The aim was to raise public consciousness about the threat of nuclear weapons and about the effects of nuclear war, even so-called limited ones, as a way to force politicians and decision-makers in the democratic Western NATO countries to resist reliance on nuclear deterrence within the alliance. The underlying assumption was that threatening to use nuclear weapons is incompatible with basic democratic values. The Dutch campaign conducted by the Interchurch Council with the goal to 'Free the world from nuclear weapons. Let us start in Holland' was a very clear example of this political strategy, almost an echo of the earlier Dutch campaign centred on the slogan 'Stop the Neutron Bomb'. A mass public opposition to deployment of nuclear weapons in the Netherlands was expected to break through in the democratic, parliamentary process and radically change the government's participation within the NATO alliance through the adoption of a more sceptical, independent role on the issue of nuclear weapons.

This political strategy was able to create mass public opposition against nuclear weapons, but it was not able to reshape policy at the governmental level. It managed the streets, but not the ballots. It both won and lost at the same time. Winning public opinion was not equivalent to prevailing over militarization.

Polls in the Federal Republic of Germany, the Netherlands and the United Kingdom showed that more than two-thirds of the populations in these countries opposed deployment of Pershing II and cruise missiles on their territories. This fact did not, however, seem to affect the policies of those governments. The lack of flexibility of democratic governments and their disregard for an adverse mass public opinion was a shock to many who had faith in Western democracy. Foreign policy in NATO countries seemed to be conducted from Washington. The NATO alliance gave very little space for independent decisions or for smaller countries wanting to remain within NATO but opposing missile deployments. National sovereignty began to seem a myth not only in Eastern Europe but also in the West. Soviet troops had been used in Hungary in 1956 and Czechoslovakia in 1968 to prevent growing democratic movements as well as to stop the search for new economic models. In the Polish crisis of the 1980s, repeated Warsaw Pact manoeuvres close to the Polish borders were used as a reminder of the overwhelming forces available to suppress undesirable developments within Pact countries. Several times since World War II the ugly face of Soviet intervention had shown itself in Eastern Europe. The lack of freedom and national sovereignty in Western Europe was different and its features were less obvious. The question about real democracy, however, turned out to be relevant for all of Europe, East, Central and West. Maps of Europe showing the military presence of the superpowers led peace movements to talk increasingly about Europe as an occupied continent.

The issue of peace was deeper than anti-nuclearism. It was not only a question of preventing deployment of new missiles or getting rid of one or another weapons system. Europe was deeply militarized quite apart from these controversial deployments. Indeed, since World War II it had been militarized in such a way that it had limited influence on its own deepest security. Decisions to use the nuclear weapons deployed on their own soil were out of the hands of European governments. The fact that the governments in Western Europe were democratically elected did not make any difference. The commitment and loyalty to a military alliance took precedence over the implied accountability towards the citizenry in democratic states.

Women's peace movements also pointed to the fact that decisions taken at the NATO Council generally denied the influence of national parliaments. The influence on this secret decision-making body in Brussels from parliaments and governments of the participating countries seemed minimal. There was a growing awareness that this body, together with its Warsaw Pact counterpart, might literally control the future destiny of Europe. Such a frightening realization gradually led peace-movement analysts to understand that 'challenging the existence of nuclear weapons necessarily involves challenging the structures within which political power is currently exercised.'[1] One further effect of this lack of parliamentary control in NATO decision-making was that women were even more absent than when these decisions were taken in governments and parliaments.

All these discoveries, experienced by broad factions of the peace movements in the West, created an awareness that East and West Europe had more than a cultural heritage in common. Limitations of democracy – especially as pertaining to self-determination and sovereignty in international relations, but also including issues of trade and cultural exchange – began to be appreciated as a problem shared by both East and West.

Freedom to Express Criticism

The question of human rights was also more complicated than mainstream media and political analysts implied. In both East and West people were imprisoned and persecuted for their critique of nuclearism. The reaction of governments had some similarities, even if the levels and styles of repression were very different. The Western democracies gave more space for expressing criticism, while in the socialist countries the reaction against dissent was open and brutal. In the German Democratic Republic and in Czechoslovakia open criticism of the deployment of nuclear weapons was almost impossible during the early eighties: the Lutheran Church in the GDR was, perhaps, the most visible exception, suggesting that limited criticism from certain sources was possible. But no Czech public demonstrations against nuclear weapons were allowed and the independent Hungarian peace group, Dialogue, faced severe difficulties in this period.

Freedom of expression was diminished in more subtle ways in several Western countries. People at the beginning of their careers were often afraid of participating in anti-nuclear demonstrations or expressing their opinions in an open form. For instance, in the Federal Republic of Germany the so-called *Berufsverbote* excluded so-called radicals from all forms of public employment. If such individuals were labelled communists, it might be difficult for them to overcome the stigma and pursue a successful professional career. The Federal Republic of Germany, especially, went through a period of deepening repression and militant reaction against citizens who were considered disloyal to the state or rejected its interpretation of security. Independent peace workers were often regarded as traitors by the governments in both parts of Europe. As a comic strip puts it: 'The governments in East and West have one thing in common. What? To discredit peace movements.' All these experiences deepened the understanding that human rights was a concern also in the Western European countries and that militarization in the West also caused serious violations of human rights, even if to a lesser and different degree. The idea that the West had 'Freedom' while the East supportered 'Peace' met a growing scepticism in the ranks of the Western European peace movements, which came to view such claims as reflecting superpower propaganda and as an expression of Cold War polarization rather than as reflecting two alternative sets of conditions in the two halves of Europe.

Cultural Roots behind Militarism and the Issue of Human Rights

The anti-nuclear movements in the West also began to discover the degree to which words were used to hide reality instead of revealing and clarifying the current situation. It became increasingly clear that getting rid of one or another weapons system would not solve problems associated with a militaristic world-view. Obstacles to a real peace politics involve more than weapons. Peace has also to do with deepening a democracy that is built on unconditional respect for human rights and the freedom to express other opinions than those held by people in control of state power. The cultural roots of the Cold War have to be analysed and challenged if one is to address the foundations of militarism. This deeper understanding was especially emphasized by women's peace movements like the Women's International League for Peace and Freedom and Women for Peace.

It was obvious that images of the enemy were often developed out of fear and lack of contact and information. The fact that the international media exaggerated negative information about the 'the other side' and sometimes even gave misleading information led to suspicions that the media operated as structures supporting the social forces and interest groups benefiting from the Cold War; these included military bureaucracies and weapon-producing companies as well as those governments interested in the pacification of their own population so as to avoid domestic challenges. Governments in both East and West relied on the fear of war and on the dark intentions of the other side whenever they needed to hide societal problems arising from declining social progress and a lack of cultural vitality.

Fear of the other has often been combined with a cult of power and strength in post-war Europe. Both East and West have justified an unprecedented peacetime military build-up in terms of the 'lesson' from the Nazi era, the 'lesson' of appeasement associated with Munich – never let your country be unprepared for military aggression from abroad. Hitler's name has been the excuse for the build-up of an extinction capacity that makes the ovens of Auschwitz seem quantitatively trivial.

The question then arises: what kind of lesson did Europe and the United States learn from Hitler? The early resistance against Nazism, which was based on an awareness that it is up to society and its citizens to discover and resist all forms of racism and anti-Semitism, has never been emphasized by the mainstream political analysts in the post-war period. The peace movements in the 1930s were often blamed by political establishments for promoting disarmament in such countries as the

United Kingdom, Denmark and Norway during the time when Hitler came to power in Germany, but these critics seldom mention the absence of adequate cultural resistance against the Nazi ideology. Very few people know that the German sector of the Women's International League for Peace and Freedom requested in 1923 that the government in Berlin expel Hitler from the country because of his racist propaganda. Observers, political scientists, military and government bureaucracies, mostly supported by the dominant mass media, have come, ironically enough in the aftermath of World War II, to adopt Hitler's own message: Military strength is what counts; to gain victory and geopolitical superiority, all means are moral. By using the natural fear of another war in Europe in their propaganda these groups have made the peoples of the continent accept nuclear weapons, a build-up of war economies and constant war preparations; security is supposed to depend almost exclusively upon a mindless emphasis on military and technical strength.

The worship of nuclearism as the centrepiece of security has its roots in Western cultural traditions. The Roman–Greek pantheons, as well as the Scandinavian and Germanic theogonies, were influenced by the Indo-European conquerors who celebrated war heroes. Cheating, lying and killing by these gods in order to gain superiority and victory was considered quite natural and even admirable, if success and victory resulted in the end. The Gandhian view, inspired by the *Bhagavadgita* and the Gospels, that means and ends are inextricably linked has never been part of the hegemonic European culture. The dominant moral standard is best expressed, perhaps, by the Jesuit notion that the end justifies the means.

This emphasis on success, victory and domination has helped the strong powers in European history not only to compose the dominant version of this history but also to create a popular acceptance of their 'necessary' reliance on immoral means to achieve military goals. The study of cultural traditions and metaphors like these has become part of the search for a deeper analysis of the background to the cold war, especially among women's peace movements and feminist groups.[2]

The fact that post-war history has made almost no moral appraisal of the wartime tactics used to defeat Nazism is also revealing. The terror bombing of Hamburg and Dresden and the atomic bombs dropped on Hiroshima and Nagasaki are sometimes mentioned as unfair methods, but very quickly explained and excused with arguments about the necessity to defeat Fascism by any means or to save the lives of the victors.

People within the European peace movements have started to question whether Fascism really was defeated. Military planners in the

Soviet Union admit openly that they have learned a lot from Hitler. Strategists in the West are more cautious and reluctant to identify such a source of political inspiration, even if their values seem derived from militaristic antecedents. The notion that state power has the right to use every means to protect its territory and its interests all over the world is rarely challenged. The core of Fascist ideology is the worship of state power and imperial domination, which seems to be very much alive in both East and West. The state has become an absolute, and in the name of security the most far-reaching insecurity imaginable has been accepted as normal.

One consequence has been the erosion of democratic practices and of human rights. To protect the security of the state, governments and military planners have assumed the right to threaten the population of the enemy with extinction but also to offer up their own population as hostage, and indeed to put at risk the future of the whole world. It is hard to imagine a deeper violation of human rights than this, but a reliance on nuclear terrorism is also combined with a more explicit suppression of human rights. People who criticize the right of the state to demand absolute obedience and loyalty have for decades been labelled 'enemies of the state' in Eastern Europe. In the nuclear age the Western democracies have moved in a similar direction by virtually excluding their own citizens, and even their parliamentary institutions and political parties, from any real participation in the formation and execution of national security policy.

The Role of Churches

Sometimes churches and other religious groups have had the best opportunities to challenge this loyalty to the state by calling upon and reactivating deeper values like the sacredness of life and our roles as caretakers of creation. The present notion of 'security' has encouraged some reformed churches in Europe and the United States to talk about idolatry in much the same way that the early Christian churches refused to worship the emperor in Rome. They have asked their members if they can properly base their security on threats to annihilate whole societies with weapons of mass destruction. The Roman Catholic Church and the World Council of Churches have helped many concerned people from different parts of the world to meet and exchange ideas and experiences on international issues of peace and justice. The possibility of drawing upon values that transcend existing power structures has sometimes created the space necessary to discuss and challenge 'security systems' built on nuclear deterrence. At the World Conference against Nuclear

War in Prague (1983), the 'Religious circle', with participants from Islam, Judaism, Hinduism, Buddhism and Christianity, was the only workshop criticizing nuclear weapons in both East and West. This attitude arose from a common understanding of life as a gift and a responsibility towards transcendent power.

The Lutheran Church in the German Democratic Republic has played a decisive role in challenging its own government's security policy. Gunther Krusche, a theologian from the GDR, suggested in Amsterdam in 1981, at the Hearing on Nuclear Weapons and Disarmament arranged by the World Council of Churches, that nuclear weapons ought to have a 'Confessional Status'. Just as apartheid was condemned by the General Assembly of the Reformed World Federation in Dar-es-Salaam in 1977, so the churches today ought to condemn the threat and use of nuclear weapons as incompatible with Christian faith. Krusche also proposed a new attitude towards pacifism:

> If the Church in East Germany today attests pacifist attitudes, she does so out of their symbolic value. Consistent pacifism can be a sign of the incompatibility of war with the will of God. Pacifism can be an imperative invitation to us not to submit to the military game against a background of worldwide distrust. Pacifism can be an expression of criticism of a stereotyped thinking in enemy categories. And pacifism can be a sign of hope, showing that there are people who refuse to capitulate to the common mood of hopelessness and resignation.
>
> It is, however, in relation to the danger of nuclear arms that pacifism is of special topical relevance. It puts to us the question whether the use of these weapons under any circumstances can be seen as comprehensible and rational. In every single case there are of course serious questions to be asked to the foundations of a decision of conscience: Is it formed by political indifference or even by a negative attitude? Is it saving only one's own conscience? In all circumstances the Church must come forward to the defence of conscience. In the same way as it struggles for the poor, whom Jesus called 'blessed', it must struggle for the 'peacemakers' whom he promised shall be called the children of God [Matthew 5:9].[3]

As a statement coming from a theologian within a Just War tradition, this is an interesting example of new thinking responsive to the special urgencies of the Nuclear Age.

Religion taken in the broad sense of 'how we come to terms with our own origins and our destiny, where we come from and why, where we are going and in what way'[4] is of course crucial for movements trying to deal with an alternative future. Religious institutions, however, are often so closely intertwined with the established authorities that they cannot even sense the deep restlessness in societal life. The overall record on

peace work among established churches is not strong, with the exception
of traditional peace churches like Anabaptists and Quakers. Nuclear
dangers have forced many church leaders to begin a process of new
thinking. In the Christian World Conference for Church Leaders, 'Life
and Peace', in Uppsala, Sweden (1983), one of the statements
encouraged support for women's special contribution to peace work as
well as giving support to civil resistance against plans for nuclear war.
The growing participation of members of churches, theologians and
church leaders in the European peace movements has revitalized the
ethical debate and helped to bring issues of democracy, of the cultural
roots of militarism, and of human rights into the peace agenda.

North–South: a Global Concern

The discovery of how the nuclear build-up and the Cold War have been
used to constrain political democracy has also increased awareness of
the interconnectedness of democracy, culture, human rights and justice
all over the world. Global networks of sister churches, political solidarity
groups and the global women's movement have facilitated another
component of the social learning process in the European anti-nuclear
movements: the increased consciousness of how closely related the
East–West conflict is to the injustice between North and South.

The Cold War between East and West in the post-war period has
obscured the deepening gap between industrialized countries, mainly but
not exclusively in the North, and countries with another form of
economy which were often increasingly dependent upon the industrialized world.

Nationalistic, economic and racial conflicts in Africa, Asia and Latin
America have been used frequently by the United States and the Soviet
Union to gain geopolitical footholds and even dominance, causing
widespread bloodshed and devastation. Weapons produced in Europe
and the United States have been exported to countries with internal
conflicts or with tensions with their neighbour countries in a way that
has sustained and magnified wars which otherwise would have been
much more limited or resolved by negotiated settlement. The war
between Iran and Iraq is an example of outside arms adding fuel to the
flames of regional conflict. 'Ninety-five per cent of the wars that have
taken place since 1945 have been fought in developing countries, with
foreign powers intervening in most of them, and 79 per cent of these
interventions carried out by Western nations.'[5]

The issue of nuclearism is also connected to the North–South conflict.
In the official rhetoric the nuclear powers claim that nuclear weapons

are not for use, only for deterrence. In the real, political world, however, nuclear weapons are not used only to deter others from initiating a nuclear attack. Since 1945 the United States has threatened to use them several times: in the Korean War, in the Quemoy/Matsu crisis, in the Vietnam War and in the Middle East conflict.[6]

The military base in Comiso, southern Italy, is a good example of the importance of bases with nuclear weapons close to conflict areas in the Middle East and the Persian Gulf. The women's peace camp created there fostered an early awareness among the Western European peace movements of the proximity of Comiso to dangerous war zones. Nuclearism is part of the present power structure in which a few dominant powers in the world shape conflict behaviour. This structure accepts the inevitability of the present world order based on bipolarity and injustice, and claims that 'peace' has existed despite the fact that 'between thirty-five and forty million people have died in the limited wars that have taken place since World War II.'[7] Even to talk about a 'post-war period' during a time when large numbers of people have been killed in a constant cycle of wars is to reveal the Northern bias implicit in this conception of 'security'. The assumption that nuclear weapons have maintained world peace since 1945 is certainly misleading. In effect, it treats the peoples of the South as of no significance.

Moreover, world peace is more than just the absence of hot war. Even where they are not engaged in a military workforce, the people of Africa, Asia and Latin America have had to cope with the ongoing warfare of structural poverty, most recently dramatized by the mixture of debt servitude and IMF penetration.

Towards Dealignment

Discoveries like these led many Western European anti-nuclear groups to understand that it was necessary to address the foundations of militarism and try to move beyond the military blocs. The military presence of the superpowers in Europe limits freedom in both East and West. A peaceful Europe would require truly democratic political societies with respect for human rights and just relations with the Third World countries. This would facilitate and be facilitated by a gradual withdrawal of Soviet and American forces of both conventional and nuclear varieties from the continent.

The Gorbachev phenomenon in the East represents a real shift in political thinking of a kind that encourages hope for a more peaceful future for Europe. Not only is Mikhail Gorbachev proposing a real nuclear disarmament with his vision of a nuclear-free world by the year

2000, he is also suggesting substantial reductions in conventional forces, including withdrawals of Russian troops from Eastern Europe.[8] Combined with the new openness towards issues of human rights and democracy, these developments will surely facilitate a loosening of the Soviet dominance over Eastern and Central Europe. Perestroika and glasnost have already shown themselves to be more than catchwords. A new domestic political debate has been emerging in the Soviet Union and it is interesting to note that one-third of the foreign-policy establishment in Moscow seems to favour a purely defensive security policy, even if it has to be undertaken unilaterally.[9]

Recent indications of economic and military co-operation between the Federal Republic of Germany and France around both conventional and atomic weapons, however, are a sign of developments in an opposite direction. While there are tendencies towards an openness between the two superpowers, expressed in the INF Treaty, that might have some positive effect on the situation in Central Europe, it has become very clear that some of the European states lack political imagination and are unable to envision security built on anything other than military strength aiming for superiority. In Northern Europe there has also been an increased military build-up. While the cruise missiles will be removed from Central Europe according to the INF Treaty, the new NATO Maritime Strategy, made public in January 1986, is causing an intense militarization of the North Atlantic and the Arctic Ocean, with submarines and aircraft carriers encroaching upon territorial waters. The US State Department has already made it clear that the United States is not going to respect neutrality in case of a military conflict. The cruise missiles are, for instance, programmed to fly over Swedish territory on their way to Moscow and Leningrad. The response from the Nordic peace movements is to work for nuclear-free harbours as a way to attack the infrastructure of this maritime strategy, and to launch the idea of the Nordic countries – including Canada – as a zone of peace.

In this complex situation, with a deeply militarized Europe but with some prospects of change, it is natural that many activists sometimes feel confusion about where to go and how to address the problem, and how to envision an alternative future. As Michael Albert puts it: 'For anyone unprepared to be moved solely out of anger vision must underlie allegiance.'[10] When activists begin to realize the interconnections between the existence of nuclear weapons and the type of economy, polity, culture and sexuality that prevail in our society, how will they address the average citizen's cynicism about protest? How will they answer the challenge 'show me something better before you risk what we have'? Dramatically to reiterate casualty figures for a nuclear war is, as Michael Albert says, not sufficient. To endure beyond the initial fervour of discovery, the disarmament movement must present alternatives. This need for vision is so much stronger today than in the sixties: 'Since the threat the disarmament movement addresses is more abstract than TV reports of massacre in Vietnam, readily visible poverty in downtown ghettos, rising unemployment and rape counts, and palpable fear on the streets.'[11] Many of the actions and projects undertaken in the seventies and eighties have had the effect of lighting candles in a church. Not only peace services, concerts and artists' performances but also rallies, seminars and conferences have had a countercultural focus: to light candles in a time of despair, confusion, and darkness.

Political analyses of this situation have not always been very clear; different groups have emphasized different approaches and created divergent strategies. This has been a period in which people have acted prior to new thinking, discovering their innovative thoughts only in reflection upon their new actions. For many of the social movements in both East and West, ideological considerations and political reflections have been the outcome of theorizing closely associated with very concrete actions in a complex political reality. It is therefore dangerous to generalize and to search for symmetrical patterns in a still unfinished web that has many threads, where maybe the most striking impression will be of asymmetry and diversity. There seem, however, to be some common tendencies and themes in the actions taken by the social movements in the early eighties: an emphasis upon cultural, professional, religious interactions and initiatives in an attempt to create detente from below.

A Common Destiny

While many governments still seem to be tied to an East–West world-view with deep loyalty to the dominant powers in their respective military alliances, many citizens in both parts of Europe are becoming increasingly aware of the interdependence between nations and peoples, most obviously when it comes to questions of the environment. Corporations, banks and government bureaucracies have for a long time been aware of economic interdependence. The stock market crash in October 1987 was only the most drastic example of an economic system in which developments in New York affect the whole world.

Long before the Palme Commission launched the terminology of 'Common Security', people in both Eastern and Western Europe were aware of the fact that security needs to be pursued jointly. The Chernobyl catastrophe that spread radioactive fallout far beyond the Ukraine made many people aware that their health and well-being were vulnerable to developments in distant countries. This deepened the appreciation of and support for collective approaches to security. Moreover, it did so in a way that brought this imperative home in a personal manner. When something happens on your own lawn, when you cannot eat your own vegetables grown in Poland, Italy or Hungary or the fish caught in the rivers of northern Norway, when the reindeer-breeding of the Laplanders in northern Sweden is threatened and injured for generations, you begin to understand the realities of interdependence in a deep psychological sense. (Chernobyl can be appreciated as the Devil's pedagogy or expressed in a more positive theological tradition as God's way of using even Evil in support of Life – if we take warning, that is!) Today most people in Europe realize from harmful, actual experience that radiation does not respect state borders. It is too early to predict whether the Chernobyl accident will in the long run convince people about the threat from nuclear power enough to overcome the economic and governmental interests in the nuclear power industry, so connected to the production of nuclear weapons. There are many Europeans who remain indifferent or can be easily seduced by talk of nuclear safety and promises of better, safer technology.

During the 1970s and 1980s there were, of course, significant differences between popular movements in East and West. The notion that the West represents freedom, sustained by NATO's nuclear-deterrence policy, committed to use nuclear weapons against any military attack from the East, was fairly often expressed by human-rights groups in Eastern European countries at informal meeting with peace activists and journalists from the West. A joke in Prague about the anti-nuclear movements in the West is revealing: 'I hope that they will succeed in getting rid of nuclear weapons, because I have always wanted to visit Paris!' The conservative or mainstream view in the West of nuclear deterrence as the only thing preventing Russia from intervening and taking over Western Europe, or at any rate exercising political blackmail, was often taken for granted among intellectuals in Eastern Europe during the early eighties, causing them to be suspicious about peace movements in the West, which they accused of naiveté and focusing too much upon the single issue of nuclear weapons. On the other hand, spokesmen of peace movements in the West sometimes argued that the nuclear issue deserved to have priority or tried to tell Eastern Europeans that their work for democracy and human rights should be subordinated to the overriding priority of nuclear disarmament.

Ideological discussions, tensions, even quarrels like these were frequently exploited by cheerleaders of the Cold War on both sides. Maybe, however, it is necessary to talk through these differences before citizens in both parts of Europe can understand, separately and together, that their respective agendas were more intertwined and convergent than they had previously understood.

Peace, human rights and green groups from both East and West in the late 1980s seem more able to listen to each other and to respect different points of view. They increasingly realize that some of the most urgent political issues are shared by the peoples all over Europe. Forests and rivers are dying. Acid rain does not respect territorial borders any more than do radioactive clouds. Critical social movements are today recognizing and acting creatively upon connections among structures, processes, and peoples that do not yet enter significantly into the calculations of conventional political actors:

> Recognizing connections, critical social movements are able to engage not only in struggles around specific problems but also in struggles that recognize the emancipatory potential inherent in certain kinds of connections and solidarities. Acting on such connections and forging new solidarities, critical social movements have the capacity to extend the horizons of our political imagination. Reacting to the intolerable, they extend the boundaries of the possible. . . . They have engaged in new forms of solidarity between peoples despite very real differences between them.[12]

Professional groups, including physicians, teachers, lawyers, psychologists, engineers, authors, ministers, and nurses against nuclear weapons have created new networks between East and West. Scientists are discussing what to do about the environmental crisis. Similar experiences linked to professional work can help to overcome ideological and cultural differences.

The growing movement to create sister cities in East and West, North and South represents another effort to build new bridges of detente from below among ordinary citizens living in small and medium-sized municipalities and towns. Ordinary people from small towns, maybe with totally different ideological views, visit each other and share cultural experiences, discuss health care and education, children and the politics of their respective municipalities. It is a deliberate means to connect people who share concerns and come to appreciate that their links are stronger than any public forces of disagreement.

When political leaders and governing bodies of municipalities and towns take initiatives to create a sister-city relationship with another city far away (or when they declare themselves nuclear-free) it is a way of expressing global responsibility locally. In fact, it is a way to act and to behave as if the future were here already, because in the future we will all have to act globally to protect our common goods, like the oceans, the ozone layer and the forests. Local responsibility is required to act globally.

Women: Pathfinders to the Future

In many of these actions necessary for the future, women seem to be the pathfinders. They are often ahead in thinking more globally and holistically, knowing that different ideological standpoints can be combined with integrity and respect for the other side. It is not necessary to think of the other as the enemy. Women more often appreciate intimacy and therefore share more readily with each other their private experiences. When women from different cultural and ideological traditions come together they therefore often share common experiences in relation to children, men, elderly people, as well as experiences in their public and professional lives. In small groups they often discover a common base and can build strong connections across borders. This is something that has been used consciously in several bridge-building seminars for women from East and West. Mutual respect and discussions of different ideologies can be developed through women's common experience. In such groups women also recognize more and more the connections between issues like child and women abuse, rape and militarism and the exploitation of nature.

One of my best friends, an artist, a drawing teacher from Ronneby, joined the peace march to Moscow in 1981. During that march she had a vision of a worldwide action involving peoples from the whole world. This vision became The Great Peace Journey. Citizens from all parts of the world formed transnational delegations. They discussed a new, expanded conception of security, encompassing basic human needs and the ecological challenge, with governments and social movements in all United Nations member states. The main vehicle for these discussions was a series of five questions which were put to prime ministers and presidents and other high governmental officials by regional delegations representing The Great Peace Journey.[13]

This movement is now active in more than one hundred countries. The aim is to challenge governmental politics and transnationalize democracy. This effort is based on a new kind of peace consciousness that draws on feminist, spiritual, grass-roots inspiration. Growing out of a mainly Scandinavian network, a wide popular network of women's groups, peace organizations, human-rights groups, humanitarian associations, churches and religious communities has been created in the space of a few years.

The emphasis of The Great Peace Journey was on North–South relations as much as on East–West relations. From the beginning, the organizers were aware of the difficulties of establishing relations with official peace committees in the East; yet this was the only form of access to governments. They contacted independent groups like the

Moscow Trust Group and the Dialogue group in Hungary and, after discussions with them, came to the conclusion that a critical dialogue with official committees would contribute to the success of the undertaking.

The women who initiated this project in 1985 and the men who became involved all emphasized the interaction between culture, religion and politics. Richard Falk – who became an ally of this movement after participating in the first follow-up conference in Ronneby, Sweden, in 1986, when people from seventeen European countries, together with peace researchers, challenged the invited governmental representatives to act upon their answers to the given questions – describes the strategy as a way to enfeeble the still-reigning war gods:

> This initiative . . . is an extraordinary attempt to build a bridge across the chasm separating old dying forms from new emerging ones. It builds on the impulse of even the most militaristic governments to strike a virtuous pose in public and give a cheap yes to peace and justice, conceived as a ritual gesture or photo opportunity, but not as a real commitment with behavioural consequences. The whole subversive motive of The Great Peace Journey is to initiate a dialogue, to insist that if a government says yes, then to ask in subsequent initiatives why doesn't it keep its word, act with consistency, fulfil its commitment to the peoples of the world, and take action. It involves a politics of seduction, to be sure, but subtly aimed at disrobing and enfeebling the still-reigning gods of war.[14]

Eva Moberg, a well-known playwright and columnist in Sweden, describes the strategy as one of conscious naiveté, when people are acting as if words of governments were worth taking seriously, turning them back in the expectation of actions. It is a way of restoring the values of words, and thereby revitalizing democracy.

To start a worldwide movement in a small town in a remote country like Sweden is to show that the world is one. To visit social movements and governments in small transnational delegations is to dramatize the fact that peace is a transnational undertaking, not only a relation between governments or between a government and its citizens. It is a symbolic, almost liturgical act.

Cultural happenings and religious services are often combined with big peace actions. The close relationship between the Solidarity movement and the Catholic Church in Poland is well known – better known in the West than the Church of England's protest against nuclearism or the critical sermon given by the Archbishop of Canterbury in St Paul's Cathedral after the Falklands War. The Great Peace Journey started with peace services on Swedish television, in the cathedral of

Trondheim, Norway, and in the medieval church in Ronneby, Sweden, after the preparatory seminar when four white buses left the little town with participants from seventeen countries on their way to meet peoples and governments in twenty-seven countries. The evening before there was a peace concert with performing artists from different countries and the day after a peace symphony specially composed for this occasion was performed in the Storkyrkan Cathedral in Stockholm where people gathered for a peace service, and later assembled for a public meeting with the Prime Minister, Olof Palme, in Kungstradgarden. In Cologne and Coventry, two cities which once tried to destroy each other, peace services were held on the same day as a result of efforts by different groups associated with The Great Peace Journey. It turned out to be more difficult to organize a similar service in East Berlin![15]

Women have been the main, but not the exclusive bearers of this vision, initiated by the journey. In its practice there has been an emphasis on culture, religion, personal relations and an effort to listen and to learn from women and men of all colours in both East and West, North and South. The visits to more than twenty regions and countries all over the world have been combined with rallies, seminars, cultural festivals and religious services, all expressing a shared concern for our global community.

Promising Signs on the Horizon

When observers talk about the disappearance of peace movements they are usually thinking of huge rallies and mass demonstrations, as in the early 1980s. It is, however, important to distinguish between invisibility and disappearance. The political strategy based on mass demonstrations was important in an early phase of the anti-nuclear movement to create a wider consciousness and public opposition to nuclearism. Today the awareness of the danger of nuclear weapons is widespread in Europe, but the task of getting rid of militarism is not over.

It is hard, however, to estimate how deep or widespread is the countercultural resistance to the present hegemonic militarist world-view. Anti-nuclear movements have changed their character, and may even have become a little institutionalized. What started out as an anti-nuclear preoccupation has anyhow deepened its knowledge and is no longer a one-issue movement, and perhaps it never was. In this process it has also become part of the party rivalry and government itself. It remains too early to evaluate the impact of anti-nuclearism on social and political institutions as such. Traditional social movements, churches, humanitarian associations, trade unions, schools and universities have all to some degree been influenced by the knowledge and questioning that arose from the peace movement. The new awareness of how issues of democracy, culture, human rights and ecology are interrelated globally has already created countercultural forces working transnationally, with women in the forefront.

In this global exchange a new receptivity to diversity and an attitude of celebration towards multiple perspectives is growing. In Europe, a successful new detente would mean a demilitarized peaceful Europe based on political and military dealignment from the superpowers and an increased exchange of ideas in Europe about culture, trade, scientific and technical research, and human experiences. This goal is part of the growing vision for social movements, not only in both parts of Europe but also in other parts of the world. Our common human destiny in the nuclear age, intensified by severe ecological threats already alarmingly present in the European area, is to create a public awareness that we need to unite our best wishes, ideas, knowledge and resources to fight against an ecological crisis instead of fighting each other. There is a cultural shift under way of great magnitude and in the direction of a new peace politics, although governments, East and West, have yet to see the light!

Notes

1. Kaldor and Falk, *Dealignment*, Oxford 1987, p. 13.
2. See, for example, Christa Wolf, *Cassandra*, London 1984.
3. See the testimony of Gunther Krusche at the WCC's Hearing on Weapons and Disarmament, Amsterdam, 1981.
4. Gibson Winter, *Religion and Politics in a Communal Age*, 1988.
5. David Dellinger, 'The Bread is Rising', in *Beyond Survival*.
6. Daniel Lang, *Patriotism without Flags*, 1974.
7. Dellinger.
8. The Hungarian Minister of Defence, Ferenc Karpati, indicated in July 1988 that Russian troops might soon be withdrawn from Hungary. *Svenska Dagbladet*, 11 July 1988.
9. Polls from the USA–Canada Institute in Moscow, August 1988.
10. Michael Albert, 'Lessons from the Sixties', in *Beyond Survival*.
11. Ibid., p. 65.
12. R.B.J. Walker, *One World, Many Worlds: Struggle for a Just World Peace*, 1988, p. 3.
13. The five questions of The Great Peace Journey:

    1. Are you willing to initiate national legislation which guarantees that your country's defence forces, including 'military advisers', do not leave your territory for military purposes (other than in United Nations peacekeeping forces) – if all other members of the United Nations undertake to do the same?
    2. Are you willing to take steps to ensure that the development, possession, storage and employment of mass-destruction weapons, including nuclear weapons, which threaten to destroy the very conditions necessary for life on

this earth, are forbidden in your country – if all other members of the United Nations undertake to do the same?

3. Are you willing to take steps to prevent your country from allowing the supply of military equipment and weapons technology to other countries – if all other members of the United Nations undertake to do the same?

4. Are you willing to work for distribution of the earth's resources so that the fundamental necessities of human life, such as clean water, food, elementary health care and schooling, are available to all people throughout the world?

5. Are you willing to work to ensure that any conflicts in which your country may be involved in the future will be settled by peaceful means of the kind specified in Article 33 of the United Nations Charter, and not by the use of or threat of force?

14. Richard Falk, IFDA Dossier 62, November–December 1987, 'On Peace and Justice in a World of Danger and Struggle', p. 27.

15. The planned service with Lutheran groups in Berlin never became a reality, as The Great Peace Journey unexpectedly received transit visas through the country only when it entered the GDR. The East German government did not receive any delegation from the GPJ in May 1985. They said they were too busy celebrating the fortieth anniversary of the victory over Fascism. Not until one year later – after the first follow-up conference, the YES Conference in Ronneby in 1986 – were they willing to receive a delegation, which then met the Minister of Foreign Affairs, Oscar Fischer. The Swedish Archbishop Emeritus, Olof Sundby, postponed a visit to the GDR for one year to protest against the GDR government's behaviour.

Conclusion

18

The Democratic Potential of the New Detente*

Radmila Nakarada

There is a widespread consensus that we are living in an age of dramatic paradoxes. The whispers of our time combine a promise of a *new* world and a threat of *no* world. We are caught up in the shadows of the old and in the rays of the new, in the revival of myths, prejudices, hostilities, and in the emergence of new insights, knowledge, and social, political and scientific linkages. The assessment of the democratic potential of the new detente and its limitations has to be mediated by an awareness of these paradoxes and contradictions.

Amidst these paradoxes one can fall into the twin traps of underestimating or overestimating its potential. Grasping fully the potential of the new detente means understanding the essential features of our time, of the particular societies we belong to, and of the global framework.

Detente is unquestionably the result of a multitude of factors, but above all of the new dramatic imperatives of reality and new insights. These imperatives are of both a negative and a positive nature. On the negative side they include the danger of exterminism, ecological degradation, economic crisis, and political failures. On the positive side are all the impulses for a transformation of civilization which come from new technological capacities, new types of emancipatory actions and agents, and above all social movements and the new human subjectivity.

New insights are evolving from the reconceptualization of past experiences and future possibilities, out of which a new image of the world is gradually emerging. The world is less and less perceived as a mechanical entity, developing progressively in a linear manner, and

---

*I wish to acknowledge the helpful critical comments and suggestions of Professor Miroslav Pecujlić.

more and more as an open system where forces of both chance and determinism are operating, a system with no hidden promises (in a form of natural or social law) of positive resolution, a system that is inherently pluralistic, containing both retrograde and progressive potentials.

If we are facing the possibility of total destruction, and if at the same time history is open and uncertain, then the potential of detente cannot be reduced to a set of tactics and political whims. In spite of all its limitations and the possible setbacks, the potential of detente should be seen as an organic part of a new evolution towards democracy. This chapter is an attempt to demonstrate this.

I use the term 'democracy' in a rather all-encompassing way to mean the development of procedures, institutions and cultural norms that allow human beings to settle conflicts, both *between* and *within* nations, in a non-violent way – through dialogue and respect for due processes of law. Democracy in this sense would mean reinvigorating existing institutions (like parliaments or the United Nations), devising new institutions so as to ensure a truly representative accountable and responsive legal framework, and the emergence or revitalization of the individual's awareness of citizenship. Hence, whether or not detente can lead to an irreversible peace – the elimination of violence or the threat of violence as a way of settling conflict – also depends on its democratic potential.

The new detente has to be understood as a combination of detente from above and detente from below, but I shall focus primarily on the latter, since it is more neglected, and indicate only briefly the problems associated with the former.

The Democratic Potential of Detente From Above and its Limitations

The democratic potential of detente from above is based on its achievements, which differ in scope, some having immediate though narrower effects, others having wider implications which are not always easy to discern. The first category of achievements consists of immediate military steps related to agreements and negotiations about arms reductions. The second category has to do with broader social achievements; the third includes cognitive breakthroughs. These achievements can be evaluated euphorically or with more reservation. However, even if one makes a more modest estimation, it is important not to neglect the fact that they contain an inherent logic of continuation.

What follows is far from a complete inventory of achievements. I shall simply try to designate those which can be considered representative. I begin with the cognitive level, because it can be seen as the first link in a chain of changes.

The cognitive level encompasses the 'new consciousness' ('New Thinking') that has evolved from several fundamental insights: first of all, from the understanding of the danger of total nuclear destruction. It is now profoundly clear that a nuclear war cannot be won by anyone. Second, there is a growing awareness that global problems can be solved only through common efforts, on the basis of co-operation and mutual respect. Finally, the two hostile worlds are coming closer together, partly because the most brutal and primitive ideological images have been discarded. There is a slowly evolving realization that opposing ideologies and viewpoints may simultaneously contain elements of the truth.[1]

On the immediate level arms reduction has begun, albeit on a modest scale, and foreign troops have been withdrawn from several areas of conflict in the world. In general the readiness for extending direct intervention has diminished; the idea of common security versus national security has gained ground, particularly in Europe. The role of the UN and its peacekeeping forces has also been somewhat rehabilitated.

On the broader social level, the following achievements are significant. First, the link between domestic and foreign problems and solutions has been established. This has redirected energies and efforts towards internal development. (The Soviet Union primarily comes to mind.) As Tucker notes:

> When the government of a great power has come to recognize that its country faces an internal crisis situation calling for thoroughgoing reform of its economic, social, cultural and political life, that government loses the need . . . to conjure up for its citizens the image of a relatively intractable external enemy. . . . It becomes free to take a less combative and more co-operative stance in external relations.[2]

Furthermore, detente promotes a broader coalition between the reformist wing of the establishment, liberal parties and peace movements, creating bridges of co-operation nationally and transnationally and potentially establishing a firmer basis for irreversible peace. Detente has also given a new impetus to scientific, technological, economic and cultural co-operation, which contributes to internal development. This can also be taken as sign of a greater readiness to accept peaceful changes in opposing systems.

The primary limitation of detente from above, other than the very restricted scope of arms reduction and the arms competition which continues behind the scenes, is rooted in the uneven linkage between foreign and domestic problems and solutions between the two superpowers. This results in an uneven interest in the process of detente, and thus in its fragility. The Soviet Union, as the economically and technologically inferior superpower, is more interested in the process of detente, faced as it is with economic collapse, dramatic social conflicts and developmental impotence. The USA, as the materially richer, industrially and technologically superior power possessing a more adaptable economic system, is still shielded from a full realization of the existential meaning of detente.

Other sources of limitation are those dimensions of social reality which work against democratic tendencies and against a firmer foundation of peace. In the Soviet Union these include the still insufficiently broad social base of the reform, as well as the negative side-effects of economic changes that may give new strength to the forces of social inertia and create a social bloc headed by the conservative faction of the bureaucracy against economic reform and against the process of democratization. In the USA internal economic problems, particularly unemployment and the dismantling of the welfare state, are also a force for conservatism, racism and nationalism – in other words, they inhibit democratic potentials. On the other hand, the USA (and Western European countries), with their privileged position in the global economic order, may be more and more exposed to the terrorism of the 'wretched of the earth'. In turn this might serve as a legitimization of the non-democratic concept of national security in the USA (and the West in general) – a new external threat, a new 'other'.

A selective retreat from the international scene could create the space for new military blocs, for instance in Western Europe, while the decline in direct and extensive military intervention could result in new modes of intervention. The best example here is the new US strategy of intervention under the name of low-intensity warfare (LIW). The 'newspeak' formula of LIW supposedly designates an armed conflict involving a low level of violence. However, the new strategy is offensive, beginning with counterinsurgency and extending to a wide variety of political, economic, psychological, diplomatic and military operations, both overt and covert. In other words, LIW is a war on the whole of society – or, as bluntly defined by one of its adherents, a 'total war at the grass-roots level'.[3]

The Democratic Potential of Detente From Below

The development of detente from below is of objective historical significance, as are its chief actors – movements for peace and democracy –

and their ongoing dialogue. We consider the established dialogue between the Eastern and Western movements to be the prime source of a novel democratic potential.

This dialogue between movements has become possible by virtue of the mutual recognition of the interdependence of two values crucial for the modern age: peace and freedom. This mutual recognition has evolved through years of dramatic controversies, bitter misunderstandings and mutual accusations, and unfortunate moments of indifference. These disputes have, among other things, reflected the severity and depth of ideological, political and cultural divisions. By establishing a process of dialogue and a linkage of societies, a firmer foundation for the new detente can be created. It is in the nature of these movements to be more consistent actors for democratic peace than governments, for they do not strive for power but for social spaces that would enable each and every one of us to be responsible for peace and freedom. Furthermore, through what they are doing and their methods of doing it, movements are demonstrating that alternatives to the existing order are possible. This does not mean, however, that movements do not have limitations, due to their own shortcomings or to the nature of the situation in which they evolve. Bearing this in mind, the ongoing dialogue between the Eastern and Western movements cannot be treated either euphorically or cynically. An analysis of both its achievements and its limitations is necessary in order to assess its democratic potential. I stress *both* achievements and limitations, for the movements do have an inner flexibility; some reflection on their limitations may therefore contribute to their democratic potential.

Since movements are not homogeneous, my attempt to assess their potential will be based on what seem to be their representative currents of thought and representative social actions.

Some Achievements of the East–West Dialogue

One of the major achievements of the East–West dialogue has been the linkage it has established between societies. This linkage is multifold – besides the East–West linkage, an East–East one is also taking place. The recent organization of East–West dialogue has had particular significance in Eastern Europe – Poland, Hungary, the Soviet Union – in strengthening the position of these movements in their own societies.

Involving the uninvolved, reaching those who were passive, marginalized, separated by ideological or class boundaries, creating opportunities for contact and co-operation, grass-roots enlightenment, are all contributions to transnational and transclass integration.

On the question of the unity of Europe, many movements have now come to a more radical position. Earlier they were inclined to accept the need to work within the Yalta arrangement, but they have now arrived at the point where questioning the existence of the two blocs is considered legitimate and plausible. The aim of transcending the blocs is radical, but the means are creatively realistic. Recognizing the sensitivity of the issues at stake, and the fact that they can be resolved only in a long-term process, the movements are mainly focusing on the grass-roots level of transcending Yalta, promoting and developing a new consciousness and a new culture of solidarity, while at the same time showing elements of openness and (cautious) support for the internal reforms in the East, 'the reforms from above', and for the achievements of detente between states.

This linkage has also resulted in the transcendence of many brutal Cold War ideological images. Movements are beginning to accept that the choice between pro-Soviet peace and pro-Western freedom is a false option. They are seeking independence or autonomy from both super-powers, and discarding to a large extent the philosophy that 'the enemy of my enemy is my friend'. They are also arguing that an exchange of an 'ill for an ill' (the Poland-for-Nicaragua type of exchange) is unfruitful.

The ongoing dialogue has, furthermore, brought together various insights:

- that the possibility of an all-encompassing solution or project of salvation is a costly illusion;

- that human relations are governed by numerous inconsistencies, among others the fact that the victims of violence and war are not necessarily partisans of peace and freedom; nor are internal principles of social organization (for example, democratic) necessarily principles of relating to the external world. Furthermore, movements are making it clear that there is no certainty that goodness and justice will prevail or that the future is secure. Uncertainty demands individual and social responsibility.

The dialogue is enabling deeper insights into problems that are not the result of this or that system but products of contemporary civilization – the problem of impersonal power, homogenization of needs and life-styles, perpetuation of inequalities (class and gender), the destruction of nature. It is creating a demand for a deeper understanding of the common underlying principles of both social systems.

The movements are increasingly overcoming a Manichaean image of reality. The forces of evil cannot be convincingly ascribed to one super-power or to one social class only. The forces of good and evil are intertwined and no simplifications can ease the problem of creating a radical alternative. Attempts to reach a deeper historical understanding of the present reality, particularly the Eastern part of it, clearly testify to this. Milan Šimečka, for instance, points out that the whole Eastern European predicament cannot be explained by the evil role of the Soviet Union:

> It's far pleasanter to pass oneself off as a guiltless nation which would show the world if it only got the chance. I just think that it serves a purpose – if only a therapeutic one – to be reminded that a lot of the evil was our own creation, and one of the reasons why the influence of the 'other civilization' was so effective was because, to a certain extent, we provided it with fertile soil.[4]

The movements have found, in the revival of the idea of civil society, the possibility of changing the existing order by building on its achievements and not destroying them, respecting the principles of democracy and legality but striving to go beyond them. To go beyond them means to transcend the dualities of socialism–capitalism, reform–revolution.

In reacting to the narrowing of social spaces, movements defend their society from the state without attempting to take power. The core of this defence lies in redefining and democratizing social spaces for new collective identities, meanings and, in particular, solidarities. Their main 'weapons' are co-operation and the upholding of ethical principles of life. Their activities take place outside the political system, in various forms, from the exchange of information to solidarity actions. The processes of linkage and the articulation of a common civil society as a goal are the two largest spheres of democratic potential created by the dialogue of the Eastern–Western movements.

Some Limitations of the Eastern and Western Movements

The limitations of the movements for a new detente do not stem from their marginality or low effectiveness. This belongs to the natural fate of movements, and in time might change. The limitations we wish to point out are to a large extent the other side of the coin of their achievements. First I shall indicate some of the limitations shared by both Eastern and Western movements, then refer to some of the limitations of the Western movements and dwell to a greater degree on those of the Eastern movements, simply because, coming from a country that is similar, I am better acquainted with them.

The following troublesome ideas are shared by both Eastern and Western movements. A common goal is a united Europe, but it is unclear what is meant by 'Europe'. Western Europe is present, Eastern

Europe, Central Europe as well, but nowhere is the south of Europe, the poor, undeveloped Europe, explicitly included. It figures as an abstraction. The envisioned united Europe seems like a unity of the rich and the intellectuals of Europe (in George Konrád's phrase, 'the international intellectual aristocracy').

Eastern and Western movements share a form of Eurocentralism, in universalizing European problems and in overestimating the division of Europe as the basis of the division of the world, the crucial source of global conflict, and the main potential detonator of war. 'Europe, like all the world, is divided within as well as between states. Europe is divided because the world is divided.'[5] There is no European solution to the European division and a democratic detente cannot evolve if it is not part of a global detente, particularly if we bear in mind the fact that the arms race is a 'theft of Third World resources' and that 'modern war has become a Third World phenomenon'. Solidarity with the Third World is insufficiently present, particularly in Eastern Europe where, besides a lack of sensitivity for the drama of the Third World due to understandable self-preoccupation, ideological reasons intervene as well. (Michnik's evaluation of Allende's programme as unrealistic and dangerous, and Gaspar's attitude towards South Africa's movements as only a question of 'exchanging one terrible regime for another no less terrible', are illustrations of this kind of ideological intervention.)

The movements are in agreement on the need to develop (common) civil society as a sphere of solidarity, legality, and pluralism as social spaces free from the domination of the state. However, they tend to underestimate the interpenetration between civil society and the state, and overestimate the extra-institutional strategy for developing democracy. They are tacitly aware that 'modern civil society is not self-sufficient', but there is a lack of a more adequate reflection on state sovereignty and on the necessary role of the reformed state for the functioning of society. Also not very well articulated is the need for institutional solutions in order to promote successfully the movement's own causes. This would include reforming existing institutions and creating new ones.

Both kinds of movement tend to ignore the complexity of the economy and its relation to freedom and peace. Among the Eastern Europeans we find two sharply differing viewpoints – one of total neglect of (even contempt for) the material side of life (for instance in the works of Kundera, Michnik, Havel) and another which considers the free market as a general solution, a panacea for all social ills. The Western movements, on the other hand (at least those engaged in the East–West dialogue) are the least creative in their actions for and visions of the democratization of the economic system, and are insufficiently aware of the participation of Europe in the reproduction of global economic inequalities.

Representatives of both movements define the existing socialist societies as totalitarian. I stated earlier that brutal ideological images have largely been abandoned, but this has not yet included the concept of totalitarianism. I do not question its previous heuristic value, but today its signification does not correspond to reality if it implies all-pervasive control, no organic connection between the system and its citizens, and a bipolar division of society between the powerful as a homogeneous category and the powerless as equally homogeneous. Analysis of conflicts within the power structure of social conflicts and change, of parallel cultures of different interest groups and so on, reveal societies more complex and rich than the concept of totalitarianism allows for. The concept of totalitarianism excludes, therefore,

> the interaction of government, historical, social, cultural and economic factors; the conflict of classes, institutions, groups, generations, ideas, and personalities . . . an array of non 'totalitarian' . . . realities from fractious political leaders and nonconformist writers to diverse social trends and outlooks.[6]

Contradictions within a totalitarian framework of interpretation are unavoidable, as Vaclav Havel's analysis reveals. On the one hand he speaks of the total absorption of society by the system, its invasion of every pore of life. On the other he describes in the following words the influence of Charter 77: 'It manages to influence the *entire sphere of social consciousness* which, normally speaking, is prey to manipulation by the regime'[7] (emphasis added).

If the system invades every pore of life, it is unclear how critical thinking can evolve at all, how groups like Charter 77 can come to life and continue to exist. In addition, when reflecting on the conditions in Czechoslovakia today he develops the contradiction by concluding that in spite of the absence of major political changes since 1975,

> some important things have happened . . . independent culture as a whole has mushroomed. There are also many other signs of movement in the consciousness of society. . . . I am forced to conclude that things have changed for the better, and that, in spiritual terms and in its consciousness, our society is better off.[8]

Opposing the totalitarian designation does not mean taking an apologetic stand towards these societies. They are undoubtedly non-democratic and authoritarian. But discarding the totalitarian concept, besides enabling us to comprehend reality in a more insightful way, means renouncing the idea of collapse or revolution as the only paths of change, and opening up possibilities for a dialogue with the moderates and reformers inside the establishment. If there is an awareness in the West that movements should develop a dialogue with 'reform-orientated parties', then the same logic could be applied to the Eastern European situation.

A few words on the Western movements and their limitations. Their perception of their own and the world's reality is to some extent reductionist, not taking up fully the implications of the fact that 'the West is deeply and decisively involved in the preservation and increase of poverty and inequality, particularly in the Third World, but also in its own societies.'[9] The movements have been criticized for concentrating on disarmament issues alone and neglecting the whole problematic of human rights. This has been accepted, and in principle the issue of human rights is recognized as an interdependent variable with peace. However, the issue of human rights has not become fully immersed in the critical analyses of the Western societies themselves. It does not fully include and problematize the questions of privilege, inequality and injustice in other spheres of human existence outside politics.

The question of internal peace between the state and its citizens is not only a question of Eastern European societies, but of the West itself. Among other things, the homeless, unemployed and impoverished segments of the Western population testify to this. Thus in order sincerely to overcome a position of double standards, eliminate all arrogance, and create the possibility of a trans-bourgeois civil society, an in-depth critique of Western societies is also necessary. In stating all this I do not wish to imply that a fundamental difference between the nature of Western democratic and Eastern (non-democratic) societies does not exist. It does. However, this fundamental difference does not mean that democracy in the West is total or definite, and that the democratic agenda and potential are exhausted. On the contrary, critical conscious-ness concerning the democratic dimensions that are being eroded or are still nonexistent (notably in the economic sphere) is important for the mobilization of a series of social actors for whom these dimensions are vital.

Two other points should be mentioned. One is the Western impatience which is sometimes expressed towards Eastern cultural specificities, towards differences which cannot be explained away by political and economic specificities. An example of this is the Western surprise at the rather subdued presence of the feminist question on the agenda of Eastern European movements. This is a sphere in which respect for the autonomy of each culture should come to the fore, and where understanding is most difficult to reach.

The last point is the question of Afghanistan. I think the Eastern

Europeans have to large extent been right in pointing out that the question of Afghanistan was not sufficiently taken up by Westerners (although things have recently changed for the better). However, I would not interpret the reason for this non-interest exclusively as part of a policy of appeasing the Soviet Union, but would be more inclined to interpret it (even though I have no proof) as a consequence of the cultural remoteness of Afghanistan. Unfortunately, often for inexplicable reasons, one tragedy sometimes carries more meaning for the world public than another, one geographical area more than another, the loss of some human beings more than others. This perhaps belongs more to a brutal reality which we cannot rationally explain than to an articulate ideological position held by the Western movements. However, since criticism has been expressed and response to it can further enhance the East–West dialogue, the Western movements (regardless of their motives) stand to be corrected on this issue.

Before beginning an analysis of the limitations of the Eastern movements, I should like to make the following statement. Bearing in mind that many of those involved in the movements for democratic peace are subjected to various forms of repression and deprivation, one can only feel respect for their admirable courage and morality. However, their ideas and approaches cannot be absolved from critical analysis in the name of the difficult conditions under which they live, act, think and communicate and the hardships they undergo.

First of all, a degree of reticence towards the peace issue is still present. It is traceable in formulations that stress the issue of human rights as the *sole* precondition for peace, and not their interdependence. Interpretations of reticence as offered by Havel are not fully convincing, and give an indication of how much this reticence is yet to be overcome. According to Havel, peace has been devoid of meaning because of ideological manipulation (but freedom is certainly as much prey to manipulation), because it presupposes an anti-West stand (why in this case should its ideological interpretation be so overpowering?), because the risk is great (so is the risk of speaking out on human rights), because it may be a new utopian promise, a new version of violence to life (freedom fighters face the same danger – violence in the name of one vision of freedom), and because peace is a poetic means of colonizing human consciousness (why is only peace a means of colonization, since the poetry of freedom has not once been used in the same manner?). But furthermore, have human beings completely lost the capacity for self-reflection and critical judgement? A more consistent interpretation would perhaps ease and enrich the dialogue.[10]

Movements are not critical enough of the Western establishment and are often wary of criticisms that movements in the West make of their own society. A good illustration is the reaction of Niemczyk and Orlos to the interview of Joanne Landy in which she dared to speak of the American aggressive imperialistic policy in the same tone as she used to speak about Soviet policy. To Orlos this was about as wrong and unacceptable as equating Nazi Germany and the USA, Roosevelt and Hitler. If there is an acceptance of a somewhat critical standpoint towards the USA then there is often an insistence of asymmetry. Havel says: 'to consider the current situation simply symmetrical, in the sense that both colossal powers are equally dangerous, appears to me a monstrous oversimplification. Yes, both are dangerous, . . . but they are definitely not dangerous in the same way.'

I am not insisting on any particular symmetry but on a more consistent democratic position, one which does not condone any forms of violence and repression in the name of one's own vision of the enemy. Symmetry is a concrete and historical concept, and outlooks would differ depending on whether a Latin American, South African, Filipino or East European is assessing the dangers from the superpowers. One should also draw attention to an illusion nurtured by Easterners that the Western establishment is particularly interested in the democratization of Eastern Europe, in spite of many proofs to the contrary.

Among the Eastern Europeans there is also widespread disbelief in the possibility of the significant reform of socialism, in the legitimation of any type of reform from above. While caution is necessary and scepticism surely has many justifications, this type of thinking is limiting to the extent that it excludes the possibility of dialogue with the reformers in the establishment, and invites a type of radicalization that may prove to be a highly destructive alternative. Šimečka's warning is instructive: 'The destruction of systems has somehow always been connected with war.'

One also comes across various types of ahistorical evaluation. The concept of Central Europe, for instance, is usually taken only in its positive aspect, while its authoritarian heritage is conveniently forgotten and the present is seen as a total historical discontinuity due to the Soviet occupation, and not as something that has to do with one's own past as well. Strained historical analogies are made, as with the Rapallo Treaty and the appeasement policy of the West towards Hitler, all of which express the domination of inverted ideological images which have not yet been fully overcome.

Finally, I should like to mention the often-echoed element of moral absolutism, the demand to live in truth (one truth), the stress on ethical (anti-)politics. This also includes the norm according to which one must be prepared to risk one's life in order to save that which gives life meaning, and lamentations that today there is an absence of heroes who are prepared to die for their beliefs. Any absolutism, including a moral one, carries a danger of experiencing one's own truth and one's own morality as universally binding. The demand to live in truth in the face of brutal, evident lies is of emancipatory potential. However, it is a dangerous demand once the level of brutal lies is surpassed and the world of multi-faceted truths opens up. As to the demand to carry one's moral position to the extent of dying for it, I pose only the following questions: today, when life, individuals, peoples, and whole societies are considered dispensable, how meaningful can sacrifice be? Can there be heroes who will live for what they believe in?

In conclusion, I should like to point out that what may seem a contradictory analysis is in fact a reflection of the contradictory ideas existing within the East–West dialogue. My attempt to distinguish their inhibiting and emancipatory implications is a hidden search not for the basis of unanimity, but for ways to enlarge the spaces for democratic peace.

The Possibilities for Developing the Democratic Potential of Detente

Differentiating between limitations that are inherent and those that are subject to change as a result of critical rethinking and engagement enables us to envisage ways of furthering the democratic potential of detente.

The significance of detente from above is crucial, but at the same time its democratic potential is far more limited than the potential of detente from below. This is because the agents of detente from above are in possession *both* of the 'war machine' – instruments of repression, irrational aggression and total destruction – *and* of the levers of economic and political power needed for radical change – that is, for irreversible peace.

Furthering the democratic potential of detente from above pre-supposes radical interventions into the core of the national and world order, into the most complex political and economic structures and relations. It is this complexity that accounts for the limitations of detente from above. Nevertheless, since establishments are not monolithic or static entities these limitations are not absolute, nor are they always identical for the two superpowers. The limitations are more or less flexible depending on political tendencies within the establishments at any one time. If the reformist wing seems to prevail over the conservative wing, the 'limits of limitations' are smaller.

Bearing this in mind, the scale of our demands has to be radically realistic – or, to use another term, responsibly utopian. This means that, on the one hand, we should be fully aware of the limitations of the detente from above, of the enormity of the task involved in the transformation of its agents and their relations, and the magnitude of the resistance to these changes. At the same time we should be conscious that the limitations are not absolute, but flexible and dynamic. On the other hand, radical realism recognizes that while the actors involved in detente from above are a determining force, they are not the only force. Society is broader than the establishment, and possesses hidden potential for transformation in its aspirations for a civilization of peace, welfare, freedom and ecological viability. A linkage between the reformist wing of the establishment and these social energies of transformation can further relativize the inhibiting limitations.

The democratic potential of detente from above depends, in part, on what happens in each of the superpowers. In the case of the USA two important factors have to be taken into account. First of all there has to be some recognition of the organic link between domestic and foreign problems and solutions. This may come about in the form of enlightened political leadership and a supportive constituency that recognizes the self-interest of the nation in promoting changes and adjustments that are more in tune with the new world order and the nature of global and internal problems. Alternatively – and more probably – such recognition may be imposed by a combination of internal crisis and external decline in the role of the United States as military, political and above all economic 'master of the world'. Since the USA is the economic pillar of the world system, it is likely that the impetus for change will come more from external pressure than from internal crisis. (The situation in the Soviet Union is the opposite.) The rebellion of the impoverished Third World countries, which may take unpredictable forms, and the emergence of the new competing economic and technological powers (Western Europe and the Pacific Region, for example) are among the key developments which already confront US imperial policy with its own limitations.[11]

Of course, the transition from a bipolar to a multipolar world can in itself be viewed as a possible contribution to the democratic potential of detente. While new powers also have hegemonic pretensions and exploitative aims towards the Third World, a greater pluralism of actors in itself creates more space for the autonomy and independence of the developing countries as well as for domestic oppositions, for all those forces opposed to external and internal domination.

This relates to the second factor which has to be taken into account regarding the role of the United States: the possibility for some innovative extension of internal democracy. The USA is facing both economic problems (the large trade deficit, primarily caused by military expenditure, and foreign debts) and social problems (millions of homeless and poverty-stricken citizens, the political marginalization of large segments of the population). But the compound effect of these problems has not become evident, nor does it seem to influence policy-making, especially in the external sphere. Internal problems are reduced to incidents that need to be covered up (for example, Irangate), leaving the imperial logic intact. In order for internal problems to be addressed more appropriately, for an awareness that reallocation of resources, efforts and responsibilities is necessary, it may be that the problems will have to become yet more dramatic if they are to threaten the imperial logic from within.

The erosion of democracy in the USA takes the form of excluding one-third of the poorest part of the population from voting, and of clandestine, covert foreign policies à la Irangate. Other developed countries suffer from the same syndrome. In principle, the extension of democracy implies the establishment of a greater degree of peace within society, and the mobilization of a greater number of citizens for peace between societies. This demands a synthesis of those forms of democracy that have previously been kept apart. In other words, what is needed is a combination of classical representative democracy, new forms of direct democracy (democracy of local councils, participatory democracy in various institutions, and industrial democracy) and a new dialectic between parties and movements:

> The multiplicity of needs and interests in civil society and the creative, democratizing potential of social movements require interaction with reform-orientated parties. But it is also true that in order to become sensitive to new public issues, in order to revitalize their identities, parties must be open to the progressive dimension in social movements.[12]

The combined implementation of all three forms of democracy would provide for more effective control of the ruling power and its foreign policy, a more massive mobilization *against* negative, pathological tendencies of development, and *for* innovative transformations of civilization, a better balance between (political) freedom and (economic) welfare, and a stronger foundation for the reformist wing of the establishment, since it would be based on support articulated in everyday life (local, communal democracy), in the workplace (industrial democracy) and in political activity (classical democracy).

The possibilities for developing the democratic potential of detente in this respect in the Soviet Union are predominantly tied to the furthering of its economic and political reforms. Faced with a major crisis, the

Soviet leadership, as mentioned earlier, has opted for the transformation of the command economy into a dual economy and of the authoritarian political system into a more democratic, socially pluralist system.

The reforms can succeed only if the base for reform is enlarged. Without activating and motivating the participation of the majority of the population, insufficient social energy will be released for the development of a democratic civil socialist society. The enlargement of the social base of reform has the following aspects. First, whether the economic transformation will alienate or activate the majority of the population depends on whether it takes the shape of a vulgar, Darwinistic, market option (which could lead to mass unemployment, astronomical price increases, new social polarization, various forms of conservative coalition – for example, between the Stalinist political bureaucracy and technocracy) or of innovative measures, which might include consistent implementation of the principle of self-management, a better balance between human needs and economic rationality, competition and solidarity, technological development and ecological prudence, and between the political and intellectual elites and the working class.

Within the political realm, the extension of the social base is conditioned by the space created for the introduction and implementation of the three dimensions of democracy mentioned earlier: indirect and direct democracy and a new dialectic between the party and the social movements. The Soviet Union is heavily burdened by the lack of democratic experience. However, the USSR has in the past had some experience of grass-roots democracy in the form of the soviets, an experience that has remained in the collective memory and can be revitalized – all the more so since this experience has a historical legitimacy deriving from the Revolution. One particularly important question is whether the party will temporarily permit the appearance of social movements as an instrument against the conservative wing of the political bureaucracy, only to suppress them later. In other words, the question is whether new forms of social pluralism can evolve so that party and movements do not attempt to destroy each other, but coexist in a creative way. Will the space for initiative and self-organization be enlarged, or will the monopoly of the party remain only slightly modified?

I should also emphasize that both for the development of internal democracy and the democratic potential of detente, the support of the West is essential, particularly in the economic realm.

The possibilities for developing the democratic potential of detente from below are more promising than the potential of detente from above. This is of course due to the very nature of detente from below, to its aims and main actors – the social movements. One radical possibility is the establishment of a system of networking between movements on a global basis, which would promote the development of alternative forms of democratic communication, exchange of information, mutual learning, and new institutions. This could enhance the understanding of global interconectedness and interdependence, strengthen respect for the diversity and specificity of cultures, and result in authentic solidarity.

Another possibility of transnational linkage is through the integration of the range of issues pertinent to democratic peace: inequality on the national and global level, human welfare, democracy at work. Perpetual revision of the agenda is also required as a response to new threats, problems, and needs. Internally the movements could enlarge social support for democratic peace by relating to the acute problems faced by different social and minority groups and by raising awareness through convincing articulation of the interdependence between resolving these acute problems and democratic peace.

On another level, the democratic potential of the movements can be furthered by the development of instruments of self-reflection and self-correction. The major instrument here would be an improvement in the quality of dialogue between movements, particularly between the two halves of Europe and between the Europeans and non-Europeans. This would legitimize the principles of mutual criticism: refraining from mutual appeasement, taking time to reconsider one's own actions, and devising innovative answers to one's own failures and limitations.

On a more practical level, movements should develop their interactions with reform-orientated parties and reform fractions within parties, but also find ways to reach those within the conservative bloc who are willing to engage in a dialogue. As a contribution to the irreversibility of detente, the movements can strongly influence the Western governments in their economic policy towards the Soviet Union; in spite of all the limitations of the Gorbachev reforms, they do present a historical chance to better the world situation and should therefore be supported. Finally, the movements should be able to articulate the dangers of all developments that have a hidden hegemonic, militaristic aspect (for instance the possibility of the creation of the new Western European bloc) and should consistently struggle for unity in diversity, against the marginalization and exclusion of any peoples or regions.

In conclusion, we can say that the problems confronting us are overwhelming, the choices facing us are dramatic, and the future is as unpredictable as ever – perhaps more unpredictable than ever. The situation demands a responsible formulation of the desirable rooted in the understanding of reality, its limitations and enormous hidden potential. It demands respect for the autonomy and dignity of *all* actors, as well as recognition of our mutual dependence and interlinkage. This is what is meant by responsible utopianism.

We are seeking solutions amidst pluralization and homogenization, solidarity and victimization of peoples, groups and countries, co-operation and antagonism, rationality and irrationality. Amidst all these contradictory forces the transformation of reality is possible, and this we not only hope for and intuitively sense, but recognize and participate in. The hidden potential in all realms of human existence (work, politics, art, leisure, family) for a peaceful, ecologically viable and more just civilization needs to be discovered and reawakened. The movements for peace and democracy have to reinforce their mutual commitment, develop their dialogue, and continue to act, living their values and sharing their strength. Together they may transform the new detente into a new world.

Notes

1. W.I. Thompson, *Evil and World Order*, New York 1975, p. 81.
2. R. Tucker 'Gorbachev and the Fight for Soviet Reform', *World Policy Journal*, vol. 4, no. 2, 1987, p. 204.
3. M. Klare, ed., *Low Intensity Warfare*, New York 1988, p. 8.
4. M. Simecka, Interview, *Obsah*, Prague 1985.
5. B. Black, 'Sources of Separation: the International Movement', *Booklet of Peace Movement in Yugoslavia*, vol. 3, no. 1, 1987, p. 12.
6. S. Cohen, *Rethinking the Soviet Experience*, New York 1980, pp. 7, 29.
7. V. Havel, Interview, *New Politics*, 1987.
8. Ibid.
9. Black, p. 14.
10. V. Havel, *The Anatomy of Reticence*, Stockholm 1986.
11. P. Kennedy, *The Rise and Fall of the Great Powers*, New York 1987.
12. A. Arato and J. Cohen, 'Social Movements, Civil Society and the Problem of Sovereignty', *Praxis International*, vol. 4, no. 3, 1984, p. 279.

Notes on the Contributors

MIENT JAN FABER is General Secretary of the IKV (Interchurch Peace Council) in the Netherlands.

RICHARD FALK is Professor of International Law and Practice at Princeton University. His books include *The End of World Order*, *Dealignment: A New Foreign Policy Perspective* (co-edited with Mary Kaldor), and *Revolutionaries and Functionaries: The Dual Face of Terrorism.*

ELISABETH GERLE, a Swede, is a Protestant pastor and singer. She was one of the women who organized The Great Peace Journey.

GERARD HOLDEN is a Research Officer at the Science Policy Research Unit, University of Sussex, and an Associate Fellow of the Transnational Institute, Amsterdam. He is the author of *The Warsaw Pact: Soviet Security and Bloc Politics.*

EGBERT JAHN is Professor of Peace Research at the University of Frankfurt, and a senior member of the Peace Research Institute, Frankfurt.

BORIS KAGARLITSKY is an activist and theorist of democratic renewal in the Soviet Union, and the author of *The Thinking Reed: Intellectuals and the Soviet State from 1917 to the Present*, which was awarded the 1988 Isaac Deutscher Memorial Prize.

MARY KALDOR is a Senior Fellow at the Science Policy Research Unit, University of Sussex, a Fellow of the Transnational Institute, Amsterdam, and the founding editor of the *END Journal*. Her books include *The Disintegrating West*, *The Baroque Arsenal*, and (co-edited with Richard Falk) *Dealignment: A New Foreign Policy Perspective*.

ANDRAS KÖVES is Deputy Director of the Institute for Economic and Market Research, Budapest.

ADAM MICHNIK is a historian, a founder member of KOR, the Workers' Defence Committee, and an adviser to Lech Walesa.

GIAN GIACOMO MIGONE is Professor of History at the University of Turin, and editor of *L'Indice*.

MAMMO MUCHIE, an Ethiopian, is Assistant Professor in the Department of International Relations and Public Law at the University of Amsterdam.

RADMILA NAKARADA is a sociologist working at the Institute of Economics, Belgrade. Her book *The Concept of Need in Yugoslav Socialism* is shortly to be published in Yugoslavia.

PAVEL PODLESNYI is a Head of Section at the Institute of US and Canadian Studies, USSR Academy of Sciences.

ISTVAN REV is Professor of Economic History at Karl Marx University of Economic Sciences, Budapest, and a founder member of the Danube Circle.

MARTIN RYLE is a writer and teacher, and the author of *The Politics of Nuclear Disarmament* and *Ecology and Socialism*.

JAROSLAV ŠABATA is a philosopher and founder member of Charter 77.

MILAN ŠIMEČKA is a former lecturer at Comenius University, Bratislava, and author of *The Restoration of Order: The Normalization of Czechoslovakia, 1969–1976*.

KATE SOPER is a philosopher and writer, who teaches philosophy part-time at the Polytechnic of North London and is a former Chair of END. She is the author of *On Human Needs* and *Humanism and Anti-Humanism.*

HANS VAN ZON is a researcher in the Department of International Relations and Public Law at the University of Amsterdam.

KARSTEN D. VOIGT is the Foreign Affairs spokesman of the West German Social Democratic Party, and a representative of the FRG in the North Atlantic Assembly.

HILARY WAINWRIGHT is a researcher and writer, former head of the Popular Planning Unit at the Greater London Council, and Fellow of the Transnational Institute, Amsterdam. Her books include *Beyond the Fragments: Feminism and the Making of Socialism* (co-authored with Sheila Rowbotham and Lynne Segal), *The Lucas Plan: A New Trade Unionism in the Making,* and *Labour: A Tale of Two Parties.*

KARIN PFEIL is a PhD student and lectures... ...

FRANK VAN VREE is a journalist in the University of ... ...

NADINE ...

HILARY WAINWRIGHT is a researcher and writer connected to ...

Glossary of Terms

ABM   Anti-Ballistic Missile
ALCM   Air-Launched Cruise Missile
CAFE   talks on Conventional Armed Forces in Europe
CDE   Conference on Disarmament in Europe
CMEA   Council for Mutual Economic Assistance, otherwise known as
   Comecon, an economic association of socialist countries
CND   Campaign for Nuclear Disarmament, Britain
CPSU   Communist Party of the Soviet Union
CSBM   Confidence and Security Building Measure
CSCE   Conference on Security and Co-operation in Europe
EDC   European Defence Community
EEC   European Economic Community
EPC   European Political Community
FOE   Friends of the Earth
FOFA   Follow-On Force Attack
GATT   General Agreement on Trade and Tariffs
GLC   Greater London Council
GLCM   Ground-Launched Cruise Missile
IKU   Inter-Church Peace Council, Netherlands
IMF   International Monetary Fund
INF   Intermediate Nuclear Forces
KSI   Club for Social Initiatives, Moscow
LIW   Low-Intensity Warfare
MAD   Mutual Assured Destruction
MBFR   Mutual and Balanced Force Reductions
MIRV   Multiple Independently targeted Re-entry Vehicle
NATO   North Atlantic Treaty Organization
OECD   Organization for Economic Co-operation and Development, an econ-
   omic association of advanced capitalist countries

PD–59   Presidential Directive–59 refers to change of targeting policies to make nuclear weapons more usable

SALT   Strategic Arms Limitation Talks

SAS   Alternative Security Policy Study Group, West Germany

SDI   Strategic Defense Initiative, otherwise known as Star Wars

SED   Socialist Unity Party, German Democratic Republic

SPD   Social Democratic Party, West Germany

START   Strategic Arms Reduction Talks

TUC   Trades Union Congress, Britain

WEU   Western European Union

WTO   Warsaw Treaty Organization, otherwise known as the Warsaw Pact

Index